FIVE hundred SUMMER STORIES

A LIFE IN IMAX®

FIVE hundred SUMMER STORIES

A LIFE IN IMAX®

Filming Adventures from
Surfing to Everest and Beyond

GREG MACGILLIVRAY

FEATURING STORIES BY
surfers Gerry Lopez, Corky Carroll, and Billy Hamilton,
writer and society sage Eve Babitz, and filmmakers Stephen Judson,
Brad Ohlund, Howard Hall, and Barbara MacGillivray.

EARTH AWARE

SAN RAFAEL · LOS ANGELES · LONDON

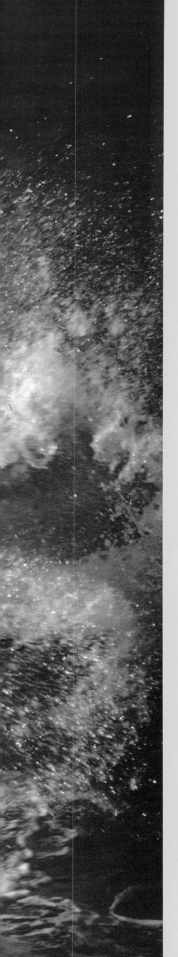

TABLE OF CONTENTS

Dedicated to the mentors who ignited my stoke for filmmaking: Jim Freeman, John Severson, Bruce Brown, Bud Browne, Stanley Kubrick, and my father.

(LEFT) Billy Hamilton at Whispering Sands, Kauai, 1966. This is my favorite surfing shot of all time. One of Laguna's finest artists, Ken Auster, put the scene to paint, he loved it so much. Billy's story: "Mark Martinson and I were the only surfers out. Seconds after this photo was taken, I turned to see Mark, his head streaming blood, ten feet away. His board had opened a one-and-a-half-inch wound. We raced to the nearby Waimea Clinic and got him stitched up." (PREVIOUS PAGE) In 1966, we searched for waves throughout all of South America. In Argentina, we hired an old man and his panel truck to drive us everywhere, becoming the first surfers to ride waves in that vast, incredibly varied country.

VISUAL MOMENTS: ENTERTAINMENT ONLINE

An Introduction
3:00   #1

Throughout this book are 40 QR-coded film clips. Simply scan each with your cell phone camera and enjoy a short video to enhance your enjoyment of the story. If your phone doesn't have a QR-enabled camera app, you can view the videos at www.500SummerStories.com.

In 2015, one of the world's best mountaineers, Conrad Anker, tests the ice at Michigan's Pictured Rocks National Lakeshore as we capture nature's beauty in 3D with the 400-pound IMAX Solido, the most sophisticated camera ever engineered.

Preface

Life changed for me on the day I turned 13. My parents had handed me a birthday present that would fire up my imagination and lead me on a lifetime of adventures filled with challenges, tragedy, heartache, and triumph. I unwrapped a priceless gift that day: a plastic Kodak movie camera. For a 13-year-old, it was like a key to open many doors to both creativity and fun.

As the child of native Californians who were later called "the greatest generation," I found myself in the perfect place at the perfect time. Growing up in the aftermath of World War II presented a unique opportunity. The times were characterized by a rising tide of optimism. Even so, when I received that 8-millimeter camera, few kids my age were thinking about a career in film. Back then, my friends thought I was strange. These days, thanks to Steven Spielberg and George Lucas, not to mention the high-definition cameras built into our cell phones, every kid can dream of becoming a filmmaker.

Over the years, I've developed a unique understanding of what works and what doesn't when it comes to telling stories in film. The underpinnings of that understanding were the experiences and lessons I learned from Jim Freeman, Stanley Kubrick, and my dad, the three mentors who are largely responsible for MacGillivray Freeman Films becoming the only documentary film company to earn more than $1 billion in box office revenues.

Sixty films later, I'm surrounded by great and true friends who for years have urged me to write about the most memorable challenges of my career. One of those friends was Brad Washburn, director emeritus of the Museum of Science in Boston, who encouraged me to make our hit film **Everest**. During an early research meeting, he toasted us by quoting Goethe:

What you can do, or dream you can, begin it;
Boldness has genius, power, and magic in it.

After that meeting, we boldly accepted the risks of making **Everest**. And now I am taking another bold and somewhat presumptuous step in offering these stories to fellow surfers, filmmakers, adventurers, and insomniacs. Join me and others who were part of what I call the "luckiest generation," as we relive the incredible adventures that came my way via the world of surfing, Hollywood, the natural wonders of our planet, and the amazing IMAX® film format.

Greg MacGillivray

In 1959, I began producing films. It was my hobby. I photographed my friends surfing. From that start, I moved on to producing films with giant IMAX cameras of friends like world champion hang glider Bob Wills (FACING PAGE).

A Near-Death Experience in 25-Foot Surf

"I was about ready to die. Then, I got my mouth just above the surface and grabbed a breath. I looked outside to see if another wave was coming. No wave. That was luck. I was saved. I don't think I could have survived it."

It's a series of rogue waves that not even the savviest Sunset Beach surfer sees coming. It usually approaches from the north during a day of sets predominantly from the west. It'll creep in and surprise everyone at that legendary big-wave spot. Boards will fly, cords will snap, and no one will ride it. It's called a sneaker set.

To a Californian like me, this kind of condition is unknown, because on the West Coast, the underwater continental shelf creates drag, slowing a wave's speed as it approaches shore and shrinking its size by half compared with those that hit Hawaii's shores. The Hawaiian Islands are volcanic mountains that have no underwater shelf to deter the waves from impacting with full force.

In late 1977, I was hired to film big surf for Warner Bros.' **Big Wednesday**. Our crew—surfing cameramen, director John Milius, and a team from Hollywood—had been in Hawaii for five weeks. This was our first day of really big surf. At 6:30 a.m., world surfing champion Fred Hemmings and I decided that, given the swell's direction, size, and wind condition, Sunset Beach was our best bet. I wanted footage of actors Jan-Michael Vincent and William Katt out on the water with the giant waves breaking behind them. This would place our stars in the heart of the treacherous action, and the stunt sequence would be much more believable if we didn't have to rely on look-alike professional surfing doubles. Even though these were popular, well-paid actors, William having just starred in **Carrie** and Jan in **The World's Greatest Athlete** and **Buster and Billie**, both could surf really well.

(FACING PAGE) Getting held underwater by a huge wave is called by surfers "the spin cycle." (ABOVE) Super-helpful assistant director Richard Hashimoto helps me launch my 35mm Panavision-lensed camera-ship.

The three of us paddled out. I was on my big surfboard, carting a 25-pound Arriflex camera with a giant lens that was protected by a Plexiglas water housing built by Warner Bros. technicians. We maneuvered into the channel, where I photographed the actors sitting, paddling, and stroking for a big wave—with huge turbulence all around us. I then wanted to show off Jan and Bill's talent for handling big surf. I wanted to film them riding a wave.

We got these shots and I sent the actors back to shore so that I could shoot the last of the roll in the surf line. Clouds had developed, changing the color of the waves from powder blue to a menacing gunmetal—the color that Milius had wisely requested. These waves weren't any more dangerous than the earlier ones; they just looked meaner. As I positioned myself to shoot the surf line, a huge cleanup set approached: the sneaker set. The first monstrous wave closed off the channel. Everyone scratched for the horizon, but the wave was breaking 400 feet out beyond the normal takeoff zone. Twenty-five

(FACING PAGE TOP) Action scenes from the biggest Wednesday ever. (FACING PAGE BOTTOM) Here I film a story moment with top surfer Gerry Lopez and accomplished actor/surfer Jan-Michael Vincent. (ABOVE) John Milius (at camera), one of Hollywood's most gifted filmmakers, taught me dramatic storytelling.

vertical feet of whitewater roared toward me. Surfboards were flying, but I had to contend with the camera as well. As the wave bore down on me, I pitched the camera and dove deep into the darkness. The huge wave spun me, churned, and held me . . . then the next wave hit. It was the dreaded two-wave hold-down.

Out of breath, I watched its whitewater pass overhead, roiling and digging deep. I swam madly toward the surface, grabbed a full breath of air, and saw that the third wave of the set was even bigger. I dove even deeper this time and watched as this wave passed, the tentacles of force agitating the water between the surface and me.

I again began my swim to the top, but this time the churned water felt radically different. Just shy of the surface, I found I couldn't get any farther. The water had been aerated, turning foamy and impossible to swim through. I kicked as hard as I could and thrust with my arms, but I couldn't make headway through the bubbles. I knew I shouldn't panic, but it was difficult to avoid.

How could this be happening? Out of hundreds of big-wave wipeouts, this was a first for me, and I feared it might be a last. Frantically thrusting with my arms and feet, with the last of my energy, I could feel that I was nearing a blackout. I made one final push and got my mouth just barely above the frothy surface. I was completely exhausted,

but I grabbed that precious breath and looked for another wave. Without warning it hit me and again spun me like a washing machine, forcefully pulling me in its vortex toward the bottom.

Convinced that I had enough oxygen to survive, I relaxed my body. Fortunately, the current pushed me toward shore, where the final wave of the set would have a weaker impact. Once it released me, I rose to the surface. Thankfully, not that far away was my big surfboard, and another 25 feet from there, the huge Arriflex water camera. I climbed onto the board and eventually paddled over to collect the camera. Paddling slowly to shore, I caught a two-foot wave and, amazingly, rode it straight to the beach, where I collapsed onto the warm sand and laid, unmoving, catching my breath. When I had recovered, I carried the board and camera back to the roadside where all our production trucks were parked. There I recounted my experience to big-wave legend and friend, who oozed the warmth and caring of aloha, Eddie Aikau. Eddie listened with eyes wide and lots of headshakes. He could relate, he said, as that had also happened to him, but only once in hundreds of days of surfing Sunset. When Pops Aikau, Eddie's father and one of the nicest North Shore locals, heard about our drama, he sympathized but laughed heartily. "Okay, brah," he said, "now you've got a couple good stories to tell!"

GROWING UP CALIFORNIAN

My dad and his friends in 1938 at China Cove, just inside Newport Harbor near Big Corona Beach, a spot named for the Chinese-inspired home on the bayfront. He (in the smaller straw hat) and his brother Don are the tallest guys in the back row. They surfed these plywood-constructed, hollow boards at the Corona Jetty. Before fins (skegs) were invented, Dad had to drag one foot in the water to turn the board.

CHAPTER 1

A Surfer is Born (and Raised)

"A glassy wave is rare yet alluring. To ride a glassy California wave is to ski fresh powder or ice-skate behind the Zamboni. On a wave like this you can do no wrong; your surfing creativity is free to be unleashed; you are gliding, floating and gravity free."

I grew up the son of a summer lifeguard. Dad's tanned complexion and engaging smile brought him friends—and responsibilities he enjoyed, like the student body presidency in high school. He'd grown up in the breezy calm of coastal California, where abalone and lobster abounded in the rocky coves. In those days, seafood feeds around a roaring barbeque fire were common. My stunningly beautiful mother was a smart and socially active student at Santa Barbara College when they met and married. The newlyweds settled in my dad's hometown, Corona del Mar, a bedroom community in coastal Orange County surrounded by rolling hills dotted with orange groves with amazing aroma. It was a wonderful life. As a toddler I would join my dad at the beach, sitting next to his lifeguard chair, playing in the sand and watching the surf. My older sister Gaye and I became good swimmers and true beach lovers.

Strange as it sounds, there was something about being held under a breaking wave that, to my sister and I, was oddly comforting. Getting tumbled, released, then bursting off the sandy bottom to catch a breath high in the air became our moment of exuberant joy. Drifting next to the big rocks of the jetty at Big Corona caused us terror, but right in the nick of time, the wave would ricochet off the

One of my specialties was shooting films while surfing behind other surfers. Oahu, 1966.

rocks, pushing us away to safety. On some days, we'd ride these wedgelike waves on inflatable mats we'd rent from a guy my dad knew at the beachside concession. To a 1950s Orange County kid, riding waves was better than anything, even better than the mock train car robbery at gun point at Knott's Berry Farm.

When I was about six, my father, who had been a navy officer in World War II, traded his nine-month-a-year job as a junior high school woodshop teacher for a new one: building homes. Though the move was a gamble, he was always a self-starting risk-taker. Working on his own was the most fun, he told me, because he could challenge himself. He loved the boldness of it.

Much of my dad's learning took place through trial and error. I saw his joy and I also saw how he embraced the total risk. Over the next 25 years, he would build 40 beautiful homes, some of them award winners. But first, there was the "learner" house. Knowing almost nothing about building except what he read in a how-to book, that first home suffered some epic problems. It was built above an almost always dry streambed, and Dad never adequately waterproofed the cinderblock construction below grade. When it rained, the underground stream would come to life, pushing water into our bottom-floor bedrooms. I remember waking up one morning to find my tennis shoes floating away from my bed!

I could always tell when Dad was building a house with his own cash, because our diet changed. With money tight, we'd have baked beans, hot dogs, and soggy canned vegetables—usually peas. I'd know when he'd sold a house, because Mom would cook steaks.

But we had plenty of fun every day in little Corona del Mar, where we could ride our bikes and even hitchhike without a care. Every morning before dawn, Sam, the Adohr milkman, would clang the glass empties as he deposited full bottles of whole milk outside our door. We'd read the *LA Times* as we ate Mom's oatmeal. "It sticks to your ribs," she'd say, and I'd wonder but never ask why rib-sticking was so desirable.

(ABOVE) These were the summer guards for Newport and Corona del Mar, 1939. My dad, Alex, is on the far right. (BELOW) In the 1930s, my dad and uncle surfed these waves at Corona Breakwater, inside Newport Harbor. Duke Kahanamoku loved the Newport area, lived there for years, and once saved eight people when their boat capsized in the surf at the harbor entrance. Duke was a famous swimmer, winning five Olympic medals. My dad was there in 1932 when Duke visited Los Angeles for the summer Olympics, paddled out, and rode a few jetty waves.

California in the 1950s

My parents had suffered through the frightening demands of the war and the heartaching poverty of the depression, but to them, these postwar years seemed hopeful, even buoyant, especially in California. Here, in this Eisenhower era, beach nightclubs like Prison of Socrates (with Tim Morgon) and the Villa Marina (with Stan Kenton) blossomed, wafting cool jazz or revolutionary folk, while artists, bohemians, and poets flocked like seagulls from the East to the West Coast, where newfound aircraft and space-race jobs abounded. To many, including my parents, it seemed like a creative Babylon, a haven full of possibilities.

I felt the hopefulness, too. In summer, I worked with my dad on construction projects. Besides me, Dad had one employee: Jim Janos. Even though he was 15 years older than my dad, Jim was full of energy. He got up at 4:30 a.m. to fish for corbina and then grill it for breakfast with a side of eggs for his sweet wife. Five days a week, when we'd pick Jim up, I'd slide to the middle of the bench seat. And five days a week, he would grab my knee and I'd leap from the pain of his vise grip. He thought this was the funniest thing ever. As he and my dad traded tale after entertaining tale, I learned something about construction—not just of houses, but of stories. How did their narratives draw me in? What made them believable? I came to realize that setup was vital, knowledge that would prove beneficial just a few years later.

My eighth summer was the best, though, because for a whole week in 1953, my grandmother, my sister, and I visited the Boy Scout Jamboree on the Irvine Ranch. To trade with 50,000 visiting scouts, I bottled Pacific Ocean saltwater and beach sand in small vials and glued on a typed label: "From California Surf." The cute novelties traded well, earning me badges from faraway states and even countries I'd never heard of before.

When I was about ten, my parents gave us the rare treat of a family outing. We piled into the Buick woody wagon and headed to the Port Theatre, which looked like a boat, with a smokestack and portholes to accentuate the nautical theme. The inside walls were wavy swirls of ocean designs. The film we saw that day, **The Glenn Miller Story** with Jimmy Stewart and June Allyson, really got to me. The idea that a man could assemble a band of musicians, create a business, and gain a rich family life, all thanks to the excellence of his art (in this case trombone mastery), impressed me. It planted a seed and got me thinking that hard and focused work could lead to the happiness, love, and meaningful life that Jimmy Stewart showed me in that film.

Like my dad, I became a project-oriented, do-it-yourself person and set about blazing my own trail. When Walkie Ray, my best friend, and I were eleven, we created a four-page newspaper filled mostly with gossip and birthday announcements and delivered it regularly to 125 subscribers in our community. One important story was reported by me

Corona Highlands, the Irvine Ranch, and my first camera, 1954. The hills behind our house became my friend Walkie's and my stage for adventure.

this way: "FIRE. A screaming fire engine came roaring up Seaward Road last Monday. There was no fire but on the way up the fire truck ran over Ricky Webb's bat. Ricky was last seen throwing it away." How newsworthy! Though my writing was terrible, my artistic lettering skills improved. My next project was building my own go-kart: designing it, buying the tubing, learning to weld, and sourcing a (to put it mildly) well-used lawn mower engine. A couple of years later, I built a darkroom and started selling enlargements of photographs—a portent of my future.

For Walkie and me, our favorite escape was the hills, most of which belonged to the Irvine

(ABOVE LEFT) My sister Lisa, 2, helps me wax, with paraffin, my first foam board when I was 13. (ABOVE) Dad works as a lifeguard as Mom keeps him and dog Pal company. (LEFT) The *Los Angeles Times* featured me in an impressive "kids as entreprenuers" story. (BELOW) My sister Gaye and her new career.

14 Part VIII-R-SUN., SEPT. 9, 1956   Los Angeles Times

EXECUTIVE ROLES — Greg, left, and Walkie put some serious thought on the editorial content of their newspaper, for which they're also advertising salesmen, revenue collectors and circulation carrier boys.

BUSINESS—Walkie Ray misses no bets in soliciting ads for the news a friend publish in Corona del Mar. Here he sells an ad to Trudy H member of the Corona del Mar Times office. The advertisement cost

Boys, 11, Hope to Reap Jamboree Passage From Weekly Newspaper

BY BOB GETTEMY

CORONA DEL MAR—Two of the Harbor area's youngest businessmen are carefully nurturing a journalistic acorn that they hope will grow into a mighty oak—and pay their way to the next National Boy Scout Jamboree.

The enterprising pair are James (Walkie) Ray and Greg MacGillivray, 11-year-old Corona Highlands residents who are copublishers and coeditors of a fortnight neighborhood newspaper called the Highland Fling.

Progress Noted

The paper got off to an inauspicious start last Feb. 16 with the first issue consisting of one page and a scattering of ads. But the hustling partners have changed that and now the Highland Fling lives up to its motto of "Onward

You can be

and Upward and Cleave to the Line" by coming out weekly with four pages and same 40 advertisers represented.

"We've got a circulation of 140 now." Walkie says, "and we think it'll grow some more."

Competitive Picture

Greg, apparently pleased with the solid position of the paper, pointed out that "Since we started, five other papers have given us competition, but they've all gone out of business, leaving us a clear field."

The lads, who share the duties of publishers, editors, advertising salesmen, collectors and carrier boys, also function as reporters, and readers keep up with community happenings from items like this:

Reporting Job

"Bob Babson, 405 Cortez Circle has got just a black stallion recently. He is very happy about the hole affair."

The trips taken by Corona Highland residents, births, weddings, parties and other items are all faithfully recorded in the Highland Fling.

One of the most popular features is the "Razz Your Neighbor" column, where subscribers poke fun at one another through items like:

"At what barbecue dinner were the steaks partly grassy because some handsome blond walked into the barbecue?"

Free Service

"We used to charge people to put things in that column," Greg explained, "but we let 'em do it free now."

With the profits from the Highland Fling the boys

only source of income. When the opportunity arises they drop their roles of editors and become gardeners, errand boys or whatever the occasion demands. The Highland Fling comes in handy when it comes to getting extra work, and jobs are solicited through ads like this:

"DO YOU NEED — Your lawn watered, mowed? Errands Run? Odd Jobs Performed? Your garage cleaned out? Your dog walked? Your walks swept?

"SURE YOU DO!. CALL GREG H. 4239W & WALKIE H. 4196."

Crises Explained

Being busy publishers and odd job men can lead to some complications, but readers are kept informed of crises through forthright announcements like:

"The editors are sorry about the late issues of the Highland Fling, but we have many other things to do. We will try to not let you down."

However, it's not all work with the publishers. The latest issue carried an item about a three-day visit the lads made to Glen Ivy Hot Springs and ended with this explanation:

"Because of this small vacation, The Highland Fling is late again."

The boys' parents, Mr. and Mrs. James D. Ray and Mr. and Mrs. James Alex MacGillivray are solidly in favor of "The Highland Fling" for many reasons.

As Mrs. Ray put it: "It's a good deal. The boys never give us any trouble about dressing up or combing their hair. When they're out selling ads or doing other work with their paper, they want

PUBLICATION TIME—Greg MacGillivray, copublisher of Corona del Mar Highland Fling, keeps the press moving on publication day. The neighborhood newspaper comes out once a week—except when boys get too busy to meet deadline.

Times photos by Rene Lauren.

Vol. 48, No. 34   Tuesday, April 28, 1964   Sixteen Pages—10c per Copy

Miss Laguna Crowned

A Laguna Niguel teenager was picked from a field of 21 contestants gathered at the Balboa Bay Club Sunday to wear the crown of Miss Laguna Beach, 1964-65.

Nineteen-year-old Gay MacGillivray, daughter of Mr. and Mrs. Alex MacGillivray of 32832 Coronation, received the crown from Chris Dsenis, Miss Laguna Beach, 1963-64.

The blue-eyed blonde, a senior at Laguna Beach High School, will compete in the Miss California contest in June.

Runners-up to Miss MacGillivray were Miss Janice Bernritter of Fullerton and Miss Vicki Hawks of West Los Angeles.

Judges for the beauty pageant were Dr. Leonard B. Stallcup, president of the Miss California beauty pageant; Francine Cheryl Herack, Miss California; Darah Marshall from Mary Webb Davis studio; Joy Brach of the Ed Harrell studio; Laguna Beach Mayor William D. Martin and Phil Jones, president of Laguna Beach Jaycees.

Program chairman was James Lawler, master of ceremonies was disc jockey Johnny Gunn, entertainment was provided by folk singer Parks Wilson.

Also vying for the Miss Laguna title were Kathi Baird, Wendy Brown, Sue Bruderlin, Carole Crosby, Mary Ann David, Kathleen Graham, Cheryl Latham, Kathy Mayer, Melody McCord, Cheryl Schroeder, Sherry Thorne, Susan Weisbecker, Lana West, Pat Wilkes, Coletta Braun, Judy Galbreath, Ladonna Walston, Chris Ganzer.

JUDGES' CHOICE—Blue-eyed, blonde Gay MacGillivray of Laguna Niguel has been selected to reign as Miss Laguna Beach for 1964-65. Miss MacGillivray was rated best of contestants at Balboa Bay Club Sunday afternoon.

Ranch. We'd hike among hissing rattlesnakes, darting roadrunners and hawks that rode the thermals by adjusting small feathers on the tips of their wings. "Be back at dark!" we'd yell as we headed out. We could walk for days, it seemed. Technically, we were trespassing, but the Irvine Ranch guards never cared. Barbed wire may have kept the 120,000-acre cattle ranch enclosed, but it didn't keep Walkie and me from using it as our playground. We followed the narrow cattle trails out through the sagebrush to hike to the twin poles up on the highest peak, now Signal Peak in Newport Coast, or to the petrified tree that lay flat on the ground, a rock by any other name, now beneath the Crystal Cove development. The Irvine Company kept making our playground more interesting: installing a single oil well one year, cultivating sheep and then buffaloes another. We were explorers, cowboys in a corner of California that today remains mostly intact, protected by the Laguna Greenbelt and Crystal Cove State Park.

Almost every house in our neighborhood had at least two kids, and they were always eager to join me in any sport out in the street. In the winter, I striped the asphalt to make a football field. In the summer, I painted a baseball diamond with a pitcher's mound and a home plate. When a foul ball broke the Browns' kitchen window for the second time, I graciously moved the "field" down the street. We'd call time-outs when cars came roaring through, but the neighbors put up with us and learned to slow down. Not even the Browns complained.

Later, we made skateboards with two-by-fours and my sister's metal-wheeled skates. We crashed-landed repeatedly, my head wound once requiring eight stitches. Blood was everywhere, horrifying my patient mother.

One summer, Walkie's dad, who was also a contractor, had just purchased an orange grove with the idea of creating a tract of houses. He allowed us to take as many free oranges as we could carry. Armed with a hundred, we squeezed until our hands ached to sell juice at Little Corona Beach, making $16 in one fell swoop.

One of our buddies was Lewis "Dukie" Baltz, whom everyone envied for being an only child. Dukie could talk his smitten parents into buying him anything, including a subscription to *Playboy* magazine, cartons of Pall Mall cigarettes, and a darkroom with a top-of-the-line Beseler enlarger so he could create beautiful black-and-white photographs.

Dukie's parents ran the local funeral parlors, so they were busy seven days a week. But in the 1950s, parenting was an afterthought anyway; kids grew up on their own. We'd hang out at his house and "read" *Playboy* interviews or watch the TV game show *Truth or Consequences* on the first television set in our neighborhood. Dukie's smoking didn't bother anyone because tobacco companies were hiring actors to play doctors and show us how good smoking was for our health. "More doctors smoke Camels than any other brand," the ads

boasted. Finally, in 1965, when the surgeon general released a stunning report stating that smoking did cause health problems after all, the tobacco companies flat out denied it and continued to push their cancer-causing products for decades more.

Shocking revelations like this made my generation skeptical of big business and its advertising. "Question Authority," read the bumper sticker that I glued to my first car. We began questioning everything, trying to find truths we could build our lives around. Dukie found his truth after attending art college, using his intellect to become a successful photographer. Sadly, Dukie died at an early age of lung cancer.

Family Strife

While we were in high school, our youthful paradise encountered a sharp turn. My sister Gaye and I suffered through years of parental marriage strife. Loud arguments carried into the night, terrifying us both. Would our parents divorce? When you're young, your existence depends on your parents and on the strength of the family bond. If that bond weakens, the world feels like it is disintegrating. Shaken, we got through it, but we were psychologically scarred. We became far less trusting of relationships and always fearful of rejection; but happily, our parents did stick together in love throughout their long lives. To cope with the pain over those years, Gaye turned to religion and beauty competitions, winning the Miss Newport, Miss Laguna, and Miss Orange County pageants, and almost the Miss California contest (due to last-second shenanigans, politically inspired by the contest's sponsor, she got first runner-up, not the crown!). Meanwhile, I doubled down on my projects and focused my mind and body toward my passions—art and photography.

The Surf Bug Bites

When I was about 12, a few of us discovered surfing at that same Little Corona Beach. At the time, surfing was a fringe sport, often shunned by respectable members of the community, but we loved it anyway. I used $15 of my newspaper publishing money to buy an eight-foot balsa board shaped by Gary Couch, a stylish surfer in Newport. Even at that price, I overpaid; the board was virtually unrideable. But I kept at it. Once one of us learned to turn and cross-step to the nose, the surf tribe would assign us a nickname. There was Roger "Rat" Zeiger, Mike "Red" Marshall, "Panda" Smith, John "Flea" Hawley. One unfortunate friend was named "Tiny Brain." I was "Bird Legs" MacGillivray; I won't bother elaborating. Since we lived a mile from the beach, I built a crude board trailer for the back of my bike using two-by-fours and some wheels from an old baby stroller. The downhill was easy, but after a day of surfing on my heavy

(ABOVE) This photo was my first published work, photographed at "Killer" Dana Point on an eight-foot south swell in 1962. (BELOW) This legendary wave was tragically ruined to make space for a boat harbor in 1971.

board, I had to push the bike, board, and leaden trailer uphill all the way home. It took me an hour and a half to go one mile. I wish I could say that muscles came from the effort.

As more friends began surfing, we found ourselves in need of durable, flexible surf trunks with a pocket for surf wax. Swimming trunks didn't cut it and "bun-huggers" like Speedos brought on fits of uncontrolled laughter. Some of the older surf rats bought custom heavy canvas trunks from the wife of Newport's chief lifeguard, so I followed suit. Plandette Reed would measure you and give you a form on which you'd crayon in the colors you wanted on the pocket, the top band, and the leg band. She would then ask for a four-dollar deposit. When I picked my trunks up a week later, I paid her the final three bucks. "Hey, are those Reeds?" friends would ask. I thought I was so "boss" that I hardly took them off all summer. I slept in them. They were so caked in saltwater that they stood up on their own. My mother was repulsed, but they lasted three years until I grew out of them.

My dad, who'd ridden a redwood plank surfboard at Corona Jetty back in the 1930s, took us camping each summer at Doheny State Beach near Dana Point. We'd stay in tents for a week or two and he'd conduct lessons on the easy waves at Boneyard or Middles, great spots for nose riding. On the biggest days at Doheny, a really old guy would paddle out on a monstrously huge board to get all the best waves, infuriating all of us "gremmies." As my skills improved, the local gang took me in and Doheny surfers Howard Chapleau, Pat Sparkuhl, Peter Van Dyke, and Danny Estrada became friends. Sometimes Jay "Sparkey" Longley, of Rainbow Sandals fame, would join us. The beach camaraderie was alluring, intoxicating, and brought me back again and again. We ruled at Doheny, we naïvely thought, and occasionally asserted our ownership with the comical slogan: "My beach, my wave, my chicks, go home!" Our own language included words like "stoked," "cowabunga," and "bitchin." We thought we were big stuff, no questions asked.

I learned better when one day I made the mistake of taking off on a nice wave right in front of a muscle-bound wrestler from Long Beach. The gorilla detonated like an atomic bomb at this breach of etiquette, leapt off his board, and tried to tackle me. I backed away, keeping my board between "Bird Legs" me and his meaty fist. Still, he must have thrown 30 punches, with a number landing on my ear and head. Danny, who was a weightlifter at Capistrano Beach High, saw this one-sided slaughter from shore and came paddling out to rescue me. The sight of Danny's muscles calmed the beast down. I apologized profusely, assuring him that I'd never even think about taking off on "his" wave again. In a strange twist, Mr. Muscles later became somewhat of an acquaintance. Whenever I showed surfing films in Long Beach, I'd make a point of letting him in for free, no questions asked.

Me (13), Gaye (14), her friend Dotty (15), Rick Webb (14), Lisa (3½), and Mom in Dad's ancient Oldsmobile convertible, on our way to surf at Dana Point.

The MacGillivray and Webb Family Ancestry

It may seem strange for a California beach family, but I am amazed to claim that we are descended on my mother's side (Webb) from William Bradford of Plymouth Colony, who in the 1600s wrote a book about abandoning England and sailing on the *Mayflower* for New England in America. The choice, he explained in his book, was well thought out: "After much thought and discourse on the subject, we began at length to incline to the idea of a removal to some other place, not out of any new-fangledness or other such giddy humour, which often influences people to their detriment and danger, but for many important reasons." I love the way he argued for the right to a better life, in particular the freedom of religion—"any religion except the one being forced on us in England." To honor our *Mayflower* past, several of my family members are named Bradford, including the notable winemaker Bradford Webb (Freemark Abbey), the only vintner to have two selections chosen for the famous competition between French and California wines in 1976. The results of the blind tasting by 11 wine experts (9 of them French) shocked the world because California wines won. This stimulated wine production in the United States and made my uncle a hero!

My paternal grandparents (MacGillivray) left Scotland for America in the early 1900s. They each settled in Los Angeles and attended the annual Scottish Games to remind themselves of the old country and how much fun it was to drink ale and toss tree trunks called cabers. They met there, fell in love, and married. After my dad and uncle were born, they moved south to Corona del Mar, bought a pair of vacant lots, and built a cozy beach house out of junked lumber, calling it "Mac's Shack." As teenagers, my dad and uncle lifeguarded at Big Corona Beach and board surfed at the Corona Jetty. The Mac's Shack property was outlined by more than 1,000 abalone shells—colorful souvenirs from my dad's many dives and resulting abalone feeds off the rocky coast of Little Corona Beach in the 1930s and '40s.

A COOL WAVE OF COLOR BY GREG MacGILLIVRAY

INTRODUCTION TO FILM-DONE BEFORE LIGHTS GO OUT...

THE ROAD FROM SANTA BARBARA TO SANTA CRUZ IS 263 MILES OF CURLING BOREDOM. AFTER PASSING THE PROMINENT TOWNS OF PISMO BEACH AND MORRO BAY, THERE EXISTS LITTLE PLEASURE IN THE DRIVE. THEN AS ONE NEARS CARMEL, HE REALIZES THAT HIS TRIP HAS BEEN WORTHWHILE. ALONG THE 17 MILE DRIVE IN CARMEL, FREE WE FOUND MANY BEACH BREAKS AND A FANTASTIC BEACH BREAK WHICH THE LOCALS CALL PARADISE. A PERFECT DESCRIPTION. IT IS PROTECTED FROM THE WIND. CLASSIC TUBES.

SO, LET'S SWINGS INTO A PERFECT DAY AT CARMELS PARADISE A COOL WAVE OF COLOR.

....

(NO NARRATION DURING SURFING IN INTRODUCTION...)

(AFTER TITLE)
(GUY IN CAR)
LET'S BEGIN OUR ADVENTURES WITH A DRIVE TO RIN ATTRACT THE ATTENTION OF A GOOD LOOKING GIR RINCON IS SPANISH FOR

DAYLIGHT TYPE

Kodachrome II
COLOR MOVIE FILM
FOR DOUBLE 8mm ROLL CAMERAS

SURF FEVER 1960

BY JOHN SEVERSON:

BIG WAVES, SUPERIMPOSE TITLE: "SUNSET BEACH, HAWAII", MORE BIG WAVES

MAIN TITLE, STILL BIG WAVE SHOT, NEGATIVE, TITLE

QUEEN'S SURF, HAWAII, JOEY CABELL, SURFING AT DUSK

SURFING CARS, FAST PAINT JOB, BUYING A CAR FROM SHRWED DEALER

MIKE DOYLE AND PIGGY BACK FOR TRIP TO HAWAII

TAMARAK STREET, MIKE DOYLE AND PHIL EDWARDS

MEXICO, VOLKSWAFEN TO AND OVER CAMERA, SCENICS OF MEXICO, MEXICAN MUSIC, SAN MIGUEL BOATS ON BEACH, MODERN ART PICTURE OF NOSE RIDE AND TURNS TO ACTION, BOYS WALKING IN FRONT OF ROCK SILOUTTED THROUGH, ZOOM FROM ABOVE, JOEY CABELL AND MIKE DOYLE, SLOW MOTION, LAP DISSOLVES AND NOSE RIDES, SUNSETS IN MEXICO AND TO CAL.

FROM BOARD, FRONT, LAP DISSOLVES, HEADDIPS

UNDERWATER, UNEXPECTED DANGER-SHARKS, NEWSPAPER OF BOY EATEN BY SHARK, SUSPENFUL MUSIC, NEWSPAPER CLOSE-UP OF WORD SHARK, GUY ON BOARD CLAMMERING TO STAY ON

MALIBU, OUT OF WHITE CIRCLE, "BULLDOG", MICKEY MUNOZ, MIKE DOYLE DEWY WEBER, MICKEY MUNOZ AND WIPEOUTS EFFECTS,--DOTS AROUND HEAD: 2:00 MINUTES

SECOS, MICKEY MUNOZ AND "QUASIMODO" FLASHY TITLE

RINCON, AREA SHOT, KEMP AABERG, 3 RIDES, PIANO MUSIC

BROOK'S STREET, DIFFERENT TYPES OF WIPING OUT, BODY SURFING, MAT SURFER

SAN ONOFRE, MARINES AND THEIR CANOE-GO BEHIND-"AIN'T NOTHIN' LIKE THE CREEK BACK HOME", KIDS- BARE BOTTOMED, CHEERING SECTION FOR PAT CURREN AND GEN. JACKRON GEN. GETS BROKEN

HUNTINGTON BEACH, CONTEST, DENNY BUELL ETC.

FLYING TO HAWAII, MONEY, POSTERS OF HAWAII, FLYING TO HAWAII, VOLCANO ERUPTING, SUNSETS, BIG WAVES SILHOUTED THROUGH WINDOW "BLACK SADDLE", SUNSET BEACH SOUND EFFECTS,"WIZZ"ETC. 1 MINUTE, DUSK SURFING, SUN OVER WAVES

WAIKIKI, DRUNK ON BE BEING SWAMP TIME LAPSE BACK TO DRU SURFERS ON

BIG WEDNESDAY 1961

TITLE, MON. TUES. BIG WEDNESDAY, BIG WAVES GROWING IN SIZE

PREVIEW OF SURF, ZOOM THROUGH TREES TO BIG WAVES, KIMO HOLL FANTASTIC WIPEOUT, STOP, REVERSE, LATER

SANTA CRUZ, TRAVELING-FOLLOWING CAR ON HIGHWAY, MICKEY MUNOZ BOARD OVER CLIFF, RIVERMOUTH IN THE SPRING

PT. CONCEPTION, CAR DRIVES ON BEACH TO CAMERA, UP POPS BOB COOPE WAXING BOARD CROSSWISE, ZOOM FROM HILL TO COOPER, HE WALKS TO SURF, "LITTLE NAN THEME", PERFECT TUBES OF BLACK VELVET, TWO CAMERAS ONE OUT IN WAT SILOUTTE OF SURF THROUGH CAR WINDOW,

TRESTLE, SCHOOL AND SCHOOL'S OUT, JOEY SEVERSON, TRAVEL TO TRESTLE, PAST ROAD SIGN, TRESTLE IN OCTOBER, OVER THE SAN ONOFRE OVERPASS TO CHURCH, JOEY SEVERSON

WEDGE, BODYSURFING TO THE WEDGE, CAMERA ON NOSE POINTING

HUNTINGTON PIER, RIDE ON SURFING BOARD, FOREWARD, THROUGH PIERS, SCREECH TO STOP

OCEANSIDE, MARINES ON RUBBER RAFS, COMEDY

HAMMOND'S REEF, REYNOLDS YATER, GOOD LINES

RINCON, FAST TRIP ON FREEWAY, RINCON, REY, YATER KEMP AABERG, "MAG.7"

VENTURA OVERHEAD, BOYS STANDING ON WATER OUTLET, "A LITTLE WATER GOING OUT AND A LOT COMING IN."

HAWAII, FAST BOAT TO HAWAII, WAKIKIK AND BIKINI, ALA MOANA, GARBAGE HOLE, YOKAHAMA BAY, HULA SHOW AND CAMERA ROUND AND ROUND, ALA MOSNO AGAIN, FAST BOAT HOME, END OF FIRST HALF

PREVIEW OF WIPEOUT, FIRST HALF OF WIPEOUTS, FLYING TO PERU

PERU, DANCING AT NIGHTCLUB, CLUB WAIKIKI, GIRLS, SURF, TRAVEL THROUGH SMALL TOWNS, CERRO AZUL, KON TIKI,

HAWAII, SUNSET BEACH, "RAWHIDE" WAVE WATCHERS, MAKAHA, HELICOPTER

HELICOPTER, TAKES OFF, "SLEEP, SLEEB SLEEP" ALA MOANA AND WIPEOUTS FORM ABOVE, WAIKIKI SURF "GINCHY" "THE BROWN BLOCKES ARE REEFS, THE OBLONG SHAPES SURFBOARDS, AND THE THINGS ON THE SURFBOARS IDIOTS" DOUBLE EXPOSURE, FIGHTING BACK VIEW OF RUNNING OVER SURFERS FROM FRONT OF BOARD, TYPES OF WIPEOUTS, LAZY SURFERS, FAST CAR TO WAIMEA, THE GUY IN FRONT HAD A FAST CAR ALSO, WAIMEA BAY SURF, SHOTS OF FACES, THE END SUPERIMPOSED OVER AIRPLANE AND SUNSET

ADMIT 1
JOHN SEVERSON'S
BIG WEDNESDAY
1961 SURF MOVIE
...SEVERSON • BOX 193 • DANA POINT • CALIF...
ADM. $1.23; TAX .02 TOTAL $1.25
No 5576

A GREG MACGILLIVRAY FILM
A COOL WAVE OF COLOR
ADMIT ONE
ADM. 1.46 TAX.05 TOTAL $1.51

JOHN SEVERSON
PRESENTS 1960
SURF FEVER
ADMIT 1
SEVERSON - BOX 193 - DANA POINT
Adm... 1.23
Tax... .02
Total-$1.25
No 6877

(CLOCKWISE FROM TOP LEFT) Kemp Aaberg at El Capitán in my first film; my grandmother with friends at Big Corona Beach, with dog Pal, 1938; my outline/study of John Severson's film **Surf Fever**; tickets from our screenings; outline of Severson's **Big Wednesday**; my narration script for **A Cool Wave of Color**, 1964.

The First Film

Before the 1955 opening of Disneyland, Orange County had been known as a mostly agricultural backwater bedroom community that offered little in the way of style or culture. The park's huge success and national recognition put our region on the map as a place worth visiting. In the midst of this makeover, I celebrated my life-changing 13th birthday. Perhaps because I'd shown an interest in taking photographs of surfers, my parents used three whole Green Stamp books to "buy" me a Brownie 8mm movie camera. At this time, all of my friends were encouraged to develop projects—and self-confidence—by our schools offering metal, wood, and electric shops—something we've sadly lost nowadays.

Motivated, I promptly started filming, using friends and my photogenic sisters, Gaye and Lisa (who was a welcome new addition to the family in 1955), as actors. I bought a secondhand editing machine for $10 and suddenly was able to compose stories with the small-gauge images. I'd never had more fun. I'd edit surfing rides with a brief story introduction, usually describing the featured surfer or the surfing location. Sometimes I'd film comedy skits to go between the sequences. Then, I'd borrow a projector, gather my friends together, charge them 25¢ admission to our garage, and show about 40 minutes of films. A couple dozen people would show up, and they loved the films, finding them funny and charming and tinged with a certain artistic feel. Their encouragement inspired me to work harder for the next screening, and gradually I started to make better and better films. Up the street, a half hour away, a kid a year older than me was doing almost the same things. I didn't know it then but our paths would soon cross, changing both of our lives forever.

By the time I was 14, I loved filmmaking so much that I decided to invest all of the $350 I had made on the newspaper in a professional 16mm camera, lenses, and a tripod. I peg that moment as the start of my career as a filmmaker; but, because I lived far from Hollywood, I had no easy access to role models or mentors. Like my dad at the start of his homebuilding career, I read any and all library books on the subject and pestered Rod Yould and Charles Jones, cinematographers who lived in our neighborhood. Charles gave me a textbook on lighting so that I could learn to shoot indoors and control the light to enhance the beauty of a scene. I visited art museums in Newport Beach to study the lighting and composition of painters like Vermeer and to pore over annual *Graphis* journals that showed the best in graphics and original photographic techniques.

I taught myself lettering and graphic design, first for Walkie's and my newspaper, and then by copying the brilliant Saul Bass, who in the late '50s and early '60s designed some of the finest posters and title design sequences in film history. Years later, Stanley Kubrick would use him to design the logo and graphics for **The Shining**, a film that would change my life. Meanwhile, my mother was quietly encouraging and perhaps the kindest person I have ever known. She never bragged about herself, or her degree, or her *Mayflower* descendants, but if her kids ever did something remarkable, every neighbor would know. When I edited a cool sequence or when we got good grades, hit a homer, or swam for a ribbon, we'd hear her weaving our accomplishment into every conversation. It built our confidence and drove my sisters and me to try even harder. But, as I taught myself artistic surf filmmaking, I noticed that producers in LA were lured by other beach attractions.

Surf Mania Meets Hollywood

In 1959, Hollywood figured out a new way to exploit the teenage market. The secret was to combine assets: bikinis on beautiful girls, nonstop injections of freewheeling California culture, and rebellious, edge-dwelling, half-naked surfer boys. It was a recipe for success, and it drew spellbound crowds of horny teenagers to box offices far and wide. The film **Gidget** was one of the first experiments, and it was a smash hit.

At the beach, it took no time at all to feel the impact of **Gidget's** success. The parking lot at Newport Pier filled up with carfuls of kids from as far away as Pasadena. The local Rendezvous Ballroom, where dances had been popular since the 1930s, suddenly added "surfing" music by Dick Dale. And the campgrounds at Doheny became impossible to reserve during the summer. I'll never forget big wave rider Greg Noll's take on the new phenomenon: "I hated this whole Hollywood bullshit deal that just brought more assholes over the hill from the valley to the beach and fucked up our scene. These bozos," he railed, "had boards in their cars, and when they waxed them they were so dumb they waxed the bottom!"

The surf craze had hit like a tsunami, drenching teenagers as far inland as San Bernardino with a wash of titillation. To be recognized as a surfer was now a coveted distinction rather than a cursed aberration. Kids from inland would strap boards on car roof racks but never take them off to use them. Being a surfer became a status symbol. Over the ensuing years, about 40 beach party exploitation films fanned the flames of sexual excitement, carrying the youthquake to extremes. But it was **Gidget** that lit the fire. Funny thing was, my friends and I never watched those films, because we were busy with school and interested in the era's more daring films like **Some Like It Hot**, **North by Northwest** and **Psycho**.

Glassy Performances

With Hollywood doing all it could to screw things up, the theme of my first film with my 16mm camera had to be unique. I looked at the

(ABOVE) The crowded Malibu surf scene, 1962. (BELOW LEFT) I'm filming Gary Propper while riding a wave—a tricky skill. (BELOW RIGHT) Johnny Fain at Rincon.

esoteric side of California surfing—its style, grace, and artfulness—a topic no other film had claimed. And because most of the early surf documentary films used the word surf in the title (**Surf Safari**, **Surf Crazy**, **Surf Fever**, **Surf!**), I named mine **A Cool Wave of Color**. My favorite surfers were stylists, not big-wave heroes; surfers who cared as much about how graceful and, frankly, awesome they looked on a board as they did about the enormity of the waves they rode. We called it "hotdogging." I was filled with admiration for Lance Carson, Mickey Dora, Phil Edwards, Paul Strauch Jr., Bob Limacher, Billy Hamilton, Joey Cabell, David Nuuhiwa, and Nat Young.

For this film, I chose to focus on California's elusive "glassy" waves that show up when there's no wind and produce a ride that is stunning to watch and sensational to experience. I lucked into an exceptional eight-foot day at Rincon (Spanish for "the corner"), a spot that rarely gets glassy because the point—or corner—sticks out into the windy Santa Barbara Channel. On shore, it was a cold winter afternoon, the sun backlighting the smooth waves. I was a bag of nerves because I knew that this was a once-in-a-lifetime chance. Johnny Fain, one of the best surfers at Malibu Point and Mickey Dora's alter ego, walked onto the beach. He also knew what a gift we'd been handed that day. I doubt there were more than 10 people in the water, and Johnny took full advantage. He rode brilliantly and I got my first perfect sequence for **A Cool Wave of Color**, a film that would highlight that distinctive California surf lifestyle.

The biggest obstacle to turning this passion, this hobby, into a real movie was being able to afford film. Each roll, good for three minutes of footage, was priced at $10, which is equivalent to about $100 today. To save money, I decided to try something risky: I'd shoot and project at 16 frames per second, rather than projecting at the standard 24 frames per second. That would save me one-third of my film budget!

Then, Bill Thomas Camera in Laguna Beach offered me a 15 percent "professional's discount" even though I had never made a movie and was far from being a "professional." I actually think they felt sorry for me. Since my newspaper route and babysitting jobs paid about $1.50 per hour, for every seven hours of work, I could buy a roll of film. Every little bit helped.

By 1961, when I was 16 and in my second year of production, my dad seriously admitted to me that he was worried. "The surf craze seems to be waning," he said. "Shouldn't you get your film out in a hurry, before interest fades away?"

It was true that the surf mania that began in '59 with **Gidget** had lost some of its energy. But I told my dad that I didn't think I needed that audience. I'd already paid for the film, I told him, and

Joey Cabell and friends.

I wanted it to be creative and to stand on its own. I still had more work to do and it couldn't be rushed. (Behind that bravado and that truth, I also was deathly afraid that the film would bomb. I kept imagining being pelted with flying bottle caps flicked like miniature Frisbees by disgruntled surfers!)

From eighth grade on, I spent nearly every waking hour perfecting **A Cool Wave of Color**. By the time I graduated from high school, I'd spent $3,000 and needed $1,000 more to finish it and book my first screenings. Thankfully, my dad had just sold a house so he was able to loan me the money at just six percent interest. I promised that the first cash from the screenings would go directly to him. Thankfully, I also had one other important helper on my side.

The Love of My Life

I always loved math. When I was 12, I was chosen to join an accelerated group of 22 like-minded students. Maybe this class full of math nerds was chosen as part of some NASA engineering program for the Cold War, but regardless of the reason, we stuck together for the next six years. On our first day as high school freshmen, I watched a new girl walk in to become part of our group: a tall, blonde, athletic young woman who, as it happened, loved math as much as I did. Barbara Smith had just moved from Washington, D.C., to Newport Beach. Her dad, an engineer, started as a scientist with the Manhattan Project, America's secretive atomic bomb program. His new job was in Newport at Ford Aeronutronic. Mr. Smith was smart and so was his daughter. But Barbara also had a lively and comical side and was constantly asking impossible but creative questions and bantering with our math teacher. She was always pushing others, playfully competing with friends to walk faster, jump higher, laugh more. Her free-spirited energy, intellectual glamour, and physicality captivated me instantly. To me, she was a goddess, with brains, humor, athleticism, and a zest for life all wrapped up in a sleek, beautiful form. I was in love.

But at 14 I had no clue how to talk to the opposite sex. It must have taken me a year to say hello to Barbara. Luckily, she thought I was funny, so I caught her attention. By our sophomore year, she had apparently grown tired of waiting for me to get up the nerve to ask her out. In what I would come to recognize as her no-nonsense honesty, Barbara invited me to a Sadie Hawkins girl-ask-boy dance. It was the best evening of my life and I set about trying to make this thing work, but it was clear that I needed every trick in the book.

Before calling her in the evening, I would prepare a list of things to talk about. "Do you think Eisenhower did a good job as president? If you were 21 (then the voting age), would you vote for Richard Nixon or John F. Kennedy? Have you ever gone surfing?"

We ended up doing a lot together, including having Barbara "act" in my early film projects. For one skit, I had her fake a fall off a ledge and land upside down in a metal trash can. With bare legs sticking out, she kicked helplessly, her fake screams amplified by the tin echo chamber of the trash can. The audience thought she was hilarious. She was game for anything and kindly put up with my definition of a date. Since all my cash at that time went for rolls of film, going out to a movie meant waiting for the 9:00 p.m. screening to begin and the ticket seller to leave the booth so that we could sneak in for free. We saw more than 20 films this way, but we always missed the opening ten minutes! So much for studying that important "setup."

In 1962, I was experimenting with my new 35mm Minolta SLR camera and indoor lighting techniques. I love the soft light of this intimate capture of 17-year-old Barbara.

Barbara knew what she wanted and didn't hesitate to express herself. She saw that I was spending 90 percent of my free time on making—and being able to afford to make—my surf film. Barbara then talked our drama instructor, Robert Wentz, into having me produce a seven-minute segment of our senior class play as a movie. My first film released at a paid event! I was hitting the big time. The evening was titled "Why Not?" and my film, **The Return of the Son of the Sheik**, was a comedy in black and white with live piano as accompaniment, just like in the silent film era. It featured a good-guy cowboy sheriff, an archaeologist professor, a damsel in distress, and many horses. The audience of students was rolling in the aisles. When I asked Mr. Wentz to explain the event title to me, with his customary smile he replied, "'Why not?' should be the response to any tough decision in life." For him, it was just like Nike's slogan, "Just Do It!" decades later. These slogans seemed to be Barbara's as well.

Being around this amazing young woman changed me dramatically. My parents could see it; I was happier, more self-assured, and more communicative. Though I was still reluctant to fully place my trust in another person, Barbara gently urged me forward.

(FACING PAGE) Barbara and me, Huntington Beach, West Coast Surfing Championship, 1962.

How a Teenager Makes a Film

SURF · HOLLYWOOD · IMAX ENTERTAINMENT · MISSION

> **"It was at that moment that I was hooked, not by the financial success, but hooked by the acceptance of me—the filmmaker."**

Though starting your first film at 14 is never easy, lots of people besides Barbara helped me with my films—actors, surfers, and drivers to get me to the surf—all for free. Mike "Red" Marshall, one of the best goofy-foot surfers in Newport, had a station wagon and I got a ride with him many times. My mom and dad would also drive. Or I'd hitchhike.

But that changed a year later, in 1961, when I got my learner's permit, and, on a beautiful December day with cold offshore winds blowing, surfer Bob Limacher and I borrowed my father's Buick woody wagon and headed for Trestles to shoot a winter sequence.

An Amazing Day at Trestles

California's San Onofre and Lower Trestles surfing area has a long and colorful history. Longboarders began surfing the rolling waves at San Onofre in the '30s and '40s. The locale became perhaps the most popular surfing spot on the coast because its slow, mushy waves were easy to ride with boards that had no fins. During World War II, after the Japanese attacked Hawaii, the US military felt that it needed a marine base along the western coastline, and they selected the oceanfront space between San Clemente and Oceanside. As a result, Marine Corps Base Camp Pendleton limited access to some of the best surf in America. For decades thereafter, the area was open only to two groups: marines and members of the San Onofre Surf Club, which was founded in 1952. My father and I stayed on their waiting list to join for years!

(FACING PAGE) In 1962, before the creation of Surfline or any way to predict when big surf would arrive, I began checking the swell every day at Newport Pier at 6 a.m. before school. Filming lines like these, at California Street, Ventura, was my obsession and mission.

In the 1970s, President Nixon bought the Cotton's estate on the bluff above the beautiful Cotton's Point and made it his Western White House. That made access even more onerous. He visited only during the summer, which happened to be when the south swells were perfect and Cotton's Point could get to 15 feet. Needless to say, all the surfers in the area were furious, since they also hated Nixon for his support of the Vietnam War, his general dishonesty, and his pale white skin. The president's walks on our beach, wearing his trademark suit and tie and hard black dress shoes, added insult to injury. Nixon did do one good thing, though: When he left office, he made certain the surfing beaches of San Onofre, Churches, and Trestles were designated a California state park, open to all.

But, to get onto the base in December 1961 required deception. I'd used my graphic art skills to forge an exact replica of the San Onofre Surf Club decal that members had affixed to their windshields. When Bob and I got to the Marine Corps guard post in my dad's car, the guard knew instantly that we were surfers by the boards sticking out the back and by our shaggy haircuts, which in no way resembled the buzz cuts of Marine Corps recruits. But, in perhaps the first example of "MacGilli-luck," he gazed at the sticker, which we had stuck on the far right side of the windshield so he couldn't get a clear view, gave us a salute, and said, "Have a great surf!" We were in! Or so we thought!

We motored along the familiar dirt road that led to San Onofre Beach, where the guard had given us clearance. But that's not where we were headed. Well past the guard post, we hung a quick right down a military road that paralleled Pacific Coast Highway. We were definitely in forbidden territory as far as the marines were concerned, but Bob had a plan: Find the area with the most trees, pull down some branches,

Bob Limacher's skill at nose riding became legendary in ***A Cool Wave of Color***, here on an amazing, cold offshore wind day at Trestles, December 1962.

cover the car with leaves and dirt, and carry our surfboards and cameras to the beach at Trestles, home to some of our state's finest waves.

The whole concept made me nervous. I was driving my dad's car, first of all. If we got caught, the marines might impound not just the car but our surfboards and my camera equipment. They'd been pulling this impoundment tactic for years because they seriously did not want us using their beaches. If we were already out in the water, they would stand on the rocks in their military-grade boots and wait for our boards to wash in. This was before Pat O'Neill invented, and my good friend Bob Nealy improved, today's surf leashes. If we fell off, our boards would surely get carried in without us.

Despite all these concerns, Bob convinced me. We successfully hid the car and started toward the beach. A six-foot swell was running so I knew I had a chance to get some epic shots of beautiful waves. But, as we walked down the dirt road, a jarhead appeared up on the hill, looking through binoculars and barking instructions to someone through a walkie-talkie. Nabbed!

I knew that if they apprehended us the consequences would be severe. Many of my friends had their surfboards confiscated at Lower Trestles. I didn't want that to happen to me. And what would they do with my camera; confiscate it forever? We took off running and ducked into a stand of trees about 25 feet off the road. I shoved my surfboard, tripod, and camera case under some tree limbs, leaves, and brush. Then I buried myself. Bob did the same, only he chose a spot closer to the road.

I heard a Jeep pull up nearby. The urgent voice of the clifftop lookout came crackling over a two-way radio. "They're in the brush beneath the trees," it yelled. "Search for them!"

I don't know how Bob felt, but I was petrified. I could hear the approaching corpsman, his heavy boots snapping limbs and crushing the undergrowth as he came to a stop just four feet from me. I didn't move a muscle.

The marine radioed back to his partner, "You sure I'm in the right spot? Could they have gone somewhere else?" He took two more steps but didn't bend down to check underneath the brush. I held my breath as he searched for what felt like an hour but was probably 30 seconds.

I finally heard the marine walking slowly back to his Jeep, calling to the guard on the cliff. "Gonna look further down near the beach," he reported, sounding disappointed. Bob and I remained motionless for another 20 minutes.

By the time our heart rate had slowed and we snuck back to the dirt road, the coast was clear, both literally and figuratively, and the waves were beautiful. Bob quickly paddled out. I set up my camera and for the next hour got wonderful shots of Bob riding the nose on crisp, wind-blown waves with cascading whitewater blown by the offshore wind coming out of the northeast. It was one of the most beautiful things I'd ever photographed. To top it off, about two dozen seagulls bobbed on the water, a blazing swath of white against the deep blue Pacific. A few more guys showed up and built a fire on the beach. I grabbed some artsy shots on this super-cold day of surfers standing around the fire, the flames obscuring the backdrop of waves with a heat wave of beauty. These shots were hard to set up, but I was patient and got a handful that conveyed the serenity of a perfect day at Lower Trestles.

When Bob came to shore, his feet and hands were blue. He said on the last few nose rides he couldn't feel his feet, so he was sure that he must have looked like a complete kook. Nothing could have been further from the truth. At that time Bob was one of the best nose riders in California, with a fluid style and grace, especially for a 15-year-old. We surfed for another couple of hours, and I even caught a few beautiful waves myself before we headed back to the car.

As we walked, I had a disturbing thought: What if the disgruntled marine in the Jeep had found our car and towed it away? I would be in big trouble and knew it would impact my dad's enthusiasm about loaning his car to me for shooting my movie.

As we rounded the corner, my heart froze. I couldn't see the car. I felt a wave of nausea. But then we got closer and I spotted the wheels and breathed a sigh of relief. Seconds later, Bob and I had made a hasty retreat from the base. That day had been a success but it could've gone very wrong. It is still etched in my mind. Now, when I see waves at my house fringed with the white of those rare offshore Santa Ana winds, I am reminded of that magical adventure.

Early Encounters with Mickey Dora

During high school, my parents gave me three "ditch school" days a year to use when the surf was really good. I met Mickey Dora on one of those days in 1960, when I was just 15. Mickey (or Miki, as he came to prefer) was already a member of surfing royalty, and I was awestruck.

Surf film producer Grant Rohloff (left) and I share ideas, Malibu, 1962.

I'd gotten a ride to Malibu with champion tandem surfer Bob Moore and had set up to wait for the best surfers. Around 10 a.m., Mickey sauntered down the beach and paddled out to catch the first of many waves. The fog had started to roll in, but I was able to photograph Mickey doing something I'd never seen before. He would take off and make a left-go-right turn; then, catlike, he'd take two delicate steps toward the nose and ride in a trim position across the face of the wave. He'd stay there, side-slipping with intentional hip thrusts that slowed his board and dropped it down the wave's face. The maneuver thrilled me but didn't surprise me, since I'd idolized Mickey for years. He was legendary, not just for his surfing, but for his stylized way of gesturing while talking, his reputation for conning others, and for taking on bit roles in films to make extra pocket change.

What Mickey had just demonstrated no one else had even tried before, so when I edited **A Cool Wave of Color**, I chose to emphasize it. Surfers from around the world who saw the film were blown away by this new way of moving along the face of a wave.

"Waves are the ultimate illusion. They come out of nowhere, instantaneously materialize, and just as quick they break and vanish. Chasing after such fleeting mirages is a complete waste of time. That is what I chose to do with my life."

—MICKEY DORA

I worried that when Mickey saw **A Cool Wave of Color** he might accuse me of being an opportunist since I played him up so much, highlighting him as if it were his name on the marquee. He certainly looked and acted the Hollywood part: dark and handsome, dramatic and scowling. To my great relief, Mickey came up to me after the screening, said, "Hey, Sport, I like what you did with that. See you again," and walked out. In that moment, Mr. Mysterioso lived up to his nickname, never showing all his cards, always an enigma.

Mickey Dora (ABOVE AND RIGHT) was the "Johnny Depp" of the time, unpredictable, wild, mysterious. (ABOVE RIGHT) My Jeep could drive itself!

Santa Cruz

Because my first film's theme was the uniqueness of California surf, I wanted to capture the waves at Steamer Lane in Santa Cruz, where the thick kelp kept the waves super-glassy all day. But Santa Cruz was a seven-hour drive, so when I turned 16,[1] I took $150 of my savings and bought a vintage 1950 Willys Jeep panel truck. I built a bed in the back with storage for my camera equipment secured beneath, and Barbara sewed curtains for the back windows. When I painted "MacGillivray Films" on the doors, I felt like I was legitimately "in the business" and ready for a long adventure! I planned a summer trip to Santa Cruz with Bob Limacher and my sister Gaye.

When school let out in June, we headed north to famous Steamer Lane, but thirty minutes short of our destination, it was my car that was steaming in the 105-degree heat. We'd made it as far as Watsonville by the time it caught fire. The only thing I could do was call home.

"Dad, the car engine exploded in flame. I ran to a used car dealership and borrowed their fire extinguisher, but the car's engine is burned to a crisp. Bob, Gaye, and I are fine. Disappointed, but fine. But we don't know what to do now!"

My dad thought for a minute, then said, "Wait right there. I'll rent a tow bar, drive up, and tow you back."

He made the long drive and lifted our spirits with his humor and stories. What a wonderful father! As we towed the Jeep behind my dad's Buick, we thought of a funny idea. What if I set up my camera in the rear of the Buick, looking back at the Jeep while Bob "drove" it to a surf spot? He could look up at the surfboards on the roof rack, concerned that they were coming loose. Then, as the car continued down the road, he could climb out the window and up onto the roof to tighten the board straps. We did it; we filmed it just that way. When I finally showed this scene in front of a live audience, the crowd howled with laughter, recognizing that that is exactly what surfers want to do when they're rushing to catch a good swell: Don't even slow down to secure the boards. The engine fire turned a bummer of a trip into a comedy film highlight. Lemons into lemonade.

Tribal Culture

In my film, I tried to convey the rebelliousness of the California surfer. We were a bunch of long-haired, bleached-blonde surf bums who had no interest in conventions. No one wanted a nine-to-five job, no one cared about conforming to dress codes or staying within the boundaries of the rules and the law. Lighting a fire at the beach to stay warm on a cold winter's day or trespassing to get to a favorite surf spot sometimes created a stir with the law and then the media. People called us vandals and truants. Some communities, like Newport Beach, tried to control us by requiring surfers to purchase a license for their surfboards. Imagine! We didn't need no stinking license! Perhaps surfer John Milius described our tribe best: "We were gods. If we weren't gods, we were certainly a race of kings. We knew no law but our own. We were not bound in any way by the manners of our times. We were outlaws, criminals, supreme anarchists, and rogues. At the same time, we had a chivalric honor more severe than anyone."

---

1 When I turned 16, it seemed like a turning point, like I was entering a new chapter of my life. I could now drive and that gave me freedom to shoot film anywhere my $150 Willys panel truck could take me. I knew what I liked and disliked. I had set goals. So I thought out a philosophy for attainment of personal growth—life in chapters of 16 years—and even though I'm now in my fifth chapter, the age divisions seem to work and help:

     0-16: Growing Up
   17-32: Finding Oneself, What Your Life Should Be
   33-48: Perfecting Oneself and Your Job
   49-64: Becoming Expert, Refinement
   65-80: Reflection and Helping Others
   81-96: Passing Your Knowledge on to Others

And surf film screenings became our tribe's favorite cultural pastime. They were boisterous, fun, and because they were so few and far between, highly anticipated; but two traditions made them stand out even more. First, they included an in-person introduction and narration by the filmmaker, who had met the surfers and lived the adventure; and second, every screening included an intermission, which meant more socializing, giveaways by the filmmaker (usually surfboards, T-shirts, or surf trunks), and the telling of more stories. (**The Endless Summer** later taught me a brilliant lesson: Put your best sequence—Cape St. Francis's perfect wave in that film—just before intermission so kids will talk about it during the break. Worked like a charm!) Though the intermission was in fact a necessity because 16mm projectors couldn't handle reels containing more than 50 minutes of film, that 15-minute break added significantly to the events. Which famous surfers had shown up? Which cute girls? And, despite our countercultural views, what were people wearing?

Some films came with printed programs, which the crowd quickly folded into paper airplanes. If a film was bad, surfers would let them fly to show the filmmaker, who was narrating from the stage, just how bad it was. I remember hearing someone yell, "This film is fucked!" during a Walt Phillips film showing—and this was when the F-bomb was rarely heard. The crowd laughed and cheered. Another filmmaker, after delivering half his narration in a squeaky voice with uninteresting storytelling, was lifted from the stage while still sitting on his chair and tossed out the exit by a gang of unruly surfers. Again, the crowd cheered, stomped, heckled, and laughed, and the film continued with its narrator locked outside. Big-wave pioneer Greg Noll released annual installments of his film series **Search for Surf**, which never really delivered. Kids who felt ripped off after paying $1.50 took revenge one day by bringing a jar of 50 moths to a screening and setting them free to flap around in the projector light, ruining the show. Noll was furious

"It was often a crude form of uplift. Firecrackers were lit and rolled across the floor to the next row of seats. Bottlecaps zipped through the air. High-decibel beer-belches rang out. A motorcyclist might blow in through the side door, ride up one aisle and down the other, then gun back out the way he came."

–MATT WARSHAW ON SURF FILM SCREENINGS
IN *THE HISTORY OF SURFING*

A Cool Wave of Color

SURF FILM

FILMED IN: 16 MM AT 16 FRAMES PER SECOND ON KODACHROME FILM

RELEASE DATE: 1964

NARRATED BY: Greg (In Person)

Since I filmed this from ages 14 to 18, I had to focus on surf I could hitchhike or drive to—in other words, California's beautiful, glassy, waves. This made the film unique and accidentally intriguing, even attractive.

A COOL WAVE OF COLOR

GREG MACGILLIVRAY'S NEW COLOR FILM HIGHLIGHTS THE FANTASTIC CALIFORNIA SURF. GREG HAS TAKEN THREE YEARS TO CAPTURE THE SIGHTS AND SOUNDS OF THE WORLD'S MOST THRILLING SPORT.

but the crowd loved it. Surfers were the very definition of a "tough crowd." But these events were ours alone, unique and more special to us than any simple movie. They were our special cultural events.

Getting to the Finish Line

In our junior year when we started to plan for college, Barbara set her sights on an Ivy League education. I couldn't understand why she would want to go all the way to the East Coast when California had so many excellent, and inexpensive, universities. (Just $1,700 a year for tuition, books, room, and board!) But I never risked telling Barbara that, even though I wished we could be together. Above all, I respected and admired her brave, independent spirit.

My parents had saved $5,000 for each of us kids to pay for college, so I might have been able to leave the state. But I needed to do more shooting to complete my film, so I applied to just one campus, University of California, Santa Barbara (UCSB), because the surf there was so good. When it came time for Barbara to fly east to study at Cornell, we could barely stand it. What would happen to us? Would our love continue with Barbara now 3,000 miles away in New York? Adding to my concern, I discovered that the Cornell student body broke down to nine men for every woman. I could just imagine my love headed to class on her skateboard, blonde hair flying.

Still, I had two objectives at UCSB: be productive during class and shoot five sequences so I could finish and release my film six months later. The army barrack-turned-dorm that I lived in with 40 other male students was a blast. Every month, the girls' barrack next door held a mixer where I'd show clips from my film, so I met wonderful friends, but I missed Barbara intensely. Though it was hard to be apart, we were each exploring what an interesting and fulfilling life might look like. We'd share those observations in our letters, however Barbara wrote actual thoughtful sentences while I made pictograms

Filming Billy Hamilton.

and decorated the envelope. The only redeeming value of that was that it made me famous in her dorm mailroom because of the "artistry" of my frequent letters to her!

Since I had a vehicle, as a break from studying I'd carry dorm friends to the commissary on the other side of campus to eat three times a day. Ten students could pile in, laughing all the way. My calculus teacher, Dr. Newsome, offered to help a few of us start the UCSB Surfing Club so that we could organize parking and trash pickup at Campus Point, which got pretty good on a four-foot west swell. I became president of the club.

Just a couple months later, on November 22, 1963, I rushed to call Barbara. John Kennedy had just been assassinated in Dallas, and I needed to process this loss of trust and confidence. She helped me through it, but JFK's death affected me for months, so I doubled down on my film, sublimating my emotions.

Around that time, a new band called the Beatles released "I Want to Hold Your Hand." The stylistically fresh song made me miss holding and just being near Barbara even more. When the Beatles appeared on *The Ed Sullivan Show* to sing five songs, everyone, yes everyone!, on campus tuned in. The show became the most watched non-sports entertainment broadcast ever, with 73 million US viewers. This was February 9, 1964, just weeks before the first screening of my film.

Though I had organized my time well enough to get good grades my first semester, I became super stressed balancing my film work and classes in the second semester. It was a struggle I'd never encountered before. But I tried not to let that get to me, because after four years of hard work, I knew I had a film good enough to be loved, especially by the most accomplished surfers, because of the esoteric style, the creativity, and the great surfing.

Because I was a "pay-as-you-go" filmmaker, I was obligated to no one. I could make my film the way I wanted, free of constraints from investors—or of any obligation to produce a profit. I loved that freedom. With **A Cool Wave of Color,** I tried to create a film that was unlike the others: original in design and execution. My only goal was to make the most artful surf film ever, and **A Cool Wave of Color** became certainly the weirdest surf movie to date, and done by surfing's youngest filmmaker. That gift of free expression stayed with me as a goal my whole filmmaking life.

Discovering the Business Side of Show Business

The business of producing a surf film back then was simple enough even for me to understand. It was the theater screenings of the completed film that proved challenging. These are the steps I would take. Three to five months in advance, I'd spend about $75 to rent an auditorium—

(ABOVE) Testing a new 385mm lens. (BELOW) Inspired by my mentors, particularly John Severson and Saul Bass, I tried several titles by designing ad pieces for my first film, which I'd later decide to call **A Cool Wave of Color**.

(BOTTOM AND RIGHT) At the 1961 Huntington Beach Championship, the tandem event got intense in 6-foot surf, and I had a chance to meet Mark Martinson.

*Suddenly It's Surfing

CALIF. SURF FILM*

FABULOUS MUSICAL SCORE • ALL IN BEAUTIFUL COLOR • FANTASTIC NEW SURFERS – MIKE MARSHALL JOHN REYNOLDS – DANNY LENAHAN – ILIMA KALAMA • FILMED IN CALIF. AT TRESTLE • DOHENY • NEWPORT • RINCON • WINDANSEA • ETC. • COMEDY • GLASSY WAVES • DON'T DARE MISS THIS SHOWING:

SAN MARCOS HIGH AUDITORIUM SANTA BARBARA
TUE. & WED. MAY 22 & 23rd. ____ 7:30 p.m.

GREG MACGILLIVRAY PRESENTS
L.J. RICHARDS   MICKEY DORA
JOHNNY FAIN   ILIMA KALAMA
BOB COOPER   LANCE CARSON
RUSTY MILLER   MIKE DOYLE
REYNOLDS YATER   MIKE HYNSON
BUTCH VANARTSDALEN DEWEY WEBER
DAVE WILLINGHAM   KEMP AABERG

The Lively Ones

WHEN IT'S HOT

MACGILLIVRAY 1118 HIGHLAND NEWPORT
ADM. $1.23 TAX .02 TOTAL $1.25

Nº 56

this was called "four-walling." Next, I'd print posters for perhaps $60, run a small ad in the local newspaper for $15, and pay a bunch of teenagers to distribute the posters at $1 an hour, for a total of $20. If there wasn't a "shoulder-hopping" surf film booked that same weekend, you might draw 225 people at $1.50 per person, for a total take of $337.50. Subtract the $170 in costs and I ended up with a profit of $167.50. At that rate, I might break even on my investment in the film ($4000) after 25 shows if I didn't account for my own labor! Not exactly a get-rich-quick scheme, but, especially for a math nerd like me, a fun way to learn the business.

A friend in my dorm, Fred Steck, became my first official employee. Fred was brave and, like Barbara, could talk to anyone—even school principals. (He would later become a highly effective investment advisor.) In early 1964, Fred and I would monopolize the dorm's hallway pay phone and, armed with a stack of quarters, call high school principals throughout California to book the film's first screenings. Fred also perfected the art of stapling a poster on every telephone pole along California's Highway 101. But we were making it up in fits and starts, so we weren't at all prepared for the reaction to the film.

The screenings up and down the coast turned out to be joyous. Even though I didn't ask them, my parents would bring my little sister Lisa and my grandmother Maud to help sell tickets, run the projector, and watch the exits so that surfers couldn't sneak in. Gremmies would invent tricky ways to avoid buying a ticket. As the film ran and I narrated from the stage, it was Lisa's job to creep down the aisle and ask me if I needed more water. She was just eight.

At the first ten screenings, as I narrated from the stage, I was a stuttering, nervous moron. Even with the lights out, I was terrified. Eventually, my timing and elocution improved. I needed to project not just my film but my personality, telling good stories and delivering laughs. Like vaudeville, I would succeed or fail based on my performance.

Then came another two instances of MacGilli-luck—a naïve, unplanned combination of occurrences that has come in handy for all of our productions. First, because my film took four long years to get right, as my dad had predicted the surf fad had in fact quieted down, which meant that there were fewer movies being made, and less competition. In 1963, because he was so focused on his magazine, *Surfer*, John Severson released his weakest film, **The Angry Sea**, wryly nicknamed by film critic Bill Cleary "The Angry Audience," and he then quit filmmaking for several years. Bud Browne slowed down production, and others, like Greg Noll, traded filmmaking in for the growing surfboard manufacturing business. That left me an opening.

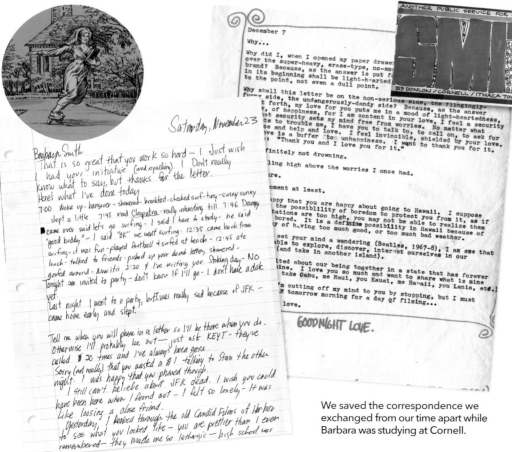

We saved the correspondence we exchanged from our time apart while Barbara was studying at Cornell.

"It seems we will sometime reach a point (I can feel it coming and it doesn't frighten me!), when we say: 'We shall devote ourselves to each other, live for one another, and build our love to the peak of possibility.' I think that this experience would be the most beautiful, rewarding, and important in one's life. (Cowabunga!)."

—FROM AN OLD LOVE LETTER TO BARBARA

Soon thereafter, MacGilli-luck #2: Bruce Brown released his tour de force, **The Endless Summer**, which was so good that it reignited enthusiasm for all surf films, including my weird movie. The stoke generated probably doubled the attendance at my summer screenings.

In 1964, the surfers at our screenings were wild and energetic and super stoked. They'd hoot at a good ride, they'd laugh at my slapstick comedy routines, and they'd ooh and ahh at the beautiful shots that I'd spent months, even years, photographing. No one was bothered by the fact that my film was projected at 16 frames per second . . . except me. I didn't like the extra flicker. From there on out, my films were shot at 24 frames per second.

For a beginning filmmaker, surfers were a great way to gauge audience approval of your techniques, and I loved this process. After some screenings, I'd re-edit the film to make it even better for the next night. Because I was showing my original Kodachrome film, not a copy, I could edit with tape splices. The timing of the comedy moments became tighter. The drama of a lead-in became more dramatically in sync with the "borrowed" musical track. I trimmed action sequences to build to a more forceful climax. I was learning from my uninhibited, extremely vocal, no-holds-barred audience! I loved so much about filmmaking, even the concept that I might fail. That uncertainty factor drove me to try harder, as it does others. For example, climbers get no challenge summiting a mountain they consider easy. When there are factors we haven't experienced before, we're forced to figure out new solutions. That's when it's fun and exhilarating.

Finally a Sellout!

By the middle of the summer, after about 15 screenings and as positive word of mouth spread up and down the coast, I had my first full sellout at the Elks Lodge in Laguna Beach, just one block from where we live today. Barbara sold tickets, learning how to collect $1.50 and give change in quarters faster than any human in history. On that hot July night, there were audience members standing in the back, sitting in all the aisles, and even up on stage with me as I narrated. It was sweltering inside, so we opened all the doors and windows, but that didn't help much. Still, the heat seemed to go unnoticed by the stoked crowd. We even turned away 30-40 people because there was no more room, and Barbara made a sign that said "Sold Out—Sorry" for the door. I still have that sign! Everyone had fun, and I discovered success like this was a turn-on. A group of hard-core surfers, including Tim Dorsey, Rich Harbour, Mark Martinson, and Roy Crump, fell in love with the movie and about 20 of them followed me around from screening to screening, from Santa Cruz to San Diego. They soon became friends.

Some crowds were extra rowdy, even drunk. In those cities, renting a high school auditorium required Fred to really turn on his

(ABOVE) My mom and dad had personality, intelligence, and style—and wonderful humor. (BELOW) Our first full "sell-out" show with Barbara, my dad, our crew, and the cash box.

OUR BIG SHOWING TRIP TO EAST COAST

6,300 MILES OF DRIVING, FUN, AND 3 SURF MOVIE LOCATIONS IN 1964

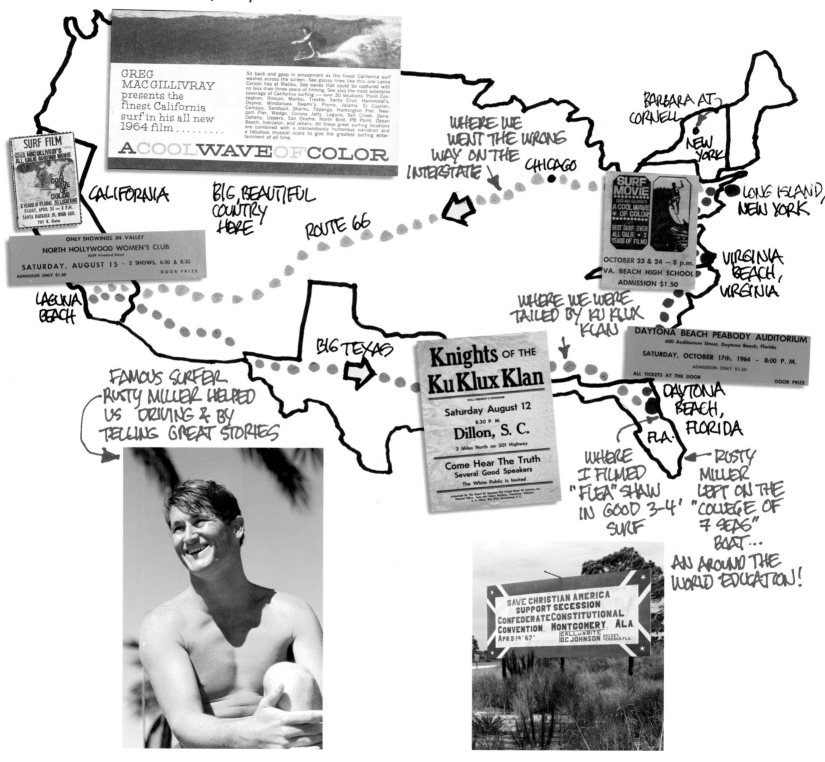

GREG MAC GILLIVRAY presents the finest California surf in his all new 1964 film . . . .

Sit back and gasp in amazement as the finest California surf washes across the screen. See glassy lines like this one Lance Carson has at Malibu. See waves that could be captured with no less than three years of filming. See also the most extensive coverage of California surfing — over 30 locations: Point Conception, Rincon, Malibu, Trestle, Santa Cruz, Hammond's, Osprey, Windansea, Swami's, Pismo, Jalama, El Capitan, Campus, Sandspit, Sharks, Topanga, Huntington Pier, Newport Pier, Wedge, Corona Jetty, Laguna, Salt Creek, Dana, Doheny, Uppers, San Onofre, North Bird, PB Point, Ocean Beach, Indicator, and others. All these great surfing locations are combined with a tremendously humorous narration and a fabulous musical score to give the greatest surfing entertainment of all time.

A COOL WAVE OF COLOR

SURF FILM
GREG MAC GILLIVRAY'S ALL CALIE SURFING MOVIE
A COOL WAVE OF COLOR
8 YEARS OF FILMING 30 LOCATIONS
FRIDAY, APRIL 24 — 8 P.M.
SANTA BARBARA JR. HIGH AUD.
721 E. Cote

ONLY SHOWINGS IN VALLEY
NORTH HOLLYWOOD WOMEN'S CLUB
5629 Vineland Street
SATURDAY, AUGUST 15 - 2 SHOWS, 6:30 & 8:30
ADMISSION ONLY $1.50   DOOR PRIZE

SURF MOVIE
GREG MAC GILLIVRAY'S
A COOL WAVE OF COLOR
BEST SURF EVER
ALL CALIF • 3 YEARS OF FILMS
OCTOBER 23 & 24 — 8 p.m.
VA. BEACH HIGH SCHOOL
ADMISSION $1.50

DAYTONA BEACH PEABODY AUDITORIUM
600 Auditorium Street, Daytona Beach, Florida
SATURDAY, OCTOBER 17th, 1964 - 8:00 P. M.
ADMISSION ONLY $1.50
ALL TICKETS AT THE DOOR   DOOR PRIZE

Knights OF THE Ku Klux Klan
WILL PRESENT A PROGRAM
Saturday August 12
8.30 P. M.
Dillon, S. C.
3 Miles North on 301 Highway
Come Hear The Truth
Several Good Speakers
The White Public Is Invited

CALIFORNIA

BIG, BEAUTIFUL COUNTRY HERE

ROUTE 66

WHERE WE WENT THE WRONG WAY ON THE INTERSTATE

CHICAGO

BARBARA AT CORNELL

NEW YORK

LONG ISLAND, NEW YORK

VIRGINIA BEACH, VIRGINIA

WHERE WE WERE TAILED BY KU KLUX KLAN

LAGUNA BEACH

BIG TEXAS

FAMOUS SURFER RUSTY MILLER HELPED US DRIVING & BY TELLING GREAT STORIES

DAYTONA BEACH, FLORIDA

FLA.

WHERE I FILMED "FLEA" SHAW IN GOOD 3-4' SURF

RUSTY MILLER LEFT ON THE "COLLEGE OF 7 SEAS" BOAT... AN AROUND THE WORLD EDUCATION!

SAVE CHRISTIAN AMERICA
SUPPORT SECESSION
CONFEDERATE CONSTITUTIONAL
CONVENTION MONTGOMERY, ALA.
APR 8-14 '67
CALL or WRITE D.C. JOHNSON BOX 524 VERO BCH. FLA.

verbal charm. Even so, some school administrators would insist on us hiring a rental cop to keep order. I'd heard bad things about San Francisco surfers, and it turned out to be true—they were the wildest. Their school district required a cop *and* a $200 damage deposit. During my show there, beer and wine bottles rolled down the aisle with noisy clanks, and I tried to hide the infraction from the guard by turning up the music; I needed that $200 deposit back!

I'll never forget that November evening in 1964 when my surfer buddies and I went to see Greg MacGillivray's first surfing movie, A Cool Wave of Color, in our little Palisades school auditorium. Greg, who appeared to be only a couple of years older than me, introduced himself as the house lights dimmed. As he narrated live from the stage, brilliant shots of glassy waves, peeling in at our home breaks, flashed onto the screen. It showed guys wearing no wetsuit knee-paddling out at Rights and Lefts on the Hollister Ranch, Hammond's Reef in Montecito and other Southern California surf spots. The surfers faded in toward the curl on the takeoff, whipping their boards around in a stylish left-go-right turn as they walked casually to the nose, hung toes, then back-pedaled gracefully, dropping their back foot to the tail block and leaning into a roundhouse cutback. Bitchen! Now this was finally something we could relate to.
—Denny Aaberg, co-writer, **Big Wednesday**

Our First Showings Outside California–a Big Step

After reading the positive review of **A Cool Wave of Color** in *Surfer* magazine, hundreds of surfers on the East Coast wrote to me begging to see the film. So I planned my first tour: a cross-country trip. I had one problem to solve first, though: I'd put 100,000 miles on my old Jeep panel truck from showing my film up and down the West Coast, and the four cylinders had gotten so loose and the valves so leaky that it now burned more oil than gasoline. I'd leave a trail of black, oily smoke every time I left beach parking lots, so I followed a friend's advice and put in 100-weight oil that was so thick it was almost a solid paste. That temporarily made the engine sound smooth and quiet enough to be worth $200 on a trade-in for a new, $2,000 Ford Econoline van. No AC, no radio, no seats in the back, but a surf vehicle par excellence.

That bare-bones set of wheels took my sister Gaye, surfer Rusty Miller, and me all the way to the East Coast to show my film five times. What an adventure; for Gaye and me it was our first time outside of California. Though I was still shy and not at all talkative, she and I really bonded during this month of laborious screenings, exotic cuisine, and strange accents. We also experienced firsthand the early days of the civil rights movement. In Alabama, I stole a Ku Klux Klan poster off a telephone pole to keep as a memento of the South, but then we were

An early review of **A Cool Wave of Color** with illustration by Rick Griffin.

A Dip into
A Cool Wave of Color
2:46   #2

followed for ten miles by some guys in a pickup truck with a notable gun rack. In Daytona Beach, we were introduced to the cheapest breakfast in the state: eggs, grits, Florida orange juice, and coffee for 25¢. We met the local hot surf kid, "Flea" Shaw, a 12-year-old goofy foot who was small enough to milk the weak Daytona Beach waves beautifully. Nearly every surfer we met fell in love with my sister, and I made it my job to fend them off. I'd tell them they were all too late since she had a boyfriend back home, and my protectiveness connected us for life.

When we reached New York, we were dazzled by Manhattan, its museums (especially MoMA), and Broadway. Feeling inspired, I even talked Barbara into a long Greyhound bus ride from Ithaca to meet me at the Plaza Hotel, where I splurged on a romantic horse-drawn carriage ride through Central Park in the cold of October—it even lightly snowed, just like in the movies.

The following night, we were invited to a wild Halloween event concocted by surfer-hustler Kenny McIntyre, my New York film promoter, who could talk faster than any person I'd ever met. Unfortunately, Barbara couldn't stay for my well-hyped screening, but I once again knew she possessed my heart. Then, after finishing that fifth screening, Gaye and I began the four-day trip home, learning every step of the way; in all, we navigated through 23 states. Gaye still has the souvenir pins she bought in each new state we covered.

FROM PASSION TO PROFESSION

Joey Cabell, recognized as a stylist, innovator, and one of the world's top five surfers, 1966.

The Groundswell

"A smiling blond surfer girl takes your ticket at the door and you are inside. There is a hush in the sounds crowds always make, a final last shudder. Darkness grows for a moment, and then the screen comes to brilliant life. You are taken into a world of sunlight, greenery and beautiful warm waves of color."

—CRAIG LOCKWOOD, AUTHOR

By the end of my freshman year at UCSB and that summer tour, **A Cool Wave of Color** was being hailed as a bizarre work of art. It had recouped four times its production budget and I had gained a cult following—probably 4,000 people who were itching to see my next film. But my success came at a price. Because I'd worked night and day finishing my film, my class attendance had suffered, and I had earned an F in one class. My first failure in life shocked and embarrassed me to no end. I couldn't tell my parents or Barbara. I came to realize that I could have avoided this situation if I had been less shy and more open to discussing my time-management troubles with my teacher or a counselor. That failure became a life lesson. Though I loved the class, the professor, and the challenge, I had taken on too much. But then I had an even bigger decision to make, and for this I needed my parents' help. When I got home for the summer, I told them that I wanted to make a second film. "Even after I pay my taxes this year, I'll still have $12,000," I said. "But I'll have to drop out of school for a year to do this."

I was pretty sure they'd object, but instead they laughed. "Why not?" they said. "What are you worried about? You can't starve or freeze in California!" I was taken aback. I hadn't heard that question since Mr. Wentz had used it for our senior class play. But I was confused. Hadn't my parents sacrificed to save money for our college educations? Then they told me that everyone was going to college, but I had a chance to do something completely different. And if it didn't work, I could always go back to school. I was shocked, but that's how my parents were: supportive at every turn. Whenever I came to a crossroads, they guided me toward boldness, if not by word, then by example. So I dropped out of school to make **The Performers**, a documentary about three surf bums in search of adventure in Mexico, California, and Hawaii. I felt the production could be done in seven months.

Dodging a Bullet (Literally)

I would soon discover that the US Army had its own production plans for me; dropping out of college had triggered an induction notice. The year 1965 had the largest draft call-up ever; President Johnson wanted 500,000 troops to prepare to ship off to Vietnam. My timing could not have been worse.

Back then, every American boy, on turning 18, was required to sign up for the military draft. They then mailed you a Selective Service card—the draft card that protesters of the Vietnam War ceremoniously burned on TV. Boys my age were panicking. Some friends, like Corky Carroll, were rejected because knee-paddling had put calluses on their knees and feet, which prevented them from wearing high-topped army boots.

On the date listed on my notice, I drove to the Los Angeles army induction headquarters for my physical. The drive seemed surreal and frightening, like I was headed down a darkened highway, as this one

(FACING PAGE, TOP LEFT) Hilarious and talented main characters, Richard Chew and Bob Limacher, pose next to my van. (TOP RIGHT AND BOTTOM) Mark Martinson and Billy Hamilton, as well as waves at Sunset Beach, made **The Performers** a success.

The Performers

FILMED IN: 16MM

RELEASE DATE: 1965

FEATURING: Richard Chew, Bob Limacher, and Mark Martinson

FILMED IN: California, Hawaii, and Mexico

AWARDS: Named "Best Surfing Film of the Year" by *International Surfing Magazine*

pivotal moment could derail my carefully calculated life. As I parked my van and walked past the winos and homeless who slept against the grimy alley walls on skid row, I was panic stricken. Nervous, I passed a longhaired protestor passing out antiwar handbills, then a group of young men standing in line, preinducted and ready to board a bus for boot camp at Fort Ord. I entered the austere brick building, and a tall man in uniform handed me an application. "Fill this in, then follow that yellow line." From there, about 100 kids stripped down to their underwear and followed the yellow brick line as sergeants yelled instructions. Every kid seemed as terrified as me. Over the next hour, we endured unimaginable tests conducted on every part of our body and brain—eye charts, strength calculations, hearing tests, and even the dreaded, abhorrent prostate exam—an unpleasant exam that was new to me. There was no talking—certainly no laughing. This was serious business and everyone knew it. Some were ready to join up, healthy and eager for a new direction. Not me! I brought a letter and X-rays from my orthopedic surgeon. After years of throwing a baseball against my neighbor's cinder-block wall, I'd had to have an operation on my throwing arm, ending my dreams of becoming the next Don Drysdale. I could throw strikes, but my elbow was permanently damaged.

I passed all the mental and physical tests, but then came the moment of truth. "Anyone who has a reason for not being in the army line up here," barked the sergeant, pointing to an area where three doctors were examining young men. I held back so I could read the doctors' vibes and picked the one who looked the nicest and most sympathetic. I got behind 20 kids in that line.

"What's wrong with you, son?" he asked. I gave him my letter, which he read without much interest. He'd seen trumped-up doctor's notes before. Then I handed him my X-rays. He held up the first and then the second one against the overhead light, gazed from one to the other, then yelled to the other doctors, "Hey, look at these X-rays. This guy is really screwed up!"

Those were the kindest words I'd ever heard. I was saved, if not from death, at least from a complete detonation of my plans for a second film. The sympathetic doctor told me to go home and that the army didn't need me.

As I drove back to Orange County, I remember feeling a little ashamed. Even though I hated the war effort, I loved my country and didn't want to let it down. I steered home in a trance. Within a week, I received my 1-Y deferment; the army determined that my elbow couldn't handle the heft of an M16. The assessment was correct. I've since had four operations on that elbow.

My First Road Trip Outside the United States

The Performers followed USSA surfing champion Richard Chew, rising star Bob Limacher, and young Huntington Beach champion Mark Martinson as they toured California, Mexico, and Hawaii. Though I had never been to a foreign country, we'd heard about a long Mexican point break at San Blas, about three hours south of Mazatlán. We decided to drive my new van down there over Easter vacation, when Bob would be on high school break. We hurried to get there, trading off drivers, sleeping in the back, only stopping for gas and bathroom breaks. Driving at night in Mexico required extra attention, because cows and goats loved to wander onto the roadway. Before cars were required to have seat belts, hitting a large animal often resulted in death—and not just of the animal.

As soon as we arrived at Matanchén Bay near the sleepy town of San Blas, we knew it had been worth the long drive. American hippies were everywhere, eating cheaply and enjoying the warmth and color of this quaint, charming village. And the waves! They were at four feet at a right point with a ride longer than any I'd ever seen before—almost a mile! Because it was also a slow wave, I could surf holding the camera and film Rich and Bob from behind, giving the audience something I figured they'd never seen. We waxed up, but before we could get to the water, we were attacked by biting bugs that locals called no-see-ums. It was an appropriate name because you literally couldn't see them, but you sure could feel 'em! We raced across the sand and dove in for some saltwater relief.

I photographed for about three hours, reloading film at the van and loving being in this new environment. That is, until after one ride, Rich looked to shore and pointed. "Isn't that our van driving down the beach?" he asked. And so it was, creeping away at three miles per hour.

Rich and I paddled to shore as fast as possible and ran after the van. When we reached it and opened the door, we found a longhaired hippie in the driver's seat drawing deeply on a giant "bomber" of a joint. Rich grabbed the steering wheel and yelled, "This is our van!"

In San Blas, Mexico, where you could drive on the hard sand beach at Matanchén Bay.

The weekly KHJ-TV show, *Surf's Up*, helped me and my film become well known.

The guy looked like he'd seen a ghost. "Hey," he said. "I thought I'd take it for a while." When I told him that was not in the cards, the hippie mumbled, climbed out, and stumbled away. We shook our heads. Only a true Darwin Award candidate would smoke weed in Mexico—if the Federales caught you they'd lock you up forever. But at least we had our van back. We surfed San Blas for a week, laughed hysterically at Bob and Rich's stories, and drove home with a great sequence in the can.

On my first trip to Hawaii, I rented a bedroom at Oahu's Sunset Point, where I stayed within my $2-a-day food budget by subsisting on rice, eggs, and pineapple juice. The kitchen supported so many cockroaches that even Raid couldn't slow them down. Butch Maloney suggested the blowtorch approach, so we upped Raid's aerosol powers with Butch's Zippo lighter, and the roaches were toast. All that was left were their charred remains outlined on the plasterboard walls.

One day during that month at Sunset Point, a lifeguard-surfer named Jim Graham called me from LA to say that he worked for a TV show called *Surf's Up* and they wanted to buy footage from me. I was all in! Over the next two years, I sold footage at such a fair price that Stan Richards, the host and something of a local celebrity, would invite me onto the show about a dozen times to promote my LA film screenings, and it helped to attract bigger, and for me, record-setting crowds.

When **The Performers** came out in 1965, it was named Film of the Year by *International Surfing Magazine*. **The Endless Summer** had received the same award the year before.

When I showed my film in San Francisco, I got a great taste of the Summer of Love. Don Ed Hardy, a friend from Newport, invited me to a Big Brother and the Holding Company (Janis Joplin) concert at the Fillmore Auditorium. Don knew the local art crowd, as he attended the highly regarded San Francisco Art Institute.

Inside the Fillmore, the energy was palpable. Even without the influence of weed it was a trip. The walls pulsed in a splash of projected organic life, dripping with paint, vibrating to the amorphous beat, matching the sizzle of Janis's searing, emotional wail. Her throaty voice lifted us off the ground with its urgent message of freedom from war, the draft, oppression and overcommercialization. Don and I danced, laughed, and sang all night.

Years later, art critics would dub Hardy "the designer who turned tattooing into art" with his hugely successful eponymous fashion line, Ed Hardy. Don stands as validation of my dad's motto: Do one unique thing better than anyone, and the money will follow.

The Backup Plan

Despite **The Performers** having tripled its investment, I still felt I needed a backup career option. After showings in California and Hawaii, I wrote to the dean at UCSB to plead for another chance, and then drove up to meet with him. Once I was inside the school office, the dean greeted me so warmly that I was confused. Hadn't I failed an important class? I had . . . but it turned out that he and his son had seen both of my films, so he understood the demands I had placed on myself. He immediately announced that UCSB would be happy to have me back. That fall, I returned to UCSB to work on my physics degree, my safety-valve plan.

To save money, my uncle and aunt offered me their spare bedroom. Uncle Don was the mayor of Santa Barbara and friendly with another politician, Ronald Reagan, who had a ranch nearby. Since my classes included political science and speech, plus calculus, chemistry, and US history, I was given a chance to shape my political positions by debating the issues with my wonderful aunt and uncle. It was fun trying to win them over to my increasingly liberal, environmental views.

The Gamble of a Creative Partnership

"Surfers live differently than other people. They live a unique, carefree life. To a surfer, only two things are important: the sun and the surf."

—FROM THE **FREE AND EASY** FILM POSTER

As MacGilli-luck would have it, my life changed at a screening of a bizarre 3D surf film. I met a filmmaker who was doing almost exactly the same thing I was, and just a few miles from me. Though for many women, including my mother, the first impression of six-foot-tall Jim Freeman was that of a painfully handsome young man, it didn't take long to realize that he had a seriously intelligent, energetic side, which explained why he was a premed student at Southern California's Loma Linda University. His parents were hoping he would follow in his father's footsteps and become a doctor, but, like me, Jim had an artistic streak and a passion for developing projects on his own. What amazed me and was convincing evidence of his industriousness was that Jim had produced the first stereoscopic surf movie, an astonishing achievement since surfing doesn't lend itself to 3D, as it happens too far away from the camera. He was obviously a brave risk-taker with an independent spirit. One particular 10-minute sequence in his film **Outside the Third Dimension** showed Jim's capacity for realizing his dreams. It was a beautiful sequence shot in the sand dunes of Pismo Beach, illustrating Jim's knowledge about film technique. When I approached him after his screening, I found that Jim was friendly and generous with his advice. We thought that we could learn a lot from each other, and our friendship blossomed. Though our colleges were 100 miles apart, we talked regularly by

phone about movies we'd seen.

In the mid-1960s, worldwide cinema was taking off into a creative vein that previously had been tempered by aging union members and heavyweight studio control. Independent films from the US and new wave films from France and Italy were widening the audience and breaking open the ways people could be entertained by visuals and music. A movie like Richard Lester's **A Hard Day's Night**, premiering in 1964 and featuring the Beatles in black and white, was a case in point. Jim and I pored over this film, as well as those by Fellini, Truffaut, Godard, and Bergman. These inventive filmmakers ignited our imaginations of what was possible in storytelling using musical sequences, nonlinear stories, flashbacks, and fantasy moments. I studied films so obsessively that I made a deal with a theater manager: I would pay one and a half times the admission if he'd let me see a film five times. When my uncle heard about my budget problem, he loaned me his mayor's pass so I could get free movie tickets in Santa Barbara.

After months of telephone conversations, Jim and I came up with a film script that we thought would speak to our contemporaries. We wanted to explore the ideas of our generation's freedom and creativity by telling the story of surfers who travel to what was a relatively unknown continent at the time, South America, on a shoestring budget in search of adventure, beauty, and self-discovery. Our first joint venture was launched, and we were off and running.

South America: Virgin Territory

Jim and I dropped out of school at the end of the semester, pooled our savings, bought travelers checks, and along with surfers Mark Martinson and Dale Struble, set off with our cameras and surfboards to South

(FACING PAGE) Jim Freeman at age 19 became the only filmmaker to make a surfing film in 3D. It was a very difficult challenge, impressing everyone. Here he films in Hawaii, drawing power from his rental car, to keep the right-eye camera and the left-eye camera perfectly in sync.

America, flying first to Guayaquil, Ecuador, on student standby rates of 50 percent off. (We used this technique until we turned 30 and the airline ticket seller asked, "Aren't you a bit old to be students?")

In the mid-1960s, surfing was unheard of across 90 percent of South America. Arriving in Ecuador, we hitchhiked to what we thought would be the most likely place for surfing. While there, we met Dorothy Jurado, who felt she could help us find surf in her beat-up jalopy. We roamed the coast with Dorothy for eight days and shot pictures of small surf, warm water, and super-friendly Ecuadorians, including Alias Ortega, Gustavo Plaza, and Christian Bjarner.

Because the waves were small and the water warm, it was a perfect time to try to teach Jim to surf. Since he'd grown up in Santa Ana, a long 40-minute drive from the ocean, he'd never tried the sport. Mark and I helped him paddle out and catch a few waves and he did well. That said, six-footers like Jim have a harder time of it. Plus, it's easier to pick up surfing during the teenage years. Jim was 21. Later, Jim contented himself with bike riding, unicycle riding, and skiing; his surfing days began and ended in the warm waters of Ecuador.

Argentina: Finding A+ Surf

After two weeks in Peru and Chile, where we found B-quality surf, we got lucky in Mar del Plata, Argentina. In this beautiful small town similar to Laguna Beach, we were driven around by a 60-year-old fisherman named Diego, who loved and coddled his prized possession—an old panel truck, with its original tires and most of the tread. Even on the terrible Argentine roads, Diego managed to keep full control, never exceeding 15 miles an hour on straightaways and five on the curves. This gave him plenty of time to watch the women go by. "I am the Tarzan of the woman!" was his only English phrase. Because it made no sense, we tried to modify his claim, to no success. This movie-inspired phrase was stuck in Diego's head!

After searching down every road that led to the beach, we located a beautiful four- to six-foot sandbar break with offshore wind. Jim and

(ABOVE LEFT) Dale Struble head-dips in Argentina. (ABOVE RIGHT) We stayed at the Hotel Grand Dorá, Mar del Plata, Argentina. (RIGHT) In 1966, we found about 20 resident surfers in beautiful Rio de Janeiro, Brazil. Now there are thousands. At Ipanema Beach, Dale Struble rides the nose.

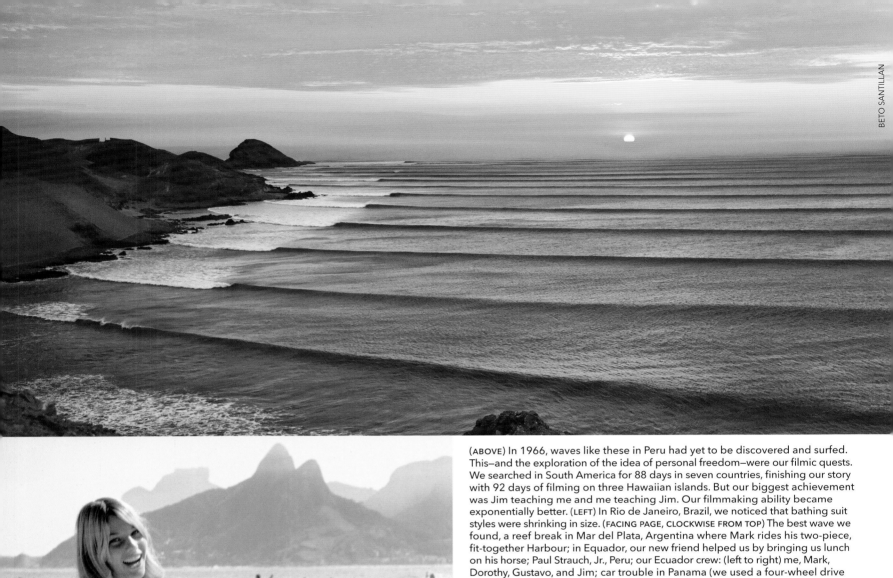

BETO SANTILLAN

(ABOVE) In 1966, waves like these in Peru had yet to be discovered and surfed. This—and the exploration of the idea of personal freedom—were our filmic quests. We searched in South America for 88 days in seven countries, finishing our story with 92 days of filming on three Hawaiian islands. But our biggest achievement was Jim teaching me and me teaching Jim. Our filmmaking ability became exponentially better. (LEFT) In Rio de Janeiro, Brazil, we noticed that bathing suit styles were shrinking in size. (FACING PAGE, CLOCKWISE FROM TOP) The best wave we found, a reef break in Mar del Plata, Argentina where Mark rides his two-piece, fit-together Harbour; in Equador, our new friend helped us by bringing us lunch on his horse; Paul Strauch, Jr., Peru; our Ecuador crew: (left to right) me, Mark, Dorothy, Gustavo, and Jim; car trouble in Panama (we used a four-wheel drive Jeep to get to a hidden point break in Panama, but the tide rose quickly and caused a disaster—which made for a good story beat).

SURF FILMS

PRODUCED BY
JIM FREEMAN
Phone: KI 3-6432
P. O. Box 1701
SANTA ANA, CALIFORNIA
Promotion: RON ADAMS

I decided to shoot two cameras from shore to get two angles we could cut together. We had walkie-talkies and after each ride we'd compare notes. "How did it look from your angle?" "Good, Greg!" "Well, how good?" "Well, pretty good!" But it was hard to communicate the success of a shot with just words, so we began using grades. "Hey, Greg, my shot was A-, how was yours?" "Mine was C+. Because you got an A-, why don't you move and get another angle?" We could really maximize our two-camera setup this way. Using letter grades was just the ticket. The system has continued to this day.

That evening, Mark and Dale tripped over to the casino. With our money running low, Dale blew $15 in a card game. Depression. Then Mark started hitting at the roulette wheel: $368. Elation! We had money to carry on. Money to eat. Money for resin to patch the boards. We headed north toward warmer waters and explorations of Uruguay, Brazil, and Panama.

Brazilian Blowout

This is the way I described my new favorite city, Rio, for an article in *Surfer* magazine: "In this, the largest Portuguese-speaking country in the world, home of the Bossa Nova, Antonio Carlos Jobim, Luiz Bonfa, Pele and coffee, you can exchange one dollar for 2,200 Brazilian cruzeiro. Brazil's main surfing beach is Arpoador at Ipanema, a left off a rock headland. Copacabana was known for rights and lefts, beach break. Mark and Dale found the local bunnies friendly and intrigued with their surfing. Rioans sashayed about in G-strings and played paleto on the sand while vendors sold mate and guarana from thermoses."

We stayed five weeks in Rio de Janeiro with the Beltrâo family of Copacabana Beach. This is where I learned to say "Agradecimento," thank you in Portuguese, because they were so generous and helpful. Their son, Irencyr, as well as Luis Leopoldo Noronho and Walter Guerra, the very first surfers in Brazil, acted as our guides. It seemed that every living room in Rio had a portrait of Jesus over the fireplace, and one of John F. Kennedy right beside it. JFK's Alliance for Progress, his Peace Corps, and his devotion to Catholicism had created a deeply held trust in all Americans. We were no longer Ugly Americans.

When we moved on to Panama, Dale's family friend, Captain Wilhite of the US Navy, drove us 30 miles north along the beach to a surfing spot he claimed was the best in Panama. Just like Malibu, he said. But we never got there, because the Jeep got stuck in the sand as the tide was coming in, and in no time was more than halfway underwater. Nearby farmers brought in their tractor for the rescue and a neighbor arrived in his uncle's bulldozer, but they also got stuck! It was a huge mess and Mark and Dale were certain we were going to jail—or to hell, whichever came first. Instead, Jim and I turned this would-be tragedy into a comic sequence for the film.

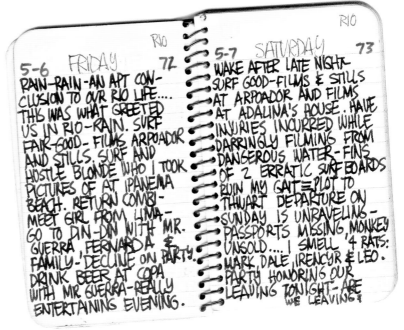

In South America, our photography, as well as the way we structured scenes and sequences, became progressively more sophisticated, and by the end of the three months, Jim and I had gone from B+ filmmakers to solid A's. We exceeded limits that we hadn't even known were there. I learned what he knew, and he learned what I knew, and very quickly, what we now knew together made a huge difference in the quality of our filmmaking.

As Jim and I got to know each other, I was always struck by how normal and calm Jim was, particularly compared to his father, who was an intense, proselytizing dictator, always warning Jim in letters of "the terrible soon-coming bloodshed and confusion . . . and of the destructive forces of fire, flood and earthquake that will soon sweep America." With such a bible-thumping father, how was Jim so carefree, positive, and creative? As our trust in each other grew, we decided to test out our new skills on the big waves off the Hawaiian Islands.

Before we left, Jim and I thought back to the first time we watched **The Endless Summer**, just weeks after I had premiered **A Cool Wave of Color**. Jim wondered how Bruce Brown, who had shown himself to be an A+ narrator and humorist (our Will Rogers) but just a B+ film artist, could have produced such an artful, stunning, fresh, and original film. To Jim and me, it was like a minor league team winning the World Series. We had to figure this out and learn from it. After researching it, we concluded that Bruce had used his advisors (Dick Metz, Hobie Alter, Bob Bagley, R. Paul Allen, and Bruce's wonderful wife, Pat) to full advantage; but he also had spent two years perfecting the film! Then and there, Jim and I agreed to find our own great advisors and to spend more time on every one of our films in order to get them perfect. We may not have reached the level of brilliance that Bruce did, but our films certainly did improve.

Haleiwa Theatre, built in the 1930s.

Aloha!

On display during Hawaii's 1966–67 winter season, the quality of surfing took a leap. Lucky for us, our filmmaking was keeping pace with those positive elements. Jim and I wanted to showcase, really for the first time, the exceptional beauty of the state of Hawaii, not just the waves. We designed the sequences as artistic explorations featuring the range of color, the dramatic, intensely green landscapes, the wide variety of flowers and trees. Hawaii represented the most diverse natural beauty we had seen, and our goal was to capture it and amaze audiences everywhere.

During our stay, Jim and I celebrated good filming days at the Sea View Inn, the most deluxe restaurant in Haleiwa. We also checked out the local movie houses. The theaters were prewar construction and films changed daily. But here, a typical screening featured an added attraction—an off-screen rat race. The local rats earned their keep by collecting popcorn, Juicy Fruit, and cracked seed candy. They snuck in, then scampered right and left, scarfing leftovers. You could follow a rat's route by tracking the lifting of feet and the muffled screams. To be honest, rat-racing was often more interesting than the film—unless a

Samurai movie was showing. New to us Californians, these blood-curdling war films were Japanese-style James Bond adventures. I think the high-pitched attack screams even terrified the rats.

An Expedition to Maui

We filmed for weeks on the North Shore and then decided to shoot an adventure sequence on the island of Maui. We selected two of the 30 or so North Shore surfers and told them we'd pay their way, cover food and lodging, and guarantee a lot of fun. Our first choice was Bill Fury of Huntington Beach, who had appeared in several surfing films before. Our second pick was a 17-year-old from Newport Beach named Herbie Fletcher. We called him "the kid," but we'd seen him at Rock Pile and Sunset Beach and we knew that he was an outstanding up-and-coming surfer.

Because very few outside surfers had ever tried the waves in Maui at that time, they thought it sounded like a great adventure—and it was! It was pretty new to us, too. Jim and I were learning to embrace the unknown and would just play it by ear. We got wonderful shots at Honolua Bay of Herbie and Bill carving the face of eight-foot surf. We shot from two different camera positions so we could edit the vantage points together. During our time in Maui, Jim and I grew to love and appreciate the honest character and creative mind of Herbie Fletcher. We hadn't been wrong about his promising future; Herbie would become one of surfing's great inventors, creating the peel-and-stick nonslip coatings that every surfer still uses. I think of his accomplishments as comparable to Hobie Alter, inventor of the Hobie Cat; Tom Morey, who created boogie boards; Bob Nealy, who designed the first surf leashes; and Bob Simmons, the father of modern surfboards. Herbie excelled at everything he tried, including being a great father and husband. It was wonderful to be there at the beginning!

While in Lahaina in 1966, I also ran into Pete Whitehead, a friend from high school who I remembered as the best writer in our class. Poetic Pete, we used to call him; his descriptions of surfing topped everything except the contemporary words of Drew Kampion and William Finnegan. Seeing him, I grew troubled. He was spaced out and disconnected from reality. I invited him to sit and catch up.

Under the huge Lahaina banyan tree, we reminisced as best we could, but Pete wasn't really there. His long hair was unkempt, he wore a trench coat and sandals, and he thought he was Jesus Christ. Six free-spirited girls kept him company. The hour-long encounter left me deeply disturbed and dogged me for days. I'd seen this happen all too often. During the 1960s, experimenting with drugs took a heavy toll on my friends and left many scarred for life. Surfers seemed to be first in line to try something new because they liked to take chances. Drug dealers got rich preying on them.

Soon after I got back to California, another high school friend called. "You're not going to believe this," he said. "Pete thought he was invincible—that he could float on clouds. He and six girls walked off the cliff at Windmills, holding hands. They all died on the rocks below."

Among the emotions that coursed through me that day were large doses of anger and guilt. Could I have done more for Pete? How did he get himself into this terrible state? Ever since then, when I read of dealers being celebrated as enlightened thinkers—the Laguna Brotherhood and Timothy Leary, for example—I can't help but mourn my friends who suffered as a result of the drug pushers' greed.

The Great Race—A Comedy Sequence

Back on the North Shore of Oahu, one rainy day, Jim and I found ourselves in a rented home thinking of ways to supercharge our film. We dreamed up the Great Race, an old-car competition.

The comic concept was that, on bad surf days, surfers would race each other from Sunset Beach to Ka'ena Point in their beat-up cars and vie for a pot of prize money. We storyboarded the race so we'd know which cuts we'd need to film, and included different comic sequences: crashes, cars catching on fire, surfboards flying off the roof of a car, even an old clunker sailing off the edge of a cliff! We shot the sequences on Ke Nui Road with no permits and no approvals. Back then, it was rare to see police on the lonely North Shore, so we were surprised to encounter a cop—and an unhappy one at that.

"Who's in charge here?" he demanded. I meekly stepped forward and was treated to an angry, loud lecture about the hazards of stunt driving. He followed that up with a very expensive ticket for reckless endangerment. I could never afford it! So when the great Butch Van Artsdalen (then known as Mr. Pipeline and considered to be North Shore royalty) walked over, I caught my breath. He proceeded to tear the paper ticket into tiny pieces, adding, "I've got friends . . . I'll make sure the cops never come after you again." They didn't.

In our best storyboarded moment, we'd set up an unidentified driver of a black mystery car: the "North Shore Tours and Pest Control" car. Who was behind the wheel?

When we were cooking up this concept, Rich Harbour came up with an idea: "Wouldn't it be boss if Mickey Dora was the mystery driver?" We agreed that Dora, the misanthrope who had a reputation for running over other surfers at Malibu, would be the perfect villain, but we figured he would either flat-out refuse or want to be paid big bucks. Jim, our resident diplomat, assured us that he could talk anyone into anything, so we tracked Mickey down and Jim went for it.

Free and Easy

FILMED IN: 16MM

RELEASE DATE: 1967

FEATURING: Mark Martinson, Billy Hamilton, Herbie Fletcher, Bill Fury, Dale Struble, David Nuuhiwa, Nat Young

DISTINCTIONS: The most popular surfing film from 1967 and 1968. Considered the "best surf film" by Corky Carroll, WSSA president Kevin Summerall, David Nuuhiwa, Mike Doyle.

Free and Easy Montage

4:28   #3

As expected, Mickey came back with, "It's gonna cost you, young man!"

"How much?" asked Jim, refusing to fold. "Two hundred dollars a day," Mickey said, as Jim's jaw dropped. "And, Laddie, I'll need a written contract and I'll need to be paid in advance." We wrote up that contract as fast as humanly possible and hightailed it over to Mickey with the $200 cash in hand. We wanted to film the next day, since the forecast again called for rain.

Despite our excitement, we were a little worried about Mickey. Word on the street was that he'd run into trouble with bad checks, deception, and larceny. Years later he would violate parole by fleeing to Europe, get arrested by the FBI, and spend time in prison. Would he take our $200 and run? Lucky for us, he showed up on time decked out in a dazzling white sport coat reminiscent of a white knight, which is what we ended up calling his character in the film.

We staged the scene and Mickey drove the black "North Shore Tours and Pest Control" car across the finish line and stepped out to greet a raucous crowd of seven surfers plus a clutch of springy pom-pom girls (footage I'd shot in high school and edited in). As he removed his sunglasses à la Jack Lemmon in **The Great Race**, the dapper bon vivant, our own White Knight, the eccentric Mickey Dora, was unveiled. Popping open the hood like a magician, Mickey shared with the cheering crowd his secret weapon: a chromed, supercharged, eight-cylinder, 350-horsepower engine (which we filmed later at a race-track!) hiding inside this broken-down sedan. And that's a wrap!

With the premiere approaching, we sent a pair of tickets to the man of mystery himself, Mickey Dora, in the hopes he'd show up for our first showing at the gigantic Santa Monica Civic Auditorium. That night Bill Bennett was one of our ticket sellers. A peculiar man arrived wearing a trench coat with the lapels pulled up to hide his face, a floppy fedora, and dark glasses. When he sidled up to the ticket window, Bill called out, "Oh, hey, Mickey Dora! How you doin'?"

(FACING PAGE) The White Knight, Mickey Dora, wins the Great Race as Jim films. Stunt drivers were Greg Tucker and Butch Van Artsdalen (BOTTOM RIGHT).

Dora spoke in a low voice: "Are these tickets that you guys sent to me any good?"

Bill said, "Of course they are and we're glad you're here. Have a good time. By the way, you're really great as the 'White Knight'!"

An Expedition to Kauai

To finish off our film, we flew with Mark Martinson and Billy Hamilton to Kauai to film Hanalei Bay. After a 50-minute drive from Lihue, this horseshoe bay that Joey Cabell had suggested to me welcomed us with a seven-foot swell. I paddled out with my waterproof camera while Jim shot from the end of the pier. After two hours of filming, I asked the one other surfer whether this was the correct takeoff spot. "Yeah," he replied, "but when it's really big, the swell shifts to the north." He pointed way outside. We stayed for nine days. Billy Hamilton's stories of that life-changing adventure follow.

Billy Hamilton Remembers Kauai, 1966

We awoke to a stormy onshore and a light drizzle that seemed to persist. We loaded the car with the day's equipment and set out for the end of the road, seven miles away. Mark Martinson and I knew each other from surfing contests and some great adventures with our mutual friend, Corky Carroll. Mark was at that time the US champion and one of the best surfers in the world. His style was compact, fast, and explosive.

As a group, we were learning about each other daily, and Mark's quick wit was a catalyst for us. We made a good team. Jim and Greg, a few years older, were exceptionally energetic and organized. Greg had an intelligent, infectious laugh and there was a constant banter between him and Jim. All in all, we were a band of happy explorers. I was seventeen but had a lot of life experience under my belt. I started drinking and smoking cigarettes at fourteen and hung around people five to ten years older. By the time I was a senior in high school, my drinking days were over, primarily because I discovered pot and LSD. Unlike former president Bill Clinton, who tried smoking pot and never inhaled, I embraced the idea wholeheartedly.

That day in Kauai, the outer reefs were showing a lot of white water, but it was hard to tell where the good waves were, and there were very few surfers to ask. Kuhio Highway, a two-lane road, wound its way up into the mountains, then down into a beautiful valley called Lumahai. A narrow river ran beneath a sweeping bridge and across a broad sand beach, emptying into the ocean a half mile distant. Kauai

(FACING PAGE, TOP) Out in front of the two-bedroom cottage we rented at Rocky Point: Jim, Rich Harbour, and I pose with our stunt vehicle, "The North Shore Tours and Pest Control" Plymouth. (BOTTOM) Making **Free and Easy** allowed us to write a wonderful story for *Surfer* magazine (and include David Nuuhiwa on the cover) and introduce Herbie Fletcher, 17, to his future wife, Dibbi, 15.

was a freshwater paradise, but in 1966, I had no idea that I would end up raising my two boys there, Laird and Lyon.

We arrived at Ke'e Beach and the ocean beyond. A narrow trail leading into the jungle made its way up to a red cottage with white trim perched on the edge of an outcropping of large black boulders and overlooking a peaceful lagoon. A magical place. Further along, on land that would mark the start of the Na Pali coastline, we found a large rock heiau, a lichen-covered stone altar that whispered of an ancient time of religious worship. Next to it was the quaint red cottage. In 1973, Duke Kahanamoku's wife, Nadine told me an interesting story about the red cottage. Nadine's narrative: "Duke and I spent our honeymoon at the charming little place. I was swimming in the lagoon one morning and the current caught me and was taking me out to sea! I was yelling and calling out Duke's name and thank God he heard me. He saved me! It was a terrible fright."

At Ke'e, we had enough weather savvy to know that when it blew onshore on the north side of the island, you went west. I remember our first surf in front of the Coco Palms Hotel. Unlike Hanalei, the wind was offshore and calm. The sun was out, and a perfect knee-high wave was peeling off the sand bar. The Coco Palms seemed very quiet; there wasn't a tourist on the beach. Mark and I played around for an hour or so . . . but Greg and Jim were not on Kauai to film baby shore break. We were here to work and discover the best new waves. Off again, this time further west.

The drive took hours. Kauai's roads were unkempt and dotted with potholes. Once in a great while we got up to 50 miles an hour. I don't remember how we found the road to Barking Sands, because even the road leading to Polihale State Park was a rough secondary road that should've required four-wheel drive. When we arrived, we walked down to the shoreline and, as we walked, our feet made the sound of a bark. It was a testimony to exceptionally clean, dry sand. (Sadly, that sound has disappeared thanks to ocean pollution by suntan oils, detergents, and other man-made contaminants.)

We set off to explore the nearby naval base. We drove up to a gate guarded by two MPs. A large American flag hung solemnly on a pole in the distance amid a cluster of buildings and barracks. The MP leaned out the window to check Jim's papers, which Jim of course didn't have. But Jim could sweet talk anyone. "We're tourists, by golly! We'd like to look at the ocean." But the MP shook his head; access denied. Jim did a U-turn and headed out to the main highway. What the navy did not know was that we were seasoned surf veterans with years of experience recon-surfing the heavily military-patrolled beaches of Camp Pendleton, Trestles, and Cotton's Point. Jim parked along the road and we grabbed our gear and headed for the ocean. We scrambled over a couple of barbed wire fences and through a forest of

(ABOVE) Mark Martinson and Billy Hamilton first fall in love with Kauai, 1966. (BELOW LEFT) Beautiful JoAnn Hamilton and two-year-old Lyon. (BELOW RIGHT) Laird at age 10. (FACING PAGE) Billy loved the energy every winter storm contained.

keawe trees. Duck soup it was not. The tree branches were covered in long spikes, and when the branches died, the spikes littered the sand, turning it into a virtual minefield. Mark and I were wearing rubber slippers called "go-aheads," because you couldn't walk backward in them. Greg and Jim had tennis shoes on. I went down first. Fuck! I sat on the sand, blood pouring onto my sandal. When I took it off, a half inch of thorn was exposed. Needless to say, it was a long walk. Mark and I walked on our longboards for the next 20 minutes.

We finally neared the ocean. A small sand dune obstructed our view, but up and over the top, voilà!, a set of three shoulder-high, glassy, barreling waves. We surfed for hours while Greg and Jim documented our first major discovery, a place we named Whispering Sands. The photos of that event captured the handful of waves we actually made. Today, with its three prime surf breaks, it is known as the spot for some of Kauai's best waves.

We returned to the North Shore bungalow we had rented from friends to finish out the winter season. After enjoying the mellow scenes on the outer islands, Kauai and Maui, Oahu seemed bustling. Pipeline, one day, had more than ten guys out! Billy and Mark stayed with Jim and me in our cockroach villa, and we all encountered the event of the season. My dear friend, JoAnn Zerfas, one of the best-educated and well-read people I'd met, besides Barbara, asked if she could stay for a week. She'd been hired to manage a helicopter tour company and needed time to find a North Shore rental before she moved over her two-year-old son, Laird. Over that week, romance simmered between Billy and JoAnn, but Billy had jobs to complete in California. Over the next years, JoAnn relished her book-crammed nest on the North Shore, and Laird's playground became the shore break at Pupukea. Like most North Shore surf rats, the ocean was Laird's best friend. He would slide down the sand bank on the broken-off nose of a discarded surfboard to collide, head on, into a crashing wave. Unaware that Laird was JoAnn's boy, one day Billy joined in his fun, body surfing the shore break with little Laird holding onto his back. After a half hour, the three-year-old Laird asked Billy, "Do you want to meet my mother?" And then showing his creative, headstrong personality even at this young age, he confessed to Billy, "I want you to be my dad." That afternoon, when Billy and JoAnn saw each other again, joyous fireworks exploded and romance blossomed. Billy married JoAnn and would indeed become Laird's father and mentor. Over the next decade, this determined and talented youngster grew to become champion big wave surfer Laird Hamilton. It was a joy to watch his maturation over those subsequent years.

The Irrepressible
Laird Hamilton
1:05   #4

By April 1967, after Billy, Mark, Jim, and I wrapped our adventure in Hawaii, we had finished our film and were ready for its premiere. All we needed was a title, and because Jim's early films were haphazardly, almost carelessly, titled, that job fell to me. Since I always preferred emotion-inducing titles (without the word "surf"), I mulled it over and settled on a phrase that may have come from my school memories of reading *Huckleberry Finn*. I wanted to convey a sense of the freewheeling lifestyle that our film represented; the vagabond, carefree life of an artist-surfer. **Free and Easy** seemed like the perfect choice, but when I tried it out on Jim, he wanted to know what it meant and how people would know that the film was about surfing. I promised him that with the poster I'd designed, they would understand. He then told me that it sounded lazy, whereas our film

was action packed, to which I said, "I came up with **Catch the Joy** for our sand dunes film, which was tied to a William Blake poem, and now you love that title. I think **Free and Easy** will work well. And besides, we're out of time!" Though Jim was 22 and I was only 21, he finally agreed to trust me, and the name worked like a charm.

When Barbara came home from school to see one of the early screenings at the Santa Monica Civic Auditorium, she brought her friend from Cornell University, the intellectual Lynne Shavelson (daughter of Hollywood filmwright, Mel Shavelson). They loved the exotic locales photographed in new and inventive ways, the evocative music, and the title, which they thought pulled it all together. The audience was blown away, but more importantly, with **Free and Easy** I had convincingly impressed the most important person in my life.

(FACING PAGE, CLOCKWISE FROM TOP LEFT) Bill Fury and Herbie Fletcher, Honolua; the brilliant Margo Godfrey, 1967; the Bixby Ranch in the old days, when you could drive the hard sand beaches; David Nuuhiwa brought a ballet-like grace to **Free and Easy**, 1967. (ABOVE) **Free and Easy** opens with this statement appearing on screen; each of the colored letters, cut by hand with scissors, were animated in a playful way. It took me 50 hours to design and execute the 20-second opening.

Zanuck, Mickey, and The Sweet Ride

After completing an East Coast driving trip in the summer of 1967 to screen **Free and Easy** at nine locations from Miami to New York City, Jim and I hurried home for a meeting with Darryl Zanuck, head of 20th Century-Fox Studios. Chico Day, the longtime production associate at 20th (and brother of actor Gilbert Roland), had seen our film and recommended us to shoot and direct a surfing sequence for Zanuck's **The Sweet Ride**, starring Tony Franciosa and Jacqueline Bisset.

We were ushered into an enormous office where Chico introduced us to Zanuck. This larger-than-life movie mogul told us that he wanted us to make an exciting sequence for a special movie about the California lifestyle. "We're gonna spend about a week shooting the sequence," he said, "so what do I have to pay you to get the job done?"

Jim did all the talking. He told Zanuck that we'd just gotten back from our East Coast successes and that we had the opportunity to make many other films. "To do this important job for you," Jim said, with all the confidence in the world, "we would have to be paid no less than $10,000 for the week." I gasped; we'd never made anywhere near that amount, let alone for a week of work! Chico stared, impressed.

Zanuck put down his cigar and said smoothly, "I don't think that we can pay that much. How about $6,000?"

I was ready to take the deal, but Jim beat me to the punch. "We can't go any lower because this is already cutting into our schedule. We would love to do a great job for you, and we would, Mr. Zanuck, but really we need to be paid $10,000." Zanuck stood, shook hands, thanked us for coming, and, just like that, the meeting was over.

Dejected, Jim and I rode the elevator down and walked to the car. As we were backing out of the parking space, Chico began pounding on our window. With a huge smile, he said, "You guys did it! Zanuck loved you. He liked that you stuck to your guns. He told me, 'Give the kids the $10,000; they'll do a brilliant job!'" I think it was the happiest day of my life up to that moment, and it was all thanks to Jim.

But the good news didn't stop there.

Later that week, Jim talked Chico into renting Hollister Ranch for a week, first because it was my favorite surf spot, and second because, since it was private property, the filming wouldn't be complicated by crowds. Jim then convinced Chico to hire at high Screen Actors Guild (SAG) day wages ($180 a day, or $1,800 in today's dollars) the surfers we most admired. We had a blast filming Mickey Dora—dressed in a wig and a mustache to look like Tony Franciosa—as well as Robert August, Herbie Fletcher, Mark Martinson, Mike Hynson, and David Nuuhiwa.

The studio put our team up in a motel in Buellton, so every morning at 7:00 we piled into a school bus for the Ranch. The surfers sat together and traded stories during the entire hour-long drive.

Mickey Dora made up as Tony Franciosa.

Robert August peppered Mickey Dora with questions about old Malibu, and Dora obliged with, among many others, a story about his buddy Greg Noll that dated back to the mid-1950s. Ten-year-old Noll arrived on his bike at the beach parking lot for his first visit ever, and his initial vision was that of a teenage surfer banging a girl on the hood of his car for all to watch. Noll told Dora, "Right then, I knew as clear as day that all I wanted to be was a surfer!" Over the seven trips to and from the Ranch, Dora amused us all with his delicious stories and wicked sense of humor.

Every day, Mickey would go to the makeup chair, get his Franciosa mustache and hairpiece glued on, and then, in character, hold court and tell us how he'd break into Hollywood parties to get free food by getting dressed in his car, he in a tuxedo and his girlfriend in a cocktail dress, and walk into the event backwards carrying a champagne glass filled with bubbly as if he'd been at the party for hours. Or about the time Greg Noll, known as "da bull" for his big-wave skills, stole the treasured swim trunks that Dora wore in **Ride the Wild Surf**, and how he'd tricked "da bull" and gotten them back. Dora's eccentric personality made the shoot a complete hoot.

On some of those rides to and from the Ranch, Jim and I would sit with the film's cinematographer, Charles Clarke, who had edited and cowritten the definitive *American Cinematographer's Manual*, the bible of filmmaking. Jim hounded him, asking question after question, but Charles seemed to like it. Chico sat with us, fleshing out the answers with insights to the studio system. These experts, tops in their fields, opened up to us generously. By the time the week's work was completed, we walked away with far more upside than the $10,000.

(ABOVE) Me shooting 35mm action of Robert August and Herbie Fletcher, Hollister Ranch. (BELOW) At the Ranch for **The Sweet Ride**, we shot at Rights and Lefts for a week with our favorite friends and had so much fun!

HANG TEN No. 1
with "Free and Easy" Producers.

Greg MacGillivray and Jim Freeman of Surf Film fame choose Hang Ten's summer turtlenecks for their road shows. Designed for Action and Fashion, Hang Ten shirts are right for YOU.

Two's Company: MacGillivray Freeman Films

"When Hollywood or East Coast clients visited, we'd buy new shoes, because Jim and I always worked barefoot. 'They may not trust us if we don't wear shoes,' Jim said."

And so it happened: **Free and Easy** had changed our professional lives forever. Thanks in part to Jim's steadfast promotion of the film to our new Hollywood friends, our photography started getting us offers to work on Hollywood films as second-unit directors and cameramen, even outside the surfing genre. We had proven to ourselves that we could make it in the big leagues.

The success of **Free and Easy** hit so quickly that Jim and I had a big decision to make: Do we commit to working together and actually become professional filmmakers? Do we forget about going back to college and hire our first employees? If Jim scuttled his plans to become a doctor, a dream that his parents shared, could he be fulfilled by making films? And I loved school, physics, math, and filmmaking. Now I had to decide which path to follow. In our travels, our relationship had deepened from one of like-minded artists to best friends, so we felt confident about cementing a business partnership. Still, we asked our family members and friends, and I, of course, asked Barbara. Jim and I were surprised by the unanimous advice: You're good at it and you love it. My parents, of course, said, "Why not try it?" So Jim and I resolved to give this huge gamble a go. But could we make it work financially, dividing our meager profits by two?

Up to that point, we had saved all of our money for film production by working out of our parents' houses or in our dorm rooms. Low overhead. Now that we'd decided to take the leap, we would need to behave like a real business with a real office—and real monthly rent. Except, of course, that we knew almost nothing about running a real business! In those days, what we now call start-ups were often short-lived and we'd seen many fail. We didn't want to become another statistic, so we started learning about running a film company by studying Bruce Brown Films, producers of **The Endless Summer** and many television sports specials. Bruce owned a small, low-cost office/studio in Dana Point, had coproducer Bob Bagley running operations, and R. Paul Allen handling PR and film distribution. It was a tight, efficient, highly effective operation. So we tried to copy them. We, too, wanted to stay away from Hollywood and the studio system and live in a place of surf and natural beauty. And we believed that talented employees would prefer that kind of environment as well.

Jim and I struggled to choose between Laguna Beach and Santa Barbara, so I told him about one of my tried-and-true decision-making methods. After I'd stood behind my tripod a hundred times trying to predict which of a four-wave set would be worth the $2 of film I'd be using up, I learned to play the percentages. I'd build probability charts with weighted negative and positive factors and come away with a quantitative comparison.[2] In comparing these two possible homes for our company, we considered about 20 factors. The final decision came down to what some might think was a small point but was critically important to us: the temperature of the saltwater! For most of the year, the ocean water off Laguna Beach was 10°F warmer than Santa Barbara's. So Laguna won out, and we began the search for an office.

(FACING PAGE) Jim's father, Paul, owned an airplane, so he flew us all over Baja California, where we hunted for great point breaks in 1965.
(INSET) Jim and I were asked by Duke Boyd to be models in a surf shirt ad for the brand he'd begun, Hang Ten surfwear—a full page celebrating **Free and Easy**! He gave us free shirts as payment.

2 The hidden benefit of pure mathematical decision-making is a reduction in stress; the need to make a major decision stops weighing you down because it's on paper rather than running around in your head and heart.

(ABOVE) Our first office, Pyne Castle. (BELOW) When we toured with **Free and Easy** along the East Coast, one screening was in Asbury Park, New Jersey, where we posed for a photo—even the surfers dressed up in coats and ties for every screening! The photo was taken by Pierre Bouret, a 16-year-old friend who helped me drive across the country and ran the projector at each of our nine events (left to right: Bill Fury, Jim Freeman, Herbie Fletcher, Greg Tucker, Rich Harbour, me, and Mark Martinson).

In North Laguna we found an historic building called Pyne Castle. We moved into this classic Normandy-style landmark that had been purchased by Laguna Beach entrepreneurs Dick Massen and Roland Greene. The rent was low—$260 a month—so we couldn't complain. Six large rooms gave us space for editing, camera storage, offices, a bedroom, and even a large living room where we could project movies. This funky old castle was a far cry from modern, plush corporate headquarters. My grandmother gave me four chairs and a sofa, all big, comfortable, and old, just like her. We had a simple business philosophy: Keep costs low and don't worry about pretension or image. Put everything we had into the quality of the films. The concept seems to have worked, because, 50 years later, most of our early films are still playing.

The Name of the Game

We searched and searched for what to call our new company, but in the end decided to keep it simple, like the rest of our philosophy, and use our last names. Although Jim and I shared all the creative roles and were equally skilled, we went with MacGillivray Freeman Films due to the fact that my first two films had been our biggest successes up to joining. Later, when Jim's photographic skills and reputation soared in Hollywood, I suggested we switch it around, but Jim turned me down. "We do already have $10,000 in envelopes and stationery," he joked.

We drew up basic concepts for how to build a unique company that could survive for at least 50 years. We'd craft our image by producing G-rated family films of immense beauty that informed audiences through entertainment. Our films would always project a positive attitude. Finally, we committed to treating every employee with respect, dignity, and friendship. We hired for attitude, not for experience or education: You had to love your work!

Once we thought we were set, we hired our first employee. Jim's boyhood friend, Bill Bennett, became our business leader (someone else might call it COO) and distribution director, helping us develop the company.

To encourage a great vibe and increase bonding, we planned events that we called "Team Action." Four to six times a year, we would host ski trips, bowling nights, and beach parties featuring, of course, surfing and volleyball.

The Filmmaking Globetrotters: 1967 to 1972

Eager to keep our momentum from **Free and Easy** going, Jim and I buckled down to develop new concepts for our next film. We decided to juxtapose the passionate surfer's never-ending quest for beautiful waves with the changes the sport was undergoing in the late 1960s. This story would be told through the eyes of Mark Martinson, whose own surfing was undergoing a similar transition. I wanted to open the film, which we named **Waves of Change**, at Southern California's Cojo Point, one of the most picturesque breaks in the world. But Cojo was located at the edge of a private cattle ranch adjacent to Hollister Ranch and was off-limits to outsiders. Jim, who had the nerves of a bullfighter, suggested that we drive around the gate and across the field in the dead of night. "We'll move slowly around the cows," he said, "and then weave our way down to the beach."

We headed north and snuck into Bixby Ranch at 2:00 a.m. A few hours later, the sun rose over the hills to reveal a beautiful four-foot swell that lifted and lowered the heavy kelp and created flawless rights off the point. It would be a magical way to open our film. After a tiring morning of filming and surfing at Cojo, we stretched out on the hot sand next to Jim's Bronco and closed our eyes. The wind was calm and all was peaceful until an immense shadow suddenly blocked out the sun and a loud, stern voice ripped through the stillness. "What in hell do you boys think you're doing?" I blinked open my eyes to the silhouette of a towering cowboy astride the biggest horse I'd ever seen. A shotgun rested across his body, symbolically punctuating his reaction to our presence. We jumped to our feet as Jim took charge. "Sir, we've been surfing," he explained.

It was Floyd, the notorious Bixby Ranch guard who, rumor had it, could get violent. Floyd made it his business to protect this stunning, untouched coastline of four point breaks and steep cliffs overhanging a hard sand beach and miles of rolling hills dotted with live oaks and eucalyptus. It was one of the most rugged and valuable coastlines in the world.

"I can see that you've been surfing," fumed Floyd, "but you're on private property. I should take you all to jail!" Jim responded immediately: "Sir, we'll pack up and leave right now." And pack up we did. Very quickly.

After five decades of developers trying to purchase and build homes on Bixby Ranch, this coastal heaven—24,000 picturesque acres of tranquility and ecological diversity—was saved by a $165 million gift from Jack and Laura Dangermond. Now protected by The Nature Conservancy, this wonderful place will be preserved forever and the public can enjoy it without fear of Floyd or his shotgun.

Our Story for Searching for *Waves of Change*

Our story for **Waves of Change** documents the revolutionary late '60s upheaval in a heretofore constant surf scene. Conventions were being challenged, surf styles debated, and boards undergoing design shifts that left the nine- to ten-foot logs in the dustbin of history. And Mark Martinson was there through it all. The story we were about to tell would begin at Cojo Point and follow Mark across the United States in a beat-up Hudson on his way to business in Europe.

Mark begins his adventure across the United States on his way to France. This was the first use of helicopter photography in a surfing film.

This is the way I described our filmic quest for *Surfer* magazine in 1968:

> *Trust me when I say that listening to four giant Rolls Royce engines driving four propellers for eleven hours straight is like scoring front row seats to a jackhammer concert. Somewhere along the flight path from New York to Luxembourg, though, my head stopped rattling and I totaled up the money we'd saved by flying Icelandic Airlines. Multiplying by four to cover Jim Freeman, Mark Martinson and Billy Hamilton, who were vibrating in nearby seats, I forgot about the deafening engines, the claustrophobic conditions and the lousy service. We didn't have a colossal Hollywood budget; we had just enough for two months of beautiful European surf.*
>
> *Because it was my first time in Europe, I can now close my eyes and remember us wheeling around Luxembourg in a painted dream of red brick farmhouses, rolling green fields bordered by gray stone edging and miles of wide-open spaces. It's difficult for us Californians to imagine such a beautiful place escaping the bulldozer, the concrete, the prefab houses (that Dukie criticized in photographs). But in beautiful Luxembourg, the inland blues are having an impact on our surfers, and "Biarritz or bust" is repeated over and over like a mantra. We head south, traversing fertile French countryside and rich Monet landscapes, passing the unearthly palace of Versailles, crossing streams shrouded by weeping willows, and catching glimpses of fishermen in rowboats. Stereotypical Frenchmen pedal along the road's shoulder wearing coveralls and berets. Cars stop along the*

Mark's adventure: It began at Cojo Point and Perkos on Bixby Ranch (BELOW), then headed to France, where he meets with Billy Hamilton (ABOVE LEFT) here stylishing turning and with Stella de Rosnay (ABOVE CENTER), and other beautiful French women (ABOVE RIGHT).

side of the road at high noon and spread out grand picnics replete with rickety folding tables, chairs, checkered tablecloths, bottles of wine, baguettes and salami.

Billy takes his turn in the driver's seat. The road is two-laned and we are behind three tiny and slow-moving Citroens. 'I'll just pass them,' Billy says, as a truck appears from the opposite direction. The driver of one Citroen has the same idea, but instead of slowing and letting us in to pass genteel-like, he hangs out of his window, shaking his fist and shouting what we presume are French slurs. The truck grows closer—and looms larger. We scream at Hamilton, who swings onto the left-hand shoulder (it could be a backside turn at Cotton's). 'What's all the fuss about?' he asks in his constant cool. We slouch into the VW seats and take deep breaths before deciding it's time for Mark Martinson to take the wheel. Billy pouts because he didn't get a long enough turn.

The Surf Scene in Biarritz

Biarritz is in southwestern France, on the Atlantic near the Spanish border. Now a fashionable and bustling resort town, it crouches between land and sea like an afterthought. Biarritz reminds us of Laguna or Carmel, stacked above cliffed coves with weaving roads and an architectural heritage rooted in Napoleonic ethos. We cruise through its complex of shops and displays, a bit lost, but with a destination: the Surf Club de France, where we're to meet Joel de Rosnay, our Basque country contact.

Joel has arranged a villa for us to rent! We leave the surf club for our temporary home: a two-story, white plaster house with red window shutters and a red tile roof. Imagine it above a secluded cove with a nice wave, far enough outside Biarritz to be peaceful at night yet close enough to be interesting by day. Call it Villa Isabel and make it ours for 1,600 Francs ($340) a month. The five of us settle into Isabel for the night and we get to know our newest member, Keith Paull: blond, reserved, well-built and 22 years old. Keith was the 1968 Australian Champion of surf and he harbored ambitions to see the world and shape the perfect surfboard. Like most Aussie surfers, he takes a lot of showers. 'He's very clean,' Billy notes. 'He also eats a lot,' Joel warns, as he bids us bonne nuit.

Next morning, the crew pops up like green shoots from dark soil. Mark, always the fairest flower, is last to appear. We down a few gobs of 'Freeman filler,' library paste oatmeal, and we're off for the Côte des Basques, the main beach of Biarritz. Along the way, Keith shows off his board. It is the first roundtail we've seen, and as Keith describes the freedom it affords, Mark becomes more and more stoked.

At the beach, a sign reads: Température de l'eau 20, de l'air 26 (water: 68° F, air: 78° F) and lists the outside times for the four-

Villa Isabel was perched on a cliff above a cute shorebreak. This was our idyllic French house for a month. In both photos, Billy, Mark and Keith.

(TOP) Keith Paull at Hossegor. Mark Martinson at Hossegor (ABOVE) and La Barre (RIGHT). (BELOW) Keith Paull, Hossegor. (BOTTOM) Billy Hamilton, Hossegor.

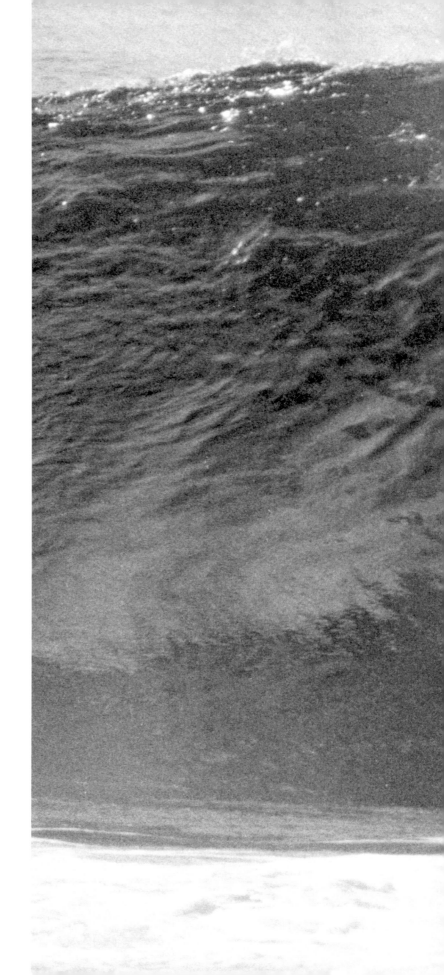

meter tide (13 feet of change). Translation: The water is pleasant, warmed by the Gulf Stream, and the tides are so radical that a surf spot can be completely transformed by the twice-changing daily tides (two highs and two lows). Mark, Billy, and Keith have no difficulty circulating among the French, as almost everyone speaks English and they get the celebrity treatment, happily accepting delicious pastries and enjoying the admiring gaze of a couple of young female surfers. Our surfers groove on the whole scene."

What follows is Hamilton's view.

Billy Hamilton Remembering Biarritz

Biarritz is a beautiful coastal town. The Bay of Biscay, which provided all of our surf, was a pleasant surprise. In July, the mistral, like California's Santa Ana winds, can blow for days directly offshore. The countryside above Biarritz reminds me of Northern California or Oregon, with a hint of Mexico. The soil is like sand and resembles snow. The people seem young and vigorous, and, judging by the sailing, water skiing, fishing, volleyball, paddleball, tennis, and golf, are passionate about their sports.

According to the French surfers we talked to, no one had ever ventured north to explore potential surf zones. I suspect this was because Biarritz was home to six surf breaks, all within a 20-mile radius, and individually, they were all excellent waves. And a 40-minute drive south to Basque region landed you at the fabulous surf of Mundaka.

From our previous experience on Kauai together, we knew that you needed to look carefully to find the diamonds in the rough, and such was the case when we went looking for a place called Hossegor that Joel said might have surf. As we drove out of Biarritz, the morning light glistened off the ocean and the mistral brushed the small swell into ruler-edged perfection.

Inside the van, we'd loaded our five boards, cameras, film and the five of us explorers. I got to drive for a while, almost killing us again trying to pass two semis and a slew of cars on a two-lane road. Our crew panicked, but this time I succeeded in passing. However, a vote was taken and Freeman took over. Merde!

We drove in and around the small city of Bayonne for several miles, counting on the road bringing us back to the coastline. Kind of lost, we then drove through a dense pine forest and, as the trees started to thin out, came upon a large cropping of sand dunes ending, abruptly, at an asphalt parking lot the size of a basketball court.

We scrambled up the sand dune hoping to get a peek at the ocean and were rewarded with a vision that is tattooed on my brain. There before us was the Holy Grail, perfect head high waves A-framing

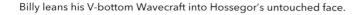

Billy leans his V-bottom Wavecraft into Hossegor's untouched face.

Hossegor's beautiful waves, unappreciated by the French until this very moment. This probably was the first day that this now legendary wave was filmed.

into flawless right and left directions. Our blood churned. We surfed the dune back to the VW whereupon Paull, with one glance at our grins, stripped off his gear, replaced the pear in his mouth with a bar of wax, grabbed his board and took off in a cloud of dune dust.

Light winds coated the ocean's surface, highlighting the swell lines all the way to the horizon. I had never put on my trunks faster. My heart was beating like a piston. I raced to the ocean with my 8' 6" x 22" wide-tailed deep V-bottomed Surfboards Hawaii, which was cutting-edge equipment that year.

The fine sand was solid underfoot. I stopped to rear up into my warmup headstand. This yogi posture sent blood to my head and instantly relaxed the limbs and torso. By controlling my breath, my senses became supercharged, warmth suffused my entire form and confidence powered my brain. Sock it to me, sea! I paddled out, Mark and Keith a few yards back and grinning like maniacs. I caught the second wave of a 15-wave set. I was late and slid to the bottom but managed to hold position. I shifted gears and, bang, was off and running on the most perfect waves of my life.

The surf and her children moved like clockwork. Paull, powerful and flowing, upright with five feet of green. Slipping vertically, trim-turning, his white wake was swallowed by the hissing curl.

Martinson was next on the line: Fade, you mother, fade! No, man, not so far! Ahh, experience rules. One sweep of aggression and some magic is displayed. The iron stance prepares for the fall line.

Crack! The curl explodes. Mark disappears into the green cathedral. Three seconds, another confession for the stocky king and he reappears, cleansed. Mark surfs as never before, trying to find a new dimension. He's become a completely different surfer since we met Keith. The waves are extraordinary, breaking in the same spot with the same shape every time. Mark borrows Keith's roundtail and doesn't want to give it back.

Another set rolls forward . . . three blue mounds. The first one? Let it go, use it as a sweeper; it cleans the trough for the next one. Next one? Do it. Two strokes? Oh, the late late show, huh? Okay, no strokes. The vertical sweep of the wave had too much to offer for my vee. I began to slip straight down, the skittering foam and fiber losing its bond with every passing second. Instinct took over. Reaching for something to hang on to, I grabbed the face of the wave. The upward charge of the curl brought a churning of foam about my fingers. Directionless in the void, my board seemed to recognize its true course. Ahh, the exalting feeling of being completely snapped!

A day of days. Virgin blue sky, warm crisp barrels glistening like there was no tomorrow. Hours passed, our bodies aching from the briny pleasure. One by one, we emerged from our blue-green canvas to the cobra-ray sands of rest.

This day of discovery was ending. The hot yellow ball shortened its radius of light to the horizon line. The air puffed around us, smelling of the land, shadows cooling sandy pockets with their lengthy strides. By the time the sun started to set, the tide had hit high mark and put the break to sleep.

Jim and Greg, aka "Free" and "Easy," organized their rolls of action, feeling a flush of accomplishment knowing that this day would be memorialized and shared with others. We sat in the sand, recharging on wine from a bota bag and relaxing into a state of euphoria that can only be experienced after a full day on the ocean.

The next morning, we retraced our steps and were again gifted with flawless conditions. That evening we celebrated at Jean Pierre's Steak House, the local hangout for young surfers and beautiful French girls. Joel and Stella de Rosnay were throwing a party for Joel's brother, Arnaud, a famous fashion photographer just home from Africa. Arnaud roared in on his motorcycle, a striking woman in tight red jeans clinging to his back. We tried to remain tight-lipped about our Hossegor discovery, but after numerous refills of sangria, our tongues started to wag and suddenly the cat was out of the bag.[3]

Years later, I returned to France as a guest of Quiksilver, which was a sponsor of the Biarritz Surf Festival. Yvon Chouinard, founder of Patagonia clothing and one of Greg's heroes, invited my former wife, Rhonda, and me on a drive to Hossegor, now considered Europe's finest wave. Returning to Hossegor was a shock! Instead of a pine forest, I found wall-to-wall houses, shops and restaurants strung out above the lonely sand dunes. I tell my friends that we explorers are always the first millionaires. We discover the gold, and then the masses overrun the place and rake in their own millions.

Billy Remembers the Bullfight of Bayonne

by Billy Hamilton (with ideas from Mark Martinson)

Our summer in France was filled with people, places, and discovery. We had gotten used to the bidet, a contraption built for cleaning yourself with hot or cold water that sat next to the toilet, which you flushed by pulling a handle on a chain; and, in the shower, to a removable spray gun for hard-to-reach spots. The French enjoyed the good things, especially family life. The people seemed to dress with their country's flag in mind: men wore red pants, girls sported blue jeans with white sweaters tied around the waist or neck. Joel de Rosnay, tall with a long, handsome face and sandy black hair, was in his late 20s and truly a stoked gremmie with a sweet tooth worse than mine. His wife, Stella, is a beautiful woman with a movie star air about her.

On mornings when the sun was out but the water was flat, most surfers would mark the day as a loss and soak in the rays. Not possible when you're traveling with two filmmaking fanatics. Greg and Jim wanted to film some of those general-interest shots. It was the kind of day when Mark and I like to pretend we're asleep or sick. Keith would soon learn. But my room was right next to the kitchen, and it was impossible for anyone to even pretend to be asleep when Greg prepared Freeman's morning oatmeal. He makes so much noise banging the pots and pans around that it drives you crazy, and I know he does it on purpose. Then he'd open my door and holler, "Hey, I'm making some oatmeal; you want some?"

He knows I hate oatmeal. When I was a kid, there was something about that guy on the cylindrical container that bugged me; not to mention the container itself. Why couldn't they just put it in a box like other cereals? Anyway, by the time Greg screamed his question, there was no chance of getting more sleep, so I got up. Jim then announced that they planned to film us at a wine festival in Bayonne. We loaded up our daily gear and headed out on another adventure, this time, to absorb French culture.

The port town of Bayonne is a picturesque place, with a large inland harbor. 'We are in the right place!' said Greg with his customary enthusiasm. "The festival is close to the center of the town square." And, bingo, through throngs of people, dogs, children, and balloons, we reached the city square. I immediately noticed four ambulances parked in the middle of the street, and behind them, a large wooden wall running across the road. Ominous. I craned my neck to look over the wall and saw about 100 berets, bobbing like a sea of black dots. To my right I caught sight of a huge bull exiting a small restaurant with a large round table atop its horns. Two white plates and a glass of wine slid off and shattered on the ground. The powerful bull bucked sharply, sending the large table cartwheeling into a group of men. Without hesitation, it charged the crowd, and everyone ran helter-skelter. Like a startled flock of starlings, the sea of berets parted, and the angry bull charged through. Electricity, adrenaline, and wild cheers filled the air. Mark, Keith, and I looked at each other wide eyed. We watched a score of near misses, then a gate at the far end of the "arena" opened and a female cow, likely in rut, was trotted out. This got the bull's attention. He followed the cow obediently. Unlike Pamplona, and Spain's "Running of the Bulls," the French version was the "Dodging of the Bulls."

Two types of color-coded tickets were being sold: blue for the stands and yellow for the participants. We bought the yellow. 'Participant?' I said, 'Participant in what?' 'In the bullfight,' Jim answered. 'What?' We convened at the nearest bar to talk things over. After a couple of rounds, Greg explained that the bulls had these leather pads on their horns so no one gets hurt. But why all the first-aid stations and ambulances, I wondered in my altered state.

3 As the story goes, Paul Witzig, Nat Young, Ted Spencer, and a young Wayne Lynch had just arrived to continue gathering footage for Paul's surfing movie, **Evolution**. They were in the restaurant that evening, and the following day, who should arrive at our secret spot? They do say that loose lips sink ships.

Greg and Jim were excited. They saw the filmic potential right away and got busy setting up cameras. Mark, Keith, and I watched as another bull entered the roundabout courtyard. The trick, we decided, was for participants to run and turn at right angles very abruptly. Bulls have poor peripheral vision and are confused by sharp moves. We thought we'd figured out the key, but for Mark and me, it didn't work out so well.

Once Greg and Jim were set up, it was time for us stuntmen to go to work. We climbed down among about 250 Frenchmen, most wearing long-sleeved white shirts and white pants with red scarves around their waist. We were dressed as American surfer tourists. Was it nerve wracking? No, it was fucking terrifying! Mark was the first to eat it. When he should have veered left, he moved right into the bull's horns! It happened very fast, but being the athletic type, he jumped up into the air as the bull approached. When Mark descended, he planted his hands on either horn like a motorcycle handlebar, except he was going backward at about twenty miles per hour straight toward a wooden pallet-wrapped tree. Mark was holding on for dear life, suspended about two feet above the ground. The bull and Mark became one with the wood pallet. *Crash!* Mark collapsed to the ground but managed to scramble to his feet and find shelter, no worse for the wear, a testimony to 20-year-old courage and natural armor. Honestly, without thinking, he quipped, "Now that's grabbing the bull by the horns!"

We were high on adrenaline and managed to dodge two more bulls. I think it was the fifth or sixth bull I decided I was going to fight. Jim was stationed at a high vantage point outside the arena with a long lens and Greg was inside with us using a handheld camera. I needed a cape and thought that Greg's black film-changing bag would work. In the movie, Greg has a shot of me walking confidently with the black bag toward the bull. I picked this bull because its left horn was broken in half. I figured if I kept circling to the right side I wouldn't get gored. What was I thinking? A black cape! Bad science. On top of that, I was wearing pink corduroy pants, which were all the rage in France that year. As I approached the bull head on, he lowered his head. I was about six feet away. He started toward me so I extended the cape to the side, just like in the movies, but something was wrong. He was aiming for my pink pants! I moved to my side stance, but he caught me with his good horn, strategically placing it between my family jewels and the spot where the sun don't shine. I was thrown into the air high enough to where I could have done a full flip . . . but instead I slammed to the ground on the small of my neck. I didn't (yet) feel anything. I was just pissed. I got up, picked up a wooden crate that was lying next to me, and ran after the bull for another go. The crowd went wild. I heard clapping and whistling. A man ran up and offered me a Gauloises cigarette, a trophy for my machismo. My neck hurt for a week.

Billy Hamilton bravely fought the bulls—and got flipped.

The next day, Greg and Jim decided to film Mark riding around on a Solex with a board under his arm. A Solex, all the rage in  France at the time because they only set you back $80, is a cross between a Honda 50 and a heavy-duty, knobby-tired paper carrier's bike. It has a 5cc engine, about the size of a model airplane engine. It has pedals, too, which are nifty for when the engine breaks down in places like Slovakia, Hungary, or Romania. There's no throttle and just two speeds: slow and fast. On the open road, they go slow, and on a narrow one-way street with a wide truck coming at you, they go really fast. In Mark's case, he was carrying his board under his arm as Greg and Jim filmed from a moving car. The road had barbed wire on both sides, and when he went to turn around, the Solex wailed and Mark went through the barbed wire, puncturing the tire and wrapping the spokes and wheel around his neck. As an untraveled 19-year-old, I'd learned far more than I ever expected I would in France—in this case, have Keith do the next cultural stunt!

The Sunshine Sea
4:08   #5

After great waves at La Barre, Côte de Basques, and especially Hossegor, our month was up. We had plenty of film for the France sequence, and plans were made to leave. The villa is cleaned: our trash, which had been accumulating for a month, was left for the trashman in a lineup of large brown paper bags that stretched twenty feet down the drive; broken lamps were glued back together; the toilet, which never worked very well, was rigged so it would flush just once for the landlord's inspection. We hoped that no count would be made on the china cups, as my birthday party took its toll. The Volkswagen was packed with boards, cameras, and food. We kissed the girls goodbye, thanked Keith for helping us with the film production (he was off for South Africa), and pulled away from Villa Isabel and Biarritz with sadness but, also, with Portugal on our mind.

As we drove through the hillsides of Spain and Portugal, Radio Luxembourg broadcast the top hits across Europe. When we heard the Beatles' "Hey Jude" for the first time, we were transformed—and it became our anthem for the trip. The Portuguese, though familiar with the ocean, do not use it recreationally. Instead, they gather at the water's edge to watch. Some fishermen use oxen to pull the red, white, and blue boats onto the sand for unloading. In the six-foot surf, Mark and I proceeded to amaze the crowd at Nazaré, unaware that this break would become famous for its big winter waves decades later. Surfed out, we returned to shore and were immediately surrounded by the curious Portuguese onlookers. Our European shoot was over.

When we drove through Paris on the way to another rattling Luxair flight, Greg noticed in *Le Figaro* that **2001: A Space Odyssey** was showing that night in 70mm. Already Kubrick fans, Jim and Greg dragged Mark and me to the show, where the only available seats were in the front row. Regardless, I'll never forget how moved we all were by the sheer brilliance of the aural-visual trip. Duly inspired, we were ready for our next filmic location.

Our first European experience had changed all of our lives, but especially Mark's. We had crossed the ocean to film Mark's development and had come with a script. In the end, we didn't need it. Organically, the development became a reality. Mark's European genesis was a turning point in his life. He could look ahead to Puerto Rico and Hawaii with a new confidence and understanding.

Puerto Rico, You Lovely (Surf) Island

The Luxair cut-rate ticket took us to New York, where Larry Lindberg had invited us to a live airing of *The Tonight Show Starring Johnny Carson* where we had front-row seats. Billy and Mark were called out as champion surfers by Johnny on air. The next morning, three of us flew to Puerto Rico to film the 1968 World Champion-

Brilliant young surfer Wayne Lynch, 16, messiah of the shortboard.

ship, while Jim headed for LA to process our European footage and check it for problems. Our three-hour drive from San Juan to the west side of the island, where Rincón and Punta Higüeras channeled waves onto smooth reefs, was punctuated by the three surfboards on the roof catching a gust of wind and helicoptering across two lanes of traffic as cars swerved to avoid getting creamed by them. Amazingly, the boards landed undamaged! At Punta Higüeras, I negotiated a month's rent with the cabana landlord. That night, Nat Young swept in donning a chef's hat, cook's apron, and his "famous" spaghetti recipe to cook for us, along with Skip Frye, who was sleeping on our veranda, Wayne Lynch, and Ted Spencer. That first night, we also learned that Puerto Rican rum mixed with Coca-Cola begins a party quickly. Exhausted by our travels and lubricated by the unofficial state beverage, we all slept soundly.

The morning waves looked small from our hilltop cabana. Mark and Ted began the walk down through the field, only to be charged by an angry bull that had gotten loose from its tether. They ran like hell to where a woman named Maria Verdes sold breakfast out of a small shack at the beach. Later in the day, everyone went off with our new friends, who were US military dependents, to buy discounted groceries at the Ramey Air Force Base commissary. I stayed at the cabana and kept my eye on the surf. During our long trip, Mark and Billy had shaped new boards with new outlines, using a lighter foam material and experimental fin designs. This was the spirit of the time as well as our film's theme: Question everything, create a new paradigm, test it, then create another. In Puerto Rico, I began riding Billy's hand-

(TOP) I often sent illustrated correspondence to Barbara. (ABOVE) Mark appreciates a shoulder-hopper. (BELOW) Billy V-turns—all in 80-degree water in uncrowded Puerto Rico, 1968.

me-down deep-V board and loved it. That day I had an experience I'll never forget.

At the reef break Balneario, the tide was dropping, the wind was dying, and as the swells grew, their darker lines latticed against the lighter blue tropical water outside. Inside, four-foot waves peeled off the reef. I paddled out on Hamilton's hand-me-down. It glided across the 80-degree water thanks to its thick 5-foot V shape, which floated the tail high in the water. A few kids sat under the trees and on the picnic tables, watching. On my first wave, I tried a "Hamilton left fade," then a top turn to the right, stalling the board with most of my weight back on the tail. The V made this looseness easy, and as the wave lined up, it was a joy to bounce from bottom to top, bottom to top, and then take a few steps to the nose. These three- to four-footers fit my style of relaxed surfing. After gliding back out to the takeoff spot, located by lining up one distant palm tree with Maria's shack, I sat feeling the serenity of this beautiful place. I could see spiny urchins on the seafloor, oily black against the white sand, a warning to never touch the bottom. I had always loved the simple feeling of waves and currents lifting me up and down as I waited, watching the horizon for the next peak. That tactile connection to nature soothed me. After a few more rides, cheered on by the kids onshore who screamed and laughed no matter how good the ride, another surfer paddled out. Linnea had come to Rincon with her husband, Bill, and she'd just begun surfing. A bit later, one of my favorite people, Skip Frye and his smooth style of nose riding joined us. We chatted, shared life stories, and traded waves until dark. For a surfer, this was the perfect day.[4]

During my trips with Jim, Mark, Billy, and Keith, I wrote to Barbara frequently. I knew my poetry could hold no candle to the brilliant minds at Cornell, so I turned to art. The envelopes and letters were comical pictograms and the women in Barbara's dorm mail room loved them. "Oh, Miss Smith, you have another letter from that California boy!" they'd tell her. Those women kept me in the game.

Our warm and happy month in Puerto Rico capped off with eight-foot waves for the World Championship, which Larry Lindberg and ABC had me filming from the water, Jim from the helicopter, and Spyder Wills from the shore for the popular ABC TV Show *Wide*

4 While in Puerto Rico, I got a letter from my childhood friend Walkie Ray, who had just graduated from Stanford and now was sharpening the business skills he'd learned when we published a newspaper as eleven-year-olds. He wrote: "I now possess an engineering degree from Stanford, and I just started at USC business school, learning how to use it. In other words, how to connive, cheat, and foreclose on little old ladies. My roommate is from Yale, and I'm constantly expecting the LA narco boys to raid us because he seems to be developing his entrepreneurial talents by selling drugs. USC has been interesting. I've almost died from the smog, I was beaten up and robbed for $100, and I miss the clear, blue skies of the Bay Area. But I am learning!" Walkie's 1968 experience was a far cry from my warm and happy month in Puerto Rico.

World of Sports. For the six-man final heat, swimming into position with my waterproofed camera became a huge challenge as the currents quickly swept me south. By the time I swam back to the impact zone, the final heat was half over! Thankfully, I got six great shots, including the 10-foot wave that won Fred Hemmings the gold. Nat, who was clearly the best surfer, came in fourth (Midget Farrelley was second, Russell Hughes third, Mike Doyle fifth, Reno Abellira sixth, and Margo Godfrey was deservedly the women's champion). The ABC show became a hit. We made friends at the network and in New York City, and then packed our bags and set off for Hawaii.

Oahu's North Shore: Our Home Away from Home

Every winter from 1965 through 1972, Jim and I rented a house on the North Shore of Oahu, where an 11-mile stretch of coastline offered at least 15 fantastic surfing breaks. One winter in the '60s, I looked around for a place to live and spotted a beautiful cabin made from wooden logs, located right in front of the surfing reef at Backdoor, next to Pipeline. The house was empty, so I tracked down the owner by phone. State senator Fred Rohlfing had an office in Honolulu and asked me to come in and introduce myself because he'd never rented this property before.

I made an appointment, cut my hair, put on my best clothes, and tried to make myself as presentable as possible. Rohlfing was a lawyer, though, and had seen enough cases of what could go wrong, so he really didn't want to rent the property. But turning on what charm I could muster and channeling Jim's powers of persuasion, I talked him into it.

The place was big enough that Jim and I could share with surfers like Nat Young and his wife, Marilyn, Corky Carroll and wife Cheryl, Johnny Fain, Angie Reno, author Craig Lockwood, Mark Martinson, and Drew Kampion from *Surfer* magazine. Drew knew more words than even Barbara did, and possessed a wild, fearless creativity that attracted me and everyone I knew. His intellect brought a refreshing breath of life to the surf crowd; he was a fountain of depth, wisdom, and humor. When he moved closer to Laguna, we became best friends. As editor of *Surfer* magazine, he shepherded its growth and ignited an inventive period of introspective commentary about surfing, its soul, and its future. His thought-provoking work would inspire both **Waves of Change** (**The Sunshine Sea**) and **Five Summer Stories**.

Every year thereafter, I could rent the log cabin because Mr. Rohlfing would only rent to me. In 1969, after we had left, gigantic 100-year storm surf and high tides hammered the North Shore for a week straight, reminding us all of the ocean's omnipotence. The cabin washed 30 feet off its foundation, but its unique construction kept the logs joined together. When I heard about it, I sent a note to Mr. Rohlfing with condolences. He replied that it was no problem,

as he had insurance, and the house would be moved back onto its foundation within six months, intact!

Here on the world's most beautiful surfing beach, our group shared a secret surf spot that is now known as Log Cabins. I have a thousand memories of parties in that house: Christmases, New Year's Eves, even the time Corky celebrated too wildly taping 100 firecrackers to Mark's favorite surfboard—the board Mark rode at Log Cabins in one of our *Surfer* magazine cover shots.

Shooting Slow Motion for the First Time

Beginning in 1966, Jim and I decided that the most original, creative, and magical thing we could do to showcase the sport of surfing was to shoot in super slow motion. Why? Because in this sport, unlike every other sport, *everything* is moving: The surfer is moving on the board, the board is moving on the water, the water is moving up, down, and sideways, and all of these moving parts are steadily approaching the shore. We felt that audiences could only appreciate the surfers' amazing balance if we could slow these things down.

We took a financial gamble and purchased two specialized cameras. One was a used Mitchell 600 frames-per-second 16mm precision device capable of running 400-foot loads, which for Jim and me was akin to a car enthusiast buying a Ferrari—this camera was a thing of engineering beauty that we couldn't stop practicing with; the other was a small Eyemo with a 100-foot load, which could be waterproofed and used in the impact zone. Jim practiced with the Mitchell, using newly developed telephoto lenses that had a side viewfinder that enabled precision focusing, and I set out building a waterproof Plexiglas housing for the Eyemo and 10 pounds of batteries. We shot tests in California and then took the cameras to Maui along with David Nuuhiwa, Nat Young, Mark Martinson, and Robert August in the summer of 1969 to finish **Waves of Change**. Arriving with us was a rare four-foot west swell, so we headed straight to Honolua Bay. Shooting from the cliff, we looked down on the surfers with the powerful 385mm lens, getting a view of the deck of the surfboards with water splashing everywhere in slow motion. No one had ever filmed in this manner before, and seeing Nat's huge feet on his Dewey Weber board was riveting. The shot moved Bruce Brown and inspired him to provide the most memorable line of our narration: "Nat has toes long enough to crack walnuts."

At about the same time, George Greenough, the unconventional son of a wealthy Santa Barbara family, was building an Eyemo camera into a waterproof housing he could wear on his back while he kneeboarded on a wave. His spectacular, groundbreaking shots went into his film **The Innermost Limits of Pure Fun**, which our company was honored to distribute. George would continue to perfect his POV shooting in years to come. Ultraslow motion was key.

Days later, we shot at Lahaina Harbor with our group enthusiastically ripping the six-foot lefts at the jetty. The Maui expression sessions we photographed impressed William Finnegan, the poet laureate of surfing. Finnegan wrote about the film's impact on him in his book, *Barbarian Days*, saying that "it was moving to the point of tears to see them surfing together, both on shortboards now, both still absolute maestros—the last dauphin of the old order (David) and the strapping, revolutionary Aussie (Nat) playing a kind of sun-drenched duet . . ."

Experimenting with and breaking in new photographic tools made Jim and me feel like we were opening a new chapter for surfing and for photography. It was a heady and stimulating period in our careers, and every day brought about new revelations.

Learning our lesson from Bruce Brown, Jim and I spent two years making **Waves of Change** and getting onto film the story of Mark's metamorphosis from a simple understanding to his complex mastery of design and surfing. We ultimately sold the film to American National Enterprises, which asked us to add other footage and release it in 35mm as **The Sunshine Sea**, a more "commercial" title for the general public. We were proud of the final product but knew we could do better. Meanwhile, other challenging film opportunities were headed our way from Hollywood.

Public Relations, aka Tooting One's Horn

To sell to Hollywood, Jim knew that communication was key. "They can't hire us if they don't know what we can do," he'd tell me. So we created a newsletter and named it *News on the March*, after the fictional Hearst-style newsreel in our favorite film, **Citizen Kane**.

We also conducted VIP screenings to gather friends and develop film assignments. To build on that concept, the wonderful New York director Tim Newman (singer-songwriter Randy's cousin) suggested that we show our dazzling Mazda Cinerama-style short film to all the New York ad agency execs at a brown-bag lunch in the city. They could get ideas for commercials, learn about our company, and enjoy a turkey and avocado sandwich on wheat bread (very California!)—all in the space of a lunch hour.

Jim and I ran with Tim's idea and sent all the agencies a mailer, followed by a personal letter. We set up our Cinerama three-screen projectors in a room at the Hilton, walking distance from the big

agencies. On the first day, thanks to Tim, about 150 agency executives showed up. By the next day, word had gotten out. We showed the film for the next four days at lunchtime in front of 200 more agency creatives. As a result, for the next five years we had more TV commercial requests than we could handle.

Growing the MFF Family

The growing MacGillivray Freeman Films team—those who have worked with us over the past 60 years—is as much like a family as a real family. From the beginning, Jim and I believed in inspiring these family members with our work ethic: playing hard and working hard. I'm sure this came about because our hobbies, the things we would happily do with or without pay, became our business. To us, the whole point was to keep it fun. If the surf was pumping, we'd tell everyone to get out there while they could and catch up on work when the surf was bad. "Let My People Go Surfing" was our mantra even before one of my heroes, Yvon Chouinard, doubled down on it at Patagonia.

Then Jim met two older crew members who would become significant additions to the MFF family. Rae Troutman was a commercial director turned grip who could mount the camera in impossible places. His partner was fellow Detroiter Pat Gilluly, a gaffer, or lighting technician. They were the best at their craft, worked 14 to 16 hours a day, and never took breaks. They formed not only a great working duo, but a hilarious comedy team. They always kept cast and crew laughing; even when things went wrong, something broke, or the clouds moved in to spoil a shot, Pat and Rae would ease the tension with their antics. When we were shooting **Behold Hawaii**, they and their wives, Ginny and Dorothy, volunteered to help Barbara by applying authentic Hawaiian makeup and tattoos to the 20 actors each morning. Little did they imagine that they'd be darkening the tan in spots where the sun didn't shine. "No butt too tough!" was their playful chant.

Pat and Rae had their own equipment rental truck with lights, generators, and everything needed to build a camera rig. It also happened to have a refrigerator and a blender. When I'd call a wrap for the day, Pat and Rae were there to hand out margaritas in glasses Pat had etched with each crew member's name. That truck helped make our domestic shoots a joy, but even in difficult places like the Soviet Union, Indonesia, Singapore, Greece, Alaska, and Hawaii, they were invaluable.

Pat and Rae were with us in Indonesia when we filmed the historic 1989 visit of Pope John Paul II to this mostly Muslim country. They met the pope and, as Irish Catholics, never stopped thanking me for the introduction. Pat and Rae have passed on now, but the joy they brought to our MFF family lives on through jokes and sayings that we repeat to this day. When we'd be in a rush to set up a shot or get to the next

After **The Sunshine Sea** was released, we borrowed my parents' dilapidated motor home and explored the coves of Baja (left to right: Cindy, me, Barbara, Cindy's brother Jeff and his wife Nancy, and Jim).

location, I'd say, "Let's hurry." Their response was always: "If you're waiting on us, you're backing up!"

Jim and I believed in producing honest films; films of the highest level of accuracy and integrity, but not preachy or boring, that celebrate the wonders of the world with a powerful subtext of conservation. The MFF team, our wonderful family, shares that goal to this day.

Reconnecting with My Soul Partner

From 1968 to 1970, Barbara and I drifted apart geographically. I was filming on location and she was studying: three years at Cornell, one in Edinburgh, and another in Geneva. I thought I'd never see her again. We wrote, but just every other week, rather than every other day. Then, out of the blue, she called.

"I'm in Newport for three days before I drive up to Santa Cruz to work on my doctorate," she said. "Want to go surfing?"

I lost my breath. I was so happy to hear her intelligent voice, quick wit, and friendly laughter. "Yes!" I blurted out. I mumbled something about the waves being good at Salt Creek, but really I couldn't stop smiling. Maybe, I thought, I could get her back in my life.

We met at the beach and I forked over a dollar to an old man named Termite so we could park along the sand. I lifted the nine-foot boards off my roof rack as Barbara admitted she might be a little out of shape. She'd spent the year in Switzerland, eating jam toast and french

fries and studying developmental psychology into the night at Jean-Jacques Rousseau Institute, in French, with Piaget as lecturer! As she tried to hide a bit of weight gain behind the surfboard, I tried to impress her with my own skills. While she was away, I'd become a pretty good nose rider. We rode waves while I tried to figure out what to say next. I came up with: "I've got a film to show up in Santa Cruz this Friday. Maybe we could drive north, share the expenses, and save some money."

It worked. On the drive, by the time we reached Santa Barbara, I had fallen even more intensely for this vivacious, stunning woman. And by the time we reached Santa Cruz, it was as though we'd never been apart. Over the next three years, I'd get involved with her classes and her friends, and she would do the same with my films. UC Santa Cruz was a hotbed of academic experimentation; it operated without grades, sports teams, or fraternities. Barbara's professors hoped to help students find new truths. After she wrote and defended her thesis, a daunting task that had even this powerful woman jangled, Barbara was awarded a PhD in the history of consciousness from the inaugural graduate interdisciplinary program at UCSC. She was a doctor!

Her studies completed, she moved south to live with me and created a path to becoming a licensed clinical psychologist. Since then, Barbara has contributed important research, photography, and a unique perspective to our films. She continues to light up my life.

Five Summer Stories

SURF

HOLLYWOOD

IMAX ENTERTAINMENT

MISSION

"We like to think that the film was able to take audiences to a spiritual place, regardless of individual faith, that conveyed to them our deep respect for beauty and nature."

By 1970, with our reputation for innovative filmmaking well established, Jim and I decided to try new filmic quests. We'd covered the surfing scene from A to Z, and felt that the behemoth up the road, Hollywood, would present us with new challenges that would help us to ratchet up our art of storytelling. We'd worked together for

David Nuuhiwa poses for a demonstation of the **Five Summer Stories** poster, painted by the legendary Rick Griffin, which became a symbolic image for the era.

four years and both of us respected and were amazed by our artistic chemistry. Emotionally, Jim and I felt confident in each other, but we also knew that we'd be moving from a career and a groove that we loved, surfing, into a field we were excited by but cautious about. Would we succeed or fail? Jim's girlfriend, Cindy, and Barbara had also developed a strong friendship built on preparing healthy food, sewing creative clothing, and sharing in the creation of beautiful images. They encouraged us to take the leap. But I worried, would the stress of Hollywood big-shot demands change our idyllic relationships? Our sensitive, quiet, but productive peace?

And to further complicate the decision, I still had a nagging desire to do one more surf film—one that would be more artful, take a few more chances, and be more unusual than any we or anyone had done before. Only problem was that we were booked solid with United Artists to do four short films that were to play with the James Bond and Pink Panther series, plus three other projects. Could we have our cake and eat it, too? One solution, suggested by Bruce Brown, was to bring in another partner to help: Bud Browne. Bud could shoot continually while Jim and I would shoot intermittently. So we were bold—and began. Bud's first assignment was filming that winter's surfing action scenes in Hawaii, while Jim and I worked on finishing a three-screen Mazda film in California. It would be a struggle, but a worthwhile one since we so badly wanted to make that final tribute film to the sport that we loved.

Over the next years, I would fly to Hawaii to help Bud, crashing on the floor of his one-room apartment at Waimea Bay. I learned that he was a true iconoclast. A former swimmer and team captain at USC, Bud became the best water cameraman in the history of surfing. His aquatic buddies nicknamed him "Barracuda" for his long limbs and slender body and his agility in the ocean. Living alone in a small

To get the sound of surfing alongside one of surf history's most entertaining characters, Bud and I taped a transmitter and microphone onto Corky Carroll. His commentary was hilarious.

apartment in Costa Mesa, he loved women but never settled down with one. He was a comfortable loner. For example, long before remote controls, he had jerry-rigged his apartment with ropes to adjust the volume of the TV, control the overhead light, and open and close the door—all without getting out of bed. He ate one meal a day (dinner) and slept like a baby. During our time in Hawaii, Bud was 60 and I was 25. He became like a second father to me.

For this special film, Bud and I wanted to capitalize on and perfect the super slow-motion beauty we had achieved in **Waves of Change**.[5] Thankfully, Hawaii's 1970–71 surf seasons were exceptional at Pipeline, so we were able to capture sequences of beauty and grace never before seen on film. After practicing endlessly with our new telephoto lenses, I became expert at follow-focusing and could keep Gerry Lopez in crisp, clear, slow motion, anticipating my focus move even when he disappeared from view inside the tube. This was the first time that Gerry had been featured in a major surfing movie, so his fresh style would surprise audience members. But I dreamed up another surprise as well.

A Soundtrack to Beat the Band

As we began the project, we planned an advertising campaign that built up the film for two years running, so that our fan base knew that it would be our final surfing film. Even the Beach Boys knew; they offered us the use of their music free of charge. Like so many others, they wanted to be part of an epic surfing film, especially one that signaled the end of an era. Happily, the Beach Boys' revolutionary recording methods played right into our plans to make this final film a defining sonic experience for the surfing world—a true spectacle. We hoped to release the first-ever 16mm film with stereo sound, generated from an in-sync magnetic tape recorder with custom speakers in every auditorium. We branded it in our advertising the "Zap Magnastereo!"

In another attempt to manage our limited, on-off production schedule, I wrote the film as a compilation of five short stories so that we could finish them one by one and toggle back and forth to work on our new Hollywood films. I called our film **Five Summer Stories**. One story we told was a hard-hitting investigation of the unfairness of surfing competitions that offered winners no prize money; it featured the scandalous treatment of Corky Carroll at the 1971 United States Surfing Championship in Huntington Beach, as well as the one-sided exploitation of surfers for commercial gain by contest promoters. Another story employed humor to chronicle the evolution of the sport

5 To do so, Bud used the small Eyemo high-speed camera in a compact water housing of his own design. It was so compact that he could maneuver in the treacherous impact zone at Pipeline, probably the hardest breaking wave in the world. Meanwhile, I used the high-speed Mitchell to shoot close-ups from shore at 200 to 300 frames per second. The combination worked better than I had hoped.

Five Summer Stories

FILMED IN: 16MM

RELEASE DATE: 1972

MUSIC BY: The Beach Boys and Honk

Five Summer Stories became a cult-film classic because of its avant-garde photographic and editing style and its controversial tone. Financed, produced, directed, photographed, and distributed by MacGillivray Freeman Films, **Five Summer Stories** played in theaters throughout the world for seven consecutive years (1972 to 1979).

The Legacy of *Five Summer Stories*
2:51   #6

(BELOW) Sequence of Rory Russell at Pipeline, one of the amazing slow-motion tubes, in **Five Summer Stories**.

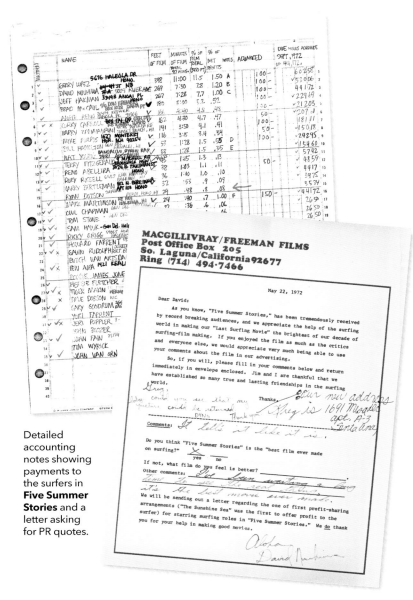

Detailed accounting notes showing payments to the surfers in **Five Summer Stories** and a letter asking for PR quotes.

Though none of us was particularly religious, we believed deeply in the connection between man and nature, particularly from a Zen 'everything in nature is sacred' perspective. So, embedded in the narration and music of the five storylines was a Christian/Buddhist undercurrent, beginning with the "creation" of the Earth and ending with "Heaven's Gift to Man: The Tunnel of Love."

Epic Outside Pipeline

Into the opening of **Five Summer Stories,** I edited rides from one particularly memorable day. When Sammy Hawk took off on an outside pipe wave that must have been 30 feet tall, the audience's anticipation built as he kept dropping and dropping down the face. Even though Bud Browne shot at normal speed, the wave was so big and Sammy's drop so long that it felt like it was shot in slow motion.

When Sammy made his backside bottom turn going left and proceeded straight back up the wave's gnarled face, it seemed like a suicide mission. The wave closed out and Sammy did a free fall down the watery cliff. By the end of that ride, everyone knew why they'd come to see **Five Summer Stories**. The stereo, clean, crisp, and powerful, was the best sonic experience they'd ever had, and the rides from that epic day reminded us of the magnificent power of the ocean's waves.

No one had seen such brazen behavior on a huge wave before, and **Five Summer Stories** managed to etch it into the collective consciousness of half a million surfers. Because the film was marketed and shown in California and Hawaii from 1972 to 1979, most surfers saw it several times. They never stopped hooting at that opening wave.

A Shocking Reaction

After two and a half years of hard work, **Five Summer Stories** premiered on March 24 and 25, 1972, at the huge Santa Monica Civic Auditorium, and the event, as they say today, went viral. The advertising hype had built to a crescendo, prompting advance tickets to sell out. These buyers filled half the seats. In an early example of misusing new technology, someone printed fake tickets using the first Xerox copiers and sold them for 50¢ each. Before the ticket takers noticed, about 400 of these forgeries had made it past the door. The 3,000 seats were full and another 400 surfers sat in the aisles or stood in the back and along the side walls. The theater manager, an uptight city employee, screamed at me, "If the fire marshal shows up, he'll shut us down, provoking a riot!" This well-intentioned man, whose auditorium had hosted the sophisticated and sedate Academy Awards so many times, would be wiped out . . . by surfers! How insulting! He was no doubt picturing his job, his pension, and his freedom (he could've gone to jail) evaporating over a mere "surfing flick." I apologized, but told him that if I tried to throw people out we would indeed have a riot on our hands. "Believe me,"

from the slapstick beach antics of 1958 to serious shortboarding of 1972, all set to Beach Boys songs over those years, from the simple "Surfin'" (1961) to the complex "Feel Flows" (from the 1971 *Rolling Stone* magazine's Best Album of the Year, *Surf's Up*). My favorite story, called "Closed Out," was written by Drew Kampion and narrated by a Richard Nixon soundalike. It documented the closing of surfing beaches due to coastline exploitation and proved to be a precursor to our emphasis on protecting the natural environment.

At the time, I was experimenting with a new fast-cut, juxtaposing edit technique that enhanced the "Hawaiian Odyssey" story, a paean to freedom and life on the North Shore, set to the song "High in the Middle," an upbeat country song written by Honk, a new band from Laguna I had grown to love. It brought a smile to everyone's face.

(ABOVE) The North Shore was amazing from 1967–1972 and we captured its essence in **Five Summer Stories**. (BELOW) Eddie Aikau on the wave of the year, 1967. By pure luck, we shot this ride from four camera positions: the point (my camera), across the bay (Jim's camera), and Bruce Brown's position near the roadside parking. But I also have this 35mm Kodachrome slide, which must have been taken by Mark Martinson with our Nikon camera! Eddie gets hammered, but it was the best big-wave ride that year.

I told him, "once Honk begins to play their short gig from the stage, the kids will be mesmerized."

He had to agree that moving ahead was our only option. So with the biggest crowd—3,400 excited surfers—ever to gather inside this esteemed auditorium, we rolled the film. As I'd promised the manager, the kids loved Honk's set. Then the screening became the most energizing event I had experienced. The film was innovative, artistic, and controversial. One of our main objectives was to leave the surfing world with a few things to think about. We promoted the film as "The Last Surfing Movie," because for us, it was. But it set us up for a wild ride into Hollywood. *Rolling Stone's* rock and roll muse, Eve Babitz, wrote a sharp, honest, and funny review of the surf event of the year:

There were three things going on Friday at the Civic. First, the audience, whose median age was about 17 and who were tan, mostly blond, clear-eyed, and radiated health in thick pulses you could almost hear. Few of them smoked cigarettes or wore glasses, and all exhibited a sense of exhilarated urgency and impatience while waiting for the movie to begin. Second, the surfers in the film, who were recognized instantly by the audience and wildly cheered as they engaged in gleaming duels of fleeting, awesome beauty. And third, the attitude of the movie, elaborately created for this night, this audience, by two guys who presume that the film will not only be shown to surf freaks but who spent thousands of extra dollars so the sound would wipe everyone out completely.

Delays in the movie's start time brought the already straining-at-the-bit kids to a point where they could hardly breathe. Flattened-out popcorn boxes frisbeed through the air, the smell of burning grass got thicker, and a blanket of smoke settled democratically down so that everyone was exposed, no one escaped.

Bolts of expectation slammed around the theater as the lights dimmed. A sudden roar rose up from the audience as the movie came fearlessly onscreen with some trance-imposing abstract colors, solarized colors in slow, slow motion turning slowly, dragging us into its rhythms and gutting us into awed silence before the whole thing changed into realer and realer color and at last was bright, blazing truth—a man sliding down the inside of a 15-foot sheet of molten green with diamonds shooting out at the top and as the wave curled lazily into itself the man drew back into the loop of air inside—the "tube"—and vanished until, at the last moment, the final moment, he pulled back out into the open. That man, Gerry Lopez, stroked the inside of a curled four-ton menace, going faster than is truly permitted in the world, too much faster. We cheered our devotion. Now I knew what everybody had been waiting for. The audience went crazy in transported ecstasy.

About halfway through the film we were dazzled by a face so

abrupt in its savagery and its vestigial traces of paradise that I figured the audience uproar was a simple reaction to the jagged beauty of the face itself. Bygone island eyes. Disheveled black hair tangled around his face and down past his shoulders like a thorn frame. Underneath the face flashed the news that this was David Nuuhiwa (New-eee-vah), but everybody in the place already knew that except me, which was why they were screaming.

Intermission. I went to the foot of the stairs where I was to meet Greg MacGillivray and Jim Freeman. I was still dazed from the smoke and the gorgeous water and the young girls' beautiful stomachs which nearly all showed tanned and hollow because the tops of their hip-high Levi's failed to meet the bottoms of their waist-low clingy sweaters. MacGillivray didn't look like a surfer nor a filmmaker—he looked like a young high school algebra teacher, and talked like one too, clear and optimistic and cheerful. Crisply-ironed shirt, economical manner, friendly, bright—no tan, no shilly-shallying, no digressions, no waste. Jim Freeman looked like a Big Sur person. More woodsy than his partner. Looking like he wanted to get back to work.

'Did the Beach Boys just give you the music?' I asked. 'Yes, Brian Wilson wanted to write the theme song, too, but we ran into a time thing and had to let it go.'

At 11:30 it was over and we were sated. Enough of slowly tunneling ocean myths, of sparkly gems flying into a child's blue sky, of boards leaving trails on clear green mountains, and of bygone island eyes. We'd screamed ourselves hoarse for Gerry Lopez, cheering him through lazy explosions that could snap him in two. We shimmered with pleasure.

The thing that Jim and I had always dreamed of was actually happening: We were entertaining our audiences and showing them a great time, but also delivering an emotional, moving experience that might just change their view of our beautiful world and their role in protecting it.

We spent two years and $72,000 producing **Five Summer Stories**. Because this was the highest budget ever for a surf documentary, we didn't expect to make our money back. We were just happy that we took this project through to completion, because it did turn out to be more than a film. It became an experience that many would compare to an epic rock concert. "You've made a beautiful, experiential film," Bruce Brown told me, calling it "a new kind of surfing film." We had followed his lead, taking our time (two years) and making it special, not ordinary. When John Engle wrote the book, *Surfing in the Movies*, he commented that **Five Summer Stories** was "perhaps the only film to nudge **The Endless Summer** occasionally off Rung One of the surf film ladder."

(ABOVE LEFT) My favorite woman surfer and best friend, Jericho Poppler. (ABOVE RIGHT) Hawaii's Kaimuki Theatre set all-time records. (BELOW) Filming David Nuuhiwa's contest comments at Huntington Beach.

Bud (center), Jim (right), and me.

Sam George, the former editor of *Surfer* magazine, recently put the film in perspective for Surfline: "During the halcyon days, surfers could hoot themselves hoarse at plenty of good surf movies, but at only two actually great surf movies. One was Bruce Brown's **The Endless Summer**, the film that, during its hugely successful wide screen release in 1966, introduced the sport of surfing to the world, and the world of surfing to itself. The other, coincidentally, also had summer in its title. This was **Five Summer Stories,** released in 1972, and judged by any informed standard, even against Brown's masterwork, must be considered not merely a great surf movie, but the greatest surf movie ever made."

Five Summer Stories saw the highest attendance for a surf film since **The Endless Summer** eight years earlier.[6] Its reputation spread like wildfire and audiences grew week after week, month after month. During the film's second run, word of mouth was so effective that polls we conducted determined that half of our audience had never even *touched* a surfboard. This is known as a crossover film effect; the appeal extends beyond the core audience to those on the outside looking in.

The success of this release meant that we were, in fact, able to recoup the costs of making the film and even to establish a new trend: We distributed 15 percent of the net profit among the 35 surfers in the film. Over the seven years that we played the film, each of those

surfers received an annual check and accounting statement. Because the shares were divvied up on a pro rata basis, and Gerry Lopez had so much screen time, he pocketed a small and well-deserved fortune. Two years later, Bud would offer the same surfer participation formula for his release of **Going Surfin'**. With a nod to enduring respect, Nat Young, a vocal critic of the photographic exploitation of surfers by surf film producers and magazine publishers, made an exception for our plan, writing: "You've treated me fairly, Mr. Easy." (A clever wordsmith, Nat would call me Mr. Easy and Jim Mr. Free!)

Jim, Bud, and I loved being part of this early age of the surfing culture. But sadly, it wouldn't last. The feeling of uniqueness and rebelliousness died away as the sport became more mainstream, organized, competitive, and finally televised. Then, in the early '80s, VHS surf videos that could be more easily watched at home killed off the fun cultural events at auditoriums forever. But thankfully, in 1972, when **Five Summer Stories** premiered to huge crowds of appreciative surfers, we were proud to be part of that special subculture and happy that we'd found a way to make one last ode to surfing and its art.

---

6 **ESTIMATED ATTENDANCE FOR TOP SURFING FILMS, 1958-1980**
The Endless Summer and *Five Summer Stories* attracted by far the most attendees.

YEAR	FILM	FILMMAKER	SCREENINGS	ATTENDANCE PER SCREENING	ESTIMATED ATTENDANCE
1960	**Surf Fever**	John Severson	25	350	8,750
1963	**Gun Ho**	Bud Browne	20	250	5,000
1964-67	**The Endless Summer**	Bruce Brown	5,420	300	1,626,000
1964	**A Cool Wave of Color**	Greg MacGillivray	28	300	8,400
1967	**Free and Easy**	MacG-Freeman	78	350	27,300
1970	**Pacific Vibrations**	John Severson	600	200	120,000
1972-79	**Five Summer Stories**	MacG-Freeman	2,280	250	570,000
1977	**Free Ride**	Bill Delaney	90	300	27,000

After 1980, the video-at-home release killed the surf film theater market.

Because my book is a filmic and business adventure dealing with risks taken, failures realized, and triumphs cherished, I am including lists of the best surf movie successes. These lists were assembled with input and guidance from: Matt Warshaw, Sam George, Paul Holmes, Bob McKnight, John Engle, Jack McCoy, Barry Haun of SHACC, and myself.

BEST SURFING FILMS, 1957-1980

1. *The Endless Summer* (Brown) 1964
2. *Five Summer Stories* (MFF) 1972
3. *Pacific Vibrations* (Severson) 1970
4. *Evolution* (Witzig) 1969
5. *Free Ride* (Delaney) 1977
6. *Going Surfin'* (Browne) 1973
7. *Surfing Hollow Days* (Brown) 1961
8. *Surf Fever* (Severson) 1960
9. *Seadreams* (Mastalka/French) 1971
10. *Free and Easy* (MFF) 1967
11. *Innermost Limits of Pure Fun* (Greenough) 1970
12. *Cosmic Children* (Jepsen) 1970
13. *Big Wednesday* (Milius) 1978
14. *A Cool Wave of Color* (MFF) 1964
15. *Morning of the Earth* (Falzon) 1972
16. *The Living Curl* (Budge) 1965
17. *Gun Ho* (Browne) 1963
18. *Too Hot to Handle* (Rohloff) 1961
19. *The Sunshine Sea* (MFF) 1970
20. *Forgotten Island of Santosha* (Yates) 1974

BEST SURFING VIDEOS, 1980-2021

1. *Riding Giants* (Peralta) 2004
2. *Blazing Boards* (Bystrom) 1985
3. *Step into Liquid* (Brown) 2003
4. *Occy the Occumentary* (McCoy) 1998
5. *Storm Riders* (McCoy, Hoole, Lourie) 1982
6. *Kelly Slater in Black & White* (Woolcott) 2004
7. *Momentum Generation* (Zimbalist) 2018
8. *Castles in the Sky* (Steele) 2010
9. *Blue Horizon* (McCoy) 2004
10. *Thicker Than Water* (Malloy/Johnson) 2000
11. *The Endless Summer II* (Brown) 1994
12. *Single Fin: Yellow* (Baffa) 2005
13. *Surfers: The Movie* (Delaney) 1990
14. *Beyond the Noise* (Kaineder) 2018
15. *Bustin' Down the Door* (Gosch) 2008
16. *Adrift* (J. Brother) 2005
17. *Sprout* (Campbell) 2005
18. *September Sessions* (Johnson) 2002
19. *View from a Blue Moon* (Kueny) 2015
20. *A Deeper Shade of Blue* (McCoy) 2011

Bill Bennett and his team became so efficient that we were selected by other producers to release their films, 1968–1980. With Brown and Severson retired from surf films, we pretty much dominated the market. Some of those films were **Pacific Vibrations**, **Evolution**, **Morning of the Earth**, **The Innermost Limits of Pure Fun**, **Salt Water Wine**, **Sea of Joy**, **Going Surfin'**, and **Cosmic Children**. For some, I was asked to design the posters, which I enjoyed doing. Unfortunately for our fun surf culture, by about 1980, VHS cassettes and video film production made it easy to see films at home and the surf film event, with its rowdy behavior, beautiful surfer girls, and stoking moments that made you hoot and ready to paddle out the next day, became a thing of the past.

Corky Carroll Remembers *Five Summer Stories*

Five Summer Stories by Greg MacGillivray and Jim Freeman is probably the greatest surf movie ever made, just for its sheer goodness. I appeared in a few of the sequences, did voice-overs for the narration, and had a little piece of music in the soundtrack. There are a number of memories I have of taking part in the production. One is staying at the infamous Log Cabin in Hawaii and pretty much blowing up my pal Mark Martinson's board with firecrackers on New Year's Eve. The firecrackers caused the fiberglass to bubble and destroyed Mark's favorite board, which was a newly invented roundtail. Mark was featured on the cover of *Surfer* magazine riding that board at Log Cabins. After that New Year's Eve party, Mark wanted to kill me, and almost did!

The best memory, though, is surfing with a microphone taped to my chest during the Pipeline sequence. One morning at the Log Cabin, Greg asked me to surf Pipeline wearing a waterproof microphone so he and Bud Browne could record the sound of what it was like to surf a wave like that. He offered me fifty bucks to do it. In those days, fifty bucks was a week's worth of food, so I said yes. A few days later, there was a clean little west swell running and Greg and I went out to do the filming. What I had assumed was going to be a tiny hidden microphone looked like a big round tongue depressor. By "wearing" he really meant duct-taped to my chest with a transmitter in my wax pocket. I set off down the beach thinking about how this was all going to work out. Once I was in the water, I grabbed a few pretty good rides and was happy with the way it was going. But Greg waved me in and told me that he couldn't use any of my rides so far because I wasn't talking. Talking? Yes, he wanted me to talk while I was riding the waves. "And say what?" I asked him. He said something like he admired my conversational skills and to be funny and engaging in order for it to work. I went back out and remember that I did get a funny in-the-water interview with famous shaper Dick Brewer, who was sitting in the lineup with me. When I took off on the waves and tried to talk, however, I found that the more I said, the less I could surf. I had to laugh when I saw the movie and I was saying, "Off the top, off the bottom," and nothing was happening!

The icing on the cake of this day was getting the duct tape off my chest. Ouch! Did you ever see Steve Carell in **The 40-Year-Old Virgin** getting his chest hair waxed? Yeah. It was like that. My scream must've been heard around the island. But the pain was worth it, because to this day people mention that microphone sequence to me; it was that unique and comical.

The Music of
Five Summer Stories
2:42   #7

One of my favorite surfers, Corky Carroll, became the first truly professional surfer by earning paid endorsements, winning more than 100 surfing contests, and being voted *Surfer* magazine's #1 surfer in 1968.

"Arriving at the Santa Monica opening late, with tender, riotous conditions prevailing, we were guided into a maelstrom of paper airplanes and surfy faces. The fans were at an explosive pitch as the film rolled. MacGillivray and Freeman, as usual, have the photography so wired that it is a technical blow-mind."

–KURT LETTERMAN, *SURFER* MAGAZINE WRITER

(ABOVE) Just two days after the premiere, Jim and I were back in Hawaii, shooting a TV commercial for Timex with Gerry Lopez starring: Remember "it takes a licking and keeps on ticking"? As I treaded the 82-degree water, Lopez would get a six-foot wave, rip it, then pull out right next to me and lean down to show, in one continuous shot, the watch's second hand ticking along. It took 25 tries, but we got an A+ shot, one that had Lopez's full-tooth smile perfectly lit. Did I tell you I have a great job? (RIGHT) Honk band members. (FACING PAGE) **Five Summer Stories**, the grand finale surf film from Jim, Bud, and myself, became a far bigger hit than we ever expected, running for seven years, 1972 to 1979. For example, it played to sell-out crowds at the Bay Theatre in Seal Beach for 7 and 9 p.m. showings for 73 nights over that seven-year span of time, joining **The Endless Summer** as the two most popular films of that early era. Barbara used to interview attendees waiting in line about the number of times they had seen the film. The most number of repeats by one surfer was 16.

Gerry Lopez Remembers *Five Summer Stories*

People might not understand how the early surf films were made. Generally speaking, much of the surfing footage featured in most of the films of the 1970s was simply the result of the filmmaker going to the beach and shooting whoever was surfing. There were, of course, instances when someone like Bruce Brown would take surfers like Phil Edwards (**Surfing Hollow Days**), or Mike Hynson and Robert August (**The Endless Summer**) on surf trips for the express purpose of filming them. More often than not, this would lead to a declining degree of tolerance for each other until, finally, they couldn't wait to go their separate ways.

When I worked with Jim, Bud, and Greg, I was completely shocked when I went to the first showing of **Five Summer Stories** at the Kaimuki Theatre in Honolulu. I saw how much screen time they gave me and had no idea they had even filmed me so much. Our relationship grew closer and closer after the release of their great film.

Five Summer Stories had a seamless flow to it, an outstanding cast of surfers, and an original soundtrack from a Laguna Beach band called Honk. Greg invited the band to his house and ran sections of the movie so they could get a feel for the film. The result was a soundtrack that knocked the socks off all the moviegoers, and the album and its single "Pipeline Sequence" became the top seller in Hawaii. The wonderful soundtrack in stereo, with major contributions from the Beach Boys, helped make **Five Summer Stories** a classic with as much relevance today as it had 50 years ago.

I was hanging out one fall day at Greg's house in Laguna when the door opened and in trooped a gang of longhaired hippies. Greg was busy at his editing table but looked back over his shoulder and said: "Hi you guys, this is Gerry . . . Gerry, this is Honk." I was watching the World Series on TV, but was stoked to meet the band because, like everyone else, I loved their soundtrack. Some of the Oakland A's players were longhaired and bearded like the Honk members. "Wow, baseball. Far out, man," one of the members commented, "Who's playing?"

And with that, the band sat down and watched the game with me. It was a very cool way to spend an afternoon.

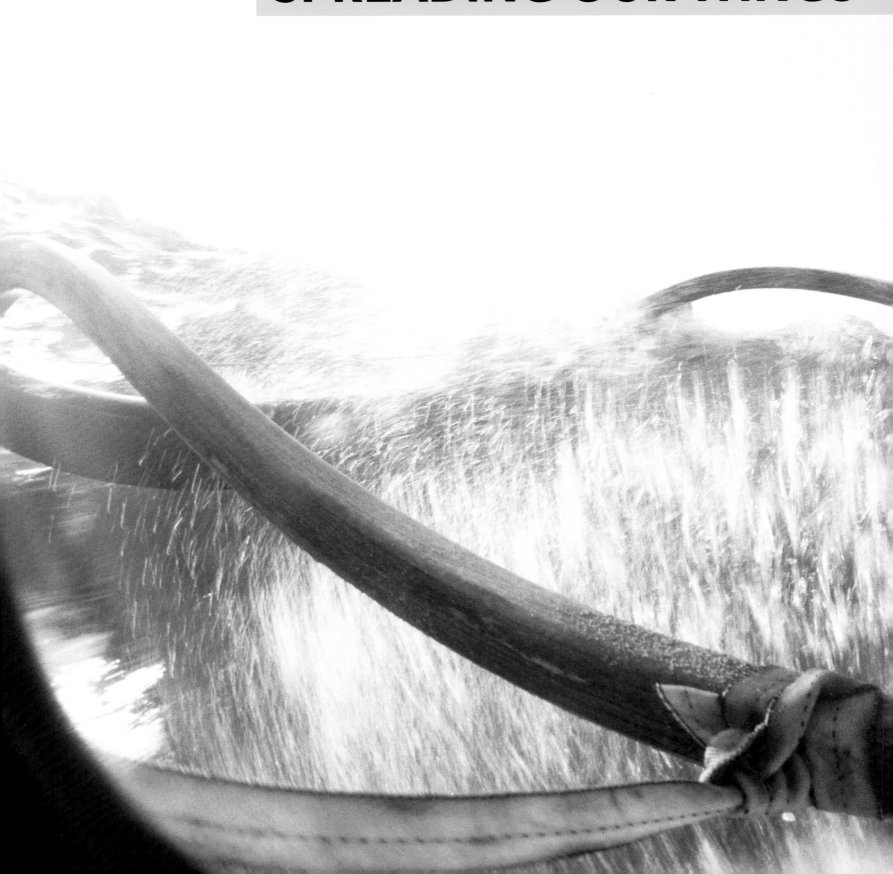

SPREADING OUR WINGS

Learning the Ways of Hollywood

> **"You have the freedom to be yourself, your true self, here and now, and nothing can stand in your way."**
>
> –RICHARD BACH, AUTHOR OF *JONATHAN LIVINGSTON SEAGULL*

Among the assignments Jim and I had early on in our two-man organizational structure, one of mine was directing our investments, and with my dad's guidance, I had chosen Laguna Beach oceanfront real estate as the best opportunity. For our first investment, Jim and Cindy moved into the four-unit house perched above the ocean that we'd just purchased from John Wayne. For years, the Duke and his band of friends had used the place as their man cave, where they would play poker, smoke cigars, drink whiskey, and use the beach as their backyard. On the night Cindy and Jim moved in, we threw an Oscars party. That night, besides the classic films **The French Connection**, **A Clockwork Orange**, and **The Last Picture Show** vying for best picture, a short film called **Sentinels of Silence** had been nominated twice, for best documentary short and best live action short. Jim had spent a couple months photographing the film, beautifully I might add, in Mexico. When the Orson Welles-narrated **Sentinels** won both of its categories, we swelled with pride and hollered as director Robert Amram and producer Manuel Arango thanked the Academy, Jim and the team. We toasted each other with multiple piña coladas because we knew that this honor would be a huge boost as we moved further into Hollywood filmmaking. We were on a roll.

To help guide us on this new adventure, we enlisted Peter Pascal to become our de facto Hollywood agent. He would scan the trade papers *Variety* and *The Hollywood Reporter* and make calls to pitch what we could do for upcoming pictures. One day in 1971, he came across a notice that producer Hall Bartlett was making a film based on *Jonathan Livingston Seagull*, that year's top-selling book. The novella by Richard Bach, a fable about self-perfection, had sold over a million copies and would remain on *The New York Times* best-seller list for almost a year.[7] That was good enough for Peter, as he'd seen the footage of seagulls we'd captured during thousands of days of beachfront shoots. He asked me to put together a demo reel.

Peter had his work cut out for him, as Hall Bartlett had already hired Jack Couffer, a brilliant wildlife cinematographer who had created many Oscar-nominated films for Walt Disney and had already begun filming seagulls for Bartlett. Trusting in our footage to make the sale, Peter lugged a rented 35mm projector and screen up to Bartlett's second-story offices. He had to set up in the lobby and wait until the busy producer got free. When he finally grabbed him for a few minutes, Peter ran the footage, saying, "My guys can do anything with the movie camera and slow motion. They can even make a seagull look beautiful." Bartlett was so impressed with the imagery that he wanted us to begin work immediately. Peter cautiously asked, "What about Jack Couffer?"

"He'll do the scenes where the seagull characters interact on the ground," said Bartlett. "I want your boys to do all of the aerial in-flight sequences."

Jim and I were stoked. At that time, consciousness-raising about nature and ecology was sweeping the world with events like Earth Day and laws including the US Clean Air Act. The story of Jonathan, a seagull trying to learn about life, flight, and where he fit, matched our developing philosophy about how to thrive on this planet. We had already

---

(FACING PAGE) **Sentinels of Silence**, a Paramount-released short that Jim photographed at Mexico's stunning Mayan historical ruins, was honored with two Academy Awards.

7 Eighteen months later, it was on every list—at the top! Sales passed 2 million hardcover copies, the most since the book, *Gone with the Wind*. In decades, more than 40 million copies sold, resulting in Richard Bach being featured on the cover of *Time* magazine.

questioned the virtues of materialism and bemoaned the meaning-lessness of authority in our films. **Jonathan Livingston Seagull** moved those themes into the poetic realm in a beautiful, almost spiritual way.

Since I was tied up shooting and editing **Five Summer Stories**, Jim was elected director/cameraman. We both knew he could handle this job at an A+ level and deliver for Mr. Bartlett. Jim's talent and recognized ability to shoot in the air had skyrocketed, as it were, so it was easy for him to pull together a stellar team including pilot George Nolan, Jim's girlfriend, Cindy Huston, as camera assistant, Jeff Huston (Cindy's brother) as production assistant, and Stan McClain as production assistant/seagull wrangler. They joined the rest of the photography team at the Holiday Inn in coastal Carmel.

Nearby, the production company had rented a huge barn where they kept the many seagulls used in the film. They'd been trapped in a humane way (approved by Fish and Wildlife wardens) at the county dump. The birds were cleaned up, given nutritious food, and grouped into the movie's four characters: Jonathan was a young male with white feathers, Fletcher was a younger male with brown feathers, Chang was an older bird with albino features, and Sally was a small female similar in looks to Jonathan. Once the birds were healthy, well fed, and camera-ready, they were taken in individual cages to the Holiday Inn, where a kind of green room had been set up. "You look marvelous, so we're ready for your close-up, Mr. Jonathan!"

How to Train Your Seagull

In a word, training seagulls was impossible. Jack Couffer had the hardest time. He'd try to coax them with fresh fish as a reward for walking from point A to point B after waiting hours for perfect lighting. Even working with brilliant bird expert Gary Gero, this method didn't work more than 10 percent of the time.

Jim's method was to take three seagulls, each in its own cage, up in the helicopter into the beautiful lighting at sunrise or sunset. George, the pilot, would position the helicopter for a great background, like a glorious sunset above beautiful clouds. Jim would then open the cage so that George could reach in with a gloved hand to grab a seagull by the legs. Instead of welcoming the opportunity for freedom, these pea-brained birds pecked at his hand and wrist and then attacked his elbow and sometimes even his face. Meanwhile, George was also trying to fly the helicopter with his other hand! When he'd finally wrangle one out of the cage, George would give Jim a countdown over the intercom—"3-2-1-Release!"—and then fling the seagull out the open door into the air current. The startled seagull would recognize that it had to fly to survive, opening its wings and getting its bearings. Then it would take a huge dump. Feeling more comfortable, the bird would fly, ever so briefly, in formation with the helicopter. Did the bird think the helicopter was its mother? Was it capable of thinking anything at all? The chance for Jim's shot lasted a hot second!

Jim was able to stretch that short formation flying by filming with a 35mm Mitchell high-speed camera with a Panavision wide-screen zoom lens. He could capture the free-flying seagull against a spectacular background at 120 frames per second. This stretched out the moment fivefold and was just enough to get some truly amazing shots. An unexpected perk was that Hall Bartlett and Paramount were now the proud owners of hundreds of outtakes of seagulls taking a dump in front of glorious sunsets.

Though comical in the retelling, this system allowed Jim to create some of the most beautiful images of birds ever captured on film. These images, and those that Jack Couffer produced with beautiful lighting on the ground, were instrumental in **Jonathan** being nominated by the Academy as one of that year's five best-photographed films! Imagine a little film about seagulls competing photographically that year with Hollywood blockbusters like **The Exorcist** and **The Sting**. Jim and I and all our friends were stoked, and our business again benefited.

Shooting with a large crew taught us so much about people and Hollywood. We learned that studio job competition is so fierce and the potential rewards so great that people regularly exaggerate their abilities. Hollywood director John Milius always said, "Actors, film-makers, and technicians will agree to do anything to get a Hollywood job. They'll say, 'Yes, I can ride a horse, or, sure, I can surf gigantic waves, or, of course I can train a seagull to do anything you want!'"

The **Jonathan** job kept getting more and more elaborate because Hall Bartlett was so pleased by what our team was accomplishing. He asked Jim to help film five important scenes, all really tight close-ups of seagulls in flight, but seen from below. Jim had gained a lot of experience with these creatures, but even he couldn't figure out how to achieve this shot. Lucky for us, help was on the way. A famous Hollywood bird trainer had talked Mr. Bartlett into hiring him to train three seagulls specifically to fly on command while facing a large wind machine. The trainer claimed to have done this hundreds of times with eagles, hawks, owls and other flyers. In retrospect, Mr. Bartlett should have been more cautious. The question he should have asked was, Aren't eagles, hawks, and owls an awful lot smarter than seagulls? If Jim had learned one thing, it was that seagulls have very, very small brains. In fact, we decided that the term "birdbrain" must have been coined by someone who'd worked with seagulls.

To get the needed close-ups, Jim aimed the super slow-motion Mitchell up at a beautiful blue sky with the wind machine just out of frame. The plan called for the now-skilled seagull, which had been in training for weeks, to lift off its perch when a bell rang. The bird appeared to float lazily in the steady wind from the fan. When another

(ABOVE LEFT AND RIGHT) Jim gets Jonathan ready for his starring role. (BELOW LEFT) Jim, Jonathan, and Gary in the Tehachapi wildflowers. (BELOW RIGHT) Cindy Huston, great assistant cameraperson.

Jonathan Livingston Seagull

FILMED IN: 35MM ANAMORPHIC

RELEASE DATE: October 23, 1973, by Paramount Pictures

DIRECTOR: Hall Bartlett

BASED ON THE BOOK BY: Richard Bach

MUSIC BY: Neil Diamond

Academy Award nominations for Best Cinematography & Best Editing.

"A beautiful and touching movie. Perfectly magnificent photography. Its camera work is so stunning that it immediately established a sensitive texture." —THE NEW YORK TIMES

The Hall Bartlett Film
Jonathan Livingston Seagull
EVERYONE'S BOOK IS NOW EVERYONE'S MOTION PICTURE

bell was rung, the bird returned to the perch for a delicious fresh fish treat—ah, anchovies. It worked beautifully! But just for safety, each of these expensive, trained birds had a monofilament fishing line attached to one foot so they couldn't fly away. Before computer-generated special effects could easily remove unwanted ropes, lines, or objects, Jim had to avoid showing the line, so he kept the bird's feet just outside the film's frame. When Mr. Bartlett saw these images, he complained. "I really need to see the whole bird against the sky," he said. "Can't the trainer do it without the wire attached?"

"Sure," the trainer said, "I can do anything!"

Jim went back on the next sunny, blue-sky day to film wider shots showing the untethered bird, feet and all. The bell rang and the obedient bird took off into the wind with Jim's camera screaming away at 120 frames per second. Just then, this "highly" trained bird spotted eight seagulls flying overhead and probably thought: "What am I doing? I'm not an actor. I'm a seagull without a care in the world." The free-as-a-bird creature flapped its wings, peeled off of the wind stream, and disappeared. We estimated that training and prepping this one bird had cost $30,000. The most valuable seagull in the history of seagulls was AWOL, and the overconfident trainer was on the next plane back to Hollywood.

Throughout the story line, Jonathan rejects the mundane aspects of daily life and explores the concept of perfect flight. He experiments with dives, rolls, loops, and terminal velocity, all in pursuit of his freedom. Since seagulls rarely actually perform such aerobatic moves, we couldn't film them using real birds. So Mr. Bartlett hired a remote-controlled glider expert, Mark Smith, to build a fake seagull. Jim, Cindy, Jeff, and Stan traveled to various locations to film these maneuvers, and then editors Frank Keller and James Galloway composed sequences that were amazingly convincing, earning the film another Academy Award nomination—this time for editing.

For Jim, shooting these scenes after years of tracking surfers with telephoto lenses came naturally, and just as with Jonathan's push toward perfection, I could see that Jim was reaching a higher plane as well. His photographic skill and artistry rose. As I observed this, I tried even harder as I edited **Five Summer Stories** and our Mazda film. Again, we were pushing each other in constructive, noncompetitive ways. I worked on my musical montages, determined to build more effective sequences. As Jim photographed aerobatics, he found ways to use these convincing maneuvers to communicate Jonathan's search for liberation, a search for fulfillment that resonated with readers, filmgoers, and Jim and me.

The Day Seagulls Nearly Burned Down the Holiday Inn

The few times when Jim needed a second cameraman, I would fly up to help. Once, after a day of shooting, the crew and I were relaxing in the hotel pool. We happened to look up to the second-floor room where the seagulls were staying. About six birds were lining the ledge of the windows, enviously staring down at us in the pool. Maybe the other residents of the Holiday Inn were shocked, but we thought it was hilarious.

A month later something happened that wasn't so funny. Because seagulls like to perch on the highest object in the room, several birds tried to climb onto a lampshade. Unfortunately, someone had left the lamp turned on. All of a sudden, the lamp fell over, and the bedsheets, which were protecting the carpet from seagull poop, caught on fire. That caused the sprinkler system to go off. The fire alarm rang for an hour, disturbing all the guests, water flooded onto the floor below, and when the door to the room was opened, the panicked seagulls scrambled out everywhere, down the hallway, flying, squawking, and terrifying everyone! The room was a disaster. The Holiday Inn management began to think twice about allowing the film crew, let alone seagulls, to stay longer. Production manager Gaylin Schultz talked the hotel manager out of anything rash. The seagulls were panic-stricken, as were a few guests, but all were safe! Years later, the hotel installed a plaque on the room door that proudly proclaimed, "Jonathan Livingston Seagull slept here!"

When **Jonathan Livingston Seagull** was released by Paramount, it was accompanied by Neil Diamond's awe-inspiring soundtrack that Neil confessed was written to represent, not Jonathan's voice, but Jonathan's heart. The soulful, poetic music and many of the songs became huge hits and the album became Neil's most popular to date, selling three million copies. The soundtrack was even nominated for a Grammy Award for best score of the year.

Learning Vital Lessons

We learned so very much from working on this film. In my study of what works in the film business, I've found that you need a staff of nine "givers" for every "taker." The givers are generous team players; the takers are aggressive and always looking for a personal win, often at the expense of others, but you need all ten. In this instance, Hall Bartlett was a taker and Jim and I watched as he played that role to his disadvantage. For example, he made a brilliant deal to nab rights to the year's most popular book, but then took it upon himself to rewrite the story against the wishes (and the contract) of Richard Bach, who had the support of millions of fans. Bartlett then hired Neil Diamond to write the wonderful score, but he insulted and alienated the songwriter by hiring another composer to work on additional music. Finally, he stretched our deal to the limits by making sure Jim worked for months longer than our contract called for and never made good on his promise of additional payments. In each instance, Bartlett took for himself; but he ended up losing a lot more than he gained. He upset Richard and Neil so much that they both went on talk shows to condemn the film the week it was released. "This is not the book that I wrote and you loved," said Richard on national TV. "Don't go see the film." And audiences didn't. The film died in the theaters and Hall Bartlett lost out.[8] Jim and I learned that good business has to be a win-win, and I'm happy to report that that philosophy has worked for 60 years.

Richard Bach and associate producer Leslie Parrish at our offices.

Jim and I had loved Bach's story of Jonathan, a seagull bored with meaningless squabbles each day who seeks a higher plane of existence. Jonathan wants to find a perfect way to fly. He does so, becoming a master of the sky, but still feels an emptiness. In the end, he realizes he needs to keep working on love. Bach wrote, "Here's to the real Jonathan Livingston Seagull, who lives within us all."

Accessing Hollywood

After we'd directed and photographed a variety of subject pieces that created quite a sensation with Hollywood and New York City studios and advertising agencies, Jim found joy in traveling to both locations to pitch film ideas. He loved to drive and he loved making friends. This new phase of our career, Hollywood feature films, was right up Jim's alley and was another example of our great partnership, as I couldn't stand LA and hated making pitches!

One of the relationships that Jim cultivated was with Nelson Tyler, who for decades had been the world's leading aerial cinematographer. He was also an engineering genius. Finding aerial cinematography jittery and unpleasant to watch on-screen, Nelson built the first stabilized helicopter mount and rendered shots from the air smooth and spectacular. His successful helicopter mount rental company, Tyler Camera Systems, established offices in cities around the world. Though Nelson had revolutionized aerial photography with his velvety artistic compositions, he had personally grown tired of filming from the air.

By the age of 23, Jim had completed the best aerial work that Nelson had seen of late, so he suggested that we team up. "Jim can do all the jobs for Hollywood features and smaller films that I don't want to do anymore," he proposed. That joining of forces set off a long and fruitful partnership with a man we came to trust more than anyone we'd ever met in Hollywood. Nelson was a giver. [9]

Meeting Irwin Allen

This new chapter in our life story thrilled Jim and showcased his outgoing, humor-laced personality. One night, as I was just finishing up edits for the day, Jim burst into the office like a five-year-old, eager to tell me about a meeting he'd had that day in LA that he thought could lead to challenging, inventive opportunities. Because Jim had such a gift of gab, of making others feel important to his story, people loved him, and so did I. Even today, people like Nelson Tyler tell me, "God, I miss Jim's exuberance." I feel the same way.

That day, Jim's enthusiasm led to a long-lasting relationship with Irwin Allen, one of the most interesting producers in Hollywood. Irwin excelled at combining simple characters and dire situations, with special effects imagery of spectacular events; it was the same combination that propelled **Star Wars** to the top. Irwin's TV series *Voyage to the Bottom of the Sea* and *Land of the Giants*, as well as **The Poseidon Adventure** (1972) and **The Towering Inferno** (1974) on the big screen, earned him the nickname, "Master of Disaster." To Jim and me, this distant mentor and friend would be instrumental in our work on **The Towering Inferno**, **Viva Knievel!**, and a never-produced volcano disaster film. Jim's photography helped **The Towering Inferno** win an Oscar for best photography and gross over $200 million, the second-biggest ticket seller that year (after the hilarious **Blazing Saddles**). During that same era, new ways to project visual experiences, like IMAX, caught our attention and would lead us on new, intellectually challenging adventures.

8 When I contacted Richard Bach months ago, he directed me to a friend who had followed the Bartlett-Jonathan disagreement closely, and it's an interesting example of how good things can go drastically and painfully bad. Bach contractually had final cut, and when Bartlett showed him the cut, Bach said bluntly, "I hate it; I do not approve." More lawyers, then judges got involved. These two normally low-key personalities wanted to kill each other. In the end, it all got resolved to Bach's benefit.

9 Nelson Tyler, genius designer and engineer, became the best aerial cinematographer when he revolutionized camera stability with his new Tyler Mount. His artistic photographic work on **Hello, Dolly!** (1969), **Batman: The Movie** (1966), **Paint Your Wagon** (1969), **Marooned** (1969), and **Funny Girl** (1968) created a sensation in cinematography circles. He received three technical achievement Oscars. He also created the Tyler Gyro Platform Boat Mount (which I used on **Big Wednesday** and **Behold Hawaii**), the Tyler Wetbike (the precursor to the Jet Ski), and about 20 other amazing inventions.

Reaching for the Sky:
IMAX® and *To Fly!*

SURF

HOLLYWOOD

IMAX ENTERTAINMENT

MISSION

> **"To Fly!** is capable of triggering the motion sickness sensors responsible for nausea . . . screaming, gasping, and getting off the ride are behaviors no longer only synonymous with a . . . theme park ride. IMAX, too, can now take a seat in the hall of the 'most visceral spectatorial experiences.'"
>
> –ALISON GRIFFITH, AUTHOR OF *SHIVERS DOWN YOUR SPINE*

During the late 1960s, new and inventive film projection systems designed to dazzle audiences with visual imagery were on display at world's fairs. Montreal's Expo 67 and Osaka, Japan's Expo 70 unveiled many formats, including six screens creating a multi-image montage; wraparound Circle-Vision 360°; 3D; and Cinerama tri-screen. These new formats enabled filmmakers to change the way people experienced visual narrative storytelling. It was a fascinating new universe and Jim and I began studying all these new techniques. We attended the world's fairs. We read everything published regarding new media. And we talked with filmmakers who had experimented with them. That learning led us to immersive results like our Cinerama tri-screen film for Mazda, **Cleared for Take-Off**, and our widescreen projection called **Above San Francisco**, an Orson Welles–narrated film that we produced for banker Charlie Crocker and book publisher and photographer Robert Cameron. That film played to tourists for a decade at the city's Cannery Theatre. We were then invited to produce **To Fly!** for the Smithsonian Institution's proposed National Air and Space Museum. This seminal project would be one of the first experiential films to be made using a new medium called IMAX®.

(FACING PAGE) The first pilots took to the air in balloons. We filmed the recreation of a 1790s flight over the untouched forests of West Virginia.

IMAX was developed in 1967 for world's fair films. The projector was immediately recognized as the new Rolls-Royce of the industry. With a price tag of nearly $2 million, the projector's output was so big, so sharp, and so bright that it felt completely immersive; it was a you-are-there experience rather than just a movie on a screen. And because the audience sat in steeply raked seats that gave a novel close-up, wide-open view of the screen, filmmakers had to create innovative new ways of writing, shooting, and editing these motion pictures.

IMAX creator Graeme Ferguson and his partners, Robert Kerr, Bill Shaw, Roman Kroitor, and Bill Breukelman, forever revolutionized film entertainment by building a camera that used 65mm film running horizontally rather than vertically through the camera. This produced an image ten times larger than we could get with 35mm. It was the largest movie camera ever made and was equipped with the same highest-quality Zeiss Hasselblad lenses that NASA sent on its moon missions.

Once we accepted the Smithsonian's invitation to produce **To Fly!**, Jim and I dedicated ourselves to becoming specialists. We practically memorized the six existing IMAX movies, interviewed audience members at the Spokane IMAX theater, traveled to Toronto to view films at Ontario Place, and interviewed Ferguson. When I saw

To Fly!

FILMED IN: 15 PERFORATION/70MM

RELEASE DATE: 1976

On the 100th anniversary of the first projection of films, the US Library of Congress celebrated by honoring the 100 most significant films from 1,100 nominees. **To Fly!** was selected as one of those 100.

"It's a National Monument."
—*The Washington Post*

his **Man Belongs to the Earth** on Spokane's 50-foot-high screen, the opening aerial shot that dove over the edge and into the Grand Canyon gave me shivers down my spine. That "ah-ha" moment changed Jim and me forever. We *loved* this new medium!

Though it was hard back then to get people in Hollywood to appreciate the power and potential of IMAX, Jim and I loved making these experimental-format films because they forced us to consider each decision without relying on tired assumptions. It was a new way to see. Rather than watching a framed picture on a wall, IMAX removed the frame and wall altogether. And since seeing is believing—IMAX created an authentic, real experience, not a movie. One film professor said we'd "exploded the frame." Our sense of independence and our desire to be unique were nourished by this new challenge. An added benefit was that we got to use our science skills (Jim from his premed days and me from my love of physics) to create amazing new experiences on screen and to design new cameras, mounts, and lenses. Every day was a joy.

Producing *To Fly!*

After our meeting in Toronto, Graeme generously began guiding us in the design of **To Fly!** using his knowledge from producing **Tiger Child**, **North of Superior**, **Snow Job**, and **Man Belongs to the Earth**. But Jim and I wanted **To Fly!** to be vastly different. It needed to show off the strength and impact of this new way to see movies, at times producing the vertigo of a roller-coaster ride, and at others the sweetness of a quiet, beautiful scene in nature. We set out to design a simple film that would follow man's ascent into the air through time, following a list of ideas provided by former astronaut Michael Collins. Mike was the director of the new National Air and Space Museum and involved in developing its leading-edge exhibits. Though not a museum expert, Mike was qualfied. Just five years earlier, Mike had circled the moon 30 times on the Apollo 11 expedition, not knowing

whether Buzz Aldrin and Neil Armstrong, who were then walking on the moon, would ever return to Mike's orbiter. Buzz and Neil's liftoff from the moon had never been tested and the odds were only fifty-fifty. Mike wrote: "My secret terror . . . has been leaving Neil and Buzz on the moon and returning to Earth alone."

Mike told me, "Bring me a film that entertains and gives the audience the true feeling of flying." When I asked how many facts and historical moments he wanted us to include, Mike answered, "I've got a thousand facts in the museum. Give me fun," adding, "and don't expect to hear from me again until the museum is fully built. See you in a year and a half." What a brilliant leader. Hire people you trust and step aside.

And so we began our most challenging film yet by planning the script with Oscar-winner Francis Thompson, the executive producer, and writers Robert Young and Arthur Zegart. Jim and I took their ideas and then simplified the structure of **To Fly!** so that it was chronologically accurate, but clear enough that the expansive visual mood wouldn't be marred by excessive narration. From Mike and Mel Zisfein's list, we included quiet helium balloon flights over untouched forests of the 1790s; 1920s biplane action; hang gliding in Hawaii. We added visual gasps: a steam train racing a stagecoach across the Western prairie; a stomach-curdling cliff drop in a Curtiss Pusher aircraft; a tight formation of Blue Angels jets above the Colorado River; and a mesmerizing kaleidoscope of 36 images filling the six-story-high screen. Because the Smithsonian wanted shows to run every half hour, our film's length was set at 26 minutes—so short that every second mattered. In our script, we began the film (imitating the wonderful surprises in **This Is Cinerama** and **North of Superior**) on a small section of the screen for the first 90 seconds. When the balloon lifts off the ground, symbolically giving its pilot a new way of seeing, "like the opening of a new eye," we cut to full IMAX size, scope, and resolution— a dramatic smash cut that audiences found shocking and spectacular.

Jim and I were used to working with large Panavision screens and Cinerama tri-screens wrapping around the audience, but IMAX was even more impactful. Even after we'd finished the script, we kept coming up with more ideas.

"Remember that story of one of the first Lumière films, **Train Pulling into a Station**,[10] where the audience screamed and supposedly bolted out of their seats? Could we do that?" I asked. And Jim, always thinking, said, "What if we built a huge mirror, placed it on the tracks at a 45° angle, and had a big train run right into it—and we'd be safely off to the side filming into the mirror?" Using the historic steam train

---

10 American inventor Thomas Edison and the French Lumière brothers are jointly credited for having projected the first motion pictures, in 1895-96. The Lumière's **The Train** was shot in 35mm and was only 50 seconds long, projected in a theater in Paris.

near Yosemite, we tried just that. What a jolt to watch a 10-ton train explode the mirror and its frame! It took our crew an hour to pick up all the pieces of the shattered mirror, but the sensational shot we got was A+ and worth every sore back muscle.

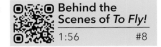

Behind the Scenes of *To Fly!*
1:56   #8

After the Smithsonian approved our script, we faced an even bigger challenge: There was only one IMAX camera in existence, a prototype. If it broke, both **To Fly!** and **American Years**, a film being shot by Francis Thompson, Inc. for the bicentennial celebration in Philadelphia, would be compromised. Francis Thompson Inc. and MFF contracted with IMAX Corporation to build three more cameras, paying our rental in advance. In just four months, we were shooting with new cameras.

As we worked on this film, Jim and I knew beyond a doubt that this was our calling, and the emotional energy we brought to the challenge recharged itself on each of the 400 days we spent on it. As we toyed with ways to improve on each giant image, from me riding in the helicopter helping to direct as Jim shot, to strategies on the ground when we double-photographed important scenes using two IMAX cameras, our friendship continued to deepen. We became not just business partners, but brothers. Our executive producer, Byron McKinney, who accompanied us to many locations, noticed the change. "Watching you two work was like watching a dance," he said later. "You rarely talked, but you communicated with ease and efficiency, each knowing the next move." At the same time, Cindy and Barbara's friendship strengthened as well.

Given our low budget, only $590,000, we hired only one trained actor, Peter Walker, our balloonist. We decided that every other role would be nonspeaking because we had to use locals, some of whom were good, some of whom were, well, not so convincing. Even Barbara, Cindy, and Jeff Blyth, our production manager, had cameos, wearing different costumes in different scenes.[11]

Once we had that first eight weeks done, and we reached our seasonal hiatus (we didn't want to shoot the super-tall IMAX images with the hazy skies and harsh light of summer), Jim and I evaluated our footage and budget and were delighted. We'd gotten through the character story points with B+ to A- image results, and were under budget to boot! Now we could do what we did best: spend the fall season on spectacular visuals, waiting for perfect light and getting A+ IMAX photographic results. But first, we had another challenge.

---

11 When we decided to use actors in our IMAX films rather than real characters, Randal Kleiser, director of **Grease** and **The Blue Lagoon**, a brilliant filmmaker whom I'd met through my great friend composer Basil Poledouris, helped me. He suggested I take classes from the famous actor Nina Foch (**An American in Paris**, **Spartacus**), so I studied with her for several months. She taught me to be simple in my instruction to actors because no actor, no matter how accomplished, can understand complicated direction. Say, "Go faster," "Say it louder," "Say it softer," or "Whisper it." And she taught me to give an actor full respect and honor their craft, which is so difficult to achieve. "Give your actor his motivation, but as simply as possible," she said. And this beautiful, talented actor helped our next 50 IMAX films dramatically.

(ABOVE) The only way to have a train run into a camera, without damaging the camera: film into a mirror placed on the tracks! (BELOW) Jim and I check the IMAX camera, mounted on the helicopter.

Summer of '75:
James Coburn Takes a Leap of Faith

We spent the summer break from filming **To Fly!** in one of the most beautiful spots in the world: the Meteora sandstone pinnacles near Kalambaka, Greece.

In 1975 we were approached by 20th Century-Fox, the studio then making **Star Wars** and which we knew from **The Sweet Ride**, to direct and shoot second unit for the feature film **Sky Riders**. Shockingly, we saw that the script called for a long action sequence of hang gliders soaring at night, over the monasteries of Meteora. With no budget to light the sky, it would have been difficult and dangerous to fly hang gliders, let alone Jim's helicopter, in darkness. Hollywood's solution would have been to shoot "day-for-night"; that is, shoot during the day and just darken it up. The results always looked phony to us, so Jim and our special-effects friend Bill Abbott came up with an idea: We'd shoot with black-and-white film and place a deep red filter over the lens. The filter would absorb the blue of the daytime sky, turning it almost black on film. Genius . . . except that 20th Century-Fox wanted proof of concept before they'd commit.

We threw together a shoot, enlisting our office crew to playact terrorists attacking our new office building, the historic Villa Bella. Secretaries and editors—even the UPS guy and our neighbor's gardener—went clamoring over the walls with their fake guns. This fun afternoon gave us a chance to beta test our concept. Once the film was color-corrected with a blue tint, the studio couldn't deny the results. It looked great and, most importantly, realistic. The film was given the green light! Since none of our team, including Jim and me, had been to Greece, we all packed excitedly for the trip.

On location we got to know the film's star, James Coburn, and became fast friends. He schooled us in the medicinal virtues of gin and tonics, which were especially tasty in the heat of a Greek summer.

One day, Coburn asked producer Sandy Howard to have us shoot and direct a special action scene that Coburn had written. Coburn's character was to jump onto the skid of a helicopter that was transporting the bad guys, and use his pistol to bring the chopper down. He insisted on doing the action himself and asked us to build a camera mount on the helicopter to show his face as he hung from the skid. To get the first shot—a close-up action cut of him grabbing the skids—we decided that I should hand-hold the Arriflex camera as the helicopter came up over a ridge, with Coburn standing in the foreground. We would duck just as the helicopter passed above us. Barbara captured this extreme, potentially lethal moment in a series of still photographs, shown on the facing page. The shot worked to perfection, highlighted the actor's daring stunt work, and became one of the most memorable scenes in the film. When we completed the scene, we held a wrap party at a Greek restaurant, dancing and, true to Hellenic custom, shattering plates on the floor. It was a fitting local tribute to the friendships we'd made over the past 10 weeks.

(LEFT) Filmimg actors in a hang-glider safely—without taking off. (TOP) The Greek Meteora. (ABOVE) Susannah York, a mesmerizing actor.

Actor James Coburn wrote an action highlight, which he wanted us to film. Coburn's idea was that he grabs onto the villain's helicopter skids, then, hanging below the helicopter, uses a pistol to bring the craft down safely. We made it work. (ABOVE) Here, I film Coburn as he attempts to grab the helicopter skid. (BELOW) Coburn taught Jim and me so much about dealing with Hollywood productions.

(ABOVE) The IMAX film format is expressed as 15-perf/70mm—each frame has 15 perforations (sprocket holes) at top and bottom and the film stock is 70 millimeters wide (2 inches by 2.75 inches)—ten times larger than a standard 35mm frame. This graphic represents a comparison of these three film formats when projected onto a theater screen.

IMAX® Screen

25 m
80 ft

70 mm Screen

35 mm Screen

(BELOW) In 1970, as I sat working at the editing bench in our first office, I was interrupted by a hard bang at the front door. Standing there were two athletic young men in their early 20s. They began talking to me with so much excitement and enthusiasm that I invited them to come inside and sit down so they could calm down a bit. They proceeded to tell me about a brand new sport they had been trying for six months called hang gliding. No one had seen this sport yet, they said, as it had started in Australia. When their enthusiastic chatter calmed down, they showed me photographs of men hanging below a kite in the sky, magically flying like a bird. I was intrigued. Since Jim was away shooting **Jonathan Livingston Seagull** for Paramount Pictures, I told him about the two pilots over the phone. He said, "Why don't you go out and film some footage with these guys just to see what this crazy new sport is?" The next month, Barbara and I accompanied Bob and Chris Wills to various California locations, filming a sequence on hang gliding. When Jim saw the footage, his imagination jumped with creativity. What if we filmed hang gliders in the air above the most magnificent locations in the world, like the otherworldly cliffs of Kauai along the Na Pali coastline? We were stoked. When Jim finished working on **Jonathan Livingston Seagull**, Bob Wills, Jim, Cindy, Barbara, and I spent a month filming in Kauai at the most glorious locations imaginable. That seven-minute clip led to the film **Sky Riders**, which we made for 20th Century-Fox and producer Sandy Howard, starring James Coburn. It also led to us being hired to direct and produce the first IMAX film for the Smithsonian National Air and Space Museum, **To Fly!**. This is Bob Wills, the best hang-glider pilot in the world, above the Na Pali coastline, Kauai, 1972.

After our Grecian summer tour, we launched back into **To Fly!** Because we were on the road to a promising new chapter in our business, Jim was even more giddy and light-hearted than usual and I could relax my focus on the tight budget and have fun creating beautiful moments of film. Our mood was serious but playful. When we'd stop for lunch at a restaurant, we'd laugh like 10-year-olds as Jim challenged me to catch the sugar packets he'd launch off his catapult-purposed spoon. Jim would compete with Barbara to see who could get the waiter to bring more lemon wedges; they each had an insatiable craving for the tangy flavor of vitamin C.

Jim loved being around friends and clients and even people he'd never met before. He'd dream up playful nicknames. Fastidious photographer Richard Hovey was "Picky-Ricky." Barbara was "Babsy-Wabsy" and Bill Bennett was "Ding," because Jim got the phone company to install a direct line between their houses. You'd pick up Jim's phone and Bill's would ring.

The fall shooting began with ground and aerial photography of a historically accurate replica of a 1790 gas balloon. Hydrogen was used in the first balloons of the 1790s. As this wasn't classic Hollywood entertainment—it would show as a documentary-style film at the Smithsonian Institution for decades—we had to be 100 percent correct. We couldn't use the more common hot-air balloon. But obtaining hydrogen was impossible and even helium was a huge problem because we needed so much. Finally, the navy agreed to help, and a tanker truck of helium met us in Parsons, West Virginia, the only place we could get an unobstructed 40-mile view of untouched forest without power lines, roads, or towers, all of which you would notice with the clarity of IMAX projection. We waited five days for the rain to abate, and finally were blessed with two sun-kissed days. The balloon pilot, Kurt Snelling, had piloted me on about 15 hot-air balloon flights while we photographed **Above San Francisco**. We'd been through many crashes, once getting stuck in an 80-foot-tall oak tree, but I trusted his skill and knowledge. These real flying shots would match into the scenes with actor Peter Walker we had already filmed in Vermont using just a wicker basket hanging on a cherry-picker crane barely out of frame.

On those two sunny days, Jim shot from the air and I from the ground, and we got enough A+ shots to make a beautiful opening sequence for the film. Over the next 10 weeks, our team shot hang gliding in Hawaii, the very first 747 airplane (gleaming new with serial number 001), stunning aerials in Bryce Canyon, Zion, Monument Valley, and the Grand Canyon, and then began editing. By June, we were ready for the premiere of **To Fly!** We couldn't wait to see the public's reaction to all of our surprises.

To Fly! Takes Off

When the National Air and Space Museum opened its doors on July 2, 1976, just two days before our country's 200th anniversary, even astronaut Michael Collins was impressed. The amazing IMAX Theatre and our film contributed to the overwhelmingly positive reviews and attendance. Just ninety seconds into the film, the audience realized that they didn't have to take notes. They could sit back, relax, and laugh their way through the film, even though the movie was being shown inside the hallowed halls of the Smithsonian Institution. As instructed by Mike Collins, we'd created a fun film, not a stuffy historical drama.

Conoco, the sponsor whose credit appears at the film's opening and closing, wanted one thing: their name to be associated with the Smithsonian, the international gold standard for museums. As **To Fly!** set attendance and revenue records, though, their investment in the film became, as CEO Ralph Bailey wrote, "the best public relations decision ever made at Conoco." Our team sent 16mm copies to all 600 independent TV stations in the United States for free public-service screenings, and this exposure helped gain an even bigger audience for the film and for Conoco. In 1981, on the fifth anniversary of **To Fly!**, executive producer Francis Thompson and I were interviewed by Tom Brokaw on NBC's *The Today Show*, so Barbara and I, with one-year-old Shaun in tow, toured New York City. The interviewers were more impressed by cute little Shaun than by Francis or me, but the TV exposure focused America's attention on how this 26-minute film had taken our capitol by storm. Five years after that, *The New York Times* arts editor claimed **To Fly!** was "the most universally popular film of the past ten years."

To the museum's Mel Zisfein, IMAX was a "quantum jump better than Cinerama, Circle-Vision 360°, and older media."[12] By 1980, every museum in the world was trying to get an IMAX Theatre for three important reasons: It was a new way to educate viewers; it gave exhausted museum guests a chance to sit down and recharge; and it produced a sizable profit for the museum.

Academy Award–winning filmmaker Kieth Merrill wrote to me at the time to say that "there wouldn't have been an IMAX industry without **To Fly!**" When, in 1995, the Library of Congress wanted to celebrate the 100 most important films of the first 100 years of worldwide cinema (film was first projected in 1895), **To Fly!** was selected to receive the honor, along with **Gone with the Wind**, **The Birth of a Nation**, **Star Wars**, and 96 others as part of the first National Film Archives. I only wish that Jim had been there to share that honor.

---

12 In her book, *Shivers Down Your Spine*, Alison Griffith noted this moment's significance by saying: "When the iconic IMAX film **To Fly!** opened at the Smithsonian Institution's National Air and Space Museum (NASM) in 1976 to celebrate the nation's bicentennial, it also marked a turning point in the status of audiovisual display technologies in museums." She was correct. Over the first four years, **To Fly!** attracted more than 6,300,000 viewers to the Smithsonian's IMAX theatre, a record.

(ABOVE) Jim and I film the helium balloon lift-off in West Virginia in both 35mm and in IMAX. (BELOW) I storyboarded the entire film so that each moment would easily flow into the next.

Losing My Best Friend

"Watching Jim and Greg filming is reminiscent of a team of surgeons. There is a certain quality of fine, deft precision that permeates their work, yet they perform it in a very relaxed manner."

—CRAIG LOCKWOOD, AUTHOR

Jim and I sat on the curb out in front of Todd-AO Studios in Hollywood. It was after midnight on June 18, 1976, and we'd just finished mixing the soundtrack to **To Fly!** on the same recording stages that had been used to mix epic films like **The Sound of Music** and **Lawrence of Arabia**. This was the zenith! As the streets emptied, Jim and I talked about completing our biggest film to date and what it meant to us. We told stories of the decisions we'd made in trying to maximize the visual and aural impact of this new type of film. We couldn't wait to see it on the gigantic Smithsonian screen, and we couldn't help but look ahead to a bright future for our company.

Two days later, Jim headed north to scout locations for a series of Kodak commercials we'd been hired to shoot in California's High Sierra, while I traveled with my whole family and Jim's mother and sister to Washington, D.C. I was going there to install a print of **To Fly!** at the new National Air and Space Museum's IMAX Theatre for the June 24 congressional premiere. Jim and I were planning to use the opportunity to celebrate the nation's bicentennial as a family. We felt lucky. After working the morning of June 23 at the museum, perfecting

the sound and picture, I was pulled away for a telephone call. I was surprised to hear Bill Bennett, who had worked with Jim and me since we were 19, on the line. Inside the phone booth, his voice was steady, but I could tell that something was wrong.

"Greg, Jim has been in a terrible accident. He was killed in a helicopter crash."

Mainly because Bill sounded so calm, I couldn't believe what I was hearing. But seconds later the words sank in and I dropped the phone. My legs actually turned to jelly and I collapsed on the floor of the booth.

Barbara came rushing over and grabbed the phone as Bill told her what little he knew. Jim had rented a Jet Ranger helicopter with pilot Bill Knott. We trusted Knott's skills because he had worked with us for months on the aerial photography for **Above San Francisco**. The pilot had taken off in the heat of the afternoon from Bishop Airport with three passengers: Jim, agency executive Ray Fragasso, and Ben Gradus, a producer from New York. As they searched for filming locations in the Sierras at high altitude, the helicopter's "engine out" light came on, signaling the worst problem in the worst location at the worst possible time of day.

Knott initiated an autorotation, a controlled descent that every pilot practices several times a year. From 14,000 feet in altitude, he picked out the nearest potential landing site: a meadow. Tragically, there were too many trees and not enough of a clearing. The helicopter crashed into several large pines.

Jeff Blyth, our production manager, was at Bishop Airport awaiting their return. When the helicopter was clearly overdue, Jeff contacted Civil Air Patrol and a frantic search began. His second call was to Bill Bennett, who jumped into a car and raced to Bishop. It wasn't until early the next morning that a rescue helicopter would locate the

(FACING PAGE) After the Wright brothers initiated powered flight in 1903, airplanes became vehicles for warfare in World War I. Years later during the Roaring Twenties, those planes and their trained pilots criss-crossed the States, selling barnstorming rides to adventurous farmers, townspeople, and, well, anyone with a few dollars. We highlighted that fun activity in **To Fly!** Here, Jim and I double-IMAX-shoot a harrowing dusting of the crowd. Camera assistant Philip Schwartz helps me, and executive producer Byron McKinney assists Jim.

crash site and report just two survivors. Jim and Ray had died at the site. It was then that Bennett called me in Washington, D.C.

Our film had its premiere the next day, but Jim's girlfriend, Cindy, was still in Laguna. I called her: "Cindy, you have to get here. We need to be together and you shouldn't be alone. Get on the red-eye tonight!"

My dad picked her up at the airport. With the premiere dedicated to Jim, the museum's director, Michael Collins, gave a stirring tribute to him, reminding us all of Jim's dreams of soaring like a bird. With his final film, Mike said, "Jim had given us what every pilot or astronaut knows and loves: the true feeling of flight, the absolute joy of looking down on Earth from near or from far." Then, **To Fly!** lit up the screen. There wasn't a dry eye for the duration of that screening.

Jim didn't get to share the immense satisfaction of watching our first IMAX film on a huge screen. What a tragic irony that this creative talent would miss seeing his best work in all its glory. As Washington VIPs, senators, representatives, and tourists lined up to experience this strange new brand of poetic documentary, I couldn't get beyond my own grieving. How could this happen? Could I handle it?

That day became a blur, but the next day I had to face another question. When I was checking everyone in for the return flight to LA, I noticed a small poster at the airline ticket counter. The movie on this flight was **Sky Riders**, the James Coburn film that Jim and I helped direct in Greece the summer before. I went to Jim's mom and explained my concerns that seeing this film again might add to her trauma. This devoutly religious mother grabbed my arm and hugged me, saying, "This was meant to be. It's what Jim would've wanted us to be watching." Her strength helped me through it.

Coming Home with a Hole in My Heart

When I got back to Laguna, my brain felt scrambled. I just couldn't put the yolk, the shell, and the white back together. Though it was tough to think straight, we all organized a gathering to celebrate Jim's life; knowing that he would have wanted it to be fun and not sad, we tried our best. That night lifted me up. Loving friends and their sympathy for the pain we were suffering supported me, helping me gain confidence. Barbara, who'd been stoic up to that point to strengthen and bolster me, broke down and wept, curled up in a corner on the floor for an hour in a catatonic state, until she was soothed and helped up by our friend Craig Thompson. Over the following months, when we would be out with others, if Barbara suddenly disappeared, I knew where I'd find her. She'd be in the ladies' room sobbing. Jim's death touched us all so deeply.

Los Angeles Times arts editor Charles Champlin wrote a moving tribute to Jim's creativity entitled "At the Height of Air and Water,"

(RIGHT) Jim loved the huge IMAX film frame. We both started our filmmaking infatuation with 8mm, now we were shooting frames about 250 times bigger!

and spoke at Jim's funeral, delivering the beautiful eulogy below. On that windless June day, just a mile from where Jim and his sisters grew up, we were all so thankful that Mr. Champlin led off the tribute, because none of us could fight off tears long enough to speak.

A Tribute: June 29, 1976
by Charles Champlin[13]

We've come together this warm afternoon in Santa Ana because it is impossible to think of Jim without smiling or feeling across the miles and the years the glow of his energy and his inexhaustible enthusiasm. Gloom was no part of him; it isn't now.

What struck me the first time I saw any of the films that Jim and Greg did was how much they said about the men who made them, and what great guys they must be, and what a uniquely California phenomenon they were in the best sense of the word. What gives California particular magic for most of us is not simply the climate; more than the climate, it is the climate of possibility, that confident feeling that if you have the idea, the energy and the dedication, you can make it work.

Jim and Greg have made it work, from what you might call a paddling start, and what they have done is to capture as art all of the excitements of life that find their clearest expression here in California.

To catch the joy—was there ever a title that said it all so well—to catch the joy of man in motion, and the lyrical beauty of it, was the challenge that made Jim and Greg realize from the moment of their first meeting in Santa Barbara in 1964 that they shared common ideals (and common minor problems like money and equipment). Jim's debut as a filmmaker came when he was student body president at Lynwood High.

Anyone who has had the pleasure of dropping by their headquarters over in Laguna Beach has had to be caught up in the contagion of people enjoying hard work. Greg was saying the other night that Jim's boundless enthusiasm combined with his own propelled them through around-the-clock editing sessions and through all the endless hours of trial and error experimentation to do things better.

What made them a matchless team was their sharing a single-minded devotion to the work. What they did for a living was their life, and that electric excitement, the exultation and the humor, the soaring sense of freedom and poetry, is in every frame of theirs we see.

We feel pangs; how can we not? But I do believe, as I said the other day, that the time a man has matters less than what he makes of that time. A life lived to the brimming full is its own precious legacy. And how enviable it is never to have run out of dreams, to have had so many more, ready and beckoning and bright.

13 Charles Champlin graduated from Harvard and for decades held the esteemed position as arts editor and head film critic for the most prominent newspaper in Hollywood and Los Angeles. Sadly, this kind and talented man died in 2014 at 88 years of age.

Jim Freeman leaves us many gifts, including all those imperishable, shining images of our time and place. But perhaps the greatest of his gifts, costly as it was, is simply to remind us all to cherish our own days and to make the most of them, as he did, to pursue the dreams and catch the joy.

Mr. Champlin expressed perfectly the hopes and dreams that fueled my friendship with Jim, and by the time he finished everyone was in tears, sniffing, some fully sobbing. Just 32 years old, Jim's death just didn't seem fair. How could he have been taken from our midst at this zenith of achievement? Gone was his ever-present smile, his handy laugh, and his engaging rapport. Everyone had a piece of their own Jim —something they shared with him that was special. I knew that Jim's death was going to change my life forever. I was heartbroken by the loss of not only my best friend but of our beautiful and unique cinematic chemistry. And I knew that the world of cinema had lost a true artist.

Losing Jim was made even more difficult by the fact that he had just gone through a period of tortuous self-evaluation and improvement. A year before, when Jim and I were directing the second-unit action crew of 30 for **Sky Riders**, we were getting fantastic action sequences of hang gliding, gun battles, stunts . . . but our elevated position with the studio (executive Peter Beale thought our footage was amazing) had gone to Jim's head. It was true. It was a heady experience because my assistant director, Brian Cook, was Stanley Kubrick's AD on **Barry Lyndon** and **A Clockwork Orange**, and our production manager was Robert Watts, who had produced **Star Wars.** We were at the top of the filmmaking mountain, so Jim should have felt at least a little proud. But his newly stimulated ego was causing strife between Jim and Cindy. Finally Cindy had had enough and left him. Jim was devastated. For Barbara and me, our core family had just collapsed. The four of us were best friends. Then, "Dr." Barbara made a wise suggestion.

"When this job is done, let's go on a head-clearing cruise through the Greek isles and the Middle East, we three in one cabin, relaxing, thinking, reflecting, and regrouping." The therapy worked, and over the next year, Jim would make dramatic changes to himself, all for the better. His focus shifted from thinking only about filmmaking to focusing on friends and family, opening up and telling everyone how much they meant to him. He also approached other friends, like Bob Baker, Bill Bennett, and Dell Haughey, and told them how he loved them. One day as I was editing, Jim came in and even though I was in the middle of a cool sequence, said "Greg, I came in to say how much I enjoy working with you. I just love it. And I love you. Thanks." And then before I could even respond, he left. Truthfully, I felt the same about him, except at

LA Times arts editor Charles Champlin interviewed us in 1975 as we were in the middle of editing **To Fly!**, the trims of which are hanging on pins in the trim bin. The show Champlin hosted would be nominated for an Emmy.

the time, before an openness that we have between males today, it was awkward to admit. I also witnessed Jim becoming nicer, fitter, more athletic, and less egocentric and prideful. Months later, when Bill Bennett called Cindy and shared news of this positive transformation, she returned to Laguna and she and Jim began dating again. Barbara and I were delighted that Cindy and Jim were back together! On Jim's birthday, June 10, they enjoyed a romantic dinner at the White House Restaurant in Laguna. Barbara and I were so happy for them that we silently crawled on the floor of the restaurant to surprise them with a cake. Just twelve days later, tragedy struck like a lightning bolt, nullifying and at the same time intensifying the love we had for this extraordinary man. Friend Mark Waxman of KCET wrote to me and said it best: "Jim was an 'active verb.' He regretted every blink for missing another frame of life. How unfair that those eyes that captured so much are now closed forever. He taught me so much joy—zest, passion, generosity, warmth, intensity. Even in his death, he taught me to seize the moment."

Two Sides of the Same Coin

Jim and I loved working together on films because we came at them from differing points of view and could push on each other in nonthreatening, constructive ways. We were confident in our perspectives but respected each other so much that the films ended up far better when we put our heads together. We often referred to that magic as one plus one equaling three. We drew strength from other teams, like our beloved Beatles, who thrived on that same alchemy. In just 12 years, Jim and I had produced four feature-length surfing documentaries, second-unit direction and photography on 10 Hollywood features, and 15 award-winning short films, culminating with **To Fly!** And now that love was gone.

For months, I didn't know whether I could go on making films. I knew that I could do it intellectually, but, the fun of a shared experience would be gone. Because Jim and I had formed such a tight team, would I be able to create film sequences at the same high level? I imagined that others had the same question. However, good friends and family— Barbara, Cindy, Bill Bennett, Basil Poledouris, Brad Ohlund, Jeff Blyth, and my parents—bolstered me and urged me on. Hollywood friends like Nelson Tyler, Peter Pascal, producer Irwin Allen, special effects guru Bill Abbott, educational film leaders Lynn and David Adams, producer Sandy Howard, and Bill Lyles at MGM; even ski film king Warren Miller, whom I had never had the honor of meeting, wrote to encourage me.

And Mark Waxman helped us by producing two documentaries featuring our strange beach-town, barefooted partnership, which aired seven times during KCET's pledge weeks over the next few years.

Even so, there was a huge hole left in our lives. Jim's death created not just an emotional hole, but a physical hole as well. Gone were his boisterous laughs, his begging to do something with a softly spoken "pretty please," his playful, almost childlike enthusiasm for a new idea for a film, or a location to photograph, or a person he just met in Hollywood. Now, it was up to me to fill these holes as best I could, but to do so I knew I'd have to learn to talk, to laugh, to engage with new people. I'd do this so that our company and its dear people—Cindy, Barbara, Brad, Bill, Jeff, Elizabeth—could move on with me, filling up part of that deep hole that Jim physically and emotionally left behind.

About two months after Jim's death, I began to get back on track when producers Van Stith and Frank Martello of the J. Walter Thompson advertising agency hired me to direct and shoot Thunderbird and Mustang automobile commercials. These fresh and demanding assignments enabled me to once again focus on the future. Suddenly, our small team of Laguna Beach crewmembers could believe that we could make it financially if we stuck together.

Van, Frank, and I traveled to Palm Springs for the Ford commercials after I'd recruited talent that just happened to be on the verge of stardom: Tom Selleck, before he hit it big with *Magnum, P.I.*; Cheryl Ladd just months before she joined *Charlie's Angels*; and Patrick Wayne, John's son, before he took on several feature film roles.

Then, as luck would have it, one of Hollywood's "insiders" and most successful entertainers offered to help, Merv Griffin. During the two years preceding Jim's death, we had worked for Merv to direct and photograph on-location interviews, now called "remotes," for his talk show, which was syndicated by more than 100 stations and ran for an amazing 24 years. Merv was a talented bandleader, actor, singer, talk show host, and creator of two of the most successful game shows in TV history: *Jeopardy* and *Wheel of Fortune*, but Merv was more than that.

When he learned of Jim's death, he called me to say that he couldn't imagine how torn up I must be, and to offer me a comeback opportunity: an hour-long slot on an upcoming show!

This was astonishing; even big stars didn't get an hour slot. So Merv interviewed me, and I showed film clips and tried to be as entertaining as I could in front of this audience of five million. That was the Merv Griffin we got to know: generous, kind, and a great businessman. This one appearance, plus the multiple shows on KCET, helped our team get film assignments for the next decade.

When it came time to decide what to call the new company, I opted to honor Jim's creativity and his immense contributions by retaining his name alongside mine forever. That way, his humor, intelligence, playfulness, joyous curiosity, and love would always keep us company as an equal part of MacGillivray Freeman Films.

(FACING PAGE) For 12 years, I had the honor of working with my best friend. We pushed each other, laughed, and sweated making our films better than we ever imagined. Here, Jim uses the Mitchell 35mm camera we loved so much. The big motor and heavy batteries would speed film past the gate at 120 frames per second, making a seagull's flight into a dance of ballet.

Back to Business with *Big Wednesday*

SURF · HOLLYWOOD · IMAX ENTERTAINMENT · MISSION

"A day will come that is like no other—a day that is so big—so grand an event of nature that it cleans everything that went before it. And nothing that happens after it will ever be the same."

—NARRATOR ROBERT ENGLUND, DESCRIBING
THE COMING BIG WEDNESDAY SWELL

I rarely got calls from the Hollywood elite, so when one came in from John Milius, the screenwriter for **Apocalypse Now** and **Dirty Harry** and the director of **The Wind and the Lion**, I sat up in my chair.

John asked how I was holding up and I answered honestly, telling him that we were making films again, but that I was finding it hard to bring myself to Villa Bella each day without my best friend and business partner there. Strangely, I felt guilt and pain to be the one left behind.

John sympathized, and told me about a conversation he'd had three months earlier with Jim about a script that John was writing for Warner Bros. When he described **Big Wednesday**, the story of the intense friendship of three young surfers in the glory days . . . well, that fell right into my wheelhouse.

"I'd like you and your team to work on the film with me," he said. "I'll shoot first unit while you produce and direct the surfing and water sequences. I know you're capable. But I've gotta know, Greg: Do you think you're up for it?"

Here was John Milius taking the time to offer me a huge opportunity and boost of confidence! I usually found Hollywood insiders to be crass, bottom-line oriented, and pushy; but this was the most caring call I'd received from a feature film big shot. I did think I was ready for a big assignment, and John's faith in me helped seal the deal. At the same time, I recognized that this was our team's chance to sublimate our pain in a cause, and Cindy, Barbara, and I could get used to a life without Jim as we all worked nonstop on this beautifully structured film.

I began making day trips to Milius's office at Warner Bros. Studios. In the adjoining office sat Steven Spielberg and his friendly assistant, the amazingly skilled Kathleen Kennedy. They, too, were working with Milius, writing and prepping the comedy feature **1941**. It was exciting to get to know these young, accomplished filmmakers as they blazed their unconventional trails through stodgy Hollywood. The unions still had incredible control over Hollywood, but Spielberg, Milius, and their friend George Lucas were challenging the status quo with their enormously profitable films.

One day, the three of them were at John's office and we were all joking around about filmmaking. I would later learn that they had each agreed to share some of the profits from the three personal projects they each had in production. Incredibly, Lucas's film was **Star Wars**, Spielberg's film was **Close Encounters of the Third Kind**, and John's film was **Big Wednesday**. They each gave away two points from the net profits that they owned in their own creations. I think this was their way to show the old-time studio bosses that a new era had begun of youthful, creative collaboration. Since **Star Wars** premiered first and to record-breaking attendance, Milius playfully tweaked Lucas's wonderful theme "feel the force" by circulating buttons to friends and our crew that highlighted Milius's **Big Wednesday** character, the surf guru, "Bear," reading: "The Bear is the Real Force!" Their friendship was strong.

(FACING PAGE) After Matt's amazing, inside-the-tube ride at "The Point," the three friends—Jack, Matt, and Leroy—follow their own paths after they've shared this one epic day of surf. This was the ending scene from *Big Wednesday*, filmed at a "set" built on the hillside of Cojo Point at Bixby Ranch, California.

ART BREWER

125

John's script for **Big Wednesday** depicted four time periods in the lives of three friends in the '60s. The four season-based periods revealed the pivotal changes in their growing up at Malibu. Since we couldn't shoot at super-crowded Malibu, our first challenge was to find an alternative. Milius had heard about a point break in El Salvador that was similar to Malibu, so Barbara and I flew down to check it out. Unfortunately, the country was in the midst of political unrest and civil war, but nearly all the fighting was in the capital city of San Salvador, two hours from the coast. John and I felt we'd be relatively safe. That May, when we knew the south swells would be marching in to a beautiful point we located, we headed to El Salvador with surfers Billy Hamilton, Peter Townend, and Ian Cairns, who were to double for actors Jan-Michael Vincent, William Katt, and Gary Busey.

Big Wednesday

FILMED IN: 35MM

RELEASE DATE: 1978

FEATURING: Jan-Michael Vincent, William Katt, Gary Busey

DIRECTED BY: John Milius

MUSIC BY: Basil Poledouris

WRITTEN BY: John Milius, Dennis Aaberg

"In this picture, the photography is fantastic . . . the views are prodigious. They make your flesh crawl, your hair stand on end. Those waves do, as someone remarks in the film, look like the end of the world."
—NEW YORK POST

Billy Hamilton Remembers *Big Wednesday*

I was hired to surf as a double for Jan-Michael Vincent, the lead actor. So, with Barbara to manage all 17 of us, we descended on El Salvador in Central America. Our destination was La Libertad, a small coastal town with abundant south swell surf, a point break, and a pier in the background to match up with the script's primary location, Malibu.

What we were not aware of was that the Nicaraguan Revolution, featuring intense fighting between the Sandinistas and the Nicaraguan National Guard, was about to explode. At the end of our first week in El Salvador, which borders Nicaragua, the police found the bullet-riddled body of the ambassador to Guatemala in a ditch a mile from where we were staying. Fifty miles inland, the military presence in the capital was evident on every street corner, with sandbags, 50-caliber machine guns and military checkpoints. One day when we had to go to the capital we were stuck in a long line of cars. The military had found a carload of rebels with weapons in the trunk. They pulled them out of the car, put them on the ground, and shot them at point-blank range. I don't know how the rest of our crew felt, but I remember being very aware of the danger that was lurking around every corner.

On another day, we were filming at the point surf at La Libertad with the helicopter and the Zodiac inflatable boat. The military sent down three troop carriers to stop what they thought were invaders! I was surfing at the time, so I was seeing this from another angle. Barbara was involved and communicated, in her excellent Spanish, with the authorities to resolve the issue. El Salvador was an exciting adventure! The stories could fill a book.

Besides the surfers, also with us were top-tier cameramen George Greenough, who would do the artistic water camera shots, and Dan Merkel and Bud Browne, who would film the impact-zone water scenes. My friend from Laguna, Spyder Wills, a renowned cameraman with a telephoto lens, would film from the beach, as would I. Ski film master Roger Brown would shoot the helicopter scenes. Knowing that it was one of my specialties, John also wanted me to photograph the surf doubles in action while riding my own board.

No sooner had our 17-person team settled into the cinder-block, thatched-roof, cabana-style motel near La Libertad Point than crew members began falling sick with what turned out to be amoebic dysentery. Ten days in, I'd established a new wake-up routine: Set the alarm for 4:30 a.m., walk to the ocean to judge the swell size, then go from cabana to cabana to find out who could work and who was too sick to even stand. Depending on the team, I'd plan the day's shots. This terrible illness persisted. Everyone lost 10 to 20 pounds. When John and Celia Milius joined us for a week of fun, they were shocked, saying we all looked like starved concentration-camp prisoners. Barbara and Celia bonded in keeping us healthy.

Despite these challenges, we shot for seven weeks . . . but the 15-foot surf we'd been hoping for never showed up. Instead, we captured two eight-foot swells that were successfully cut into the film by editors Robert Wolfe and Tim O'Meara.

Spielberg had always been enthusiastic about **Big Wednesday**, calling it **American Graffiti** meets **Jaws**, two hugely successful films. But when John and Jeff Blyth showed him the El Salvador footage, he was underwhelmed by the surf size and asked whether we could find bigger surf, 20- to 30-foot waves of apparent danger that would

(CLOCKWISE FROM UPPER LEFT) Peter Townend and Ian Cairns, wonderful surf doubles; our wrap party—Loyann Townend, Cindy Huston, Barbara, and Mark Martinson; A tired and ill crew—George Greenough, Paul Gross, Scott Coffman, Mark Martinson, and Bud Browne; Cindy and Gerry Lopez; Sunzal surf, ski film director Roger Brown and George Nolan in the helicopter.

Because the film ends on "Big Wednesday"—on that magnificent day Matt (Jan-Michael Vincent) gets the wave of his life—we wanted to use Greenough's inside-the-tube shot, photographed with a camera mounted to George's back as he crouched on his kneeboard inside a tube. To match this exceptional shot, John and I needed a tube ride shot from shore at slow motion in close-up! Because the rights at Sunset Beach rarely offer up such a tube, I'd have to photograph at the *left* at Pipeline, and then in editing simply flip the shot! So I hired goofy-foot Jackie Dunn, who looks like Jan, made a board with a reversed Bear logo, and waited for the perfect Pipeline day. When it came, director of photography Jack Willoughby and I trekked with Jackie to Pipeline, set up, and started filming. Because I had more experience than anyone filming slow-motion images at Pipeline from shore, Jack allowed me, the director, to operate the camera. I told Jackie that I needed him to crouch inside a big tube, come out, and then have the worst wipeout of his life!

So Jackie got the wave of the day, did exactly as asked, and threw himself into the worst over-the-falls wipeout I had ever seen. As I photographed, I honestly thought that he'd probably broken his neck. I was so relieved when he popped up in the whitewater. When he swam to shore, he jogged up to me and asked, "Hey Greg, do you need it again?" It took Jack and me more than a minute to stop laughing. Then, I said, "No, that was perfect—and I'm giving you a bonus!" That was the final scene shot for the film. Just days later, Gary Busey dyed his blonde hair black, put on black horn-rimmed glasses, and became Buddy Holly in the film that would earn this talented, fun-to-be- around, crazy friend, an Oscar nomination as best actor.

129

(CLOCKWISE FROM TOP LEFT) George Greenough films Jan-Michael Vincent; I get stitches for a slashed skull caused by a rogue board in the surf; Greenough and I discuss a waterproofed camera to be aimed at a paddling William Katt.

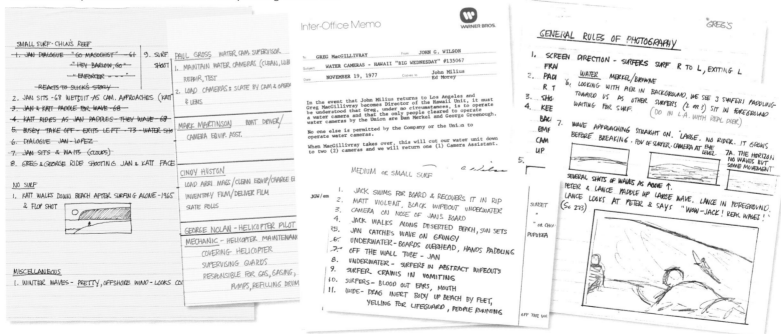

terrify even the best of the best. I agreed; we needed killer surf. We needed Hawaiian big waves.

To make our film super exciting, we flew to Hawaii to film. John was nearing the end of his production budget and had just enough left to cover five weeks of shooting. John and Denny Aaberg had written a script of friendship that everyone on our crew loved, mainly because it reflected the deep respect we shared with each other. In filming these big waves, you have to trust each other. Every day, former world champion Fred Hemmings and I would check the surf and decide where to film, pushing ourselves every day.

One day, Billy Hamilton and Jeff Johnson (singer Jack's dad) pitched a stunt to us: Get an old outboard engine and a 12-foot speedboat, paint it like a lifeguard rescue craft, dress up as two lifeguards and take the rig over the falls on a 20-foot wave. "It'll be the film's highlight moment, and all for just $10,000," they gushed. Milius said, "You'll get killed." They said, "Perhaps." I said, "Let's do it." Over the next few weeks, as we waited for a huge swell, the boat was readied, and on the final day of shooting **Big Wednesday**—December 14, which happened to be a Wednesday—we went for it. And Billy was right; it was an action highlight and, because surfers always enjoy making fun of authority figures, including lifeguards, the sequence became a comedic highlight as well.

Big Disappointment

We worked hard to make **Big Wednesday** superb and realistically thrilling, but the film disappointed surfers and film critics alike. Some thought the dialogue didn't ring true and that it was too over-the-top. When the terrible reviews and small crowds had delivered their verdict, John picked up the phone. "I'm calling everyone who poured their hearts and souls into **Big Wednesday** because the reviews stink, Warner Bros. is pulling it, and I'm sorry I let everybody down. I won't leave the house because I don't want to run into any friends. Hollywood devours its weak and failed competitors; it's merciless!"

I told him that his true friends would stand by him. Making the film was an effort that we believed in because that era, that unique time for surfing, was worth celebrating. Those of us who were part of that time were establishment rebels and proud of it. Though **Big Wednesday** ran for only a couple of weeks, it is now considered a cult classic, partly because the corny dialogue now sounds reasonably representative of the early '60s. As for John's sharing of points with Spielberg and Lucas, **Close Encounters** became a huge hit—and **Star Wars** set records, becoming big wins for my friend Milius. But Spielberg would joke about this arrangement to me later: "The deal worked out better for some than for others." Then, with a twinkle, "We haven't repeated the practice!" And he laughed. Even so, "the force" was with all three of these revolutionary filmmakers. And, thanks to Milius, our small team

of Laguna friends now knew we could handle any big assignment, even without Jim, our best friend, with us.

We paid tribute to John Milius in 2018. He'd suffered a stroke but still had that famous smile and three words: "That's really great." We held a discussion panel, which I moderated, with Gerry Lopez, the hilarious Gary Busey, William Katt, Denny Aaberg, Rick Dano, and Lee Purcell. That night Barbara shot 30 minutes of video of John with a gigantic smile on his face. The tribute to one of my greatest Hollywood friends, the ever-original and comical John Milius, was well worth the effort.

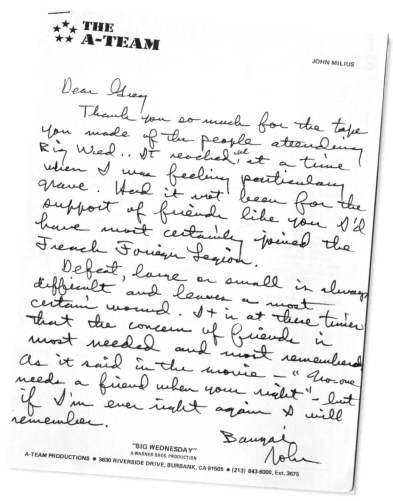

131

CHAPTER 11

Stanley Kubrick, *The Shining*, and a New Direction

SURF

HOLLYWOOD

IMAX ENTERTAINMENT

MISSION

> "Greg, good to hear your voice. My production manager, Brian Cook, has told me all about you. I'm wondering if you would be interested in working on my film **The Shining.**"
>
> –STANLEY KUBRICK, DIRECTOR

My secretary had buzzed me to say that someone claiming to be Stanley Kubrick was on the line. I suspected it was one of my jokester friends, since they all knew what Kubrick and his films meant to me. But the voice was soft, direct, with an air of self-assurance that made me think twice. I played along. "What did you have in mind?"

"Brian tells me that you work as hard as I do, so I know you're a little crazy. But I need someone to do the opening sequence for my film, as well as maybe 10 others. We're shooting the main action here at Elstree Studios near London. Can you come over for a few days?"

By this time, I knew it was the real Stanley Kubrick and I'd gotten my jaw back in place well enough to accept gracefully and suggest the following week for a trip across the pond.

When I got to Elstree Studios, I was awestruck by Roy Walker's and Stanley's set design, art direction, and authenticity. Then, to impress me more, director of photography John Alcott, who had won an Oscar for the innovative lighting in **Barry Lyndon**, showed me around the unique illumination scheme for **The Shining**. Using controlled dimmer boards, Alcott could dial in any number of lighting conditions for each room on set. He and Stanley would spend time after the crew went home doing test shots and assigning numbers. This allowed Kubrick to shoot a scene in one room, study the dailies, decide how he wanted to improve on it, and go back a week later to shoot more, knowing that the lighting and color-temperature scheme would match what they'd photographed earlier. This was especially helpful because, as a minor, Danny Lloyd, the boy who could "shine," was only allowed to shoot 40 days a year. If it was a "Danny day," Alcott and Kubrick could pick up scenes from various sets and match them perfectly from a lighting standpoint. John explained that they first built scale models from cardboard to test lighting schemes and wall colors, then spent months wiring up the wall and ceiling fixtures to create one master-control dimmer room. As the Steadicam traveled through the set, John could control the light by radioing the control room.

This was incredible; the light could be imperceptibly changed during the shot! No one had ever done this to this degree before. Leave it to Kubrick and Alcott. These clever innovations explained why Kubrick was able to spend 13 months, about four times the average schedule, to shoot **The Shining** on a relatively low budget.[14]

Here I was with this secretive, famous but facially anonymous, mystery of a genius—my favorite filmmaker—inside his den of creation, learning from my hero. Kubrick's directorial style was known to be famously obsessive, with him calling for take after take. This might have driven Jack Nicholson and Shelley Duvall a bit crazy, but it went with the territory given the schizophrenic nature of a movie that is

---

(FACINIG PAGE) Shelley Duvall, Danny Lloyd, and Jack Nicholson—a family on their way to a tortuous winter at the Overlook Hotel.

14 I was always amused that Stephen King hated Kubrick's scripted adaptation of his book, as well as the resulting film, and when Kubrick's exclusivity period on the book rights ran out, King helped remake the story into a terrible TV movie, which I hated. I think that one of King's complaints to Kubrick was that the topiaries, which moved in a terrifying way in the book, were wisely omitted from the film because special effects of the time were not sophisticated enough to make them believable. They would have looked hokey and unreal, not scary, as King had written in his wonderfully frightening book, which is rated as the 3rd most popular and 3rd best-selling novel for this prolific writer of 40 books! For Kubrick, **The Shining** became his most profitable film ever.

(CLOCKWISE FROM ABOVE) Stanley Kubrick at Elstree Studios near London; Stanley and I are in the kitchen set just after filming Jack Nicholson getting dragged into the storage locker; script supervisor (and really nice person) June Randall gives comical Nicholson his next lines; I told Shelley, "Go check if I'm in sharp focus; executive producer (and Stanley's brother-in-law) Jan Harlan and Stanley.

still considered, along with **Psycho** and **The Exorcist**, to be one of the best horror films ever made.

I found Nicholson to be a complete delight. Trapped on location in London for more than five months already in a precable TV universe (no CNN), he flashed his trademark Jake Gittes grin and immediately begged to know how his beloved Lakers were doing. It was fun getting to know Shelley Duvall and young Danny Lloyd, too.

My arrival on set must have seemed like a breath of fresh air—everyone was so welcoming. The crew had been shooting six days a week for months already but were still energetic. I watched as they shot and reshot a close-up of Nicholson's hand removing a vacuum tube from the Overlook Hotel's two-way radio. By 8 p.m., they'd shot 28 takes, and Jack joked that if Stanley weren't so cheap he'd have hired a hand double and Jack could've gone out on his date. But in the end, Jack and Stanley were very respectful of each other, understanding that they each relished pushing the limits of their craft in subtle or even invisible ways.

The next morning, a Sunday, I met Stanley at the studio at 10 a.m. He had been there for two hours, going over shooting plans with Roy. Stanley casually asked me whether I wanted to watch the dailies with him. I considered this a great treat, as my favorite moment in the filmmaking process is seeing footage for the first time.

Watching Kubrick's dailies with him was something else. Maybe we were alone in the screening room because all those close-up takes of a vacuum tube, indistinguishable to all but Stanley, bordered on the terminally boring. But I also got to watch other scenes, including elaborate Steadicam "follow" scenes. One was a lengthy 30-second shot that gave the audience a sense, like in IMAX, of being there, because there was no cut to interrupt the experience. John's lighting, using actual in-the-scene chandeliers and windows, would dim and brighten during the shot to eliminate cameraman shadows and to improve the scene's dramatic effect. One light panel contained 860 1,000-watt PAR flood lamps and created so much heat that you'd faint if you were near them for longer than a few minutes. It was dangerous but beautiful, just like

(ABOVE) To simulate sunshine streaming in the huge Overlook Hotel windows, these light panels could rotate left and right to cast shadows representing morning, noon, or afternoon sun direction. That's Kubrick!

The Shining

FILMED IN: 35MM

RELEASE DATE: 1980

FEATURING: Jack Nicholson. Shelley Duvall, Scatman Crothers, Danny Lloyd

DIRECTED BY: Stanley Kubrick

MUSIC BY: Wendy Carlos, Rachel Elkind

CINEMATOGRAPHY BY: John Alcott

"For one thing, it has a wonderful opening sequence that promises the kind of movie we are hoping it will be."

—PAULINE KAEL, *THE NEW YORKER*

real sunlight. Any of the dozens of takes of each scene would have been good enough for most filmmakers, but not for Stanley Kubrick. His rationalization for all those takes? "Film stock is cheap, but remarkable quality will pay dividends forever."

I asked how he knew when to move on to his next shot. He thought about it for a minute before divulging what must have been Kubrick's number one trade secret: "Don't walk away until it's perfect." The moment reminded me of a similar lesson I'd learned from Jim Freeman. We'd been watching dailies of his stunning aerial photography for **Jonathan Livingston Seagull**. After one spectacular shot where everything lined up—the sunset, the bird, the background, the helicopter move—I mumbled something about it being perfect. Jim shook his head. "Nope," he said, "if it was perfect, there'd have been a twinkle in the eye of the seagull."

Stanley and I went to lunch at the raunchy sandwich shop at the entrance to the studio. Back in 1978, the British were no foodies and the meal was nearly inedible, but the conversation made up for it. Stanley was intensely interested in everything. We talked about emerging film systems like IMAX, film emulsions, lenses we owned, films we'd seen, and what was going on in Hollywood. He was especially intrigued by Steven Spielberg and his burgeoning career. I shared with him what I'd learned through Milius.

In later years, Stanley and Steven established a strong friendship. They would even collaborate on one project, the film **A.I. (Artificial Intelligence)**. They'd been developing the story together, in fact, when Kubrick died suddenly in 1999 at just 70 years of age. Spielberg spoke with emotion at the Directors Guild tribute for Kubrick. Steven revealed how close they'd become while creating the story for **A.I.** and of Kubrick's obsessive need to instantly reach Spielberg with ideas, even insisting that he install a fax machine in his bedroom. After months of nightly fax conversations, Spielberg's wife, actor Kate Capshaw, had had enough. She demanded that the noisy "Kubrick machine" be removed from the bedroom so they could occasionally get some sleep!

I had brought along a 35mm reel of demonstration aerial scenes to show Stanley. I figured we could use them as the basis of discussions about lenses, style, lighting, and movements for shots of the all-important opening sequence: Nicholson's yellow VW Beetle traveling up the mountain road toward the ominous hotel. I held my breath as the projectionist threaded up my demo reel. While we screened the footage, Stanley kept silent, pensive. I wondered what was going through his mind. When we looked at the reel again on the flatbed editing machine,

> **"Working with Kubrick was an exploration through a forest of ideas and visions, always in search of a solution that was not just the best, but the most original. I left London inspired and excited."**
>
> –GREG MACGILLIVRAY

Stanley scratched at his beard, his dark eyes narrowed, and he studied every detail. When he looked up, he said he loved it and that this was just what he needed to confirm he'd made the right choice. Phew!

Shooting *The Shining*

Just days later, our "family" crew descended on Montana's Glacier National Park for the shoot. What a place: a series of glacier-carved valleys, towering granite peaks, and breathtaking lakes snaking down the middle. While I would direct, produce, and shoot the ground shots, I was supported by Barbara, my girlfriend, as production manager and double for Nicholson as driver of the Yellow VW, Cindy Huston as my long-standing camera assistant, Duane Williams as our helicopter pilot, Jeff Blyth as aerial cameraman and production manager, and Bruce McGregor as assistant cameraman. Kathy Blyth drove the van back and forth over the mountain passes to replenish our stock of jet fuel.

St. Mary Lodge was our home for the month and its parking lot was our helicopter staging area. The rangers agreed to allow us to film so long as we didn't land the helicopter inside the park. With no traffic control, we were always on the lookout for the last tourists straggling out of the park, and only began shooting when the road was clear.

Over the long days, the crew passed around a copy of Stephen King's book *The Shining*, which reminded us that our hotel, just like the Overlook, was getting ready to shut down for the winter. The weather changed constantly so we had to be quick on our feet. Some days began sunny, with a calm, glassy lake. By 11 a.m., it might be raining, and

by 3 p.m., blowing snow could change the scene again. With our ability to turn on a dime, though, our small team was able to shoot a huge quantity of film in just four weeks.

Every three days, Stanley called to see how we were doing, and the two of us had long conversations about what we'd shot and with which lens. Once he'd seen the footage, we would talk again. He would call late in the evening London time, after he'd returned from working Nicholson to the bone, again. No other A-list director worked as long or as hard as Kubrick; of that I'm certain.

Stanley asked me to shoot some background plates to be used in rear-screen projection, showing Glacier National Park (doubling for Colorado) whizzing by behind Jack, Shelley, and Danny inside the VW in close-up. "Use your Arri 2C," Kubrick said, "and have your steadiness checked." I mentioned that the test, done in Hollywood, would take time. "No, no; you can do it," he answered, and proceeded to teach me how to perform the test myself. I felt honored to get a crash course in Camera Steadiness 101 from this expert.

We had great luck in Glacier, but because the weather changed every other minute, I wanted to extend my stay to get shots that matched each other better. I made Kubrick an offer he couldn't refuse: We would not charge him for waiting-for-weather days; only for filming days. This also gave us time to wait for the fall chill to turn the trees bright yellow. I think he liked our plan because it fit with his motto of "Don't walk away until it's perfect." After a month of watching and waiting through variable weather and not-quite-perfect filming conditions, we awoke one day to sensational colors and a glassy-smooth lake mirroring the dramatic mountains. I returned home thrilled with the way the visuals looked.[15]

London, Take Two

When I returned to London, I was anxious to see the footage. I hadn't seen it yet because Kubrick had wanted it processed at the London laboratory so the developing chemicals would match the rest of the film footage. When I walked onto the enormous set of the Overlook Hotel's kitchen, the welcome and praise I got from the cast, the crew, and Kubrick himself told me that they must already have seen our Glacier dailies. I kept thinking they were overstating the case. Isn't everything exaggerated on a film set? They were probably so bored, cooped up on those soundstages for seven months, that they were desperate for some outdoor scenery, even if it was in the small Elstree screening room. But they said the footage was perfect and I guessed that it was for one reason.

---

15 **The Shining** was honored by the National Film Registry in 2018 as one of the best films in history, and was later also listed by the American Society of Cinematographers (ASC) as one of the "100 Milestone Films in Cinematography of the 20th Century."

Back when we were working on **To Fly!**, Jim and I developed what we called our "flying belly mount." It was a long platform that was slung under a Jet Ranger helicopter, between the skids. In front was a rotating tilt plate that could hold the heavy IMAX camera. For **The Shining**, we mounted two 35mm cameras, one with a 9.8mm lens and one with a 16mm lens, side by side. The beauty of this rig, built for us by Nelson Tyler, was that it looked forward and down. And, because it was designed for the centerline of the helicopter, the footage gives audiences a feeling not just of flying, but of banking like a bird in flight. I felt that it would match perfectly with Kubrick's forward-moving Steadicam shots on the London sets, performed by the master, Garrett Brown. For a horror film, this approach is much more engaging than a panning perspective and side camera angle. It engages audience members as edge-of-your-seat participants and not just as onlookers. Kubrick obviously liked what he was seeing.

"I want you to stay here for a while," he said, "because I want you to do more: shots in Florida, scenes of Scatman Crothers flying into Denver in the snow, Scatman crashing his car in Florida after getting a 'shining—a message.' Can you do it?" I had to say yes, I thought to myself; but I'd need to reschedule all kinds of other work. "I'd like that," I told Stanley. So I hung out with them for two weeks, mostly chatting with Vivian Kubrick, Stanley's 18-year-old daughter, who was shooting a documentary on the filming in 16mm.

While I was there, Kubrick and I mapped out the unscripted scenes that he had just invented. Art director Roy Walker worked with me to find locations and develop ideas from the research stills and maps they'd assembled. After I'd been there for a few days, I asked Kubrick if I could shoot some stills of the sets. The super-secretive director said, "I don't normally allow that, but I'll say yes as long as you don't put them in *American Cinematographer*!" He knew I'd written technical articles for this Hollywood publication, but he trusted me, which was nice because we now have these rare casual photos of Kubrick and his team at work.

During this visit, I stayed with Brian and his wife. We'd become good friends when he worked as my assistant director in Greece, years before. From Brian, I caught some uncommon insight into Kubrick's passion for perfection. Let me explain. Brian wanted me to learn from shooting the ballroom dinner scene, a huge, complicated day with a hundred actors that Brian had spent weeks setting up. Two days later, Kubrick announced that the scene would have to be delayed because Jack wasn't ready. Brian cursed, and then confided in me. "Jack's ready to do the scene, but Stanley isn't. He hasn't yet figured out how to stage it!" In fact, Kubrick would postpone three more times until he'd planned out an amazingly effective and original way to stage the impressive 100-person scene.

(ABOVE) While I was in London, the art department made 10 doors with "MURDER" spelled backward, from which Kubrick could choose. Shelley checks out one of the test doors—ready for Jack's ax. (BELOW) Cindy Huston and Bruce McGregor assist me in Montana; our helicopter belly-mount gave me a forward-flying sensation that matched Kubrick's use of the Steadicam.

As he, too, waited for the big scene, Leon Vitali found himself assigned to me by Kubrick. Leon was a talented actor who had played a leading role in **Barry Lyndon** and now worked on Kubrick's staff as his associate producer. Among many other duties, Leon took care of Kubrick's camera and editorial equipment, and he would even later handle casting for **Eyes Wide Shut**. According to Jan Harlan, Stanley's producer and brother-in-law, Leon was Kubrick's "right-, left- and all-hand man."

> **"I should like to comment on the wonderful sequence which Greg MacGillivray shot from the helicopter in the first sequence of the picture. It was a great introduction to the film and some of the most beautiful helicopter work I've ever seen."**

–JOHN ALCOTT, CINEMATOGRAPHER ON **THE SHINING**

Leon and I spent a day going through the Glacier footage on the Steenbeck flatbed editing machine. I was elated, particularly because of one shot we'd gotten near the end of our shoot. The belly-mounted camera is flying low, skimming the mirror-smooth water of St. Mary Lake, when it picks up and tracks with the yellow VW Beetle. We had rehearsed this shot every day for four mornings at daybreak, waiting for the perfect sunrise, the tree leaves to hit peak yellow, and glassy lake conditions. The shot lasted two minutes and was flawless from start to finish. Don't walk away until it's perfect? Indeed!

I knew Kubrick wouldn't begin editing for another six months, so I wrote him a note and posted it on the emulsion of the shot. I wrote another on the box of film the shot was stored in, and a third directly to Kubrick. Each one implored him to use the entire shot, saying: "It's the best helicopter shot anyone has ever seen. Use it as the background for your opening credits." I knew he'd pay attention, because he sought input from others, especially from those he knew really cared about films. I may have overstated by a bit, but in the end, Kubrick was as excited about the shot as I was.[16]

Kubrick the Producer

Ryan O'Neal, who starred in **Barry Lyndon**, used to say that Kubrick knew how to make the most of a budget. This was true. **The Shining** budget was $15 million. Of that, Nicholson and Kubrick were getting about $2.5 million each. To manage to shoot with a cast and crew for over a year, with huge sets on

Barbara drove the yellow VW Beetle.

rented studio stages for that entire time on just $10 million, was a remarkable financial achievement. Even with his high shooting ratio, Stanley was much more efficient than other Hollywood producers I had worked for. His money-saving secret? Get the best people to work at cut-rate prices because they knew the job would: 1) be a feather in their cap, 2) shoot for a long time and 3) result in an historic film.

As they were completing the film, I got a call from Jan Harlan, the film's executive producer. "Stanley wants to get your credit right on the film, so can you send us what you'd like?"

A month later, he called again. "Stanley wants to give you more than what you requested. He loves your work and he'd like to give you a second credit." I was astonished. In Hollywood, it's commonplace to fight for credit when you negotiate your deal. Here, the world's most famous director wanted to give me another credit over and above what was called out in my contract.

When our family crew gathered again at Warner Bros. Studios to preview the film, Stanley had another surprise for us. In the plans, there were to be two trips by the yellow VW, one with Nicholson alone in the car, and a second with Jack, Shelley, and Danny when they move into the Overlook. The first trip was photographed exclusively by helicopter. The second, in which the VW tows a small trailer filled with the family's belongings, was filmed with ground-based photography. When we previewed **The Shining**, however, we discovered that Kubrick had apparently thrown out that notion and had used more of our helicopter shots to represent the second trip. The rub was that, in those shots, the VW had no trailer! Stanley had deliberately ignored the error and inadvertently sparked conspiracy theorists to wonder how the family had so much luggage when they arrived![17]

---

16 Years after making **The Shining**, Kubrick got a call from Ridley Scott, who was finishing his epic film **Blade Runner** starring Harrison Ford. Turns out the producer of the film hated the ending and was demanding a change. To this news, Kubrick said, "Call Greg MacGillivray." So I met with Ridley and the producer one day in Hollywood—and ultimately became the mediator! We talked story solutions, and because they were low on money, I gave them options: Hire us to shoot the newly agreed upon ending, or cheaper yet, buy a shot from Kubrick's stash of great shots we'd done for **The Shining**. This idea saved the day, calmed their director-producer relationship, and improved the film's ending by 1 percent. And, maybe, I helped a bit in making that beautiful film.

17 Over the years, as the popularity of **The Shining** has grown with the public, critics, historians, and film buffs alike, crazed fans invented ways that the "mysterious" Kubrick hid special meaning in the film's scenes. Even my friend Tim Cahill wrote in *Rolling Stone* about this "serious, critical reevaluation process" in 1987. Then, the documentary film **Room 237** recounted those preposterous conspiracy theories. To Leon Vitali, who knew Kubrick best, all the theories were "fake news" and laughable. One of them involved us—four frames of a helicopter shadow that theorists attributed to the devil, I believe! (It was simply an editorial mistake.)

Those of us who'd worked on these scenes realized that Kubrick had chosen the beauty of these shots over continuity of story. "Always choose the strongest visuals, even if it defies explanation," was another motto from the master.

I'd learned so much on this exciting assignment about directing, about actors, and about photography. But I also knew how difficult it was for the actors to work with Kubrick. He was trying to find the most realistic and cinematic way possible to portray Jack's descent into madness within the supernatural horrors lurking at this immense hotel. And he achieved what he sought, producing a powerful and enduring film. I'd personally seen the intense, harsh way Kubrick directed Shelley Duvall, at times driving her to tears. I tried to console her. But, as Nicholson would say, Shelley had taken on the toughest job of any actor he'd seen. Kubrick beat Shelley into that performance. At the end of this stressful filming experience, Shelley jokingly presented Kubrick with recently departed clumps of her hair. But truth be told, her performance was eerie and intense. As Nicholson has lovingly said, "she'd nailed it."

Spending time with Milius and now Kubrick, I'd ask myself, "What would Jim have done to make this relationship more rewarding? This sequence a better story? Or an overall better film experience?" This exercise would give me greater confidence and a strength to move on.

After Stanley passed away in 1999, I experienced sadness and regret. Our love of film and the standards we set for ourselves were what we shared throughout our association. Kubrick's movies and personality were so unusual, so outstanding, and so thought provoking, that they caused everyone involved to reevaluate; to dig deeper within themselves and find more room for improvement. You could not meet him, even casually, without gaining one remarkable insight or sharing at least one laugh. Millions of fans, including myself, miss him and his inventive films.[18] I wish I'd kept in closer touch with him and thanked him more profusely for what he did for me. When the Directors Guild held a tribute in his honor, Jeff Blyth and I were invited and were proud to see that our "perfect" helicopter shot was the first scene shown in a collection of classic and historic Kubrick moments.

18 I was always amazed when, every five years, Stanley Kubrick would release another artistically revolutionary film, surprising all of us filmmakers and raising the artistic bar again. How did he do so with each film being radically different in subject, style, pointed commentary on life, and genre? I studied his films, all so leading edge: **Killer's Kiss** (boxing drama), **The Killing** (crime drama), **Paths of Glory** (war drama), **Spartacus** (costumed historical action), **Lolita** (sexual tension), **Dr. Strangelove** (satirical black comedy, anti-war), **2001: A Space Odyssey** (science-fiction/art piece), **A Clockwork Orange** (commentary on youth, edgy thriller), **Barry Lyndon** (quiet costume drama), **The Shining** (horror), **Full Metal Jacket** (anti-war shocker), and **Eyes Wide Shut** (sexual odyssey). Because of Kubrick's variety of genres in his career, I strived to do the same in my career, going from one subject and style to another with each film: **Five Summer Stories** (sports action), **To Fly!** (comedy), **Behold Hawaii** (historical fiction), **The Living Sea** (poetic science story), **Dance of Life** (art and culture documentary), **Everest** (action thriller), **Coral Reef Adventure** (conservation documentary), **Dream Big** (life story drama), **America's Musical Journey** (musical history), and **Into America's Wild** (an astronaut's life journey). Variety is truly the spice of life.

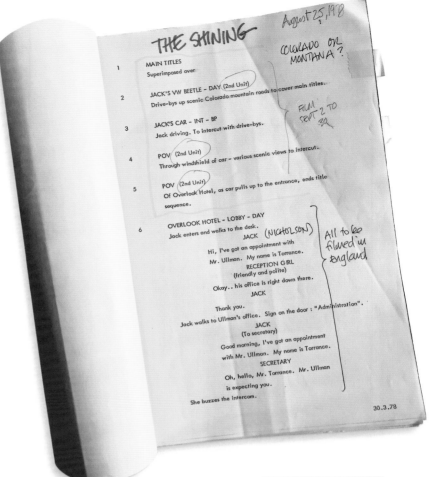

(ABOVE) The script for **The Shining**. (BELOW) Filming the opening sequence for **The Shining** at Glacier National Park, in which Barbara's silhouette often doubled for actor Jack Nicholson, 1978.

Making *The Shining*
3:03   #10

The Best Years of My Life

From 1960 to 1976, Jim and I had worked seven-day weeks because our job was our hobby and our hobby was our job. We didn't think it was excessive. In fact, we loved it so much that we didn't take our first break for a vacation until 1973, after we'd finished the Mazda film. Barbara and I chose to ski in Europe and Jim and Cindy planned a camping trip in the Sierras. Five weeks of total joy, with no movie cameras in sight!

Even after Jim's death, I continued to work long hours. But by 1979, when I'd proven to myself that I could make a contribution to major producers like Milius and Kubrick, I grew more assured and finally felt like I could take a breath and work less, reducing my hours from 70 to 50 per week. Barbara and I even decided that the time was right to take some other big steps. Barbara chose to apply her doctorate as a clinical psychologist focusing on children. And we committed to sharing the earth-shattering experience of having children of our own! But we had a question: Should we also get married?

We had been living together for seven years—living in sin, some would say. When Barbara successfully got pregnant, we consulted with lawyers about how marriage might provide more legal protection for the child. "No one has ever come to us with that question," they replied. "Come back when you want a divorce!" Undecided about the wedding plunge, we did want to celebrate our joyous news with everyone.

So in September, when Barbara was three months along, we threw a black-tie party at our office. We called it a "Celebration of Summer" to keep the real theme a secret. Friends and family members showed up all decked out. They dined and danced to cool jazz from the 1930s, including our love song, "You Made Me Love You." Then the local band Honk played from the stage, and every guest was given a special fortune cookie. Each written fortune was the same: "Two of your friends have started a family." After sharing some quizzical looks, it sunk in and rippled through the room that the two friends must surely be Barbara and me.

In December, just three months before Shaun's due date, Barbara started feeling what she called "the need to nest" and quietly made plans for us to get married. She asked my brother-in-law, the well-known lawyer Dave Brobeck, if he could arrange for a judge, but the year's end was a tough time for this. One judge was available on December 24, which Barbara liked, since she knew I'd never forget that date. But the judge, who was seriously religious and overbooked on Christmas Eve, could only spare ten minutes! This would be a shorter ceremony than even we had envisioned.

Barbara and I, along with our good friends Bobbie and Basil Poledouris, joined the judge in his chamber. The judge said, "Are you expecting anyone else?" Patting her stomach, Barbara said, "Not

Our big and comical wedding day.

for another few months!" The pious judge, not amused, responded curtly, "Let's get this done."

That evening, for my parents' traditional Christmas Eve dinner with 20 family members and neighbors, Barbara and I had promised to bring dessert. When my mother saw what we'd placed on the table, she started to scream and yell. I guess the huge, white wedding cake with a baby buggy on top did the trick. Everyone jumped up to hug us and my grandmother started crying uncontrollably—she was that relieved and happy. I wasn't going to have a bastard son after all! To make the evening even more celebratory, Cindy Huston then stood up and shyly raised her glass. "I also have a big announcement: I'm now engaged to Jeff Hartman!" All 20 of us erupted in joyous cheers because Jeff was outstanding. We could not have been happier.

Three months later, Shaun, named for a surfer I admire, Shaun Tomson, was brought into the world legitimately! And three months after that, Cindy married a wonderful attorney from San Clemente. But even as a devoted wife, she promised to continue as my assistant cameraperson for years to come.

Meghan came along two years later, and for the next 20 years our family traveled as a foursome, shooting movies and having adventures. When Shaun and Meghan were eight and five, respectively, they accompanied us on several shoots to Indonesia. On the remote island of Lombok, the native kids would follow them around and join them in games of soccer and beach volleyball, often touching their blonde hair as if it held magic. Shaun and Meghan taught dozens of young Indonesians how to fly a Frisbee. As they played, they tried to learn the island dialect, Bahasa Indonesia.

Our house, which sits above a surfing spot called Thalia Street Reef in Laguna Beach, became the "beach club" for Shaun and Meghan's friends and their surfboards. When I came home from the office I'd find at least seven kids munching on the healthy treats that Barbara kept in the refrigerator, or surfing out front, or studying around our dining room table. It was the best time of our lives. I'd often think how Jim would have loved it. He would have been a great father . . . and a playful uncle to Shaun and Meghan.

Barbara and I wanted the kids to get part-time jobs to practice being responsible, being on time to work, and delivering on a schedule,

A perfect home for a surfer with little spare time—right at Laguna's best waves.

but in contrast to when I was young, there were very few jobs open to kids. Dishwasher, gofer, and other minimum-wage jobs were being filled by adults. So I set up a summer work program for them at our office and had them sign contracts. Meghan's read: "Your hourly compensation, starting July 6th, will be $6.50 per hour. You will receive a special bonus at the end of the summer if you come to work on time (9 a.m. to 1 p.m.), do not take too many days off, and work hard." Each summer, they worked in a different department under a different supervisor. They learned about distribution, marketing, accounting, postproduction, and production. Some bosses were nice, some were demanding, some were critical. And the kids learned how to deal with them and be good employees.

In 1989, when the kids were six and nine, our IMAX theater industry held a convention in Holland. With their blazing blonde hair and huge California smiles, these two became the cute hits of the gatherings. Days later, as we watched on TV as the Berlin Wall began to topple, Barbara, ever eager, said let's go there! She promised she'd make it happen, and four days later we were in Berlin. How she does these things, I'll never know!

The western side of the wall, plastered with colorful graffiti and slogans, was already starting to be demolished. As we looked on, two East Germans approached us. One said in heavily accented English, "I rent you hammer and chisel?" The other man chimed in, "You vant buy Soviet Army hat?"

I said yes to both, figuring we might as well encourage their capitalistic initiatives. For the next hour, we took turns chipping away at a literal and symbolic wall that I never expected to see fall. When an East German policeman appeared on the scene, the entrepreneurs vanished and left us holding the illicit tools. Meghan remembers the fun we had swinging a hammer, while for Barbara and me this was a pivotal and emotional moment in our cold-war life. It impressed the boy in Shaun for entirely different reasons, as he wrote, in his own grammar, in his daily journal to share with his school class back in Laguna:

"Thursday, Sept. 13. In Berlin, we chipped off a piece of the wall it was so much fun. Berlin was so neat because it was boomed in the war and there was bullet holes in everything."

A Costa Rican Scare

One summer, our family took an adventure trip to scout two places for a film that conservationists had told us about: Cabo Pulmo in Mexico, and further south, Costa Rica. Both maintained their thriving environments by preventing overharvesting on land and sea. Tourists came to see the sustained beauty; fishermen and farmers profited by managing their natural assets; and the government earned tax credits for positive results. Everyone and everything wins.

In Mexico, Manuel Arango, the producer of **Sentinels of Silence**, gave us the grand tour, and we were blown away by his generosity and concern for the region's ecological health. He and others in the community had done much to preserve the area's plants, animals, and natural beauty in the Sea of Cortez.

In Costa Rica, we were joined by the Ostensen family and four surfboards. Because the land and sea have been prudently cared for, the surfing was magnificent, but that same pristine sea would soon bring me one of the worst days of my life. Derek and Justin Ostensen and Shaun and I surfed six-foot peak swells all morning on waves that were perfect for my long, drawn-out turns and sweeping cutbacks. After a three-hour session, we walked back to our bed-and-breakfast, a quaint colonial two-story beneath a 100-foot-tall fig tree. After lunch, Barbara and Meghan, and Joy and Kay Ostensen left for a girls-only nature walk and poetry reading beneath the forest canopy. Shaun, Derek, and Justin walked back to the beach to catch more waves and I used the free time to indulge in my guilty pleasure: reading books that have nothing to do with work.

Two hours later, I was jolted out of my reverie by the urgent sound of horse hooves and a man screaming in Spanish. I could understand only a few words: "Blonde boy . . . shark . . . blood!"

I grabbed our passports and all the cash I had, jumped into our Jeep, and tailed the galloping cowboy through cane fields, onto and along the beach to a local surf spot. We must have looked alarming, skidding from 50 miles an hour to a full stop on the sand.

Shaun lay on a makeshift bench, bleeding profusely from seven-inch-long shreds on either side of his ankle. Derek couldn't look without hurling; Justin was worried that Shaun would lose his foot. As I wrapped

the ankle in a clean, white T-shirt, I asked the cowboy to guide us to the nearest hospital. He said he could never find it, that there were too many turns, but he knew a person who could. I told him I'd pay him $50 to be our interpreter and his friend another $50 to get us there as quickly as possible. As I was loading Shaun into the Jeep, Derek told me that Shaun hadn't lost much blood because, as unlikely as it may seem, a beautiful topless girl rode up on a horse and gave Shaun a Valium, which calmed him down, lowering his heartbeat. What luck! And then we were off—the cowboy, his buddy the navigator, Shaun, and me, all piled in the Jeep. The hour-long drive felt like ten minutes because of the adrenaline surging through my body. Every time we hit one of Costa Rica's many potholes, Shaun yelped in pain, while I concentrated on taking each turn without rolling the Jeep.

When we arrived at the cinder-block medical clinic, the cowboy took over, demanding instant attention from the one doctor, who led us into the "operating room." Laying Shaun on one of two cement tables, each with a large bare light bulb suspended above it, the doctor went to work. "Tiburón," he said, immediately identifying the shark's teeth marks in Shaun's skin. The big concern was damage to the Achilles and other tendons. In a shock-induced fog, I saw my son's future flash before me: He'd never walk again, he'd quit sports, hang with dopers, lose interest in school, and turn into a homeless vagabond at 20.

Shaun looked at me and said, "Dad, you should lie down, too. You've turned white." I lay down on the second operating table until, thankfully, my dizziness subsided. Two hours later, the operation was over and Shaun hobbled back to the Jeep with 100 stitches in his leg. We were hopeful that his tendons had been saved, but just in case, I had made a sketch of the open wound so that a doctor in Laguna could evaluate the extent of his injury. The bill from the Costa Rica clinic, including surgery, pain pills, and antibiotics, came to $25. In Laguna, we had the wound reopened, recleaned and restitched. The bill was $8,000!

Shaun spent the next month with his foot elevated, reading and watching videos. Lea Abel, his friend since preschool, would bring him daily treats, friends, conversation, and humor. It was during these encounters that Shaun learned how to talk to girls instead of freezing up as I had when I was his age. So, as always, there was a silver lining. Shaun now has an awesome story, the scars to prove it, a beautiful and talented wife, Katie Matheson, whom he met in college, and three wonderful children.

Catching the Bug

When it was time for our kids to go to college, Shaun decided on an economics program at Emory University in Atlanta, while Meghan studied English at my alma mater, UCSB. Near the end of Shaun's senior year, Barbara and I went back east for one of his soccer games. He admitted to us, rather anxiously, that he didn't believe he wanted to spend his life as an economist sitting behind a desk. "I'm thinking that being a filmmaker might be more challenging and interesting," he said.

Barbara and I were surprised but secretly elated! We'd never pushed the children toward any career, knowing full well that it would probably drive them in the opposite direction. At that moment, our hearts were bubbling with excitement. But now it was my turn to be anxious. "Do you have a plan?" I asked. "You do know how hard it is to be in the film business today."

Shaun revealed that he'd already applied to the USC School of Cinematic Arts and thought he had a good chance of getting in. I couldn't have been prouder that he had taken the initiative to think things through and plan out his near-term future.

The USC graduate program taught students for six semesters (three years) and kept classes small, admitting just 50 students per semester. Shaun told me that his professor addressed the class honestly on the first day: "There are many areas of film you can go into, but today, because so many students want to be filmmakers, the grim reality is that only one of you will make a decent living making films. So which one of you will be that filmmaker?" Shaun said that 50 hands reached high, showing the enthusiasm each of these classmates possessed. Two and a half years later, Shaun graduated with honors from the best film school in the world, and of course I asked him to come work for our company.

Meghan did especially well at UCSB and went on to earn a master's degree in English from Chapman University. Barbara and I were bowled over when she announced that the summers she'd spent working at our office were so much fun that she wanted to come back. She applied for a job and I gave her the hardest one of all: production manager. Ever since, she's done a better job than anyone who came before her. People love working with her and she's found a way to balance work and home life (with husband Louis and two adorable kids) with incredible grace.

Shaun was promoted to president of MacGillivray Freeman Films just as he began a film project to pay tribute to the 100-year anniversary of America's best idea ever: the National Park Service. I am so proud of the way that he put this project together. After a year and a half of photography, the film turned out amazingly well and in 2016 became the year's highest-grossing documentary film in any format.

National Parks Adventure is one of my favorite films. Much of the quality of the final film derives from the fresh style and new approach brought by its young producers, Shaun and Meghan, along with the new generation of the MFF family team!

> **Our Friends Making Films**
> 2:52   #11

(ABOVE) Meghan acted in **The Discoverers**, playing 8-year-old Maria Sautuola, who discovered the Altamira Cave Paintings in 1879. (BELOW) Shaun sets the exposure. (FACING PAGE) The kids learned life lessons in Indonesia, Singapore, Kenya, Tanzania, Israel, Egypt, Greece, and Spain—all great filming locations.

Disney and the China Experience

"Lazily waving my white feathered fan
  Naked to the waist in the midst of the
    forest's green trees
  Hanging my cap on a rocky crag
  Baring my head
  To the wind that blows through the pines"

—CHINESE POET, LI BAI, *A SUMMER DAY IN THE MOUNTAINS*

In 1974, Jim and I created a Cinerama tri-screen presentation for Mazda. The unusual film was designed to play for one night in Las Vegas in front of a thousand of the company's top car dealers to motivate bigger sales that year. We utilized amazing multiscreen techniques, but we also needed a great, emotionally impactful soundtrack. Jim called Neil Diamond, with whom we had worked during the making of **Jonathan Livingston Seagull**, and asked whether we could "pretty please" use one of his songs. Diamond told Jim that his timing was perfect because Neil's daughter had just turned 16 and needed a car, so if he could get his hands on a new Mazda, we could use all the music we wanted. "Deal!" replied Jim in one second flat.

Five years after Jim's death, in 1981, Disney was designing EPCOT Center for its new park in Orlando, Florida, and asked to see the somewhat famous Mazda film. The designers were specifically interested in multiscreen concepts. Filmmaker Jeff Blyth and I drove up to Burbank and showed the Mazda film to Randy Bright, Marty Sklar, CEO (and former Rams pro football player) Ron Miller, Don Henderson, and others. They loved it and decided that we were the best choice to create a nine-screen, Circle-Vision 360° film for EPCOT's China Pavilion. Since I would be working on two IMAX

films at that time, I asked Jeff to direct this project. He threw himself into it, researching China, its history and people, but especially its scenic locales.

For Disney, this project should have been called their leap of faith, because China was just emerging. Since the 1930s, the country had been in turmoil, first struggling with the Japanese occupation of their lands, then suffering through a raging civil war between Nationalists and Communists (Mao), and finally, trying to implement various economic and social plans while its poverty-laden population surpassed a billion. In the 1950s, my sisters and I grew up with the admonition from Mom, "Finish the food on your plate. Think of the starving children in China."

By 1981, when EPCOT was being built, most of China was still inaccessible, secretive, and unknown. It was also still impoverished, but Disney needed the world's most populous country to be represented. Unlike the other pavilions lining the World Showcase Lagoon, whose countries paid (from their tourism marketing budgets) to be included in EPCOT, Disney offered to foot the bill for the China Pavilion, promising a replica of the Temple of Heaven; history, cultural events and dances; an authentic Chinese restaurant; and our Circle-Vision 360° theater—but on one condition: China had to give us access to their locked-tight country. Given this backdrop, Jeff and I viewed the project as a risky undertaking; forty years ago China was nothing like it is today.

Jeff traveled to China for a lengthy scout. We would be the first Westerners to shoot in a country that had been off-limits to outside news media for decades. We expected, and got, extra scrutiny and burdensome government protocols. Once they were resolved, Jeff scheduled shoots in fall, winter, and spring for a total of four months of filming. Though the film was only 20 minutes, we needed a lengthy shoot

(FACING PAGE) A portable house, a yurt, with our one actor playing the ancient Chinese poet, Li Bai, in Inner Mongolia, China, for the filming in Circle-Vision 360° for Disney's **Wonders of China**.

(ABOVE) The Circle-Vision 360° camera links nine cameras, each shooting up into 45° mirrors, here at the Great Wall; (BELOW) I taught the Tibetan kids how to say and signal "A-OK!"

because transportation systems were so unreliable and infrequent in China. We also had to keep in mind that our Chinese crew members were only a few years removed from the brutal effects of the Cultural Revolution. As Mao had only been dead for five years, men in the streets were still wearing Mao jackets. As such, our Disney crew encountered an endless parade of many cultural, transportation, housing, and food issues.

Even so, we were committed to covering as much of China as we could, from the frozen north to the tropical south, from the cities of the east to exotic regions of the west. We came up against numerous state security obstacles, including our desire to film in mountainous Tibet and the far-off provinces of Xinjiang and Inner Mongolia. Also complicating matters was the fact that the Chinese worried that Disney's 360° camera could see around corners, through mountains, and into the nooks and crannies of faraway military installations. Getting permission for each shot was very difficult, especially if it involved what our hosts deemed to be strategic targets: railroads, tunnels, bridges. You know, the interesting places.

We wore them down with our persistent—and ultimately successful—efforts to share China's majestic beauty with the rest of the world. By the end, I was amazed that they allowed us to shoot a scene of farmers and their water buffaloes right in the middle of an army base. We even shot a scene on a moving train, coming out of a tunnel and crossing a bridge! Three strategic no-nos. We came away feeling good about having won them over to the project.

As the photographer and producer, my main concern was that the monochromatic tone of the scenery made it a challenge to shoot a beautiful movie. Scenes with white or gray skies on a circular screen

(ABOVE AND BELOW) Circle-Vision 360° at Tiananmen Square, Beijing, 1981.

JINJIANG HOTEL, LEON CHOOLUCK, GREG
MACILLIVRAY, ROOM 215
CHENGDU

HAVE SCREENED FIRST SHIPMENT. GREAT STUFF. REGARDING YOUR QUESTIONS:
GRADUATED ND WORKS GREAT. NO PROBLEM.
NO GRIP IN ANY SHOT
SUNSHADE IN LAST 2 TAKES OF SCENE NBR 7 BUT NOT OBJECTIONABLE.
FAR FROM OVERT. THERE WAS SOME FLARE IN PRIOR
LANTURN AND STORYTELLER AT DESK ARE BOTH
DYNAMITE.
SLO-MOTION HORSEMEN VERY NICE. ABOUT 1/2 IS SHARP, 1/2 IS
SOFT FOCUS.
I PERSONALLY WOULD PUT THINGS CLOSER TO THE CAMERA, AND THE
CAMERA LOWER. JUST AN OPINION - SOMETIMES IN FRANCE I WORRIED
I HAD THINGS TOO CLOSE, BUT LATER NEVER
I HOPE I'VE ANSWERED YOUR QUESTIONS. PER YOUR REQUEST, I'LL
TRY TO RESPOND TO EACH SET OF DAILIES. REGARDS
RICK HARPER

COL NIL   V3358

would wash out all nine images. To improve the frequently troublesome skies, I came up with an idea to use adjustable neutral-density graduated filters over the lenses that could darken the sky in the 360° view. I could slide the filters up or down to give a matched, customized look to the landscape, continuously blending from one image to the next, making the sky prettier, darker, and bluer. This worked well and was worth the half hour that it took me to set up filters for just one shot. After we shot our first images, I had Rick Harper, an outstanding filmmaker who was working on another EPCOT film about France, view the footage in LA. Long before fax or email, he telegrammed me in China: "Graduated ND works great." Thanks Rick!

Up to that point, all of Disney's Circle-Vision 360° films had been straight travelogues with simple voice-over narration and beautiful imagery. In our experiential films, IMAX and others, we'd found that incorporating a story, no matter how basic, helped audiences connect emotionally to the film. I pitched this concept to Randy Bright and, though he was concerned that a character story might detract from the you-are-there experience, he agreed to it. Jeff came up with the idea of creating a story line using the ancient words of Li Bai, an eighth-century Chinese poet. An actor in a Tang dynasty costume played Li Bai and made five appearances to guide viewers through the locales as his poetry formed the basis for the narration.

In addition to our crew of five Americans and our Chinese "minder," we were joined by two Peking University students who spoke English well enough to be our translators. Production began in Inner Mongolia, where we shot a wonderful sequence of riders on ponies among yurts in the rolling grasslands. We got impressive shots cruising along the Yangtze River through the Three Gorges, and in Beijing at the Temple of Heaven and Tiananmen Square. In every city, we were celebrated with a formal welcoming dinner with regional Communist Party leaders, events that took place entirely in Chinese. For hours we bowed, smiled, toasted one another's country with wine, and ate mysterious thousand-year-old eggs. I quickly learned that, if we followed my mother's rule to finish the food on our plate, the Chinese would immediately pile on more just to prove the abundance of everything, including their hospitality. They'd finish the state dinner with gifts—including cartons of Panda cigarettes.

It was a fun shoot, especially in Tibet, which was like the Wild West. Towns were filled with mountain men from the untamed lands beyond, dressed in animal hides, dirty, rough-edged, and covered in long, matted fur. In the dirt streets of Lhasa, kids swarmed us as if they'd never seen a white person. They would run up to me giggling and follow me around while pulling the hair on my arms because body hair was so unusual. I had fun showing them the hand-signal for "A-OK" that was the rage of US astronauts. Despite the attention we received, we got great shots on the roof of the famous Potala Palace and in Tibet's towering mountains, the tallest in the world.

I called Barbara every four days—an hour-long task in those days. Shaun had just turned one and Barbara's back had seized up under the heavier load. Finally, with her back calmed and both of our mothers elaborately scheduling coverage to watch the baby, Barbara joined our adventure in the then-mysterious China. By the time she arrived in Beijing, however, I had contracted hepatitis from eating bad shrimp on our Yangtze riverboat. For the first week of her stay, I lay sweating, feverish and very weak. Barbara treated me like a king, though I knew what a disappointment the trip was becoming for her. I insisted she see the Great Wall, the Temple of Heaven, and the Summer Palace; sadly, as the crew traveled to Guilin, the most spectacular location, Barbara and I flew home. I remained in bed for the next month, sicker than I've ever been. Jeff and the crew carried on brilliantly and completed the shooting.

Wonders of China opened at EPCOT in 1982 to great acclaim. Standing outside the China Pavilion on opening day, Jeff heard two kinds of responses that justified all the hard work: "That settles it. Now we must go to China," and "Well, now that we've seen China, we don't need to go there!"

As we finished this film in the early '80s, a recession was also beginning, slowing the progress of filmmaking opportunities. Needing to protect our financial position, the China film bolstered our reputation for experiential filmmaking. More than 100 million people saw the film in that one theater over the next 20 years, as EPCOT, with about 12 million visitors annually, grew to become the fourth most-attended theme park in the Unitied States.

At the same time, I encouraged Jeff to move to Los Angeles and advance his own directing career in Hollywood. Meanwhile, our team doubled down on immersive entertainment, continually working on new ways to amaze our audience members. In one example, we filmed in IMAX an almost impossible-to-believe aviation accident involving expert piloting skills, for our second film for the Smithsonian, **Flyers**. As *Smithsonian* magazine reported, "An aerial stunt in the Air and Space Museum's new feature film, **Flyers**, is leaving viewers aghast and almost disbelieving." In a scene to represent the barnstorming era of flight, when air shows featured biplanes with a wing walker balancing on the top wing, we recreated the story of one wing-walker who fell off the wing, to then be caught in mid-fall by a diving rescue plane. This had actually happened! It was true, you-are-there IMAX! Director Dennis Earl Moore filmed the scene above the Grand Canyon with IMAX cameras mounted on the two airplanes—all real, without special effects. Expert skydiver Kevin Donnelly performed the fall, while stunt pilot Art Scholl, who worked with us on **To Fly!,** flew the catch plane.

In our film **Flyers**, director Dennis Earl Moore reenacted the fall of a wing walker off an airplane, then to be rescued by a diving Stearman biplane. Our team filmed this scene, live-action (no computer special effects), above the Grand Canyon.

Spectacular Stunt over Grand Canyon
5:44   #12

"One of my greatest pleasures of my work as director of the Smithsonian's Air and Space Museum was engaging with Greg MacGIllivray on an IMAX film, **Flyers**. If I were to make an IMAX film tomorrow, I would immediately select MacGIllivray Freeman to make it."

—Walter Boyne, founder, *Air and Space* magazine, and former director, National Air and Space Museum

Trying to Grow the IMAX® Brand

SURF
HOLLYWOOD
IMAX ENTERTAINMENT
MISSION

"The secret was to take full advantage of the overwhelming size and clarity of the screen and to immerse the audience in an intense, you-are-there experience. Finding and filming those moments has never been easy, but it has been my quest for 40 years. It is a perfect marriage of technique and story."

One thing Jim and I learned early was that there is an invisible pecking order in the film business, related to how much you're paid per day per project. The unions have codified this order. At the bottom are crew members working on low-budget industrial or educational films, then local TV, PBS TV and documentaries, then network TV, above that TV commercials and IMAX documentaries—and at the very top studio feature films. Everyone is reaching for that brass ring, the high-profile feature project.

Four years after Jim's death, while riding the wave of accolades we received for brass-ring projects **The Shining**, **Big Wednesday**, and **China**, I found myself at a crossroads: Should I continue to direct Hollywood second-unit shoots and TV commercials, which were interesting, profitable, and challenging, or commit to pushing the IMAX format with creative filmmaking? I'd learned a lot working with Kubrick, Milius, and Disney on their films, but because Jim and I had had such

fun making **To Fly!**, and because I'd always loved taking risks, I decided to go for the less certain business path and try to grow this industry newcomer into something far bigger. Adhering to my dad's motto, we would try to become the best at this one specific and new way of making movies, while hoping that the money would follow. So, MacGillivray Freeman Films, still carrying Jim's name out of respect for his artistry and contributions, committed itself, its savings and its energy to growing the IMAX brand by producing films that would be a positive force for all IMAX theaters for at least the next decade. It was a long shot, but hadn't I learned to say "Why not?"

The plan was to make truthful, accurate documentary films that were emotionally impactful and memorable, not just through the stories but by harnessing the breadth and power of IMAX technology. Since it was just me making this monumental decision and failure was a distinct possibility, I decided to create a plan of action for the entire decade of the 1980s.

We would combine high-quality filmmaking with solid promotion of those experiential films in each community developing an IMAX theater. But we had no assurance that the number of theaters would grow beyond the 14 that were then open and operating. It was common knowledge that Cinerama, the spectacular tri-screen, 146° wraparound presentation of the 1950s, had expanded quickly to 20 theaters only to fizzle and fail. Friends and advisors wondered whether IMAX would go the way of Cinerama. Though I felt in my gut that IMAX would succeed because of its astounding quality, I studied the reasons Cinerama had collapsed and tried to build on what I felt had earned that format its initial success. In doing so, I almost killed my company.

I had concluded that if I combined spectacular action (as seen in the Cinerama hit film **How the West Was Won**) with great,

(FACING PAGE) One of our three main characters in **To The Limit** was rock climber Tony Yaniro, who besides having outstanding upper body strength, possessed decision-making intelligence to perfect moves on cliff faces such as El Capitan and here, at Red Rocks. To film this "fantasy" falling scene, cameraman Mike Hoover hired a trapeze-rigging team from Circus Circus, in nearby Las Vegas, who stretched a net just below the frame line. To test that Tony wouldn't bounce out of the springy net, we dropped into it a 150-pound sack of rocks. And they didn't fly out! Even so, we told Tony, "Grab the net as soon as you hit, just to make sure!" The shocking moment became the highlight of our trailer for the film.

"From the moment I began making films, I've been driven by the need to exceed the audience's expectations. Is the experience worth more than the price of admission? The answer has to be a big yes, and that's why we've always insisted on making original and surprising films."

inspirational stories (as seen in IMAX's **Man Belongs to the Earth**), we'd attract a wider audience than for a normal, impersonal historical or wildlife documentary. So when I pitched the Smithsonian to make **Flyers**, and the fast-food chain, McDonald's to make **Behold Hawaii**, both of which were fictional, actor-driven, inspirational dramas, I could not have been more misguided. In my drive to expand the appeal of IMAX and grow a bigger audience, I missed the main point of IMAX: the authenticity of nonfiction storytelling, of taking the audience to a real place and giving them the actual, not fictional, experience as if they were there! While both films brought A-quality visuals and spectacular action sequences, including a never-before-photographed stunt, the acting couldn't stand up to the magnification and clarity of IMAX. You could tell that our character actors were acting almost as clearly as you can tell when a sneaky car salesman is jiving you; you see it in his eyes! And those all-telling eyes were ten feet tall on the IMAX screen!

Though both films gave a boost to the IMAX name, I had clearly blown two big opportunities. I believed so strongly that I was correct that I missed the point, as did famous director Jean-Jacques Annaud when a few years later he spent $12 million making **Wings of Courage**, a fictional drama, in 3D IMAX. We'd committed unforced errors because our films were made-up inventions, not authentic experiences. But after this trying experiment, I now knew the true power of IMAX and how to amplify that power in our next films by creating images that went beyond the ordinary. But for that I'd need some revolutionary cameras.

The Equipment Can Help

Since the time that Jim and I first bought our Ferrari-like Mitchell high-speed camera, we had loved what a unique camera can do to make a film more amazing, like slowing down the graceful fluttering wings of a seagull in flight. But when we began producing films in the IMAX

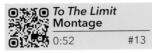

To The Limit
Montage
0:52   #13

format in 1974, there was only one very elementary camera available called the Mark II. To build it, Graeme Ferguson had commissioned camera designer Jan Jacobsen, who combined salvaged parts from an old 65mm, five-perf camera with an innovative, new movement. Bill Shaw, the genius projector designer at IMAX Corporation, marveled at how Jan had fit so much in a small space. He told Graeme that Jan's Mark II achievement was astounding. It was a simple and wonderful camera that got the job done—the same design IMAX used for the three cameras built for us in 1974; but it was noisy, heavy, and could only shoot up to 55 frames per second.

When we began producing **To The Limit** and **The Discoverers**, I needed new tools to achieve new things. First, I wanted to shoot in real slow motion—110 frames per second, or twice as fast as the IMAX Mark II camera. Second, I needed a camera light enough to carry on a Steadicam in order to become part of a fluid scene with characters. This would be impossible with the current camera, so I called Bill Shaw.

This man was one of the nicest, most creative people I have ever met. Humble, soft-spoken, and with a wry sense of humor, Bill jumped at the chance to design and build these two cameras, but even Bill said my dream of running 65mm film at 110 frames per second was an unreachable goal. Experts at Kodak said their film would tear apart if it was transported at that speed—four times faster than normal. Camera companies warned that the complex mechanics might explode. Metal scientists said the pull-down claw would warp and break.

Still, Bill and I liked a challenge, so we put together a set of construction parameters for camera designers to follow. Nine months later, we were testing the heaviest IMAX camera ever, but one that was fully capable of running Kodak's Estar plastic film at true slow motion. What was remarkable about this high-speed (HS) IW-8 camera was that every frame was registered by two pins sliding into the film's sprocket holes and then sucked flat by a vacuum against a pressure plate, which prevented buckling, vibration, and jitter. Imagine that happening 110 times per second. We used it to film super slow-motion images of downhill ski racer Maria Walliser in Aspen; of Olympic gold medalist Carl Lewis sprinting and long jumping; and of ballerina Nina Ananiashvili leaping through the air on the Bolshoi stage. To film-industry insiders, this was revolutionary and stunning. No one had believed that 70mm images could be shown with such crispness and beauty. The project was a surprising success. I loved everything about this camera—except lifting it onto a tripod. It weighed more than 130 pounds!

Not one to rest until something was perfect, I'd asked Bill about designing a lighter Steadicam-accessible camera. A week later, I got a call at 10 p.m. from Bill in Toronto, more excited than any kid could be. He'd learned about a new design that could save weight by using one pull-down claw rather than two. We quickly recruited Jeff Williamson

---

(FACING PAGE) Over the past decades, Greenland's ice caves have been warming, turning the crystalline ice into running water. Here, Luc Moreau descends deep to study climate change for our film in a location perfect for the IMAX experience.

and another genius designer, Jack Tankard, for our team. Together they built a single-claw, 25-pound 15/70 camera light enough to mount on a Steadicam. I tested it out on my next film, **The Discoverers**, and was thrilled to find that I could move fluidly while filming reenactments of historical figures like Isaac Newton in his laboratory uncovering the elemental properties of light. The sequence was mesmerizing and drew the audience into the action, much as Kubrick had done with his use of the Steadicam in **The Shining**. These two cameras are responsible for achieving revolutionary advancements for the IMAX industry and they have produced many a visual treat for audiences.[19] Bill Shaw loved designing for the IMAX system that he adored.[20]

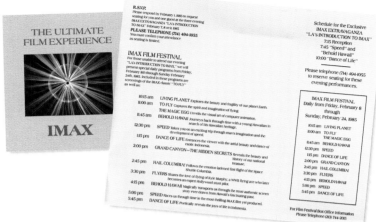

Struggling to Grow the Brand

Even with these new cameras and a handful of new films, the growth of the IMAX theater network stalled in the '80s. We had all hoped that Hollywood fat cats would invest and rescue the company, but only a few had seen IMAX in its mainly eastern locations. Finally, by 1985, Los Angeles had an IMAX theater at the California Museum of Science and Industry, and we financed and hosted a two-week film festival called "LA Introduction to IMAX," where we showed our three IMAX films, along with four others, to about 10,000 producers, students, reviewers, and trendsetters. Arts Editor Charles Champlin wrote in Southern California's largest newspaper, the *Los Angeles Times*:

> *Now the screen has gone fantastically high, wide, and handsome to enrich the movie-watching experience—and, as before, lure us out of the house. Viewers who have not yet been exposed to the vast IMAX screen can hardly imagine quite how different the visceral response is from the customary commercial movie-house experience. It is a quantum leap beyond even the startling dimensions of early Cinerama. One of the films in the festival series is Kieth Merrill's **Grand Canyon —The Hidden Secrets**, which is to previous travelogues what a picture postcard is to a mural. Some things can't be faked, and the wooden boats, bucking and ducking beneath the furious whitewater, and capsizing in the raging river, are a gut-tightening spectacle. It's some of the most*

thrilling live-action footage I've seen, and it demonstrates what the IMAX dimensions can do at their best.

As we waited for IMAX to attract investors, I felt especially worried for Graeme, Robert, Bill, and Roman Kroiter. We realized we were in a tricky "developing" business in a tricky time. I watched in dismay as my good friends at Francis Thompson Inc., the leading producer of world fair films, winners of the Academy Award for the superb film **To Be Alive** and executive producers of **To Fly!**, struggled and went out of business as lending rates went to 20 percent, causing investments in films to dry up. These examples made me very conscious that the bottom may fall out at any time.

Then came a temptation I regret not taking. Kubrick called to offer me the opportunity to shoot and direct second-unit on the film he was beginning, **Full Metal Jacket**. I had to tell him I was too committed to this new medium to help, even if IMAX was at that time an even bigger long shot.

As the public's awareness and comfort level with giant-screen projections grew, I would call Graeme, Bill, or Robert at IMAX and we'd bolster one another's confidence. But I knew success would take every inch of our combined creativity.

Maximizing the WOW Factor of the IMAX Screen

When we were awarded the contract to make a 22-minute IMAX film for a new amusement park in Michigan called AutoWorld, I knew that we needed to maximize IMAX's ability to put the audience in the throbbing heart of the action by focusing on the evolution of speed —the innovations that have allowed humans to travel faster and faster since the dawn of time—concluding with super-sonic flight.

I titled the film simply, **Speed** (the one that came long before the 1994 Keanu Reeves action thriller). Our company had worked with the

---

19 The third camera that we developed was the W4, the quietest and most precise-focusing studio-style camera of all the 15/70s. With its sound-blanketing cover, we could film sync-sound situations with the 30mm fish-eye lens just two feet from a character without recording any camera noise. The W4 had a unique mirror-shutter viewing system, which allowed me to focus much more precisely. Unlike other cameras, the sweet spot for focusing at 12-power magnification occurs in the frame about one-third from the bottom, not in the center of the frame. This feature also allowed me to slide the lens so that the sharpest part of the lens, its center, was repositioned on the optimal area for the audience. I could shoot sharper images much more precisely and deliver a better product to IMAX dome theaters.

20 While the IMAX format was growing in popularity, a hybrid system known as Omnimax or IMAX Dome, made use of the same projector, but on a domed screen, with images surrounding the audience that, if shot properly, could be intensely engaging. As audiences voiced their enthusiastic approval, MacGillivray Freeman Films became known for this challenging, difficult style of photography that utilized our three advanced cameras to maximum effect.

(FACING PAGE) **The Discoverers**, based on a Pulitzer Prize-winning book, was the #1 attraction at Expo 92 in Seville, Spain. Here, historical scientists discuss evidence proving that the Earth is round.

Speed

FILMED IN: 15 PERFORATION/70MM

RELEASE DATE: 1984

Played at 12 IMAX/Omnimax theaters in its first year, a record for simultaneous release in 1984.

The film was released with a special "sonic boom" soundtrack that, when combined with large speakers and amplifiers, produces an enhanced low-end vibration that can literally shake the audience.

"**Speed** will knock your socks off! The big screen effect is electric. You'll find yourself leaning into the turns, grabbing onto your chair. You may literally be dizzy."

–JOHN CORCORAN, KABC-TV

(ABOVE) Our 15/70 IMAX camera on a Steadicam. (BELOW) A wide, low-angle view of a bicycle racing at a velodrome.

Blue Angels demonstration team on our film **To Fly!**, and the navy admirals and their public relations team had loved what that film did for the recruitment of new pilots. They were so enthusiastic about shooting with us again, they convinced the McDonnell Douglas engineering team to build an IMAX camera mount for the nose of Blue Angel's jet number seven, which would fly behind the traditional six-jet formation. On a beautiful morning in Pensacola, Florida, we were wheels up at 8 a.m. to film maneuvers. I was in the back seat, behind my pilot. We were both wearing flexible rubber "g-force" suits that monitor when the airplane is beginning an intense turn or dive. To avoid blacking out, air is pumped through the suit, squeezing your arms and legs like a tourniquet so that blood is not pulled away from your heart and head, avoiding dire consequences like passing out.

For our fourth shot, we had lined up directly behind the other jets when the lead pilot in jet number one—"the boss"—ordered the use of the air brakes—flaps that rise to slow the jet instantly. My pilot, who at that very moment happened to be asking me a question, did not hear the command, so when the air brakes came up on all six jets in front of us, he had to react swiftly by shoving the joystick hard to the side. We immediately flipped upside down and went into free fall. Had he not done this, we would have run into the tails of three of the jets, resulting in sure disaster. Close call!

After that scare, we ended up twisting and turning and diving and accelerating at 500 mph for about 40 more minutes. I had to direct air jets at my face to keep from throwing up. Hearing that, my pilot quipped, "Sorry about that, Greg. How're you feeling back there?"

"I feel okay," I said over the intercom, adding, "I've never been airsick, carsick, or seasick before, but I can tell you're working on it!"

When we landed, I remember vividly the difficulty of climbing down the narrow ladder from the cockpit to the ground below. My legs had gone to jelly, having been squeezed by the rubber suit so many times through four g's positive and one g negative turns. When I got to the ground I bent down and kissed the tarmac. What pilots go through shocked me into something I never do. I drove directly from Naval Air Station Pensacola to my hotel room, lay down, and took a three-hour nap at eleven in the morning! I felt more depleted than I had been since surviving that two-wave hold-down at Sunset Beach so many years before.

Maximum Intensity: A New Sound System

Because we wanted **Speed** to be shocking and impactful, to really sell the IMAX experience, I decided that it would be good to incorporate new elements into the sound system at AutoWorld's permanent theater.

(FACING PAGE) The spectacularly talented Blue Angels in an IMAX wow-moment.

(TOP) Our rented tiger, Johnny. (ABOVE) Shaun was Johnny's target, so he had to watch from the car. (BELOW) Carl Lewis in super slow motion.

After talking with technical authority David Keighley and the sound experts at IMAX Corporation, I hired a company called Sonics with engineer Evans Wetmore to design the system. Of the six IMAX sound channels, we decided to use the rarely utilized channel number six as a discrete sub-base channel to drive a row of eight 12-inch woofers on the theater floor, aimed up at the audience. When certain actions in the film, like the breaking of the sound barrier, called for an extraordinary sound effect, we could trigger the speakers to create a low-frequency sonic *boom*! The concussion wave would pulse from the front of the theater and bounce off the audience's chests, creating an actual physical impact. Kids screamed! Adults laughed!

Anticipating the fun of this shock, I wrote into the script 15 moments to incorporate such impacts. I remember them well: our hero car crashing through a banner being installed in a 1930s town, running into a stack of tires that cascade down the street, and clipping through a field and knocking over a couple Burma-Shave billboards.

Thrilling Stories on the Giant Screen

While filming **Speed**, we rented Johnny, a full-grown tiger, for a scene of a caveman being chased, comically illustrating the most elementary reason for going fast: survival. Every time our four-year-old, tow-headed Shaun appeared on set to watch us film, the tiger strained at its chain, trying to sink his teeth into this golden-haired bite-sized morsel. We had to keep Shaun locked in the car, watching out the rear window, whenever Johnny was near.

In the most difficult shot in my storyboard, the tiger had to chase the caveman through the trees; and because in IMAX there was no way to composite the two elements together with special effects, I had to shoot it *real*. The trainer, Monty Cox, told me he had it all worked out, but, recalling our seagull-trainer experience, I had my doubts.

"I'll tie two slabs of fragrant meat to the inside of my animal hide costume," he said, "which will get Johnny to chase me and no one else. As I run, I'll tumble into a fall, just as you wanted, then jump back up and keep going. My assistant will wait next to my truck with the hatchback wide open, I'll leap in, and he'll drop the lid. Then he'll calm Johnny with a juicy T-bone steak and chain him up." It sounded far-fetched to me, but Monty was convinced it would work. Amazingly, it did! With Shaun watching studiously from the car, we filmed three takes of this action, and each time, Monty escaped Johnny's teeth just in the nick of time. By the fourth take in the hot sun, Johnny had figured out the program, was tired, and wouldn't move until Monty dangled a fresh, bloody steak in front of his nose. A pissed-off Johnny chased after him one last time—and nearly got him. Even from the back of the car, that chase was one that Shaun would never forget.

Tiger Chase from *Speed*
1:36   #14

Another of my sequences was called "We Have Just Begun to Crawl." The story point was how much more we humans have to learn, and on the title card, which was animated in a jazzy, high-tech style, I thought it would be charming to have a simple scene of a crawling baby inching its way along, crawling in a timeless natural setting. "Talent agent" Barbara suggested our daughter: "Meghan would be perfect, but you'd better hurry up, because she clearly wants to walk!" So on a cold December day, we took one-year-old Meghan down to the rocky beach in front of our house to shoot the scene against the wide ocean view. As the noisy IMAX camera rolled, she felt proud to be the center of attention and started to stand up. Barbara was off to the side, yelling, "Get down and crawl!" So Meghan did what could be called a "stink-bug ambulation," half crawling, half walking. After many tries, we got the shot and she was the highlight of the final scene of the film. Little could Barbara or I ever dream that these brief touches with filmmaking would lead to Shaun and Meghan choosing film as a career years later.

In the MacGillivray Freeman film **Speed**, *the huge screen envelops you, overwhelms you, edges out any other reality. It can quickly induce motion sickness (or uneasiness) as you whip along a winding road. MacGillivray and his partner, the late Jim Freeman, got their start doing surfing films (there is an homage to the firm's beginnings in* **Speed**, *a rousing surfing sequence). But the power is in the breathtaking grandeur of those IMAX vistas—vistas that give to film what one viewer rightly called a sense of the divine.*
—Charles Champlin, arts editor, *Los Angeles Times*

Since **Speed** was my third IMAX documentary film, and in each of the previous two I'd experimented with ways to up the intensity of the filmic event, I now needed an editor who could grasp this medium's potential and stay with our company over the next decades. This key creative individual would help me push IMAX's popularity and reach. The writer-editor on **Behold Hawaii**, Alec Lorimore, introduced me to Stephen Judson. Steve's films were imaginative and unconventional, and thankfully I was able to pull him away from Universal Studios, ABC, and Hollywood to edit and co-write **Speed** and **Dance of Life**. He even moved to Laguna, remodeling a historic residence so beautifully that it has been featured on our community's annual Charm House Tour. Steve was perfect because he possessed an incredible brain, and he worked long years to make it even better at Yale, then USC. As our composer Steve Wood would say, he became our "intellectual janitor," in charge of making everything more deeply interesting, always adroitly looking for inventive new ways to tell stories. Over the past 40 years, Steve has graced our films with his brilliance and insights. His perspective on the medium helped IMAX succeed.

Joining the Team: a Memory by Stephen Judson

When I moved from LA to work for MFF, I lived in the unit above Greg and Barbara's house. (The price was right.) One Saturday, I sat with Barbara at Main Beach, watching a volleyball match. She had their baby daughter, Meghan, snuggled peacefully into a carry basket. Without warning, Barbara said "Watch Meghan!" and jumped up and sprinted off. I was so shocked and terrified that all the women nearby started laughing. "Out of my element" doesn't begin to cover it. I was stupefied! What if Meghan started bawling?!! (She didn't.)

Having worked for producers and directors who were not devout film aficionados, I was struck by the intensity of Greg's approach. For one thing, whenever we projected dailies, he gave every single shot a letter grade. (An A+ was as rare as a snow leopard.) Greg was so diligently studious of the 15/70mm format that he verged on being a cinema nerd. He had thought deeply about the unique demands of giant-screen films and how to shape a movie for a gigantic screen.

I edited 15/70mm footage on a screen no bigger than a desktop computer; but the audience would ultimately see those images six stories tall. Greg realized how this jump in size made IMAX film-watching a fundamentally different experience. It was the difference between observing a location and experiencing it up close. One major adjustment for me as an editor was learning to trust the A+ shots and let them play, and play—and then play longer. Greg understood that the giant screen amplifies the immersive power of aerials and POV shots by an order of magnitude.

He also understood how sound, even in the earliest IMAX theaters, could impact the pace of a film. When I was editing **Speed**, *he made me double the length of several shots. When I first saw the film projected on the giant screen, I saw the wisdom of this. In the decades since, Greg and I have had countless creative disagreements, but I learned early on that betting against his gut about pacing for the giant screen was a losing prospect. To this day, whenever Greg says "let it play," I listen.*

Using Music More Impactfully

Steve and his luminous storytelling skills matched with my command of inventive visuals assisted IMAX through the rough 1980s, and by the 90s, IMAX had opened 80 theatres. To push this big screen acceptance further, I felt we needed bigger names—celebrity reach—star power! But how do we engage highly paid stars with our miniscule budgets? Maybe we could entice musical luminaries with the exceptional quality of our sound reproduction strengths.

When I was a kid and just discovering movies, it was assumed that directors would hire a composer to write an original musical score to fit the film. Starting in the 1960s, innovative directors began experimenting; they sought to tap into the cultural zeitgeist by using prerecorded songs instead. Films like **Easy Rider**, directed by Dennis Hopper, and George Lucas's **American Graffiti** used this approach to great effect. With the soundtrack albums from these revolutionary films producing millions of dollars in profit for their studios, a new revenue source was born, and original scores took a back seat to contemporary hits. Better yet, those songs contributed exponentially to a film's long-term emotional impact.

Jim and I had been using both prerecorded and composer-created music in our films from the very beginning. Halfway through shooting **The Living Sea** years later, it occurred to me that if IMAX could offer the finest audio experience of any movie theater in the world with its six-channel sound, the best speakers and source equipment available, magnetic film and Dolby noise-reduction systems, wouldn't many rock 'n roll artists, like our friend Neil Diamond, want to showcase their music in our sonically inspired theaters to create a bigger fan base for both of us?

I wrote to five of my favorite recording artists—cold calls, to be sure—and got positive responses from Sting, Paul McCartney, and Phil Collins. They could see how a collaboration would give them access to our captive IMAX audience of 10 to 30 million people per film.

In a first for the IMAX documentary film industry, MFF collaborated with Sting and his team to create the soundtrack for **The Living Sea**. Steve Judson and I selected his hit "Fragile" for the main cue. We utilized his purely instrumental recordings for other sequences and audiences loved every bit of it, connecting to the sequences more quickly and creating emotional memories that enhanced the success of the film. Sting also benefited by releasing the soundtrack album on A&M, his record label.

The film created a stir that led to a memory of my own. We had escaped for a few days of family skiing at nearby Mammoth Mountain. I'd just climbed the stairs to the Warming Hut when I got a message to call our office immediately. On the other end of the line, Alice Casbara excitedly cut to the chase: "Greg, you better sit down! **The Living Sea** just received an Academy Award nomination for best short documentary!" I almost dropped the phone. And that afternoon, I've never skied better; I actually think I may have floated down the mountain. Barbara, the kids, and I couldn't stop smiling. And I still think that Sting's beautiful music had much to do with that Oscar honor.

For subsequent films, we mined the talent and libraries of composers and songwriters including Crosby, Stills & Nash, the Moody Blues, Sting (again, for **Dolphins**), Queen, George Harrison, Paul

McCartney, Dave Matthews Band, Aloe Blacc, and Lindsey Buckingham (Fleetwood Mac). For each artist it was a win-win, as our IMAX fan base of well-educated and affluent museumgoers heard the songs in connection with an entertaining and mission-driven film. Some managers, like Sting's Miles Copeland, felt that it was one of the most effective things they'd done to broaden these amazing artists' reach.

And there were other ways we improved our soundtracks. Because our IMAX visuals require a lengthy postproduction schedule, we could use that extended time to perfect the score over a twelve-month period. The extra time also allowed musicians to compose specifically for our films. Sting wrote the title cue to **Dolphins**, Brian May of Queen recorded brilliant, soaring guitar elements for our film **The Alps**, and Justin Hayward and John Lodge of the Moody Blues wrote and recorded the title song for **Journey into Amazing Caves**.

One of the most heartwarming musical explorations of my career was when I decided to use songs by George Harrison, the innovative Beatles guitarist, as the score for **Everest**. Many of George's compositions celebrated Eastern religions and were spiritually driven and very powerful. Since the people of Nepal and Tibet consider Mount Everest to be sacred—Tibetans originally named it Chomolungma, or Goddess Mother of Mountains—I thought that George's songs would be an ideal fit. Even though he wanted to be involved, when I asked him for permission to use "Here Comes the Sun" as a closing element in our story, he didn't like the idea. After we showed the finished film to him and his wife a year later (Olivia and Bob Dylan's wife saw it at a private IMAX screening we arranged in Los Angeles, while George, then in treatment for cancer, saw it on video), he told me that we just had to use "Here Comes the Sun" in the film, as "it would be perfect." George's team gave us the 48 tracks of a live concert in which George had performed the song as an encore. As it was the end of a long night, his voice was raspy, one of the background guitars was out of tune, and the audience was chanting wildly. Nonetheless, score composer Steve Wood did a fantastic job of cleaning it up for Jeff Lynne of ELO and the Traveling Wilburys, who came to our mixing studio to make certain that all of George's cues, along with their six-channel spreads, were up to snuff. George and Olivia loved the film and its message, and appreciated the way we had used his music. Sadly, the cancer took this creative and sensitive human from us in 2001.

For some of our films, my favorite composer, Steve Wood, collected instrumentalists and singers representing each region; a spicy stew, as he called it. Sometimes, Steve would accompany us to filming locations to gain firsthand perspective. In Papua New Guinea, he recorded the music of native tribes to give audiences for **Journey to the South Pacific** the sonic vibe of this exotic oasis. As always, staying true to the culture was a critical element of our success.

(CLOCKWISE FROM TOP LEFT) Composer Steve Wood brilliantly worked on 31 of our films; Sting composed **The Living Sea** and **Dolphins**; Jon Batiste and Dr. John on **America's Musical Journey**; Paul McCartney on **To The Arctic**.

Only a thoughtful composer like Steve Wood, one of the smartest people I've ever met, could have walked the line of creativity with the various artists we've used in the soundtracks of our films. He had an impressive ability to respect and manage the sometimes fragile, sometimes oversized egos of these famous artists, and he produced what I feel were some of the finest soundtracks ever done for films, working with Ken Teaney, Marshall Garlington, and Andrew DeCristofaro, in my opinion the best sound mixers in Hollywood. This trio created the inventive sound design and mixing for all 28 of our films during those years.

Steve Wood's Musical Journey
5:33   #15

New Leadership at IMAX

By the mid-'90s, so many people had enjoyed the experience at museums that the IMAX brand was recognized as the undisputed leader in premier movie-watching experiences. The founders of the IMAX Corporation decided that it was time to retire and put the company up for sale. CEO Robert Kerr asked me to join them and a few other IMAX champions in the sale. I couldn't afford to invest at the time, but I still appreciate the friendship and generosity of Robert, Graeme Ferguson, and Roman Kroitor. They sold to an investment banking group led by Rich Gelfond and Brad Wechsler, who would later take the company public.

In 1997, when we knew that **Everest** would become a bellwether for the IMAX brand, I traveled to New York to brainstorm with Rich and Brad and discuss how we could all benefit from the publicity and push that this film could create for their system. I suggested erecting a giant Times Square billboard to highlight the film and the IMAX brand. They loved the idea, but didn't have the budget for a five-month campaign. In the hopes that it would create a stir among the New York City–based media giants, we took the plunge and spent $90,000 to install the billboard. As a result, Peter Guber's Sony Theatre sold out show after show of **Everest**, leading IMAX to brag in its June 1 press release: "**Everest** has grossed more than $1.6 million and has been seen by over 200,000 people on the one (Sony) screen. It is the highest gross for any film that has run at the Sony IMAX theater to date." We had outgrossed even the big feature films![21] At that time, in 1998, I think we all now understood that we could make it in the big time, that IMAX would not become the next Cinerama, and that all of our hard work would pay off.

The Engineering Genius of IMAX

When we premiered **To Fly!** in 1976, there were just four IMAX theaters in the world. Today, there are 1,700 located in 75 countries. What a fantastic accomplishment for the IMAX Corporation! And just a few years ago, IMAX created a most amazing innovation: The IMAX laser projection system. Since IMAX laser projection eliminates the traditional prism, the image is sharper, whiter, and has better color and contrast range than any digital projector I've seen. That's why I am so enthusiastic about the future of the IMAX theater process. The company's engineering team, led by Brian Bonnick, has done it again, and the creative leaders, Rich Gelfond, Greg Foster, Rob Lister, Megan Colligan, David Keighley, and Brad Wechsler, deserve high marks for carrying on the tradition of excellence that I have enjoyed and shared over the years.

IMAX has teamed with many filmmakers to push the limits of filmmaking. One of my favorite filmmakers, Stephen Low, has delivered with films including **Beavers**, **Rocky Mountain Express**, and **Across the Sea of Time**, as has Howard Hall with **Deep Sea 3D**, Graeme with **The Dream Is Alive**, and Toni Myers with **Space Station** and **Hubble**. Robert Zemeckis, in his film **The Polar Express**, created a dreamlike 3D snowfall experience. Hollywood filmmaker Christopher Nolan photographed parts of **The Dark Knight Rises**, **Interstellar**, **Dunkirk**, and **Tenet** in IMAX. He also projected his films in 15/70 film in about 100 theaters worldwide, driving word-of-mouth attendance. These presentations became "road show" special exhibitions with an emphasis on raising awareness about quality, much the way David Lean's 70 mm films, **Lawrence of Arabia** and **Dr. Zhivago**, did a generation earlier, and as a result, increased their attendance by about 30 percent. All of these creative forces have loved working in the IMAX medium—and the audience has loved the amazing viewing experience.

---

21 It wasn't long before chains like Regal, AMC, and Edwards decided to install commercial IMAX screens to attract customers to an expanding number of multiplexes in shopping malls. This worked well for a time, but those theaters needed more highly publicized films, not just 40-minute documentaries. Rich and Brad, who, like the company's founders, were creative leaders, felt that the best way to grow the IMAX brand was to combine it with the entertainment value offered by feature films. They and their engineering team invented DMR, a clever process that transferred 35mm films to digital, enhanced them, and then printed the image back onto an IMAX film frame for theater exhibition. **Apollo 13**, directed by Ron Howard and starring Tom Hanks, was the first film to get an IMAX rerelease in 2002. The DMR enhancement process worked like magic. All of a sudden, feature films could look as if they were shot on 70mm. For a producer or director, this was like found money. In addition to releasing films to conventional 35mm theaters and TV, they could be shown in state-of-the-art IMAX theaters. The problem was that most of the IMAX theaters were still in museums, and only a handful would program Hollywood features, because dramatic, mainly fictional films were not aligned with their educational mission. That led Rich and Brad to a creative solution: Why not install a new version of IMAX theaters in multiplexes? The plan was to remodel the inside of an existing multiplex theater, installing the largest screen that would fit and steeply raked stadium seating so every customer had an unobstructed view. High-tech acoustic treatment for the walls, A+ sound reproduction, and dual digital projectors would complete the redo and, they hoped, eclipse existing digital and 35mm projection. The most attractive part was that they were offering this package to the theater chains at no cost to them; IMAX would recoup its investment through a percentage of ticket sales. This created another hard-to-refuse freebie for the movie theaters. Unfortunately, the new version confused the IMAX fan base. The screen was smaller and the quality of the image didn't match what audiences had come to expect from 15/70 film projection, which was bigger and sharper. Critics labeled it "Lie-Max," not IMAX! The new concept did, however, offer an upgrade from 35mm quality. As a result, for the past 10 years, most big Hollywood productions have been offered to all IMAX theaters in this digital format. Before putting this new technology on the market, Rich and Brad, concerned that it could hurt existing production groups working in 15/70 documentary films, drove down to Laguna Beach to tell me about this new process. It was considerate and thoughtful of them to let me know in advance so that I could plan ahead if DMR was going to impact my business. I'll never forget this kindness.

(FACING PAGE) The best IMAX sequences put the audience IN THE ACTION!

Dance of Life

Near Death in New Guinea

SURF · HOLLYWOOD · IMAX ENTERTAINMENT · MISSION

"The Dani live in thatched huts and are the most interesting people I've encountered. The women wear only grass skirts with no tops and the men, a simple gourd to cover their privates. They rub pig fat on their skin to repel mosquitoes. They seldom bathe. The stink is repulsive and memorable. Until a decade ago, cannibalism was common. When we arrived, we were told that every Dani with whom we met had tasted human flesh."

West Papua is one of two Indonesian provinces comprising the western half of the island of New Guinea. The middle of this island, one of the most remote and untouched places on earth, is home to the Dani tribe, which has existed largely isolated and unnoticed within the dense forests and high, inaccessible mountains since time began. Until a decade before we arrived, cannibalism was common. In 1961, Nelson Rockefeller's son, Michael, was rumored to have been killed, cooked, and eaten in this region by natives while on a scientific mission. Why would I want to go there? Well, let me tell you.

In the mid-1980s, we were selected to produce an IMAX film about the history and culture of the 13,000 islands that make up Indonesia. This film would fit perfectly with my newly acquired knowledge of taking an audience to a unique location and allowing them to feel as if they were there. **Dance of Life** would play at the largest IMAX theater in the world: a 900-seat arena being built at a Jakarta cultural park called Taman Mini Indonesia Indah.

Indonesia is the fourth most populous country in the world and home to hundreds of cultures, including primitive tribes. For this production, I wanted to feature the old and the young using a unifying and very visual theme that centered on the "circle of life" concept long before Disney's **The Lion King**.

I'd seen an anthropological report featuring a photo of a dance the Dani people performed prior to going to war. It was a circular dance, and this fit our theme perfectly. Because of the unpredictable nature of the Dani, it took months to get permission to film. The Indonesian Education and Cultural Ministry felt it would be too dangerous. I took the chance anyway. Although the government had forbidden the people to do this dance or to go to war with each other, they finally relented. Word spread like wildfire to the ten regional tribes that this historical ritual would be carried out one final time for our film. The warriors were delirious. To the Dani, this was the Super Bowl of their culture . . . plus, the warriors had missed the excitement!

We flew in on a rickety airplane and landed on the short dirt runway of Wamena, the main village in the Baliem Valley. Production manager Alec Lorimore, cameraman Brad Ohlund, and I stayed in thatched huts that only slightly repelled the rain. We slept fitfully, trying to ignore the nibbles and scratches of the bugs. At 7 a.m. we woke to chanting from the surrounding forest. Troupes of men and boys, clad only in their penis gourds but decorated from head to toe with tribal war paint, paraded out of the forest, down to the valley where the dance would be staged. Twenty men came from one region, 30 from another, 50 from somewhere else, and they all converged on the field next to the main village. At our request, the tribal members had built a 10-foot-high platform out of tree limbs for our IMAX camera. The tribes stood in their groups, chanting and singing and stomping their

(FACINIG PAGE) The poster for our lyrical paean, **Dance of Life**.

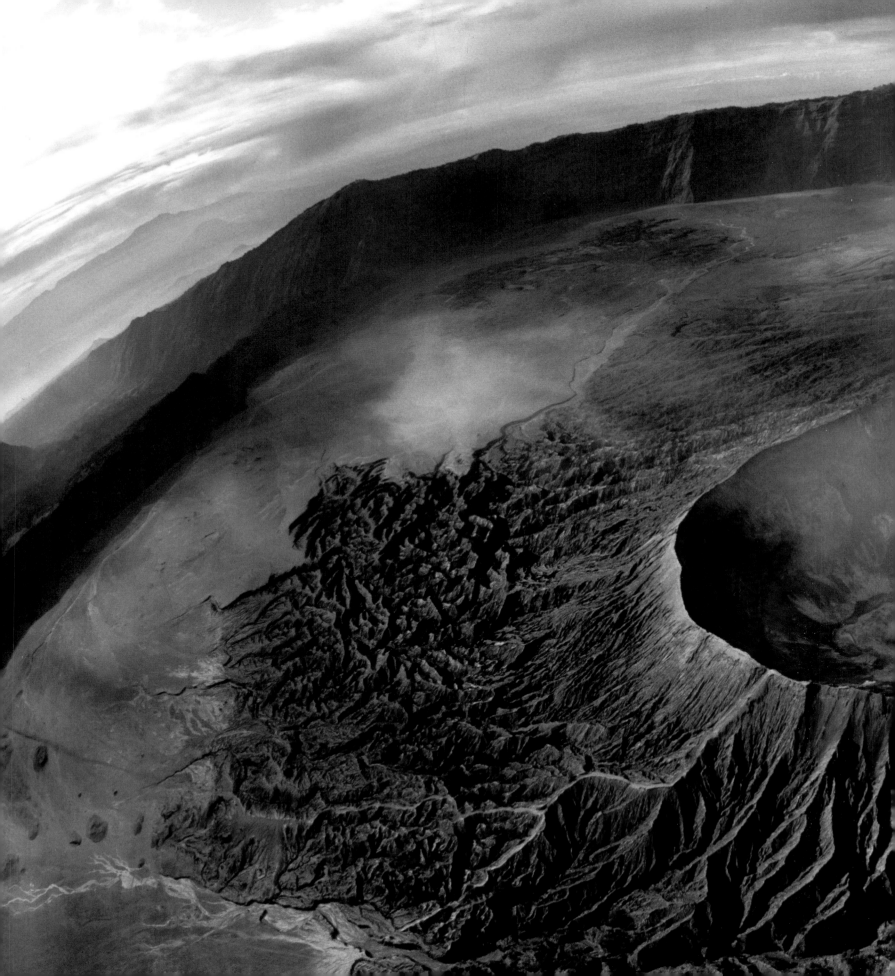

(ABOVE) Thankfully, we had help from our new friends. Each heavy box carried two 15/70 magazines with just 6 minutes of film. (PRECEDING SPREAD) The circular Mount Bromo fit my film's visual design.

feet. The hyped-up warriors looked like they hadn't slept in days. Their eyes were bloodshot and glassy. You could almost smell the testosterone. Having chewed a strange root and smoked an exotic tobacco-like herb, they looked scary, stoned, and jumpy.

Before we started filming, I grabbed my Nikon camera and headed toward one group of chanting warriors. Everyone carried either a bow and arrow or a 10-foot-long spear. Suddenly, a boy of about 18 broke away and raced straight at me. He raised his loaded bow, aiming the arrow squarely at my heart. As if in a trance, he stood, quivering and intense, poised to shoot. I slowly turned sideways and edged away, hoping that he wouldn't let fly. Knowing that these arrows were rumored to be tipped with poison, my life really did flash before my eyes. Time passed as if in slow motion and I thought: What an idiot I am to approach a war party all alone! It was like I had accidentally shaken nitroglycerine. I remember thinking, "I'm thin, maybe he'll miss me." Miraculously, the boy put down his bow, turned, and dashed back to his group. Our anthropologist, Nora Surianti, later told me that I'd experienced a testing ritual often practiced between tribes. This "choosing-off" frightened me, but it showed me that, to the Dani, life is cheap—and short. Life expectancy is 35 or 40 years in their world. Mine was unimportant to them. If I was shot and killed, so be it.

I retreated to the relative safety of the camera position on the scaffolding. Nora and I gave the signal to start the dance. About 150 warriors began to circle a large pole, praising the chieftain who stood

atop it. The chanting was rhythmic; a magical song designed to induce a war trance, a numbness of thought, a hunger for the kill. We filmed for the next two hours from numerous angles, even some low to the ground, and achieved a powerful sequence that resonated deeply with the circle-of-life message of this exotic and poetic film.

As Nora and I walked back to the village, we passed a native woman who had one naked breast that was normal looking and another that hung low, the nipple reaching her waist. The deformity shocked me. Nora explained that one breast was reserved for her baby, while the other was for the family pig, who, Nora giggled, "did not like to let go of the nipple." For the Dani, a pig was a cherished source of protein. If a family owned a pig, it was considered wealthy. Because pigs were eaten only at special annual events, they were revered and nurtured, including being suckled by the women of the house.

Living with the Dani in thatched huts, breathing the smoke of their constant fires meant to drive away mosquitoes, was a fascinating experience. They were simple, smiling, and reserved, but an evolutionary chasm of 1,000 years separated us. We could never really understand or communicate with them. They were as capricious as children. We were documentarians, but living in their skin proved to be impossible.

A Developing Country

The inside look at Indonesian culture in **Dance of Life** brought one million viewers to the theater that year. Decades later, the film continues to screen daily in the world's largest IMAX theater in Jakarta. Gaining the trust of the president of Indonesia through this filmmaking venture presented me with a moral dilemma. Suharto had been president for 18 years, had amassed power, but had also allowed corruption to spread throughout the government and the military. At the same time, he had done much for his people, and as we saw in visiting his home, he lived modestly. Though our films helped educate Indonesians at the cultural park created by the Suhartos, I wondered whether working for a tarnished system was moral. Barbara, my team, and I stewed over this question for years. We went ahead with the release, but also committed to doubling down on our conservation and humanistic film programs.

After **Dance of Life** became a runaway hit, the Indonesian government hired us to make three more films. To find the best story, Barbara and her team did months of research, talking to anthropologists and historians. Drawing from what they learned, we wrote a very personal script as our second film to tell the stories of seven children of progressively older ages, each in a contrasting culture. I wanted to highlight both their cultural diversity and their linked humanity. The theme would parallel Indonesia's motto: Bhinneka Tunggal Ika, or Unity in Diversity. The film would be called **Island Child**.

The Dani people were the most interesting, colorful and distinctive I've ever encountered.

Of all of the stories, the most shocking to our Western tastes took place in a remote paradise. Long Nawang, the Dayak village where we wanted to film the second child, a five-year old boy, is tucked into the highlands of Indonesian Kalimantan, as far from the coastline as you can get. During World War II, Japan occupied the region after killing and imprisoning the Dutch colonists. As the United States and its allies moved across the Pacific, trying to dislodge the Japanese, British paratroopers landed high in the forested mountains and secretly organized the Dayaks into blowgun brigades to attack the Japanese. It worked. When the Japanese departed, partly because of their remoteness, the Dayaks reestablished their practice of ritualistic headhunting. A man could not marry without presenting his future father- in-law with an enemy's head. No building could be constructed without placing an enemy's head in the foundation to ward off evil spirits.

Getting to distant Long Nawang was not easy. We had to fly our crew and gear in on helicopters, but one tank of fuel wouldn't get us there. We needed somewhere to refuel. At the halfway point, we set up a storage depot in a clearing of the thick rainforest. Using my rusty math skills, I calculated how many 55-gallon fuel drums we would need to stockpile at the depot and in Long Nawang to cover eight trips to and from the village over the three-week period.

At our destination, in the center of the rainforest, we set up an encampment that was right out of **Swiss Family Robinson**. Our toilet was a hole in the floor of a shed we built over the river. Water was piped in from 100 yards away using split halves of bamboo. At night, the sounds of the jungle, with its millions of insects buzzing and chirping, snakes lurking, and unnamed animals grunting and groaning, were terrifying, exhilarating, and nearly deafening. The crew members who were afraid to use the facilities chose constipation over comfort. Every morning I knew it was time to get up when Pat Gilluly walked noisily down the bathroom path and over the rickety rope bridge wearing nothing but his towel. Meanwhile, Rae Troutman would be sipping coffee and wearing a red plastic clown nose to amuse the native kids.

On the day we filmed a scene of our five-year-old subject paddling his dugout up the Nawang River, I had to insert a new roll of film by opening the camera and laying the lid on the dry leaves around my feet. When I popped it back on and gazed through the viewfinder to focus for the next shot, I jumped back and screamed. A gigantic 30-foot-tall

dinosaur was staring back at me. Brad and Pat leapt to my side. "What's wrong?" they asked. "A dinosaur," I shouted. When they looked into the viewfinder, they recoiled, too . . . until we realized that a small lizard had crawled into the lid while it had been on the ground and had been magnified by the lenses, terrifyingly real—and very much alive—an inch from our faces. This canny reptile had played a cruel but hilarious joke on these out-of-town city slickers.

An Unexpected Visitor

Six days after our arrival, a missionary plane landed and we were shocked to see another white person stroll into camp: actor Richard Gere! He was traveling with his Brazilian girlfriend, Sylvia, who was straight out of a fashion magazine. Since I'd worked briefly on **An Officer and a Gentleman** and was friends with the film's director, Taylor Hackford, I tried to be as welcoming as I could be in this difficult location. They had flown in from Bali to see the canoe races we had helped to organize and film for that day's Indonesian Independence Day celebration. Clad in shorts, tank tops, and sandals, and carrying a small shoulder bag, they had no food, no extra clothing, no rain gear, and apparently no plans. Gere told us that they had just come from a visit with the Dalai Lama, though, so I imagine they were feeling pretty invincible.

Our production manager, Ira Abrams, introduced them to our homemade jungle shower that drew water from a nearby stream. I had two women villagers boiling water all day long so the crew wouldn't get sick from tainted water. Every morning, I invited Gere to our kitchen for some of the oatmeal and coffee Barbara had prepared for the team. I asked how long he thought he'd be staying.

"A few days," he said. "Eat, then," I said, "and good luck."

Gere wanted to take Sylvia for a walk through the rainforest to the next village, Nawang Baru, about a four-hour trek. I suggested leech socks for the muddy paths but he wasn't interested. They returned that night covered in blood-sucking leeches. After two days he announced that he was desperate, he had to get out. "My girlfriend is driving me crazy with her crying and her depression," he said. "She hates the rainforest!"

When I told him that I wouldn't have a crew helicopter going out for another week, he asked to bum a ride off the military helicopter that was leaving the next day. I explained that I would never allow our crew to fly in it because the pilots were inexperienced and the Sikorsky was old. It was used only to ferry fuel, supplies, and equipment. He didn't care.

The next morning it was raining, but by 10 a.m. the clouds had parted and we started filming. At 11 a.m., I heard the helicopter depart. That night, our crew's anthropologist, Tim Jessop, used our shortwave radio (we had a kid climb a 100-feet-tall tree to mount our antenna) to

check with the airport in the coastal city of Balikpapan and confirm that the helicopter had arrived. The airport had not seen hide nor hair of it.

I knew that meant trouble and was worried sick. We learned that they had flown into another rainstorm and the poorly trained pilots had gotten lost, used up all their fuel, and been forced to set down in a small clearing in the middle of the thick rainforest. When I saw him again, the helicopter captain told me that two hours after they landed, Gere's girlfriend was crying so much that he and his crew demanded she get out of the helicopter and take shelter underneath it. Gere was chivalrous enough to join her for most of the night.

I sent our private helicopter with its well-trained pilot to fly a grid-patterned search path. By five the following afternoon he'd located them, dropped off some fuel, and transported the unhappy pair to Balikpapan. Our pilot later recounted the end of the story.

"When we left them at the airport," he said, "Gere and the girl ran for the first commercial plane they spotted leaving. They actually stopped it on the tarmac and climbed aboard. He must have used his big smile to get a seat." We were all relieved that they were safe.

Diving for Dummies

For the seventh and final island child, we hired 18-year-old Sandy Vulukora, who was studying oceanography in Jakarta. We then traveled to an isolated atoll in the Banda Sea called Lucipara to film underwater. As a surfer, I was completely comfortable in the water, but as soon as I'd do a dive, I'd start thinking of shots and camera angles and forget about being underwater. That flaw would almost kill me.

Thankfully, I'd engaged the talented Ron Taylor, who had filmed the ravishing and elegant underwater scenes in Randal Kleiser's **The Blue Lagoon**, to join the team. We began 21 days of glorious diving.

(FACING PAGE AND RIGHT) The "circle-of-life" Dani war dance, Papua New Guinea, performed one final time for our cameras.

One afternoon, I was waiting to get a shot of Ron and Brad Ohlund carrying flashlights down to a 110-foot vertical underwater wall of colorful coral. I was positioned at the mouth of a cave stabilizing the huge IMAX camera on a three-foot-high undersea boulder. It was a stunning scene because a couple of eight-foot reef sharks were circling nearby. But Brad and Ron had to get new batteries for their flashlights, and the wait put me at a depth of 110 feet for longer than was safe.

They made it back and I got the shot, but by that time nitrogen had seeped into my brain and given me a high called narcosis, the "rapture of the deep." Without enough oxygen, my brain was functioning at 80 percent capacity. It was like being drunk, but not nearly as much fun. I also was almost out of air but was too silly to know it. As we headed to the surface, I handed the huge camera to Ron and Brad. Big mistake! Without that extra weight, I was ascending way too quickly. By the time I reached the surface, I could feel my extremities tingling.

"You're very lucky," the ship's doctor said after examining me. "If you were fat, you'd have a serious case of the bends." Because I'm so thin, the nitrogen bubbles had dissolved in my bloodstream and escaped my tissues. The doctor gave me aspirin and wished me luck. I felt like an idiot. No, I was an idiot. But at least I was alive.

After another day of filming on our underwater sequence in the Banda Sea from our inflatable boat, Ron Taylor spotted in the distance about 100 animals splashing the surface and wanted to check it out. Then the churning water began to move toward us. "I don't know what they are, but let's meet them!" Ron yelled as he turned the boat into their path. We'd already finished a full roll of film so we had nothing left to shoot the experience to come, but we were excited. As the creatures charged toward us, all we could do was wait. "What are they?" asked Brad. "Don't know, but they're big!" Ron shouted, "Let's get underwater and have them go over us." We grabbed our snorkels and all four of us jumped in, swimming directly into their path. I held my breath and dove down 15 feet. I was shocked by the squealing, high-pitched sound of all these animals vocalizing. These powerful animals swam like darts quickly over our heads in mere seconds, faster than any animal I'd ever seen. The sound became deafening. They loved to talk. Or scream! When the last passed overhead we all rose to the surface. "What were they?" I yelled to Ron. "Big pilot whales—I've never seen that many before," Ron joyously answered. We were all elated. Smiles, chatter— we yelled, hooted, laughed. After we clambered back into the Zodiac, Ron said, "No one will believe us, but still I can't wait to tell Keith [Shackleton] and Peter [Scott]," both of whom had been with us on the dive boat. These two English gentlemen were relatives of the famous South Pole explorers Ernest Shackleton and Robert Falcon Scott. They were in the country to snorkel, count fish, and enjoy their sixties with lay-science observations of these rarely dived Indonesian waters. I had been having dinner with them and their witty wives every night because they told such amazing stories. These expert ichthyologists seemed to know every imaginable species so we looked forward to describing our pilot whale experience. Sure enough, when we reported back to the fish experts they didn't seem impressed with our powerful sea life encounter—they completely denied it had happened, teasing us sarcastically. I knew that they were really, really jealous! Over the weeks we were together with these four Britons visiting the pristine, world-class dive spots now considered bucket-list worthy, like Lombok, Komodo, Roté, Banda, and Cowo Cowo, they never let go of that jealousy, continually asking: "Young man, are you resolutely certain that you saw that many pilot whales?"

Never Let Your Guard Down

After 60 straight days of success on this film, Brad and I had one last shot to do, and it was underwater. Ron and his wife, Valerie, had gone home. I wanted a shot of the unique and colorful starfish at Ambon. Because it was our last day, our safety protocols were lax and as a result the IMAX camera was not properly sealed—my mistake. When I began the dive, all of a sudden the camera started pulling me down. The housing was filling with water! It now felt like it was filled with lead!

Fortunately, the sandy bottom was only 25 feet down, where the housing and I landed with a *thud*! The air was bubbling out of one of the housing's seals so I knew it wasn't quite full of water yet. I lifted the camera case and pushed hard off the bottom, kicking frantically for the surface. Brad was on the boat as I pushed the 300-pound camera over the gunnels. How did I manage to do that? I do not know. Adrenaline must have been racing through my body because I had strength I never knew I had before. Later that day we disassembled the entire flooded camera, oiled each part, and reassembled it. Thankfully the camera was still working, but we learned a lesson about making simple mistakes at the end of a shoot.

Another example of this syndrome was when our friend, hang glider Bob Wills, was killed while shooting a television commercial. He had been working with a novice action director and they'd finished all their required shots. Then the director called for one more: an unplanned and, frankly, unnecessary scene. They literally winged it. This ill-planned shot cost Bob his life when his kite flew through unexpected rotor wash from the helicopter filming him. A fatal mistake.

I've always tried to set an example for my crew to be extra safe and prepared—particularly when you think you're done, and especially on the final day of a shoot—because that's when you're most likely to let down your guard and make an error that could be very costly, even tragic.

(FACING PAGE) Stand-up paddling warriors in Papua New Guinea.

Shooting in the Soviet Union

SURF

HOLLYWOOD

IMAX ENTERTAINMENT

MISSION

"Throughout the night, we chatted, drank wine and fell in love with the spirit of the Russian people. We were able to see that, regardless of where we're from, we are all alike. There really is no reason not to get along."

In 1986, we were selected by the Museum Film Network, a group of 16 science museums with IMAX theaters, to create a film that would explore the highest levels of human performance. **To The Limit** was conceived as a revolutionary science-based film that would tell the story of how the human body responds to challenges during peak effort. Using advanced endoscopic and microscopic photography, we'd show how the heart, lungs, blood vessels, bones, our senses, and our brain can work together and even improve themselves to produce a masterful performance.

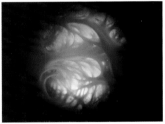

To personalize this science story, I wanted to film the best ballet in the world. Barbara and I spent a year in search of a dancer who could leap to extreme heights. We attended performances by every company that came through Los Angeles. We traveled to New York to see the American Ballet Theater and the New York City Ballet. By the end, we had seen 12 companies and still hadn't found our dancer. One night, when I was in Colorado shooting the skiing sequence for the film, Barbara called me in a tizzy: "I think I found her! You have to see her leaps. She's only 22 years old and I think she's the best in the world."

(FACING PAGE) Nina Ananiashvili dances the playful, active stepping section in *Don Quixote*, one of the 20 dances we studied. As perhaps the best ballerina in the world in 1988, we chose her to demonstrate how practice and repetition leads to precise performance–the amazing human body adapts, changes, and improves if we treat it well. In 2002, Nina was named "Best Ballerina of the Year" by *Dance Magazine*. *(ABOVE)* IMAX view of the miraculous heart.

I was delighted to hear the news, but daunted by the prospect of shooting her dancing for the Bolshoi in Moscow. "This won't be easy," I predicted.

In the 1950s and 1960s, the cold war, the Cuban Missile Crisis, and the space race created competition between the United States and the Soviet Union that could not have been more fierce. By the 1980s, threats and even Black Sea ship provocations had upped the tension. The election of right-wing president Ronald Reagan was the icing on the cake. Reagan increased military spending and began a second cold war. Then in 1980, our Olympic team boycotted the Moscow Games to protest the Soviet invasion of Afghanistan; four years later, the Soviet Union responded by boycotting the Olympics in Los Angeles. Reagan ratcheted up the hostility by calling the Soviet Union the "Evil Empire," imposing economic sanctions, and, in 1986, justifiably criticizing the Soviets' inept handling of the Chernobyl nuclear disaster and the accidental downing of a Korean Air Lines passenger jet.

I knew that, even with the help of our executive producer, *Nova* (the PBS science series) and powerhouse partners Dr. Jeffrey Kirsch, Paula Apsell, and Susanne Simpson, getting permission to film during this fraught moment would be no easy feat. But Barbara, undaunted, would get up at 5:30 every morning and begin calling the Russian Embassy in Washington, D.C., hoping that one day they would surely answer their phone. After months she got through, and we set up a meeting with the cultural attaché in Los Angeles. He gave us all the yeses we wanted, but they proved to be empty words.

Then we met with the Bolshoi's artistic director, Yuri Grigorovich, in Washington, D.C.. More yeses and shots of vodka, but no result other than a pleasant buzz. We were witnessing a glimmer of why Communism was doomed to fail: It was a system in which no one was willing to take

(ABOVE) Derek, Ludmilla, Nina, and me. (BELOW) In perhaps the most dramatic editorial cut in all of IMAX documentary films, in **To The Limit** we juxtaposed about 3,000 New York Marathon runners with blood cells moving in the same direction in a human capillary, a shocking and thought-provoking moment.

a risk for fear of being blamed by a party leader. It was far safer to say "yes, of course," and then delay until the problem—in this case, our entry and filming request—went away on its own.

Frustrated and depressed, I called Mike Hoover, a producer of astonishing climbing films. Mike had worked for years with Occidental Petroleum's Armand Hammer, who had cultivated privileged access inside the Soviet Union. Mike was sure that Hammer would love this challenge, so he introduced me to Derek Hart, who worked with Hammer and happened to be a ballet dancer and filmmaker. I had admired and studied Derek's work, especially his documentary, **Backstage at the Kirov**. Derek promised to get Hammer to call Mikhail Gorbachev, then leader of the Soviet Union, to get our permit rolling. Amazingly, two days later, Hammer came through and, after a year of legwork, Derek and I were suddenly Moscow-bound. We scouted sites and planned the logistics for a three-week shoot, including two days of filming on the Bolshoi stage. I would be able to shoot with 25 dancers and a staff of 35 stagehands and cleaning ladies. Incredible!

How Do You Cajole the World's Best Ballerina?

At 4:30 a.m. on the first day of shooting, our team arrived at St. Basil's Cathedral, next to the Kremlin and Lenin's Tomb. It would take us an hour to set up 40 feet of dolly track and a crane to carry the IMAX camera. We got ready in the dark, lighting the location to add more beauty to an already beautiful spot. We waited for our star ballerina, Nina Ananiashvili, to arrive at 7:30. When she showed up at 9:30 a.m., I thanked her for coming and suggested we do the shot quickly before the lighting conditions changed. I got a B+ shot, but the lighting at 7:30 would have made it an A+.

I sat Nina down on the curb along with Derek and Ludmilla, our dancer-translator, to talk privately. I didn't want to make a big deal about it, but production tardiness had to be addressed.

"Nina, we were ready for you at 7:30. Did you have difficulty getting here? Should we send a driver?" I needed to make sure we could correct the problem for future work days.

Nina said, "I am sorry, but my schedule with the Bolshoi has me beginning at 10 a.m. for a four-hour performance day. For me to come earlier doesn't make sense, since I'm only paid 16 rubles per day."

I was amazed that the world's best ballerina—the Bolshoi's most famous dancer at that time—was being paid only $25 a day. And, deceptively, our contract with the Bolshoi guaranteed eight hours of her time each day. I asked her: "What if I personally give you special gifts every day that you arrive on time and work longer hours? Would you then think it was worth it?" She thought it would be.

That evening I went into the Friendship Store at our hotel, a place where Russians could not make purchases. I brought Nina a bottle of

Chanel No. 5, my own mother's favorite, with my personal cash that I'd brought with me to buy gifts for friends back home, and gave it to her the next morning. She hugged me for nearly a minute. I said, "Nina, we need you for another three days. I promise that every day my personal gifts to you will get better and better!"

I felt awkward offering these gifts from my own funds, but I learned that this was the way things got done in Moscow. When individuals are not paid what they deserve, they learn to compensate. People have a will to survive.

Thwarting the KGB

Every day of production brought surprises. For us, it was exciting—and a bit like playing James Bond. Back then, everything was secretive and government controlled. People had few rights, little food, and limited freedom of travel or thought. For filming, we brought walkie-talkies so that we could communicate on location. Turns out the KGB, the state's secret police, didn't like people talking to each other.

After five days of filming in various Moscow locations, we moved on to the practice stage at the Bolshoi Ballet Academy. Penny Marshall of television fame joined us there. She was alone in the country and, understandably, felt the need to be around some Americans. She was keeping all of us in laughter and good spirits until, suddenly, in barged a KGB officer, yelling in Russian. The young officer, it turned out, had been scouring Moscow trying to locate the "subversives" who were using American-made Motorola walkie-talkies and who no doubt were intent on overthrowing the regime. Eugenie, one of our Soviet production managers, asked him why it took so long to find us, since we'd delivered our daily schedule to the government months earlier.

"Well," he said, "I have no car, so I had to listen in, locate the signal, plot it on a map, and take the bus to an area away from the signal so I could triangulate your position. By the time a bus got me to that spot, you had gone somewhere else. Very suspicious behavior."

Eugenie showed him our government permits, which included the right to use walkie-talkies. He then invited the officer to watch a ballet rehearsal with five beautiful ballerinas, including Nina. This calmed him. Later that afternoon, he enjoyed the lunch we served and the vodka we poured. Penny also tried to get him to laugh, using her broken Russian. The two of them sat for three hours watching us film a lovely sequence with Nina, her coach, and the team.

The First Worker's Strike at the Bolshoi

Days later, at the Bolshoi Theatre, we filmed elements from the romantic ballet *Giselle*, which I chose because it features eleven haunting ballerinas in long white tulle dresses. The fabric itself is

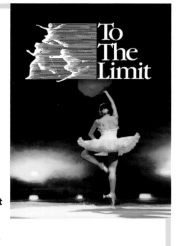

To The Limit

FILMED IN: 15 PERFORATION/70MM

RELEASE DATE: 1989

NARRATED BY: Richard Kiley

FEATURING: Tony Yaniro, Maria Walliser, Nina Ananiashvili

To The Limit was featured in more than 70 theaters internationally and viewed by more than 14 million people in its first 6 years.

Grand Prix du Public— La Géode Euromax Film Festival

"The images are stunning. **To The Limit** is more exciting than the Indiana Jones picture."

—GENE SISKEL, "SISKEL & EBERT"

Making *To The Limit*
2:16   #16

mesmerizing to watch as it wafts in sync with the dancers' sinuous moves. Nina's performance was spectacular, as was that of our male dancer, Irek Mukhamedov. They executed stunning glissades, classical pirouettes, and soaring grand jetés as we captured in slow motion, with our new camera, the best ballet form in the world.

Everything was going smoothly on the stage until the middle of the sixth take. Suddenly the fire curtain came crashing down. *Clunk!* I was filming from the front row of the Bolshoi Theatre balcony and I yelled out, "Hey, what happened?!" I thought it was a stagehand-cueing mistake or an equipment failure. My interpreter from the Bolshoi, a delightful former ballerina, came running.

"I am so embarrassed, Mr. Greg. This has never happened to us before. The workers are calling a strike. They will not work until they get paid in cash. They love working for you, but they have been cheated in the past by film studios."

I had to laugh; the people were finally expressing themselves! Gorbachev's new policies were changing things. These workers were feeling that new power. But, Eugenie and Alec informed me that it would take a lot of time to work this out using "proper" channels, and we could not extend our shoot because the Bolshoi stage was booked tight. We were stuck!

"It's Saturday and the banks are closed," I said to my interpreter. "How can we get money to pay in cash?" Eugenie pulled me aside. "How much cash you have, Greg? In pocket. Right now."

Was this a shakedown? I carried about $2,000, but that was for our crew's expenses.

"What exactly do you have in mind?" I asked quietly. He told me he knew a place on a Saturday where he could exchange trusted American greenback dollars for lower-worth but much more useful Soviet rubles.

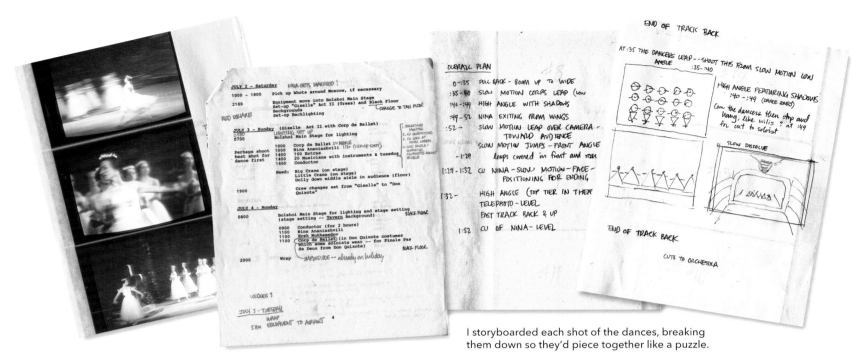

I storyboarded each shot of the dances, breaking them down so they'd piece together like a puzzle.

"You mean black market?" I whispered. Eugenie nodded, held up one finger, and then five. I took that to mean he'd be able to multiply our sought-after dollars by a factor that would turn my two grand US into ten grand local. It would be enough to pay everyone. Since it was our only option, I pulled out my cash.

"Okay," I said, cautiously, "but on one condition. We tell everyone in the company, all the stagehands and dancers, exactly what you are going to do." I wanted to make sure that this little deal was well known to the others in case we never saw Eugenie again.

We assembled all 60 people on the stage and I made a short but impassioned speech about the importance of this project. By the end, many had tears in their eyes. Eugenie left the stage to fierce applause. He jumped on his motor scooter and within two hours we had a six-inch stack of rubles to count out for the workers, who lined up in front of a cardboard table. This was capitalism at its finest. Each worker came up to me with a huge smile and shook my hand.

After we'd finished the ballet sequence, I still needed a couple of scenic views of Moscow. For a dramatic sunrise shot, our American and Russian team gathered on the roof of one of the Stalinist buildings next to the river to get a night time-lapse shot looking down at the city. Knowing the KGB couldn't bug us at this remote spot, Iriana and Eugenie, our Soviet team, opened up to us for the first time. Iriana asked whether it was true that everyone in America owns a gun and shoots each other if they get angry, and Eugenie added that they read in *Pravda* that we're irresponsible cowboys. We laughed and asked some equally naïve questions. That peaceful, joyous, and simply romantic night we learned, as Sting had sung, that the Russians love their children, too.

On the final days of the shoot, I purchased with my own funds and gave to Nina a VHS cassette player and a 40-inch Sony Trinitron television, both forbidden items, as the KGB did not allow its citizens to see uncensored Western life. Nina broke down in tears and I figured that she was happy because she'd get great use out of them. Wrong.

"Greg," she said, sniffling, "these gifts I especially love because I can sell them on the black market. Even wealthy Communist leaders can't buy these, so I could get $15,000 US. Do you understand? This will be my parents' retirement fund for the rest of their lives. Thank you so much. I have loved working with your team, not just because of this, but because of, well, everything." Five years later, Nina defected to London to dance, then joined the ABT in New York, where she finally was paid a fair wage. Today, she is back in her native Georgia, which became an independent country in 1991, revitalizing their national ballet program, and inspiring kids to become the next Nina.

To The Limit paved the way for science museums to use IMAX films as teaching tools. Its visual power allowed audience members to look at health issues differently; but for me, it convinced me that we needed to continue to cast subjects like Nina. Bill Shaw of IMAX Corporation told me that **To The Limit** was the first IMAX film in which he felt emotionally moved by a character. At that moment, I realized that I had finally achieved my goal of making my characters look real on that super-detailed, unforgiving IMAX screen.

(CLOCKWISE FROM TOP LEFT) Nina dancing as Giselle; our team waits patiently for Nina to show up at St. Basil's Cathedral, Red Square; at the Ballet Academy, where 12-year-olds learn flexibility; Nina checks the scene.

A Love Poem to the Sea

SURF

HOLLYWOOD

IMAX ENTERTAINMENT

MISSION

"No matter where on Earth you live, with every drop of water you drink, every breath you take, you're connected to the sea. Health for the ocean means health for us. The blue heart of the planet keeps us alive."

–DR. SYLVIA EARLE, OCEANOGRAPHER,
ONE WORLD ONE OCEAN BOARD MEMBER AND ADVISOR

Ever since I sat on the beach while my dad lifeguarded in Corona del Mar, the ocean has had an intense effect on me. Yes, it's big, covering 71 percent of the earth's surface, but its hold on me went beyond physical size. Whenever I was away from the ocean, I became less focused and more anxious and would find any way I could to get back to it. I was in love with its awesome beauty and mystical allure.

I had a visceral need to communicate that powerful connection, so in 1993, I decided to make **The Living Sea**. Though I was open to starting the process using my own funds, I hired John Jacobsen and Jeanie Stahl of White Oak Associates to help explore other funding options. They recommended that we meet with the developers of the Nauticus museum in Norfolk, Virginia, a large facility with a planned 200-seat theater. Nauticus had budgeted $2 million for a film and ours was going to cost $5 million, so John and I convinced them that we should team up. We would make the full film and also create a powerful 20-minute version for them to show in their fabulous theater. Nauticus would get a better movie, exclusive rights to it in the state of Virginia, and a return on the distribution of the film elsewhere. They were stoked!

Human Ingenuity to the Rescue

To showcase the incredible forces at work in one interconnected ocean—tides, waves, currents and subaquatic life—**The Living Sea**

(FACING PAGE) The violent wave at Mavericks, near Half Moon Bay, California.

would feature sequences from around the world. We decided to focus on the US Coast Guard's storm rescue boat operations. Training exercises take place at the mouth of Washington State's Columbia River, at Cape Disappointment, so named for the hundreds of ships that have run aground there. A quarter-mile-long sandbar produced by silt from the river causes big north swells to break and provides trainees an opportunity to learn to pilot the boats in heavy seas.

These rescue boats are amazing and unique. They can withstand 50-foot surf, but they also can flip upside down and then right themselves without taking on water. At the same time, they have the capacity to rescue up to 10 people and keep them safe and secure, seat-belted in a watertight compartment below deck.

The captain and the pilot, decked out in helmets, full-coverage dry suits, gloves, boots, and harnesses, drove the boat while standing on an elevated bridge. They were strapped in at two places, so that if the boat flipped they would not be washed overboard. This rescue boat was ready for serious action and I couldn't wait to join them.

We filmed with the captain of the training team, Mark Cady, for four days in five-foot surf and good weather conditions and got great footage; but the waves weren't big enough to warrant shooting from our rented helicopter. On the fifth day, in what Brad Ohlund says was a prime example of MacGilli-luck (a term he famously coined), we awoke to 15-foot surf, the biggest swell they had seen all year. We readied the camera and fastened it to the rear of the boat in a waterproofed housing. The special mounting had required six months of work and more time for approvals from the federal government. Two of the cadets checked out the surf from a crow's nest and approached Captain Cady. "Sir," one of them said, "we don't think it is advisable to go out into these conditions.

We believe it would put us all in danger and the boats at risk."

Cady replied, "Son, this is what these boats are made for and this is what you are here to experience. We're lucky to have these gigantic waves today." It was music to my ears.

I got into my safety outfit and clipped in alongside the captain. Brad left for the airport to strap into the Tyler Monster Mount that we'd built for **To Fly!** with our IMAX camera in the side hatch of the helicopter. When the boat reached the big surf, we skirted some of the waves by moving into the channel, but then spied a 20-foot monster coming from the outside.

Captain Cady barked, "Come around! Let's crash through it."

(FACING PAGE) Nothing illustrates the delicateness of the ocean system and its ecology more than a swarm of jellyfish, each swimming up and down in the water column in their daily chase of the sun. We chose Sting's tender song "Fragile" to accent this message of interdependence. (ABOVE) Tough boat, tough crew.

The 300-horsepower engines muscled us up the face of the wave, which had already broken. Our boat shot into the air and then crashed down the back side of the wave with a gigantic splash. It felt as if we'd rocketed 10 vertical feet. The helicopter was right above us and Brad radioed that he'd gotten a great shot. We probably repeated this feat 10 more times with both IMAX cameras capturing the action.

One of the cadets yelled, "Sir, we have a warning light for hull damage! We'd better check it out." This time the cadet had it right. Some rivets had loosened on one of the hull's panels. We were slowly taking on water and agreed that it would be wise to head back to the dock. All in all, everything worked out great: The cameras ran properly, and Captain Cady was delighted.

"I wasn't a believer at first," he said, "but I think you've got a great sequence that's going to make our Coast Guard outfit very proud."

These unique rescue boats are stationed in over 170 coastal locations around the United States to help protect our shores and rescue sailors who have been washed overboard in heavy seas. Over the past 50 years, they've saved hundreds of people and tens of thousands of dollars whenever they tow a stranded boat back to safety.

The Living Sea

FILMED IN: 15 PERFORATION/70MM

RELEASE DATE: 1995

NARRATED BY: Meryl Streep

MUSIC BY: Sting

SCORE BY: Steve Wood

Inducted into the IMAX Hall of Fame, voted in by members of the Giant Screen Cinema Association, September 2007

Nominated for an Academy Award for Best Documentary Short Subject, 1995

Gold Award—Worldfest-Houston International Independent Film & Video Festival

Gold Camera Award, nominated for Best of Festival—U.S. International Film & Video Festival

Certificate of Merit—The Chicago International Film Festival

The highest grossing documentary film (of any format—15/70 or 35mm) of 1995 and 1996.

"No movie released this year is likely to contain more spectacular or astonishing images than **The Living Sea** . . . a truly ravishing experience . . . like the best documentaries, it's a potent plea for preserving the environment."
—*CHICAGO TRIBUNE*

 Making *The Living Sea* 2:20 #17

Wind Power in Palau

For a year, we traveled the globe, photographing whales in Maine, 30-foot tides in Nova Scotia, big-wave surfing in Hawaii, and more. To round out the picture, I needed one last transformative tale set in a magical location. My choice was the rarely seen South Pacific islands of Palau. My friend Paul Atkins had shown me pictures of Palau's unforgettable green, mushroom-shaped islands that balance in the crystal-clear Philippine Sea.

Part of the film's story focused on a young oceanographer's trip to an island lake that was home to millions of jellyfish. Howard Hall, Bob Cranston, Mark Thurlow, and Brad Ohlund had already photographed the underwater scenes. Now I just needed the air-to-air scenes showing marine biologist Laura Martin getting to the lake.

The seaplane was owned by ex-US Air Force pilot Spike Nasmyth, who had spent six years as a prisoner at the Hanoi Hilton (with John McCain) during the Vietnam War. After seven days of flying with him, I could see that his wartime experience at the helm of an F-4 Phantom fighter jet had turned him into one of the finest pilots I'd met. But I needed someone else to pilot the camera plane from which we'd shoot Spike's seaplane landing with Laura inside. Coincidentally, two Air Canada pilots happened to be staying at our hotel. They were

(ABOVE) **The Living Sea** storyboards I crudely drew so the crew could prepare.

(BELOW) Jack Tankard mounts the IMAX camera on the wing in Palau as Shaun and Meghan pepper him with questions.

touring the islands in a rented single engine Cessna, and unlike the local pilots, spoke fluent English. For air-to-air shooting, communications are critical, so I hired them for a day, had the doors of the Cessna removed, and put my dear friend and stellar photographer, Jack Tankard, in the back with me to assist while the two pilots took the controls.

Because of how we lost Jim, I am super cautious about aerial photography, so before we took off, we went over the seven shots I wanted. As we prepped, a 30 mph wind began blowing. It was steady, so we figured it wouldn't impact the stability of the camera. After an hour of shooting, it became clear that these big commercial jet pilots had never flown formation before. And that wasn't all.

For my sixth shot of the seven, our camera was tracking the seaplane as it landed on the water. We were 100 feet up. Looking through the camera's viewfinder as I photographed the scene, my eye was drawn to something that looked a lot like a tree. But wait, weren't we over the water?

Shocked, I looked up to see an island cliff and even more trees filling the front windscreen. We were just 20 feet from crashing! Thankfully, our Canadian pilots looked up as well, then jerked the controls full right to avoid certain disaster. We had no more than a couple of feet to spare.

I'm sure Jack's heart was in his throat, just like mine. We exchanged a "holy shit" look as I spoke slowly and calmly over the headset. "Climb to 2,000 feet. Let's finish off this seventh shot and go home."

Back at the main airport in Koror, we talked it out. The crosswind had blown our plane sideways over the island. Because the

(ABOVE) On our way by sea plane to Jellyfish Lake, a closed off place where Laura Martin (BELOW) could study jellyfish.

In Palau, I featured a family story of Palauans Francis Toribiong and his kids.

pilots were intent on keeping the seaplane in the center of the shot, they were not looking ahead. Big mistake. One pilot should have been looking sideways, tracking the seaplane's position, while the other should have looked straight ahead. We said our goodbyes and I walked to the commercial side of the airport to greet Barbara, Meghan, 11, and Shaun, 14, who had just flown 23 hours to join us on location. "How's it going?" Barbara asked. My knees were still a little shaky and all I could muster was a partial truth. "We're getting great shots."

Released in February 1995, the film became the fourth most successful IMAX film ever, with a worldwide box office gross of $125 million. Despite that close call on Palau, **The Living Sea** turned out to be one of my favorite films and best family experiences ever.

> **"I have seen The Living Sea and personally gauged it as the best nature movie I have ever seen."**
>
> —DR. BERND WÜRSIG, DIRECTOR, MARINE MAMMAL RESEARCH PROGRAM, TEXAS A&M AT GALVESTON, AND SCIENTIFIC ADVISOR ON **DOLPHINS**

Don't Dream It; Do It

by Stephen Judson

Writing and editing the film **The Living Sea** will always be a great memory because, even more than most MFF movies, it was truly made in the editing. Not only was the imagery inspiring, but Greg had a very simple mantra for the film: Make people fall in love with the sea. To me, rescuing the ocean with a film was a lovely pipe dream. But Greg had

no doubt that if he could make people fall in love with the sea, there would be a real and lasting impact. It would be one of Greg's first movies designed to protect the environment, but certainly not his last.

Editing is an obsessive, intensely focused process that saps one's mental energy. To replenish those reserves, I rely on that revered substance: coffee. One morning, while shaping **The Living Sea**, I emerged from my editing cave for a cup of joe, hoping to exact sympathy from anyone who'd listen. Greg fell victim. I explained that I was editing each sequence to a great piece of music (and hoping to buy rights later) and that each music cue was great by itself. But the musical mixture made the film feel disjointed. Wouldn't it be great, I said, if we could use the music of just one artist like Sting or Paul Simon throughout the movie?

I was kvetching. It's what editors do. We blow off steam and go back to our cave to resume the process, reinvigorated. It never crossed my mind that using a single artist might be a possibility. But early in my caffeinated diatribe, Greg's gaze wandered and his mind went elsewhere. It was literally the next day that I learned that he was already on the hunt to sign up Sting.

All of us have fun dreaming up ideas, but we rarely take it beyond the what-if stage. Not Greg. He's quick to go beyond dreaming, quick to ask: Why not? That impulse has powered his company.

The optimism of **The Living Sea** went beyond Greg's love for the ocean. I sometimes felt, in our first decade working together, that Greg was channeling the spirit of Jim Freeman. Nowhere was that more evident than during the making of **The Living Sea**, where Greg included a surfing sequence in Hawaii filmed from the air and gloriously choreographed for the giant screen. It was vintage Jim Freeman, a joyful and exuberant celebration of his talent and spirit, soaring across the ocean with the greatest of ease. Greg and I never spoke about Jim's presence. We didn't have to. I knew what was going on. The sequence called for music that went deeper than happy. It needed something spiritual and quietly joyful to express this elegant rapture, this euphoric dance with the sea. I chose "Love is the Seventh Wave" by Sting.

There is a deeper world than this
That you don't understand
There is a deeper world than this
Tugging at your hand
Every ripple on the ocean
Every leaf on every tree
Every sand dune in the desert
Every power we never see
There is a deeper wave than this
Swelling in the world

(ABOVE LEFT AND RIGHT) Shooting with the huge IMAX camera in the impact zone at Banzai Pipeline was a daunting challenge. (BELOW) Hobie Cat joy, one of the many benefits of a healthy ocean.

CHAPTER 17

Flying into the Eye of a Hurricane

by Brad Ohlund, Director of Photography

"If I roll too early, I miss the arrival into the eye. If I roll too late, I miss the buildup. I make an educated guess and roll the camera 30 seconds before I think we will penetrate the eyewall. Just then, the winds diminish slightly, the sky gets a little brighter, and 30 seconds later we emerge into an utterly peaceful, sun-filled cirque; a heavenly, cotton-walled nest. A wall this well defined is beautiful to behold."

—BRAD OHLUND

"Gentlemen, we have a situation up here, and I'm going to need your help getting us home tonight." The voice coming over the intercom was that of the pilot of *Miss Piggy*, the P-3 aircraft assigned to NOAA Corps, the team that flies into hurricanes to gain predictive information. How strong will it be? Where will it hit land? Because hurricanes are dangerous killers that destroy lives and billions of dollars of property, understanding the physics and mechanics of these massive storms helps NOAA mitigate the impacts. Science at its best.

MacGillivray Freeman Films had become the leader in communicating true stories to the public through IMAX films. We'd learned how to explain complex science to 6-year-olds and 86-year-olds, while making it exciting and sometimes thrilling. We'd done so film after film, resulting in more students wanting to become scientists. To us, these films had important missions.

The boss, Greg MacGillivray, had tasked Jack Tankard and me to go down to Tampa, Florida, where we were to report to MacDill Air Force Base. The mission: Fly into the eye of a hurricane and film it from the inside with IMAX cameras, showing the process of science and data

collection. And then, of course, come back. Shouldn't be too tough; a hurricane is only one of the most powerful forces on earth.

We were making a film entitled **Stormchasers**. It was our second film for the Museum Film Network and *Nova*, the PBS science series, with partial funding from the National Science Foundation. **Stormchasers** told the story of the dedicated scientists who defy dangers to protect us from life-threatening weather: Dr. Bob Sheets, who predicts hurricanes; Dr. Howie Bluestein, who tracks and predicts tornadoes; and, a team of meteorologists who study the biggest storm system, the monsoons in India. Each of these storms is difficult to photograph, but the hurricane was the most intense. And we wanted to get inside one! So here we were in Florida.

To our surprise, the NOAA team was not overjoyed about us being there. We had arrived just ahead of hurricane season, which runs from June 1 to November 30, and they had a lot to do. Plus, we had a few unique requests. We wanted to mount cameras all over the plane. And not little cameras; we were shooting IMAX!

The first and most important of the mount shots was out the side window of the airplane to get the you-are-there-inside-a-hurricane's-eye feeling that IMAX theater audiences have come to relish. Months before, at huge cost, we'd replaced the port with a new, unscratched window. The other mounted camera shots featured the scientists collecting data during the storm.

Our first contact was with the loadmaster. He said the mounts would have to be built, installed, and approved by his maintenance chief. "Good luck with that," he added slyly.

The maintenance chief had been with the hurricane team for a long time and he did not suffer fools. To him, we probably looked like just that: a couple of California filmmaking fools. But we had a

(FACING PAGE) After a month of chasing storms and tornado-like events every day, we finally got amazing shots like this. As dramatic filmmakers we were hoping the twister would demolish the barn, but it missed!

Stormchasers

FILMED IN: 15 PERFORATION/70MM

RELEASE DATE: 1995

NARRATED BY: Hal Holbrook

MUSIC BY: Patrick Williams

"Stormchasers really does capture the feeling, excitement, and danger of flying into the eye. My hat is off to the filmmakers."

-DR. ROBERT SHEETS, FORMER DIRECTOR OF THE NATIONAL HURRICANE CENTER, VETERAN OF OVER 100 HURRICANE EYE PENETRATIONS

Into the Eye of a Hurricane

3:13   #18

secret weapon: Jack Tankard, boy wonder. Besides being a well-respected aerial cameraman, Jack could build pretty much anything. He'd just built our Steadicam IMAX camera! I knew that he and the chief would get along. Everyone loves Jack, and sure enough, the two of them teamed up on the mounts like they'd been working together for years. The chief would complain; Jack would listen. Perfect arrangement. The mounts got built, approved, and installed and we were ready to go flying. But then . . . we waited.

We sat on the ground in Tampa and watched as two or three hurricane flights left and returned. The television crews were getting first dibs, which was logical because the dangers had to be communicated instantly to the public on TV news. But we needed to figure out a way to get in on the action. I recalled from our orientation that, on these flights, there's no food or water offered on board; you bring your own. I thought, what if we showed up with food, not just for ourselves, but for the whole crew? Everyone likes to eat. And if we had something a little better than PB&J, then maybe, just maybe. . . . So we went shopping. We bought a slew of high-quality cold cuts, cheeses, spreads, condiments, bread, and lettuce; everything needed to make someone a nice lunch. As I was trolling the aisles I noticed, among the pickles and such, small jars of caviar. I thought, what the heck. We packed it all up and were good to go—we hoped.

We checked in early the next morning with the loadmaster. This day, he said, "It's looking good for a flight." Still, he wasn't sure we'd be able to get on. Ever so casually, Jack and I said, "Well, just in case we do get on the flight, we brought fixings for everyone to make sandwiches. Utensils, paper plates, paper towels, you name it. Nothing to get in the way of flight operations."

The loadmaster turned to his colleague and said dryly, "These IMAX guys aren't such a pain after all." We shrugged and said in an off-handed way that we were the new guys in town so we wanted to

offer up a goodwill gesture. He looked at our platter of food, overflowing like a cruise ship buffet. I pointed out the roast beef, turkey, and different cheeses, mayo, adding, "we even have a couple jars of caviar."

He looked at me with a big grin and said, "I'm on today's flight and I love caviar."

We both knew what had just happened. We'd made new friends, and were now almost part of the team like the TV guys.

On our first flight we discovered that the interior of the P-3 is a standard military bare-bones operation. It is not designed for comfort. It's painted military green, shows its age, smells like grease and fuel, offers seats with no padding, is ridiculously noisy, and vibrates and shakes like crazy. And it's really cool. The old-school, spartan feel gave us the sense that we were deep into the weeds of hardcore methodological scientific research. It added an air of excitement and adventure to an already fascinating experience. They say that flying is mostly boredom bookended by a few moments of terror. These flights were just that.

Over the years, several flights ended in disaster, with the plane literally falling from the sky. The team loved telling me about one flight years before. One scientist in particular was not doing well. Even though the plane was intensely bouncing around, he unbuckled and started to head back to the toilet in the rear of the aircraft. But it was so rough he couldn't walk, so he got down on all fours and started to crawl. Then it happened. The aircraft began to drop so fast that the guy crawling down the middle of the plane was lifted off the floor and literally pinned to the roof. The plane dropped 10,000 feet. At about 1,500 feet in altitude, the cockpit crew was finally able to wrestle back control. It was close. And as the plane settled down, the scientist was rudely deposited back on the floor, where he reportedly didn't miss a beat and just continued his crawl, eventually reaching his destination and some relief.

Over the next months, we gradually were accepted as an unofficial part of the crew. The loadmaster and our new best friend even made up NOAA flight suits for Jack and me complete with name patches and the plane's *Miss Piggy* logo. (We flew in the P-3 called *Miss Piggy*. Their other backup P-3 was named *Kermit*.)

Every time we went up, we'd take our positions and strap in. This was where the fun began. The ocean's surface churned below. Foam, whitecaps, and blowing spray reminded us of the powerful and furious forces spiraling around us. We heard the navigator request a slight course correction to avoid a particularly nasty thunderstorm. And we were still five miles from the eye! Sheets of rain lashed the windows. You were violently bounced and the straps holding you in your seat were straining like a mad dog. Someone quipped, "You ain't seen nothin' yet," and suddenly, we got that feeling in our stomachs as the plane dropped like a lead balloon about 1,000 feet. Think of the worst turbulence you've experienced on a commercial flight and then multiply by ten or more. This went on for longer than we'd have liked; trust me. We felt weightless as a lightning strike flashed through the darkness, so close we could hear the thunder over the cacophony inside the plane. The propellers were screaming, the rain was pounding, and the plane was bouncing around in every direction. As we moved through the storm, wind speeds increased. Just outside the wall we felt the strongest winds yet. Amazingly, crewmembers were still moving around, securing what had come loose, assisting scientists, and preparing to launch dropsondes, expendable reconnaissance devices that are tubes filled with sensors dropped from the plane to transmit back to scientific instruments all sorts of details, including the all-important water temperature. Colder water, smaller storm; warmer water, an intensification of the storm. With these and other data points, the scientists were locating the precise center. This proved invaluable inside the National Hurricane Center, where Dr. Bob Sheets would predict when and where the eye might make landfall.

The shaking, rattling, and roaring built to a fever pitch. Then, a bit of brightness. The pound of rain fades away, and suddenly . . . you're floating. Entering the eye of a hurricane is a remarkable, indescribable sensation. It's as calm as could be and it happens in an instant. It's awe inspiring. Spiritual. You are in the loving embrace of nature. Yee-hah!

We took a beat, only to have the plane punch through the other side of the eye and return to bucking-bronco status. Shake, rattle and roll! The plane flew through the storm until it reached the outer bands, at which point it lined up for another pass through the eye from a different direction and altitude. We did this four to six times per mission. Simultaneously, Dr. Sheets used our data to track all the storms that cross the Atlantic Ocean and the Gulf of Mexico each year. When the wind reaches 70 mph, it becomes a Category 1 hurricane. As it continues to increase, the storm is upgraded, up to a Category 5 when sustained winds reach 150 mph. Katrina reached 185. Patricia, one of the strongest storms on record, registered wind speeds of over 200 mph.

Despite our successes, we still hadn't achieved the holy grail: a shot of a perfectly formed eyewall. And time was running out. Then, on a flight with Dr. Frank Marx from the National Hurricane Center directing the mission, we got lucky. As we approached the storm, from his radar visual, Frank announced that it had a pretty sharp wall.

"This one should be good," he said calmly. He told me that even after about 300 eyewall penetrations, he still gets a knot in his stomach as he approaches the wall. The stress is intense.

ETA to the eyewall: three minutes. It was getting bumpy. At every workstation, scientists and crewmembers were holding onto anything substantial to keep from being bounced around uncontrollably. Jack and I were next to the window camera. It was mounted on a steel framework that had been bolted to the floor. It was rock solid in the midst of chaos. We could see the angry clouds and rain whipping around outside. I rolled the camera to get some of this intensity. Jack and I were excited. The voice on the intercom announced that we'd be breaking out in two minutes. Now this is where IMAX differs from any other format. We only have three minutes of film in the camera, and I've already shot one minute. I rolled the camera 30 seconds before I thought we would penetrate the eyewall. Just then, the winds diminished slightly, it got brighter, and 30 seconds later we emerged into an utterly peaceful, sun-filled cirque; a heavenly, cotton-walled nest.

A wall this well-defined is beautiful to behold, but it also meant that the storm was building strength. As the boss, Greg MacGillivray, has said, "There are so many things working against you in IMAX that it's amazing we ever get anything." In this case, it turned out to be a great shot—as Greg would say, an A+.

However, the ride, and the excitement, weren't over yet. The captain had a serious concern. Flying into a hurricane was predictable. Flying home through thunderheads was not, and it was now nighttime. It would be tough to pick a path around these deadly storms. The captain told the scientists that they were going to have to help him navigate through these dangerous formations. Well, that was like offering honey to a bear. They quickly gathered around Frank's workstation. On the screen were the clouds and the position of the airplane. They would discuss for a few seconds and then, every 30 seconds or so, call out a course correction. "Ten degrees starboard," then, "20 degrees to port," and then, "Straight and level."

Only during the brief lightning flashes could we see the monstrous clouds towering over us. Otherwise, all was pitch black and unsettling. Up front, the pilots couldn't see the clouds either. And flying into a thunderhead is what pilots try to avoid! For this, our final flight, it was a long, stressful, scary trip back. We finally landed and disembarked. Because we had to get our gear off the plane, Jack and I were the last ones coming down the stairs. We saw that everyone was bunched up around the nose of the aircraft. When we joined them, it was apparent what fascinated them all. *Miss Piggy* was peppered with burn marks— the result of too many lightning strikes to count. I don't know if we were lucky to be alive or not, but who would have thought that the most dangerous part of flying into a hurricane would be getting home through a lightning storm?

After spending two years chasing storms, we had ourselves a really good film, which our team released with branching educational programs. Unfortunately, the high budget, special-effects heavy film **Twister** was scheduled to be released just months after **Stormchasers**. Though our film did well, **Twister's** portrayal of six tornadoes in one day, all artificial but very convincing, made the real thing feel less adventurous. It was yet another reminder that timing is everything.

ODE TO THE EARTH

How *Everest* Changed Our Lives

"Our cinematographers were neither war correspondents nor newsreel cameramen. Their first instinct when tragedy struck was not to grab their cameras and photograph the suffering, but to help those in need. They acted nobly, if not heroically, risking their own lives to assist climbers from other teams, climbers who were near death."

When the number of worldwide IMAX theaters approached 40 screens, I saw the potential for a new business opportunity. I asked, "What if we were to invest our own money in a production that we had a passion for, like we had done with our surfing films way back when, and then lease this passion project directly to the museums? Could we repay ourselves and, theoretically, return a profit?" This was a huge gamble; one that no one else was taking. I was alone in the decision making, but I recalled Jim and my company philosophy of "passion over profit." And, though I took comfort in how my father had enjoyed (and for the most part profited from) investing in his own house projects, my company depended on this idea succeeding. We needed to do everything right.

To guide me, I put together a Blue Ribbon Advisory Board[22] that set about polling theater customers to discover why, exactly, they liked IMAX documentaries. Were the reasons different in different cultures, for example North America versus Europe versus Asia? Mary Pat Ryan, a marketing genius at IMAX Corporation, had conducted a serious but small-scale survey that concluded that people liked IMAX films that created a "fun learning experience." She felt that all three components were critical: FUN = entertaining, LEARNING = educational, and EXPERIENCE = putting the audience in a location (you-are-there!). Using Mary Pat's findings as a basis, the advisory board created a one-page, easy-to-use questionnaire for 2,000 IMAX theater patrons at six theaters across three countries as they waited in line for the next film. Because they were waiting anyway, most spent a focused five minutes completing the survey and yielding honest, valuable data.

After tabulating the results, we felt fairly certain that we understood why our millions of customers would do a seemingly crazy thing: drive to a museum theater and pay an impressive $6 to $11 per ticket to watch a 40-minute documentary film. We learned that compared to general filmgoing audiences, our customers were older (average age 44 versus 32), much wealthier (family incomes of over $100,000 per year), and far more interested in educational rather than escapism entertainment. We also learned that the you-are-there visual experience in a nonfiction story was vital and that our fans expected us to deliver unique experiences not seen anywhere else, like on free TV.

Using this eye-opening and gold-plated data, I created a list of 10 passion projects for IMAX documentaries. Following the success in 1995 of **The Living Sea**, our first film using this new, self-financing model, we began recruiting investors and experts for our second film. This time we'd focus on the tallest mountains on earth: the Himalayas.

The story of climbing the Himalayas—with the tallest mountains projected onto the tallest screens—seemed like a perfect fit. Taking our

---

22 My first Blue Ribbon Advisory Board was composed of the best talents from the museum and theater world at the time. I was so fortunate to engage the experience of Freda Nicholson of Charlotte, Jack Kahn of Chicago, Jeff Kirsch of San Diego, David Ellis of Boston, Peter Giles of San Jose, and Jim Edwards (my high school friend, of Edwards Theatres of Newport Beach). They all helped me immensely.

(PREVIOUS PAGE) Ed and Paula Viesturs mountain-bike in Moab to condition their bodies for high-altitude climbing. (FACING PAGE) Boudhanath Stupa in Kathmandu, Nepal, a Buddhist tomb that can bring your wishes to reality.

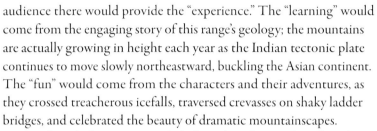

Everest

FILMED IN: 15 PERFORATION/70MM

RELEASE DATE: March 4, 1998

FEATURING: Ed Viesturs, Jamling Norgay, Araceli Segarra, Sumiyo Tsuzuki, Roger Bilham

NARRATED BY: Liam Neeson

MUSIC BY: George Harrison

SCORE BY: Steve Wood

Inducted into the IMAX Hall of Fame—September 2009

Best Picture of the Year, Best Score of the Year, Best Cinematography of the Year—1998 Maximum Image Awards

Best Marketing Campaign of the Year by a Distributor—1998 GSTA Achievement Awards

Highest grossing IMAX documentary film of all time

audience there would provide the "experience." The "learning" would come from the engaging story of this range's geology; the mountains are actually growing in height each year as the Indian tectonic plate continues to move slowly northeastward, buckling the Asian continent. The "fun" would come from the characters and their adventures, as they crossed treacherous icefalls, traversed crevasses on shaky ladder bridges, and celebrated the beauty of dramatic mountainscapes.

Though the topic seemed ideal, our board warned us of two huge obstacles. First, typical mountain climbers were mostly driven males with testosterone pushing them higher and higher for their own glorification. And second, since mothers typically make the decision to attend a museum with their children, we needed to make sure that our story would resonate with an audience of which most of the adults were female. How could we do this when most Everest climbers were male? The solution was to find three men and three women, each from a different part of the world, each with an altruistic climbing goal that went beyond merely proving themselves to be risk-takers.

Selecting Our Character Stories

Our research led us to Sherpa Jamling Norgay of India, who dreamed of climbing Everest to honor his father, Tensing Norgay, the first to summit Everest with Sir Edmund Hillary in 1953. Then we heard about Sumiyo Tsuzuki of Japan and Araceli Segarra of Spain, two respected women climbers, both of whom had long hoped to summit Everest. We made casting tapes of them, and I was immediately struck with the sincere charms of Araceli and Sumiyo. Ed Viesturs, from Seattle, Washington, was probably the strongest and best-known American climber and, coincidentally, had set a goal of climbing the mountain without supplemental oxygen. That would be an interesting story point,

but Ed came with what he felt was a liability: He was going to be married a week before the start of our expedition and, respectfully, he didn't want to leave his new wife back home. Creative minds got to work, and his wonderful bride, Paula, agreed to come with us as our base camp manager, a position she had filled on other expeditions. We rounded out the team of six with Roger Bilham, an English geologist studying the impact of Everest earthquakes on the local population. In coordination with Nepalese scientists, Roger hoped to install the third of three GPS receivers to measure the plate movement to an accuracy of three millimeters. Our climbers would attempt to position Roger's receiver near Camp Four, 26,000 feet up the mountain.

Scriptwriters Tim Cahill and Stephen Judson cleverly wove Paula and Ed's forty-degrees-below-zero honeymoon into the story, adding another layer of human interest to the film. The writers worked hard to include humor, depth, purpose, and personality in the development of each character, so that, even when they were hidden by parkas, masks, oxygen tubes, and hats, the audience would feel connected to them. As we got to know the climbers better, we identified personal traits that the writers worked hard to highlight:

Araceli: Loves chocolate, has charming Spanish accent

Ed: On his honeymoon on uncomfortable Everest, so determined that he's called the "Chevy truck" of climbers, loves the strange, undietary Spam (plenty of fat to burn at altitude)

Jamling: Buddhist, quiet and sensitive, climbing to pay tribute to his father

Paula: On her honeymoon with Ed, no nonsense base-camp manager, intelligent and well-organized, concerned about Ed's safety

Roger: Scientist, English accent, geologist

Sumiyo: Japanese TV producer, videotaping mountain events and her climb for a Japanese TV show

Our Bodies, Our Brains

As part of the educational element of our IMAX mission, we wanted to expose the audience to the two most common climbing styles. Some climbers, like Araceli, focus on rock climbing, which requires strength (even in the fingertips), balance, conditioning, and an ability to zero in on individual moves. The other approach, exemplified by Ed, Sumiyo, and Jamling, is to become an alpinist skilled at planning lengthy assaults on peaks at altitudes above 15,000 feet. In these ascents, endurance and determination are key. Climbing Everest requires the latter skill set.

Even to an alpinist, though, this mountain is a potential death trap. Lack of oxygen and the bitter cold will test the limits of every

(ABOVE) The best team on the mountain in 1996 gets ready in Kathmandu in April. (BELOW) In Cabo San Lucas, Mexico, Araceli Segarra conditions her body for the climb of Everest, hoping to become the first Spanish woman to do so.

climber. Base Camp alone is at 17,600 feet; there, a lungful of air contains just two-thirds of the oxygen we breathe at sea level. The same lungful at the summit (29,029 feet) delivers a mere one-third of the oxygen, presenting a real threat. The brain doesn't work as well; some climbers become nauseous; others are hit with serious conditions like pulmonary or cerebral edema, or swelling. But here's the cool part: if a climber treks from 9,000 to 20,000 feet slowly and methodically, over a month's time, the body almost magically acclimates. New red blood cells are produced, boosting the blood's oxygen-carrying capacity.

But climbers can make mistakes even after acclimatizing. Climb too fast and you risk mountain sickness, which causes headaches, nausea, sleep problems, weakness, and shortness of breath. For this reason, most climbers carry supplemental oxygen to use as they approach the so-called death zone above 24,000 feet.

I wanted to include this complex and incredible story of the human body's ability to adapt, so we hired Dr. Charles Houston, a mountaineer, a physician, and an early expert in the field of high-altitude impacts, to help write this part of the story. At the same time, I engaged mountain expert Brad Washburn as an advisor and he made sure that we defined the project, not as a climbing film or a travelogue about Nepal, but a film about the human spirit. It was about boldly setting heartfelt goals and possessing the will to carry them through.

Climb Everest with an IMAX Camera? Why Not?

A year into our story development, I set two must-do objectives: Tell a great story of human determination to reach an altruistic goal; and take audiences to the top of the world in IMAX fashion so that they can be right up there with us, looking down at all the rest!

To achieve the latter, we needed a cameraman who had the skills to be able to operate a camera in high-altitude, low-oxygen conditions with the wind blowing and a windchill of minus forty degrees. Among the finalists was filmmaker David Breashears, who was particularly impressive because he had accomplished some of the most imaginative and challenging filmic events on Everest, including broadcasting the first live video signals transmitted from the summit. Despite Breashears having been described to me as aggressive and opinionated, I hoped that I could get him excited about my dream challenge: getting IMAX film images from the top of the world! I wasn't wrong.

When I met David, he came across as an energetic and intelligent man ready to do something memorable. He had climbed Everest twice before, so his first reaction to getting an IMAX camera to the summit was not entirely unexpected. He tried to convince me that shooting with a lighter 35mm movie camera would be good enough. I insisted that, to capture the real you-are-there experience, we had to have the

ten-times-sharper images in IMAX. Once he realized that I wouldn't budge, he signed on, fully committed. In just a few weeks, we developed a plan to build a lighter 15/70 camera and test it on Everest in the spring of 1995, then mount a full expedition with 30 people in 1996 with a backup for shooting in 1997. We projected the release for 1998.

Because we didn't want to build a giant camera and have our team of five sherpas carry it to the top only to have it fail, we hired Kevin Kowalchuk at the IMAX Camera Department to rebuild the IMAX Mark II camera. It had to be far lighter (from 80 pounds down to 42), able to be easily disassembled, carried in five separate backpacks, and reliably operable at 29,000 feet.

Kevin made several design changes to accommodate our needs. He replaced rubber belts, cables, and lubricants with synthetic materials that wouldn't freeze, stiffen, or shatter, and he added a hand crank like the ones on the earliest movie cameras to free up the movement in case it froze overnight. I remember the day, after months of work, that Kevin and Gord Harris put the modified camera in a minus-40-degree cold storage room. When they went back four days later, wrapped up in parkas and gloves, they turned on the camera and it ran instantly. When they called me, I hooted like a stoked surfer!

In April 1995, David and Kevin took the new camera and a small team to Everest to shoot 30 rolls of film and test our plan. The trip was also an opportunity to train David, who until then had only shot in smaller formats, on how to shoot film for IMAX and IMAX Dome screens. This beta test run gave us great insight into some very serious potential on-mountain problems.

One was the scratches on the film emulsion caused by the fine dust found throughout the Khumbu Valley. This dust has been blamed for a nagging respiratory affliction among climbers known as the Khumbu cough, which can lead to bronchitis. To protect the film from dust, we created a special bag to use when we had to change rolls. Another problem was the difficulty of loading the heavy and unwieldy 1,000-foot rolls of film with cold hands. We decided instead to use 550-foot loads, magazines with hinged lids and enlarged controls, and special gloves. The third issue was film shrinkage from the cold that risked film breaks, so we opted for the most expensive Estar plastic film, which did not shrink. Fourth, the camera's nickel-cadmium batteries lost efficiency in the cold, so we ordered special lithium batteries. And finally, like even experienced cameramen when first shooting IMAX, David had made framing and lighting mistakes that just wouldn't do on our giant, unforgiving screens. In Laguna, David and I watched the test footage again and again, sitting close to our large screen to try to replicate the IMAX theater experience. I shared what I'd learned in shooting dozens of IMAX films, and with this vital lesson, David learned how to shoot effectively in IMAX.

Ready, Set, Shoot: Nepal, 1996

I had planned to go to Nepal and codirect **Everest** up to my climbing altitude limit, which was probably the top of the Khumbu Icefall; but when our film about the Blue Angels was delayed and was going to overlap with Nepal, I had a decision to make. I could put off the **Everest** shoot or I could send Steve Judson and cinematographer Brad Ohlund in my place. Brad and Steve knew the IMAX format well and could help David with IMAX-specific issues.

I gave the go-ahead to the production, and stayed in close contact with David, Brad, and Steve from afar. We communicated over a satellite phone, which was amazing in its clear and reliable transmission. Out of necessity rather than choice, this would be the most collaborative film of the 60 that I've made. David directed on the mountain during the two-month expedition, and again on an aerial shoot in Nepal a year later, while Steve helped in Nepal and guided the writing and editing. As the third director, my job was to focus on the big picture: the overall story and film.

The team left California for Nepal in March 1996. Brad landed in Kathmandu, armed with 75 cases of film and equipment. He was met at customs clearance by our expedition leader, Wongbu Sherpa, who had his own way to get our equipment through customs by downplaying its value. When Wongbu departed with the paperwork and then reappeared a few minutes later with a stamped approval, Brad was stunned. He definitely wasn't in Kansas anymore!

As I'd learned while working on our films about the US Navy, we'd need redundancy if we wanted to eliminate potential problems of shooting at the top. Robert Schauer, a brilliant Austrian cameraman who had already climbed Everest, would assist and provide backup for David in case he became sick or injured. We also had a spare IMAX camera rental sitting in its box at Base Camp. Since we knew that we could not afford to fail, we were the best-funded expedition on the mountain that season. We had the best communications, medical facilities, contact with the outside world, and Sherpa personnel of any expedition. We even had a teacher! In 1996, the Internet was in its infancy, and in a first for a film adventure, Liesl Clark posted online updates of our stories of science, exploration, and adventure from Base Camp headquarters every two days for students and teachers. I hoped that by utilizing this new communications platform we would extend our educational impact and build anticipation for the film. I negotiated a deal with *Nova*, the PBS science series, to distribute these updates live and direct to all American schools through *Nova* online. Also reporting that year from Everest were *Outside* magazine online (Jon Krakauer) and Sandy Hill on NBC Interactive. This would be the most covered climbing season in history!

(ABOVE) In Kathmandu, the spiritual aspects of life affect all. (BELOW) By ascending to 18,000 feet slowly, your red blood cells multiply. It's called acclimatization.

MOUNT EVEREST
29,028 ft   8,848 m

South Summit
28,710 ft
8,751 m

Lhotse
27,890 ft
8,501 m

Northeast

Dashed section of route
located behind ridge

South Col
26,000 ft
7,925 m

Camp IV
26,000 ft
7,925 m

Geneva

Spur

Nuptse
25,790 ft
7,861 m

Bei Peak
24,878 ft
7,583 m

West

Camp III
24,000 ft
7,315 m

Khumbutse
21,867 ft
6,665 m

Camp II
Advance Base Camp
21,300 ft
6,492 m

Western

*Rongbuk
Glacier*

Lho La

Camp I
19,500 ft
5,943 m

Lingtren
22,142 ft
6,749 m

Pumori
23,507 ft
7,165 m

Khumbu

*Khumbu
Icefall*

Base Camp
17,600 ft
5,364 m

Khumbu

Cho Polu
21,965 ft
6,695 m

Our competent team knew that we had a solid contingency plan in place. "Get everything you can this season," I told them, "but take no risks that might injure someone. If the weather blocks our singular goal of summiting, we have a budget for returning next year." I wanted to make sure that there was no pressure that would force anyone to move up in the death zone, where bad decision-making is common.

As a further protection, we wanted the camera team to shoot only vital scenes (like the ones at the summit) at high altitude, so Steve, Tim, and I designed the shot list carefully, guided by previous climbing films. Shots were prioritized: a rating of 10 for the most important and zero for least. A complete storyboard was given to everyone, so the entire team knew exactly what it needed to photograph.

Every week, the exposed film was boxed in special containers, strapped to the sides of a yak, accompanied by a Sherpa for three days, then flown from Lukla to Kathmandu and loaded onto a flight to LAX. Amazingly, not one of the total of 113[23] rolls was damaged or lost. Within two days, I would watch the footage on a big screen, evaluate the quality of IMAX imagery, and fax the team my graded shot report. From this they knew which scenes were complete and which would have to be redone.

One day, I saw a shot of Araceli slipping and falling backward as she set a ladder over a crevasse. David felt that the shot wasn't usable because it looked like she was too clumsy. He wanted to reshoot it. But I loved it because that spontaneous and natural slip would help build her character even more. Steve wrote a great line for Araceli: "I want to get my slipping done early so I don't have to slip later on." The audience chuckled at Araceli's self-deprecation.

We had succeeded in our meticulous advanced planning and had everything in place. We were only missing one critical component: We didn't have enough money. We had prelease advances from six theaters and a sizable grant for children's science education from the National Science Foundation, but we had no major partners to cofund the film. I couldn't deny what worried investors were telling me: Any climb of Everest is dicey, let alone one with heavy equipment. They all said essentially the same thing. "The financial risks are just too big for us to stomach. We can't help you by investing."

In the end, I decided to go forward with the project. "I'll take the gamble and pay for the rest of the budget myself," I told the team. Sometimes you have to have your back against a wall to make a tough business decision ("Why not?"), and the one I ended up making that year turned out to be the best one of my life.

---

23 These valuable 113 rolls (65,000 feet) became the heart of the film story, but were amplified by 175,000 additional feet of 70mm film shot to provide highlight action sequences, aerials, and story texture later in Utah, Baja, and Nepal.

(LEFT) Nepalese climbing route up Everest; illustration courtesy National Geographic Books.

Unforgettable, Undefeatable Everest

The story of what happened during this historic and tragic year on Everest was brilliantly documented by Jon Krakauer in his best-selling book *Into Thin Air*. There were 16 expedition teams at Everest Base Camp in 1996, and scheduling of the ascents was critical so that the Hillary Step and the Lhotse Face, two areas of slow progress, didn't get jammed up with too many climbers. Our team was chosen to approach the mountain and begin its final climb on May 9. But on May 8, as our team reached Camp Three (of the four camps), David and Ed grew concerned. They watched relentless winds roaring like a jet engine, tearing off snow at the top, blowing a plume of white off Everest's peak.

David's radio was patched through to me. I could hear his hoarse voice from high on the mountain, at 23,500 feet on the Lhotse Face, just below the death zone. David told me the team had planned to go up to Camp Four and try for the summit the following day, but it was very windy near the summit. He felt that not only would it be unsafe, but he probably wouldn't be able to hold the camera steady enough in the fierce wind to get good shots. I again stressed that we had a budget and a schedule that would allow us to come back a year later if we didn't make the summit. I wanted no dangerous gambles. "Don't force it," I said. David agreed.

"There were many, many fine reasons not to go, but attempting to climb Everest is an intrinsically irrational act—a triumph of desire over sensibility. Any person who would seriously consider it is almost by definition beyond the sway of reasoned argument."

–JON KRAKAUER, *INTO THIN AIR*

David and his team left the IMAX camera up high in our tents and returned to Camp Two to wait for the winds to subside. As the long shadows crept up the Khumbu and night fell, they learned that Chen Yu-Nan, a member of the Taiwanese team, needed help. During the night he had plunged 70 feet down Lhotse Face, severely injuring his head and face. David and Ed rushed to his aid, but tragically it would be too late. David gently closed the climber's eyes and helped drag him back down the mountain. Chen's death cast a pall throughout all the camps and set an ominous tone of things to come.

Not long after, Ed and David were passed by two friends leading two expeditions, Rob Hall and Scott Fischer. These two teams reached Camp Four, spent the night, and on May 10 tried for the summit. Because the experienced and able leaders of these teams had commitments to their climbers, who had paid $65,000 for a climb to the top, they felt great pressure to ignore the storm threat that David had rightly feared. Later that afternoon, the storm unleashed 40 to 70 mph winds and frigid air that proved to be largely unsurvivable. As the blizzard moved in, it caught 19 climbers high on the mountain and trapped them for the night. People like Beck Weathers collapsed along the route and were abandoned. Beck's story would become part of our film, and he would write about it later:

> On the evening of May 10, 1996, a killer blizzard exploded around the upper reaches of Mount Everest, trapping me and dozens of other climbers high in the Death Zone of the earth's tallest mountain. The storm began as a low, distant growl, then rapidly formed into a howling white fog laced with ice pellets. It hurtled up Mount Everest to engulf us in minutes. We couldn't see as far as our feet. A person standing next to you just vanished in the roaring whiteout. Wind speeds that night would exceed seventy knots. The ambient temperature fell to sixty below zero.

Even before he joined the Rob Hall expedition, Beck was aware that fewer than half of Everest expeditions put a single member on the summit. But this amateur climber wanted desperately to complete the heralded Seven Summits, the highest peaks on all seven continents. He'd already climbed five. Beck loved mountain climbing, and even as his worried wife and children waited at home, praying for his safe return, he kept going back for more. May 10 broke the spell. This one night would change Beck Weathers forever, and for the better.

After the storm closed in on Beck, he hunkered down in the deep snow, and as the cold took hold, Beck fell into a hypothermic coma. Other climbers came upon his bulk, checked for breathing and a pulse, and finding none, left him for dead. His wife received the shocking and terrible news in Dallas: "Beck's dead." But the impossible happened. Hours later, miraculously, he opened his eyes! As he explains in our film, "I stood up and said to myself, I'm going to keep walking down, into the blinding snow, until I either walk off the mountain or into camp." And somehow, snow blind and stumbling, one hand bare to the unimaginable cold, Beck turned his back on death, made it to Camp Four, and began a shaky start to the rest of his life. In that transformative moment, he would dedicate himself, not to his self-centered climbing goals, but to his wonderful wife, Peach, and their two children. As an inspiration to everyone, he went on to become an amazing motivational speaker, one of the best in America, recounting his experience and redemption on Everest.

Meanwhile, as the ongoing mountain tragedy unfolded, I had a sickening feeling of guilt. I had instigated our expedition, talked everyone into it, and now I felt like an army general sending his troops

On May 10, 1996, Everest turned deadly.

(ABOVE) Jamling on that fateful day. (BELOW) Only a heroic, death-defying helicopter rescue at 21,000 feet in altitude saved Beck's life.

into a hopeless battle. I was a bundle of nerves, and even back in warm Laguna, I couldn't sleep. It was one of the worst times of my life.

The next morning, in the midst of chaos, our team attempted to save other climbers. The first thing Ed, David, and Robert Schauer did was to help Beck Weathers down the Lhotse Face. Debilitated and barely able to see, Beck stumbled down the mountain, his frostbitten hands useless. The rescue was a three-man job. Ed guided him with a rope attached to his harness. David was roped to him in front while Robert moved Beck's feet for him. During the slow descent, Beck remained in good spirits. In what might have been a side effect of the low oxygen levels, Beck reacted to their preposterous condition, breaking into an impromptu rendition of the song "Chain of Fools."

The threesome helped him down the steep and icy cliff to the middle camp, where a rescue helicopter piloted by Lt. Col. Madan K.C. performed the first high-altitude rescue in history. At 21,000 feet, on a section of hardpack snow where Araceli had drawn a large "X" using red Kool-Aid, Lt. Col. Madan loaded Beck and a Taiwanese climber, Makalu Gau, into the helicopter. It is doubtful that Beck would have survived had the helicopter not been able to land. Beck's wife, Peach, was notified that he hadn't died after all, but was in bad shape. Lt. Col. Madan, whose initials, K.C., identify him as a member of the "Khatri Chhetri," the revered warrior caste in Nepal, would later receive the highest honor for international pilots, an award for skill and heroism that was given to him in a ceremony at our office in Laguna Beach. On that day of so much suffering, this man's brave heart, strong spirit, and flawless piloting skills prevailed.

Meanwhile, as the storm raged on, Rob Hall radioed that he was at the South Summit and unable to move through the treacherous winds. A call was patched through to his pregnant wife, Jan Arnold, a doctor in New Zealand. Rob and Jan told each other how much they loved one another, and chose the name of their unborn baby, landing on Sarah. With his last words, the brave Hall, one of climbing's most cautious and most beloved, told his wife: "Sleep well, my sweetheart. Please don't worry too much." When the story of that emotional telephone call was shared via the Internet by Liesl, the 100,000 armchair travelers following the action from all over the world were tearfully stricken. Rob and seven others perished that night, victims of the wrath of the mountain and its weather.[24]

24 As a positive footnote to this tragedy, as he documented the event, Brad Ohlund had recorded with our quarter-inch Nagra one of the conversations between Jan and Rob. Years after the event, I wrote Jan, telling her that we had the tape, and she instantly wrote back saying how much it would mean to her to have a copy, knowing that Sarah would gain a better understanding of her father's nobility and courage by hearing it later in life. In 2007, when we were filming at Everest Base Camp for a new IMAX film studying hypoxia and its cures, Jan, her mother, and 11-year-old Sarah met with us to share stories. Jan was there on Everest to show Sarah why Rob felt so strongly about the mountain, its beauty, spiritual power, and why he risked his life to share it with others.

(ABOVE) The Khumbu Icefall is the mountain's most deadly location. This danger zone is where 12 Sherpa were killed in an avalanche in 2014. You try to climb through it quickly. (BELOW) Our tents at Base Camp were at the foot of the treacherous Icefall.

(ABOVE) After being left for dead on the mountain, Beck Weathers stood up and miraculously walked back to Camp Four in a raging storm. Back in Texas two weeks later, we photographed him receiving aquatherapy, which helped save his ability to walk. He never regained use of his frostbitten fingers. (BELOW) Before leaving on the final attempt, a puja ceremony helped bring our team a break in the weather and a clear route to the top.

In the extreme conditions on Everest, it is difficult to motivate oneself to do anything—even to put one foot in front of another—let alone to help someone else. Every moment is spent trying to conserve energy, to eat or drink the small amounts that your body can handle, and to force your brain into working out the next decision. There were still climbers on the mountain who had depleted their supplemental oxygen containers during the night. Signaling a gallant allegiance to the "brotherhood of rope," David radioed permission to any climber at the High Camp to cut into our tent where the heavy IMAX camera and magazines sat protected in special backpacks. Our 25 reserve oxygen bottles and food were given to the needy climbers. The effort our crew gave to the struggling and desperate climbers was remarkable. I have never been more proud of one of our film teams.

Meanwhile, our climbing team had retreated to Base Camp to recover from the shock and the physical strain. They were dizzied by the intensity of this epic disaster, which caused the highest daily death toll ever on Everest. They'd lost best friends and acquaintances and had seen with their own eyes people who lay dead on the path to the top.

David and Brad were not battle-tested war cameramen. For them, it was a struggle to shoot video of Jamling, Araceli, and Ed as they shared their most profound emotions. But I encouraged them, and these video scenes added incredible honesty and heart to our film.

Permission to Ascend

Once our team reached Base Camp, I was certain that they would give up on another attempt to summit. They'd already climbed part of the way up—no easy feat—and come all the way back down. Most teams were departing for home, leaving the sacred mountain. It would have been natural to conclude that the gods were against climbing that season and that our chance had passed. Members of our crew were dealing with the tragic deaths of two close friends, Rob Hall and Scott Fischer. Ed and David had climbed with them in the past. They were physically, emotionally, and spiritually spent. Even the stalwart Paula had such a strong negative premonition that she had to leave Base Camp for a couple of days. I was ready for them to announce that they were heading home. And then they heard from Beck Weathers.

After having his right arm amputated below the elbow and losing most fingers and his thumb on his left hand, Beck tearfully told the team via phone from Dallas how grateful he was for their help in saving his life. He called them heroes—and the "strongest team" on the mountain. About the same time, Jamling Norgay heard from his monastery and then from the rinpoche, the region's religious leader. They encouraged him spiritually and gave him hope. In something I never expected, the team started to rally. By the time Paula returned to Base Camp and heard that Ed was pondering another attempt, she gave

Ladders are used to cross otherwise unpassable sections of the Khumbu Icefall. To get the shot [BELOW], David lowered himself and the IMAX camera on ropes as Araceli cautiously crossed the deep chasm.

him a shot of confidence and encouragement, telling him that if he went, he should climb the mountain "as he'd never climbed it before." The group's energy rose, the sherpa team replenished the high camps with new supplies, and our determined team decided to give it one last try. Their feeling was: "We've come here to do a job and we should complete it—if, and it was a big if, the mountain will let us."

On May 24, two weeks after the disaster, they began their ascent anew. David had succumbed to the Khumbu cough, making it difficult to talk, but he realized that if they didn't go now they probably wouldn't be able to try again until next season, a year away. Digging deep, they set out from the Middle Camp and up the Lhotse Face to Camp Three. They felt stronger and in their hearts were sure that they could do it. When they reached Camp Four, the winds subsided and they knew that they were in luck. Sumiyo Tsuzuki had several cracked ribs as a result of her own hacking Khumbu cough, so she volunteered to stay at Camp Four as a safety communicator.

Into the Death Zone

Ed decided that he would lead the way, so he left the camp at 11 p.m. He climbed by the light of his headlamp, trying to be the first to ascend the mountain after the most devastating disaster ever to hit Everest. Following Ed an hour later were the five Sherpas (Wongbu Sherpa, Jangbu Sherpa, Muktu Lhakpa Sherpa, Dorje Sherpa, and Thilen Sherpa) carrying the camera equipment. Then came Araceli Segarra, Jamling Norgay, David Breashears and Robert Schauer. As Ed continued climbing out in front, he broke trail through waist-deep snow, hoping, as was the original plan, to summit without the aid of supplemental oxygen.

By 7 a.m., after seven hours of climbing, the team had reached the Balcony, a somewhat flat area where David assembled the five components of the IMAX camera. In biting cold, he and Robert shot a roll of Jamling and Araceli climbing toward the top, just as the sun kissed the peaks of Lhotse beautifully framed behind them. But David's throat was getting worse. It took another five hours of struggle before all ten members of the team reached the top. At that very moment, I was at a formal fundraising dance for a group called SchoolPower, which supports public schools in Laguna Beach. When I was summoned to the phone, I couldn't believe what I was being told. Surreal doesn't begin to describe it.

"Greg, we've reached the top," came the words over the satellite phone connection. "It's so beautiful. Thank you for having confidence in us. Now our job is to get down safely."

At 7 a.m., just after sunrise on one of the longest days of the year, the team reached the Balcony, where David and Robert assembled the five pieces to the IMAX camera and photographed Araceli and Jamling.

Every day you hear the rumble of avalanches. This one David filmed from Base Camp with the winterized Mark II camera.

Standing in my tuxedo, I told them how proud I was of their courage and the strength of their humanity in helping save the lives of others. What a positive example they set for the children of the world.

At the top, the team, meanwhile, was concerned about the 1 p.m. turnaround time they had set for themselves—a hard deadline. David had lost his voice completely, so Robert helped communicate. They set up several shots but had to wait an hour for a battery being carried by one of the Sherpas who was having a bad climbing day. The crew shot another roll of film for a grand total of just three minutes; not much, but those images would move the world.

The team then carefully descended to Base Camp, where a worried Paula waited with open arms. After all, they all joked, this was her honeymoon! For many following the Internet words of Liesl, Sandy, and notably Jon, this was the adventure story of the decade.

Steve Judson and I, with an assist from writer Tim Cahill, would spend the next 21 months editing and perfecting these touching moments on film, trying our best to relate this remarkable tale of heroism with the respect and honor it deserved.[25]

Later, when I recorded Beck's voice for the film, I asked him whether, if he had it to do all over again, would he go. He surprised me by saying that he would; that in those mountains, he had traded his hands (now just stumps) for something more valuable: his family and his future. For the first time in his life, he was at peace and comfortable in his own skin. "I searched all over the world for that which would fulfill me," he said, "and all along it was right here in front of me at home. And better yet, I now know it."

The tragic storm had turned our simple story into an emotional epic, but few of my staff and partners understood the value in refining the story points to the degree Steve and I did. With so much attention focused on the tragedy, they felt that getting the film out quickly was the more prudent move. "Take advantage of all the free press," they said. But we saw it differently. This was not a climbing documentary and it was not meant to sensationalize the challenge. As Brad Washburn had boldly challenged me, it was a film about chasing dreams, about heart, about testing the limits of the unknown and honoring those we love. Remembering what Jim and I had learned from Bruce Brown decades before, I knew that we needed to tell this story with artistry and sensitivity, and that, more than anything else, requires time.

25 When in 2015 Universal released a film that usurped our title, **Everest**, an actor-centered recounting of the 1996 tragedy in 3D, climbers and filmmakers like myself were incensed that they made Rob, Scott, and other climbers appear as foolhardy, when really Rob had acted heroically, staying with his client, Doug Hansen, as the two were trapped by the storm high on Everest. In an ice cave, they waited for the storm to diminish—and when it didn't, they died. This dramatic film made them out to be stupid macho men, and I resented this portrayal. They had also completely missed the positive stories, like Beck's and others, in which the tragic and pivotal experience changed climbers into better people.

(ABOVE LEFT AND RIGHT) Brad Ohlund and Steve Judson on Everest to help with the 15/70 shooting; the SpaceCam gyro-stabilized IMAX camera was a revolutionary tool for IMAX films, invented by Ron Goodman (LEFT), here with (L-R) Bob Nehnert, me, and ace pilot Jim Gavin. (BELOW LEFT AND RIGHT) Bill Bennett, distribution sales leader; added to the sales team were Mike Lutz and Bob Harman. (BOTTOM LEFT AND RIGHT) On a cold New York morning, the film premiered and David, Jamling, and Araceli joined me on a bench outside; I brought the team to Laguna for a week of surfing—Tim Cahill, me, David, Robert Schauer, Ed, Araceli, and Paula. We were happy to be all healthy and safe.

Timing Is Everything

Shortly after our team had successfully summited the mountain, I got a call from television producers Howie Masters and Betsy West from the award-winning ABC show, *Turning Point*.

"We are going to do an hour-long special on the tragedy on Everest," said Howie, "and we would love to have you and your team involved."

I immediately saw this as a huge opportunity. Our film could get major network publicity as well as exposure on other ABC talk shows like *Good Morning America*. I made Betsy and Howie an offer that they couldn't refuse.

"We'll give you access to our climbers, our filmmakers, and all the footage we've shot, at no charge. In exchange, we just want a significant mention within the one-hour show. Whenever any of our footage is shown, we get a six-second on-screen credit over that shot." Howie was thrilled. Within an hour he'd called me back to confirm. "We have a deal, and my boss wants me to come out to Laguna Beach tomorrow to meet with you and plan our strategy."

A video crew from *Turning Point* flew to Nepal ten days later. They met our team and filmed them on location. When I brought the team home in early June, we scheduled a week of interviews for them in Laguna Beach. That broadcast became *Turning Point*'s highest-rated show of the year. It ran three times, including just before our premiere on March 4, 1998. Host Forrest Sawyer closed with this message: "If you liked this story and want to see more, but on the gigantic IMAX theater screen so you can feel as if you are there, go see MacGillivray Freeman's film **Everest**, which begins in IMAX theaters this coming Friday." We could never have afforded this kind of plug. Our company's philosophy of treating people well had come back to us in spades.

An Editing Marathon

I love editing. You've already shot the film, and now there are at least 1,000 ways to put it all together. Your job is to find the single best way to tell your story. To do so we would test-screen the film five times, patiently get viewers' feedback, and then re-edit. As you read and revise, read and revise, you eventually find the best way to tell this effective and powerful story, all in 44 minutes. Telling the story in 90 minutes would have been ten times easier.

Because the film was so complex, **Everest** became the most difficult editorial challenge in my 35 years of filmmaking. **Everest** recounts the complex and true stories of six well-defined characters. But it also incorporates scientific, cultural, and religious content, not to mention philosophical themes that gave it more depth than other IMAX films.

In the first edited versions of the film, we gave our four climbers equal screen time; but the test-screening questionnaires showed two trends developing. First, the film received a higher "quality of entertainment/experience" rating from men than from women. That was a problem. Second, Jamling was far more effective than we'd expected. This spiritually impactful character with his quiet personality was resonating deeply with audiences, particularly women. This surprised me at first, but then it became clear. Jamling, more than any of the other characters, was climbing the mountain not for himself, but for his family. I told Steve that we needed to reconsider every filmed outtake that included Jamling. We then flew Jamling from India to California to shoot new opening and closing sequences: the butter lamp ceremony at the monastery when five-year-old Jamling is first inspired by his father, and a matching moment at the film's end. The subsequent re-edit did the trick; now we'd succeeded in our goal of getting women to enjoy the film even more than men did.

Over the years, I've learned that a truthful and realistic story is much more emotionally fulfilling than any fictional movie. Real life is so attractive to audiences today, especially in IMAX. Because of the clarity of the image and the distinctiveness of the sound, viewers believe in IMAX more fully. They know it's real and not a bunch of special effects. I love knowing that our story of **Everest** touched people in this unique, honest, and powerful way.

A New Kind of Release for a New Kind of Film

As we edited **Everest**, I was also preparing for the film's commercial launch. Our Laguna team of 25, aware that our film would have an immediate and urgent appeal that would go well beyond any previous IMAX film, planned an industry first: a simultaneous "day-and-date" release. This meant that our sales team had to convince some 40 independent theater directors to release the film simultaneously, and add in another 60 theaters over the first three months, rather than adopting the usual trickle-out release system. Because our story had such momentum and energy, we wanted it fully released to 100 theaters within three months. To achieve this goal we hired Mike Lutz to help Bill Bennett with sales in Asia and the United States and Bob Harman to cover Europe. Then, we scheduled a 7 a.m. screening on the huge IMAX screen on September 21, 1997, during a conference of the Giant Screen Cinema Association (GSCA) in Vancouver.

In spite of the early hour, some 400 IMAX theater executives were treated to what was probably the most electrifying IMAX showing I've ever attended. After introductions by Bill Bennett, climber Ed Viesturs, and me, we ran the film. By the end, there were very few dry eyes in the house. For the first time in my experience, this normally critical and blasé crowd gave a film a standing ovation.

But for me this was also a test screening. (Remember: "Never walk away until its perfect.") From the questionnaires we received from each theater director, Steve and I made about 40 changes to the film.

FEBRUARY 1997 calendar (handwritten daily tasks for the Everest film production)

TITLE/DISTRIBUTOR	Reported Box Office 5/22-5/28 (full week)	Number of Theaters This Week	Number of Theaters Last Week	Weeks Avg $ Per Theater	No. Weeks Release	Domestic Box Office Cumulative
Godzilla (Sony)	$62,771,776	3310	—	$18964	2	$81,306,243
Deep Impact (Par)	23,398,372	3250	3192	6891	4	101,925,519
The Horse Whisperer (BV)	17,494,429	2049	2039	8538	3	36,076,361
Bulworth (20th)	12,422,324	2047	2	6066	3	12,650,661
Quest for Camelot (WB)	7,206,197	3107	3107	2319	3	14,667,834
Fear and Loathing in Las Vegas (U)	5,500,490	1126	—	4884	2	5,500,490
Titanic (Par)	4,248,586	2008	1990	2115	24	577,635,895
City of Angels (WB)	3,946,798	1967	2245	2007	8	71,194,115
He Got Game (BV)	2,084,978	1244	1414	1676	5	19,459,251
Everest (MacGillivray Freeman)	1,670,569	46	40	36316	13	15,085,360
Paulie (DreamWorks)	1,647,774	1502	1812	1097	7	22,416,391
Sliding Doors (Miramax)	1,642,244	522	522	3146	6	8,341,695

(ABOVE) Making the top ten on the *Variety* Box Office list was a milestone for IMAX filmmaking. (LEFT) From my early years, I've kept a daily record of tasks each day so I can be certain that we're accomplishing enough each month. Since most of the storytelling moments in our film **Everest** had to be finished after the main on-the-mountain event, we carefully planned these scenes for staging in Utah at Moab (Ed and Paula mountain biking) and Snowbird ski resort (the tent scenes, the night climb through deep snow, and the avalanche).

Making *Everest* 4:08 #19

We even doubled the length of time at the top, giving that moment a more riveting, you-are-there sensation.

As something new to our industry, we committed to spend about $2 million for public relations, sending Jamling, Araceli, Ed, and filmmakers David and Brad across the country to do 100 TV and radio interviews. We also published our coffee table book *Everest: Mountain Without Mercy*, which became one of National Geographic's best sellers, with 400,000 copies sold. Bringing out the book two months before Christmas helped our film become a runaway hit. And an eight-page article in *National Geographic* magazine exposed the film to its eight million readers. It was the kind of marketing you just can't buy. We increased awareness and attendance, and the film recorded the highest audience numbers ever for an IMAX film, not only at museum theaters but also at commercial multiplex theaters. We were trying to help IMAX expand its market reach, which in turn would help us with our business. Even though we only receive about 15 to 20 percent of the box office gross, the PR spend paid off.

Everest premiered to unprecedented acclaim in New York for the media and then again in Boston for all of our partners. Then coproducer Alec Lorimore and I decided to plan a star-studded LA premiere in an effort to create a similar Hollywood stir. We felt this would help our (and IMAX's) reputation and build a strong future in Hollywood for both organizations. Our friend Peter Guber at Sony had the best Rolodex in studioland and helped us with the VIP invitation list. The reaction was over the top: Trade papers raved, and the MFF family hobnobbed with Dustin Hoffman, Sting and Trudie Styler, Carole King and John Badham, Jeff Goldblum, Richard Dreyfuss, Jared Leto, Ravi Shankar, and **Field of Dreams** director Phil Alden Robinson. It was an historic night for the IMAX theater industry.

Sharing Our Success

When **Everest** premiered on March 4, 1998, I decided to report, for the first time, our box office numbers to *Variety* for their list of the top 50 films of the week. Our team thought the listing could help IMAX Corporation by encouraging new theater sales. Though **Godzilla** and **Titanic** were playing on over 5,000 screens and **Everest** was playing in just 46 theaters, we became the first IMAX film to place in the top ten. This success got the attention of Dick Cook, president of distribution at Disney and one of the nicest people in entertainment. He wanted to know how a 44-minute documentary could produce such huge attendance, and with very little income drop week after week.

"It'll take me two hours to tell you," I answered. Within days, he was visiting me in Laguna and planting the seeds for what would become a 20-year relationship and friendship. The result of that meeting was that Disney found a way to use IMAX theaters to promote **Fantasia 2000**, a pet project of Walt Disney's nephew, Roy Disney. Today, MFF and Dick Cook are still working together, dreaming up wild concepts for tomorrow.

6 IMAX FILMS.

EVEREST - **Test Screening Questionnaire**   September 23, 1997

Please circle: <u>Your Age</u>:   Under 13   14-24   (25-50)   50+   (Male) / Female

We are still shaping this film; we will be making changes, so please be truthful. Please circle your opinion.

		Very Good	*Average*	*Weak*

1. How would you rate the film, with 10 being

2. Rate the sequences: (they are in this order i...
    A. Opening of young Jamling, the dangerou... training.

    B. Ed and Paula training (mountain bikes) i...

    C. Kathmandu: Introducing team, who talk...

    D. Helicopter Ride into the mountains.

    E. Computer graphics of India and Asia, ho...

    F. The Trek up to the base of Mount Evere... our bodies adapt to high altitudes.

    G. Base Camp: kitchen tent, map of the da...

    H. Climbing the cravasses in the Khumbu...

    I. The storm hits, the tragedy unfolds, and...

    J. The aftermath sadness, and re-energizin...

    K. Starting over -- Climbing the Khumbu...

    L. Setting up the GPS at the High Camp a...

    M. The Night Climb.

    N. The Daytime Climb - summit day.

    O. Ed summits.

    P. Jamling and Araceli summit.

    Q. The ending -- Jamling reflects.

3. How entertaining was the film?

4. Did it contain enough science and educa...

5. Was it visually exciting enough?

6. Please name which scene you found wa...
    COMING DOWN -
    SHOW MORE

7. Were there any sections that were especially boring for you?   YES   (NO)

8. Which ones?
    _____
    _____

9. Do you think that we mentioned Rob Hall too often in the film (he's the close friend of Ed who died on the mountain)?   YES   (NO)

10. Do you think that Mel Gibson would be a good choice to narrate this film?   (YES)   NO
    And how good, on a 10 point scale, 10 being very good?   10 (9) 8 7   6 5 4   3 2 1

11. Did you understand the main purpose of the expedition well enough (to put GPS receivers on the mountain to learn more about earthquakes in Nepal)?
    Very Clear   Average   Not Clear
    10 9 8 (7)   6 5 4   3 2 1

12. Were you satisfied and excited when the team reached the top?   YES   NO
    - NOT ENOUGH / SHOW MORE

13. Did you want to see more from the top?   (YES)   NO
    Or had you seen enough from the summit?   YES   NO

14. Would you want to see this film again?   (YES, Definitely)   Maybe   NO, Once is enough

15. Would you recommend this film to a friend?   (YES)   NO

16. Are there suggestions you want to make? (Use reverse side if necessary)
    • SHOW MORE OF THE DIFFICULT ASPECTS OF THE FINAL CLIMB
    • SHOW MORE OF ED AT TOP
    ✳ • THE RIDGE - VERY DRAMATIC FROM DISTANCE BUT WHEN SHOWING THE CLIMB ON THE RIDGE, NEEDS TO SHOW IT MORE DRAMATICALLY.

2

While editing **Everest**, we conducted several test screenings at our office and then one final test on the giant IMAX screen in Vancouver's Canada Place Theatre. From that morning's show to 400 industry insiders, Steve and I made many significant changes, making the film's story more clear, more emotionally told, and with a stronger conclusion at the summit. We also learned that we needed a stronger narrator than Mel Gibson, so we selected Liam Neeson, who did a wonderful job.

IMAX THEATRE FILM TOPIC SURVEY

We are deciding which films to produce over the next five years and we need your help. Of the following topics, please **RATE WHICH FILMS YOU WOULD COME TO SEE** on a 10 point scale. Score a 10 for films you would DEFINITELY want to see, and 8 or 9 for PROBABLY, 5 for maybe and 1 for NEVER

SCORE
(10 – 1)

TITLES AND DESCRIPTIONS

8 — **MYSTERY OF THE NILE** ① 536/68 = 7.88
Past the Great Pyramids, the Sphinx, and the riches of Luxor, we venture into the heart of Africa to follow in the historic footsteps of explorer Richard Burton, to find the source of one of Earth's longest rivers.

4 — **OCEAN PLANET** ③ 521/68 = 7.66
On an adventurous journey, follow scientist Alexandra Boehm from the peaks of Italy's Alps to the ice fields of the North Pole to the coral reefs of Tuvalu Island in search of an answer: Do the people of earth have enough water?

7 — **JOURNEY TO INDIA** ⑨ 403/68 = 5.93
The historical sweep of India, its cultures, inventions and treasures - - culminating in the science of building the most amazing tribute to love ever constructed - - the Taj Mahal.

8 — **EVERGLADES ADVENTURE** ⑧ 446/68 = 6.56
Migrating birds sweep across the sky, crocodiles snap at divers' feet, air-boats wisk across the glassy marshland as scientists study the freshwater cradles of life of the Everglades and the Mississippi Delta.

6 — **TO THE ARCTIC** ⑥ 505/68 = 7.43
Robert Peary's historic 1909 expedition to the North Pole is the backdrop for a modern-day Arctic journey, where adventurous explorers encounter polar bears, walruses, whales and more.

7 — **GREECE: SECRETS OF THE PAST** ④ 513/68 = 7.54
An intrepid archeologist explores the high mountains and deep blue seas of Greece and its islands, and examines the ancient ruins of a colony (some say it was Atlantis) destroyed by a volcano 3500 years ago.

4 — **HUMPBACK WHALES** ⑤ 507/68 = 7.46
Follow a group of scientist-divers as they travel to Fiji, Hawaii and the Caribbean to study the endangered humpback and try to unlock the mystery of these majestic animals' haunting "singing".

7 — **SPACE JOURNEY** ② 526/68 = 7.74
Follow a woman astronaut and a male astronomer as they search for knowledge about Mars and the insights this neighboring red planet can provide about the possible existence of extraterrestrials.

2 — **SOCCER – THE WORLD GAME** ⑩ 310 68 = 4.56
Explore the exciting culture and spirit of soccer, discovering what drives different people from all all across the world to love this sport. Culminates at the exciting Men's and Women's World Cup Championships.

8 — **AFRICAN ADVENTURE** ⑦ 488/68 = 7.18
Three adventurers trek across part of the Masai homeland in Tanzania, a rugged, isolated environment rarely seen by outsiders. Encounter wildebeests, elephants, buffalo and their predators – lions, hyenas and cheetahs.

Our Topic Testing: To determine the appeal and attraction of various topics for IMAX films, every two years we'd conduct a survey of our IMAX customers as they stood in line for another IMAX film. This way, we'd know what our distinct customer would want to see. Each test presented ten topics in the exact same format, so we could compare 1998's test with 2004's test. Sports films (soccer, golf, the Olympic Games) were least attractive—and strongly visual locational films were most attractive (Nile, space, ocean, Greece). This is one such test, from one theater from a Thursday crowd of 68 people (of 2,000 people tested in 6 theaters). This customer was male, 30-39 years old, with a graduate degree, earning $100,000 to $300,000 per year, who had seen 6 or more IMAX films including **Everest**. A devoted fan!

*In IMAX, size of the screen is not enough, and state of the art technology is not enough. We must be state of the heart—with stories coming from what's on the page more than the size of the stage. With **Everest** (even in 2D), the film never gets off the human focus, never chooses the sigh-producing "wow" over the "sigh" of the heart. It inspired me, because our success all starts and ends with the customer. We need them to be RAVING, AVID FANS, and with **Everest**, those expectations have been exceeded.*

—Peter Guber, Sony Pictures, excerpted from his "Where We Should Go" speech at the 1998 Large Format Cinema Conference

Everest ended its three-year run as champion with distinction, becoming the top-grossing documentary of all time and being inducted into the IMAX Corporation's IMAX Hall of Fame. The film earned top honors in every category: Best Film, Best Script, Best Music, and Best Photography.

> **"It may be hard to believe, but when we went to Nepal to shoot Everest, Araceli Segarra was very quiet, subdued, and shy—for two solid days. It turns out she felt intimidated by the presence of legendary climbers. But in the end, irrepressible people are . . . well, irrepressible."**
>
> –STEPHEN JUDSON, CO-DIRECTOR, CO-WRITER, EDITOR

In a June 1998 press release, Rich Gelfond, co-CEO of IMAX, said, "**Everest** is a phenomenon that has drastically raised the profile of IMAX theaters around the world, bringing more people to IMAX theaters for the first time and generating record box office results. IMAX has clearly been a beneficiary of the remarkable success of MacGillivray Freeman Films' **Everest**. The film's performance is stimulating an increase in business activity for IMAX in terms of new theater inquiries, broadening of existing relationships and new film projects."

Jamling, Araceli, David, Sumiyo, Ed, Roger, Paula, Robert, Brad, and Steve, our five summiting sherpas: Wongbu Sherpa, Jangbu Sherpa, Muktu Lhakpa Sherpa, Dorje Sherpa, Thilen Sherpa—and the support staff—will have my love forever. As for that decision to move forward without financial partners, let's just say it turned out all right! What's more, it set us up for a new era of mission-centered filmmaking dedicated to the conservation of our natural world.

Remembering Everest: The Right Risks
by Stephen Judson

I grew up in the sticks. Movies were a big deal. When I was eight years old, my parents drove me 45 minutes to the big city to see a documentary called **The Conquest of Everest**. It had a huge emotional impact on me. The images haunted me for many months.

Forty years later, when I wandered aimlessly into Greg's office, coffee mug in hand, he asked me what I thought about making a 15/70mm film about an expedition to Mount Everest. His question tapped into my boyhood dreams, so I reacted with a loud burst of unbridled enthusiasm. Days later, it struck me what a momentous question Greg had asked—and how much he had on the line. If Jim Freeman had still been alive, Greg would have asked him, of course. Maybe I was the next best thing. Greg also consulted with Alec Lorimore and Bill Bennett, who, unlike me, had a good feel for the business equation. But it wasn't the same. The three of us had no skin in the game. Greg was on his own.

Looking back, it's easy to see the trajectory of MFF's success as somehow inevitable. Greg did what no one else managed to do: He kept a 15/70 production/distribution company thriving for decades. He rolled the dice on producing **Everest**, even though the risks were real and the outcome entirely uncertain. Besides financial risk, **Everest** carried a risk of death that lurked in the background.

Fast forward to editing, where telling the story of the tragedy was a difficult puzzle. Much of the audience, having read Krakauer's book, would be expecting certain story points. We simply didn't have the footage to do justice to the full story. I had to make it elliptical, merging images, music, and words. But the sequences still didn't come together. Greg pushed me again and again to simplify the story. It finally clicked. This was just one of a thousand times over the decades when Greg helped my storytelling by urging me to simplify.

Everest was a watershed film, not just for MFF and the giant screen industry, but for Greg personally. In the early films, I sometimes sensed a vacuum, like an empty seat at the table. I sometimes wondered if Greg caught himself absentmindedly turning to seek advice from the friend who wasn't there. But after the massive effort of producing and promoting **Everest**, I never felt Jim Freeman's shadow in the same way again. Greg had taken a huge calculated risk with **Everest**—the right risk, as it turned out. Having climbed his own mountain by dragging this movie into existence through sheer force of will, Greg had proven himself to be his own man.

(FACING PAGE) Araceli's artistic eye loved the unmistakable beauty of the icefall. Here she tries hard to climb smoothly, so that the three ladders lashed together don't topple.

CHAPTER 19

Taking Our Filmmaking to a New Level of Import

MFF GIANT-SCREEN FILMS	GROSS BOX OFFICE THROUGH DECEMBER 2019
America's Musical Journey	$2.5 million
Dream Big	$16 million
National Parks Adventure	$32 million
Humpback Whales	$22.4 million
Journey to the South Pacific	$14 million
To The Arctic	$26 million
Arabia	$8 million
Van Gogh: Brush with Genius	$9 million
Grand Canyon Adventure	$31 million
The Alps	$20 million
Hurricane on the Bayou	$23 million
Greece: Secrets of the Past	$17 million
Mystery of the Nile	$52 million
Coral Reef Adventure	$67 million
Top Speed	$9 million
Journey Into Amazing Caves	$55 million
Adventures in Wild California	$21 million
Dolphins	$100 million
Everest	$155 million
The Magic of Flight	$45 million
Singapore: A New Day	$4 million
Stormchasers	$19 million
The Living Sea	$110 million
Indonesia Indah IV	$4 million
The Discoverers	$19 million
At Sea	$4 million
Eureka!	$2 million
Emeralds of the Sea	$3.5 million
Homeland	$5.5 million
To The Limit	$81 million
Race the Wind	$12 million
Island Child	$4.5 million
Dance of Life	$9 million
Speed	$52 million
Behold Hawaii	$13 million
Flyers	$39 million
To Fly!	$135 million
Films 1960-1976	$8 million
Cumulative Box Office	**$1.2 billion**

"It stands to reason. A super-sharp image looks more like real life than a blurry one. Our brains tell us that. People love sharp images because that's what real life looks like, and they'll continue to vote for quality with their purchasing decisions. It's that simple."

The release of **Everest** in a record-breaking 250 IMAX theaters enlarged our core customer base and enabled our team to proactively build on that momentum by creating the Great Adventure Film Series, an annual series of science-based adventures, like **Everest**, filmed in exotic locations. Each film was marketed to the hilt, was paired with educational branching elements to reach students, and was released yearly in late February to play through December, a repeating pattern our audience loved, resulting in record attendance.

During this time, 1999 to 2012, however, our industry was weathering big storms. First, things got difficult in the early 2000s, with commercial theaters falling into bankruptcy due to overbuilding. Then the terrorist attacks of September 11, 2001, put a virtual halt to travel and museum attendance from tourists. To compound matters, IMAX stock hit an all-time low of about $.75 per share on September 25, 2001, and some uninformed theaters panicked and resorted to screening cheap 2K digital 3D films blown up to IMAX size, with blurry images on-screen. As I told my staff, these things seemed to happen every ten years, just when you were feeling comfortable!

To get a handle on these challenges, and create a new paradigm for our industry, we invited our Blue Ribbon Advisory Board to a winter meeting in a warm location. Fifteen theater advisors gathered with us at the Rancho Mirage golf resort near Palm Springs in early 2003. Shaun, who was now 22 and studying business economics at Emory University at the time, had spent six months interviewing theater directors, discussing possible solutions, and gathering demographic data that would become part of a business analysis to predict the future profitability of our industry. He asked to present his conclusions at our Blue Ribbon meeting. That morning, he borrowed my only sports jacket. When it came time, he was more nervous than I had ever seen him—more so than during a championship soccer game when his team was tied going into the final minutes. His shirt and my coat were soon drenched with sweat. He apologized, but he should have recognized how little I cared about my wardrobe and how proud Barbara and I were of his presentation. Our son impressed everyone and showed that he understood our compact industry better than we did.

As a result, we created a new model for producing and marketing IMAX documentaries, and once we overcame the recession, attendance grew, and in 2010, our small company and its Great Adventure Film Series passed a revered Hollywood benchmark: $1 billion in ticket sales. We proudly issued the following press release:

LAGUNA BEACH, CA (September 2, 2010)—Pioneering giant-screen film producer/director Greg MacGillivray has joined an elite club of filmmakers whose films have cumulatively earned more than $1 billion in ticket sales at the worldwide box office. Approximately 100 feature filmmakers have attained this level of box office success in the history of cinema according to industry trackers, but

(FACING PAGE, TOP ROW) Our main characters in **Grand Canyon Adventure** were adults and daughters: Shana Watahomigie and daughter, Cree; Tara Davis, Wade's daughter; Kick Kennedy, Robert's daughter. (FACING PAGE, BOTTOM) Ready for an action-packed run down the most difficult rapids in the Grand Canyon, Lava Falls, Wade Davis and Shana Watahomigie check the IMAX camera.

MacGillivray is the first documentary filmmaker to join the group, a benchmark celebrated by the entertainment industry's trade journal, Daily Variety, *in a special feature now hitting newsstands.*

In that highlight periodical, *Daily Variety's* Iain Blair wrote:

The film business is full of showy sprinters: filmmakers and movies that flash by as they ring up impressive box office numbers, only to leave little of substance in their wake. Then there are the dedicated long-distance specialists, like Greg MacGillivray, whose thought-provoking documentaries—including **Everest**, **To The Arctic**, **To Fly!** *and* **The Living Sea***—play for years, even decades at a time. These giant screen labors of love may not have made MacGillivray a household name, but over the past four decades, they've entertained and educated millions around the globe, and recently—in a hare-and-tortoise scenario Hollywood should envy—quietly passed $1 billion in box office. While most filmmakers would be ecstatic about reaching the milestone, MacGillivray is not one of those people. "I'm actually a little embarrassed, as it's the educational value of our films and the kinds of changes they've helped bring about that are the most important thing to me," says MacGillivray, 65, who co-founded MacGillivray Freeman Films (MFF) back in the '60s with partner Jim Freeman.*

To me, this financial milestone signified longevity and perseverance more than anything else. We're the first to acknowledge that our films are not normal documentaries, but specialized experiences. Just like some of the highest-grossing films in Hollywood history, including **Avatar** with its spectacular 3D effects, **2001: A Space Odyssey** with its 70mm-wide screen, and **This Is Cinerama** with its wide tri-screen wraparound WOW, our films benefited from a superior, specialized presentation that audiences couldn't get enough of: the clarity and brilliance of the IMAX theater 15/70 projection.

Most importantly, this 2010 financial benchmark proved that we could take another big risk, utilize our new business model, and delve into projects that we were most passionate about: those focusing on conservation. And it was the Great Adventure Film Series that set us up. The series began with **Everest**, then the Academy Award-nominated film **Dolphins**, and was followed by **Adventures in Wild California**, **Journey into Amazing Caves**, **Coral Reef Adventure**, **Mystery of the Nile**, **Hurricane on the Bayou**, **Greece**, **Grand Canyon Adventure**, **Arabia,** and **To The Arctic**. From those stellar films, shown on the following pages, we created a new goal to turn people on to nature. But what stories would we tell?

(FACING PAGE) To give the audience highlight 3D sequences in the Colorado River rapids, we planned two "you're-getting-splashed-in-the-face" shots using the giant Solido 3D IMAX camera, which was worth $1 million. We didn't want to flip the raft! (RIGHT) The bottlenose dolphin.

Dolphins (2000)

(LEFT) Kathleen Dudzinski holds her breath to videotape postures and record matching vocalizations of spotted dolphins in the Caribbean. (ABOVE) Dean Bernal with his friend, a bottlenose dolphin named JoJo. (BELOW) The study of dolphin intelligence by Louis Herman and his staff in Hawaii led to greater protection for this perceptive, keen-minded animal.

Troy Hartman, the best skysurfer, over San Diego and filmed by the best free-fall cameraperson, Joe Jennings. We waited for months to get a perfectly clear day, after a rainstorm, to shoot this in IMAX.

Journey into Amazing Caves (2001)

Nancy Aulenbach and Dr. Hazel Barton (LEFT) repel, then swing themselves into a cave opening at the Grand Canyon. Taking an audience member to magnificent places was enhanced by the high quality of our photography, but there was also another trade secret. Unlike all Hollywood films and all our competitors' IMAX films, our film prints looked better projected on the giant screen! Everyone noticed this because rather than fourth-generation prints made from copies of copies, all our prints were made directly from the camera-original film—so they looked sharper, less grainy, and more realistic. I feel that this hidden secret accounted for a bit better audience satisfaction— maybe by 5 or 10 percent!

Coral Reef Adventure (2003)

The Marrakesh Express

by Howard Hall

Bob Cranston, Mark Thurlow, and I descended through clear waters outside the Tiputa Pass, a deep channel through the reef that connects French Polynesia's Rangiroa Atoll with the open Pacific. The incoming tide slowly began carrying us toward the mouth of the channel. Once we entered the pass, we knew the current would become a screaming torrent as the tide rips through the deep blue water toward the shark cave below.

At 150 feet I signaled Bob to close the gas intake valve on the massive camera housing. The maximum operating depth for the camera system was 140 feet, but we were descending to 240 feet. At that depth, the housing would crush like an aluminum beer can in the grip of a weightlifter—if not for the valve. A few minutes later we settled in front of the cave, then turned seaward to gaze out into the cobalt-blue open ocean. From there we should have been able to see clouds of grey reef sharks. Instead, we saw only a dozen or so. Where were the sharks? Rangiroa's spectacular schools of grey reef sharks were the main reason we had come to this remote atoll in French Polynesia. We hoped images of the schools would become a key sequence in the 2003 MacGillivray Freeman IMAX feature **Coral Reef Adventure**.

We waited at the mouth of the cave for another twenty minutes, but no other sharks approached close enough to warrant a shot. I signaled to my friends that it was time to head up the slope and into the pass. This was the fun part. As we rose up the slope and entered the mouth of the pass, the current began to increase. Both Mark and I reminded Bob to open the valve on the camera housing as we approached 150 feet. Soon I saw bubbles pouring out of the housing's exhaust valve and I stopped worrying about the camera blowing apart.

There were deep canyons in the bottom of the pass at about 100 feet. As we raced through the pass I began to see grey reef sharks hovering deep in these canyons. I decided to drop into the next canyon and try for a shot. I took one handle of the camera housing and Bob, Mark, and I dropped down to the bottom, skimming close to the coral. As we passed over the rim of the next canyon, we swam hard, straight down, struggling against the buffeting turbulence. When we reached the calm water below the rim I looked up to see that the canyon was filled with hundreds of sharks. This was the shot we were looking for!

Mark followed us as Bob and I slowly swam through the canyon. I triggered the camera and captured a great scene as swarms of sharks spilled past us. Then I dropped down deeper into the canyon for a short second. There was a tight group of sharks hovering near the far rim of the canyon. As I raised the camera, one of the sharks arched its back dramatically and pointed its pectoral fins nearly

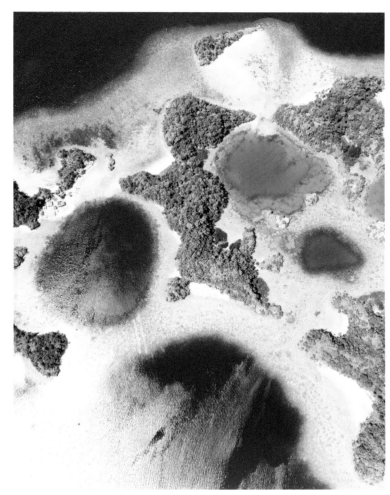

(FACING PAGE) On Rangiroa Atoll, the team finally located the famous gray reef sharks. (ABOVE) The reef formations in the South Pacific.

The Marrakesh Express

1:13   #20

straight down. Scientists call this behavior "defense posture" and it is often followed by a lightning-fast attack. I've had two friends badly bitten by gray reef sharks that had exhibited defense posture. In one case, the attack had been triggered by the flash from an underwater strobe. I knew that we were in serious danger. As much as I would have liked to include a shot of a grey reef shark in defense posture as part of our shark sequence, I knew to slowly and quietly back away.

In **Coral Reef Adventure**, Greg MacGillivray and Steve Judson brilliantly cut scenes of our underwater film crew flying over the coral through Tiputa Pass accompanied by the Crosby, Stills, & Nash song "Marrakesh Express." Few can watch this sequence and not be thrilled by the sheer joy of underwater flight. Now and for the rest of my life, every time I hear that song I will be transported back to those amazing dives flying through the Tiputa Pass with my friends at the Rangiroa Atoll. It was the ride of a lifetime.

Mystery of the Nile (2005)

In the first source-to-sea navigation of the Blue Nile River, Pasquale Scaturro and Gordon Brown risked death by gunfire from shiftas, attacks by hippopotamuses, and wind driven storms on Lake Nasser. In four months, they succeeded in the great adventure through Ethiopia, Sudan, and Egypt to reach the Mediterranean, and the film, **Mystery of the Nile**, became the year's biggest IMAX hit. (ABOVE) Tissisat Falls, Ethiopia. (BELOW) Blue Nile rapids. (FACING PAGE) Passing the Italian Bridge.

Hurricane on the Bayou (2006)

The wetlands of Louisiana are the largest in America, but erosion has caused them damage, and over the past decades, their important role in slowing a hurricane as it approaches from the gulf has diminished. Storms like Katrina have devastated the area near New Orleans. Our goal was to encourage funding to restore the wetlands—and our film succeeded. After a congressional screening at the Smithsonian, the US Congress funded a new program.

Greece: Secrets of the Past (2006)

Grand Canyon Adventure (2008)

(ABOVE) The Great Adventure Film Series takes you places. (FACING PAGE) In IMAX, we tell the story of the three ages of early Greece, the birth of Western civilization, and the creation of democracy.

How *Grand Canyon Adventure* Inspired Change

Our films are collaborations between filmmakers and sponsors who care deeply about helping the planet. In **Grand Canyon Adventure**, our partners were Teva and Kohler—whose team helped us to implement national, regional, and grassroots promotions bringing awareness to fresh water conservation. The campaign reached millions of people and generated early word-of-mouth excitement about the topic. In marketing terms, there were an estimated 86.8 million impressions for national and regional publicity, plus an estimated 21.9 million impressions for local publicity in 33 markets.

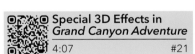

Special 3D Effects in *Grand Canyon Adventure* 4:07 #21

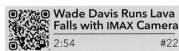

Wade Davis Runs Lava Falls with IMAX Camera 2:54 #22

Kohler coordinated water conservation events. They put low-flow toilets in the lobby as a comical photo-op. They even provided theaters with 213 new water-saving fixtures to promote the film's message, saving 1.4 million gallons of water a year. And each audience member recieved a written list of ways to save water at home.

The film inspired local river cleanups and environmental education—and film proceeds helped to bring fresh water to thousands of African school children.

Arabia (2010)

(LEFT) The astounding sharpness of the IMAX projected image allowed each one of the hundreds of thousands of hajj participants to be seen at Mecca in the yearly pilgrimage. (ABOVE) Henna hand painting is a customary ritual at weddings. (BELOW) Over the centuries, camels have been the desert mode of transportation, particularly on the frankincense trade route from the Indian Ocean through Arabia to the Mediterranean Sea.

To The Arctic (2012)

The North Pole

SURF · HOLLYWOOD · IMAX ENTERTAINMENT · MISSION

"We were documenting a moment in time that could foretell, not just the end of an ecosystem, not just the keystone species that live there, but the ability for indigenous human populations to survive. We were documenting the potential for something so monumental that it could ricochet around the planet."

Three of the Earth's most vulnerable "canaries in the coal mine" are the Great Barrier Reef, the Amazon, and the Arctic. Impacts to any one of them could alter fundamental attributes of life on Earth itself. In 2010, we reinvented ourselves from a mission of educational adventures in the Great Adventure Film Series to a mission-based media company specializing in saving the environment and protecting the wonders of the world. For our final Great Adventure film and our first conservation campaign, entitled **To The Arctic**, we were spurred on by one undeniable fact: Average temperatures in the Arctic were rising twice as quickly as anywhere else in the world. This canary, it seemed, was already on life support!

What exactly might this mean—what did it already mean?—to the animals and people living there? What could it mean for the rest of us? Once we got answers, we were bound and determined to share that information in an IMAX film.

One significant milepost inspiration was **An Inconvenient Truth**, the impressive 2006 Oscar-winning documentary by Al Gore, Laurie David, and Davis Guggenheim. The film made the topic of climate change a dinner-table conversation in millions of US households. It also acknowledged that global warming is a difficult problem to solve, and that any solution leaves one powerful industry holding the bag: big oil. When **An Inconvenient Truth** came out, the oil industry fought back by dishonestly attacking the science, just as the tobacco industry had denied its connection to lung cancer decades earlier. Within a few years, the public became so confused by the oil industry's campaign that belief in climate change decreased. Greed had won out. We had to do something.

In 2010, we had some heavy hitters on the team. Our first Arctic partnership came when Robert F. Kennedy Jr. called me on an early prototype cell phone from an airport somewhere.

"I've just flown back from Alaska with Tom Campion," he said, "who owns Zumiez, a huge skateboard and clothing company, and he wants to—" and the line went dead. He called back: "... he wants to finance a film with you on the Arctic

(FACING PAGE) Marine mammals, the mother polar bear and her cub. (RIGHT) Insulated by my "orange puffy" coat, I filmed images of our icebreaking ship.

because—" and again, dead. On the third try, I got the whole story: Tom Campion loves the Arctic and wants to save it from rampant and unnecessary exploitation. A great way to do that, Bobby had informed him, was to partner with us on an IMAX film. Over the years, Tom had paid for senators and representatives to visit the Arctic and experience its beauty. Once they saw it, they wanted to save it. But Bobby told him, "An IMAX film can reach a thousand times more people and is even better than being there. It is that convincing and real."

Bobby had seen the power of IMAX firsthand through our film, **Grand Canyon Adventure**. It featured Bobby and his friend, Wade Davis, along with their daughters, Kick and Tara, taking their last father-daughter trip before college, an adventure down the Colorado River. This film had convinced audience members of the importance of conserving fresh water. Bobby believed that one of our films could do the same for the Arctic; and he had found us a sponsor: Tom Campion and the Campion Foundation.

I was used to filming in harsh and dangerous environments, but we had never gone somewhere so remote, so frigid, and so dangerous. Have I mentioned that I don't like the cold? In comparison, Everest was balmy! The Arctic is the harshest environment on earth, where temperatures drop to -40°F. If we were to fall into the 28-degree water without proper gear, we would die in three minutes flat. And even with protective gear—so-called survival suits of heavy neoprene that fit like sausage casings—we could not stay alive for more than forty-five minutes. If our ship were to hit an iceberg and sink, we would quite simply perish, no questions asked—and quickly at that.

After nine months of research and watching every video made about the region, we crafted our story based on the experiences of three photographers who had interacted with the Arctic in unique ways. Over the next four years, we would visit seven times, braving the elements for eight full months. **To The Arctic** would become the longest shoot in MacGillivray Freeman history. As the process unfolded, it also became the most animal-centric IMAX film we'd worked on since **Jonathan Livingston Seagull** in 1973.

Our first characters were Leanne Jeffries and Karsten Heuer, a husband and wife filmmaker and biologist, respectively, who had spent six months tracking, photographing, and living with a huge caribou

To The Arctic

FILMED IN: 15 PERFORATION/70MM

RELEASE DATE: April 20, 2012

NARRATED BY: Meryl Streep

SONGS BY: Paul McCartney

Giant Screen Cinema Association Award: Best Film of the Year

By partnering with Coca-Cola, this campaign resulted in $4 million in donations to Arctic conservation.

"Its breathtaking photography has a purpose beyond pretty pictures: to remind us that climate change is causing the frigid Arctic to melt . . . a visual treat, and an important reminder." —SEATTLE TIMES

herd on its annual migration in northern Canada and Alaska. Their mission was to understand what such an arduous trek is like from the animals' perspective. At 800 miles, it's one of the longest land migrations of any animal. After making the grueling journey on foot, they created a film and accompanying book called **Being Caribou**. For our film, they revisited the area, and we recreated part of their journey.

But finding the caribou was harder than expected. Because the area the caribou traverse is so wide, it isn't easy to intercept the speedy herd midmigration. Years ago, scientists wondered why the caribou were able to move faster than any other hooved animal. They carefully locked one on a treadmill to study its gait with slow-motion cameras and discovered that caribou have unique, spring-loaded hooves that snap back after each step, allowing a faster stride. What's more, this amazingly simple interplay of bones, tendons, and the cohesion between tissue layers produced a distinctive clicking sound that we duplicated in the film.

Filming *To The Arctic*
2:15   #23

Our team was out in the wild for a month, waiting, wondering, listening for clicks, until one day they were awakened by a herd of clicking caribou serenely sauntering past their tent flaps. They shot some wonderful close-ups and then followed the herd as it made a challenging river crossing.

These caribou, also known as wild reindeer, helped us to demonstrate how climate change impacts wildlife. For example, the hotter summer resulted in rivers flooding earlier in the year than usual, and the now-wider rivers slowed the annual migration of the 400,000 to 500,000 animals. Because 90 percent of caribou births occur over the same 10-day period each year, the migration delay—in this case three weeks—meant that some babies would be born on the hoof, or before the mothers reached their birthing ground destination. These newborns would quite literally have to hit the ground running and

---

(FACING PAGE) Sniffing for prey in the Arctic. There is ice and water for thousands of miles. No trees, plants, earthworms—nothing except seals, birds, walruses, and 20,000 polar bears. That's why polar bears are hard to find—they're spread out over an area the size of China, continually searching for food. That's their job. Polar bears are eating machines, even more so than great white sharks. When we were filming, we sensed one strong feeling: We knew that if we fell out of our icebreaker, there was nothing we could do—we'd be eaten within seconds. The mothers need food so they can produce rich milk to nurse their cubs for their first year of life. After that, the moms and cubs catch seals together—and then cubs are off on their own. Polar bears live for about 30 years.

ford rushing rivers. They were thus more vulnerable to drownings and polar bear predators than ever before, and not all of them made it.

As we shot our film, we came to see that with a family of caribou, walruses or polar bears, there was a common truth: it was the mothers who were doing the heavy lifting in the Arctic. These splendid creatures never got a day, or even an hour, off. The entire time they travel with, nurture, and protect their young, they are on the lookout for predators. With this realization, we'd found our main theme. I told our writers, "This is *gold*: we'll tell the story of motherhood. This is a great, emotionally riveting theme for everyone."

The Stars of the Show

After years of filming, we had imagery that would depict the impacts of climate change on the brave mothers of the Arctic wild. But then a miracle happened aboard a 130-foot, steel-hulled icebreaker called the MS *Havsel*. She was moored at Norway's Svalbard islands, the northernmost set of inhabited islands closest to the North Pole, and we rented her from a captain who had been plying the waters of Iceland, the North Sea, and the Arctic Ocean for decades.

The wise captain suggested we travel north to where a whale had died, its carcass becoming a treat for several polar bears. Each day at about noon, they'd come for lunch, so we set up our IMAX camera on shore, framed the shot to include the tasty vertebrae, anchored it to the ground with heavy-duty chains, tested our radio-controlled trigger, and waited safely in a small boat.

About noon, a mother and her baby cub arrived. What luck! But alas, the new, strange object on shore with a shiny lens and a tantalizing rubber eyepiece intrigued the cub. First it gnawed at the chain, then it slowly climbed up a tripod leg to finally sit on the top of the IMAX camera and magazine itself, where it sharpened its teeth on the lens housing. I watched this in horror, hoping that the cub's weight wouldn't topple the camera into the water. Finally, after five minutes, the cub decided to join its mom, who was eating meat off the vertebrae, allowing us to start the camera and get a cool shot.

A Polar Bear Cub Gets a Close-up
2:52 #24

The next day, on the luckiest leg of the adventure, the *Havsel* would take us to the spot where icebergs crumbled off the ice shelf—and where we would unexpectedly meet our story's headliners. MacGilli-luck had been present from the start, but on this last leg of filming, it showed up in spades. An unusual wind from the east had pushed hundreds of icebergs together, forcing all of the region's polar bears to gather in close quarters for about three weeks. This gave us once-in-a-lifetime access to perhaps 40 bears and their subtlest habits.

(LEFT) This is the image photographed by the IMAX camera that the cub balanced on top of—we triggered the camera wirelessly from the boat.

(ABOVE) In the early years, Jim and I narrated the films with our own voices. We could tell the stories most convincingly. But later, when our subjects and stories changed, we needed better storytelling voices and a more mature emotional delivery. For the light-hearted **The Magic of Flight**, I chose actor Tom Selleck, here with Steve Judson, Jack Stephens, Mary Jane Dodge and me. (BELOW) For the story of Jawi in **Journey to the South Pacific**, I chose the sensitive voice of Cate Blanchett, and for **Dream Big**, the wide-ranging skills of actor Jeff Bridges, here with (left to right) a studio mixer, Shaun, Barbara, Jason Paul, Steve, and me.

Making *To The Arctic* with Meryl Streep
2:24   #25

But it wasn't until we met MB, aka Mother Bear, who traveled with her two seven-month-old cubs, that we found the heart and soul of our story. While the polar bears we'd photographed until then were camera shy, skittish, and wary, MB was oddly comfortable with us. She allowed the boat to drift very close to her family—sometimes as close as 30 feet—and for five days, she simply did her thing for our IMAX cameras. The cubs did their thing too, playing, nursing, and scampering around the ice floes. In those five days, we got to know them by their personalities, their whimsies . . . and their frequent races to avoid being killed.

The only bear predators in this vast, white wonderland are other polar bears. The most carnivorous of all bear species, when they emerge from their five- to seven-month hibernation, they emerge famished. Separated by space and water from the seal population, adult males will eat bear cubs without batting an eye. MB's main occupation, all day, all night, all the time, was to sniff the air for predators and prey. She was constantly on call, trying to feed her babies and keep them alive. One day, she repelled four separate raids by much larger males as our team kept shooting and kept rooting for her, knowing that we could not interfere.

The centerpiece story of **To The Arctic**, because it so magnificently exemplified the heavy lifting of an Arctic mother, was a nail-biting, four-mile escape by MB, during which she instructed her twins and managed logistics. The chase culminated in her turning the tables in a daring showdown. Because this encounter was so unusual, I wrote a lay-scientific description of what occurred and sent it to the 30 or so polar bear scientists around the world.

To capture this sort of rare footage, we had to stay alert at all times. Lead director of photography Brad Ohlund who, with **To The Arctic**, notched his 90th on-location shoot with our company, explained: "We took shifts, with someone always on the bridge of the ship keeping an eye on the bears. We would sleep with our clothes on. It was like being a firefighter. If something happened—maybe a male was on the prowl—we'd get a knock on the door and we'd throw on our boots and jackets and race up to the deck. The camera was all set up. We'd just put our eyes to the viewfinder and start shooting away."

Shaun knows exactly what Ohlund means. "The crazy, amazing, rewarding thing about wildlife filmmaking is that moment when you get it right," he says. "All the variables line up: the perfect light, the animals, the action, the angles, the incredible beauty, and the story attached to it. You hardly ever have that opportunity, but when it happens, it's magnificent."

A Story Told by the Best

Once we began editing this story of motherhood, I realized that there was only one person whom I felt could narrate it: Meryl Streep. We'd

(ABOVE) The Arctic glaciers are melting quickly. (BELOW) Filming IMAX beneath the ice.

worked together twice before, and I felt that this intelligent mother of four talented children would present the climate problem most effectively. But Meryl's schedule was chock full. She was promoting and shooting several new films. She only had one day available for the narration and it was the day after the Academy Awards. She had earned a nomination that year for her portrayal of Margaret Thatcher in **The Iron Lady**, and her performance—indeed, her complete transformation into Dame Maggie—thrilled and mesmerized audiences. Most deservedly, she ended up winning. Sitting at home, I worried that she would be out late celebrating, so I contacted her assistant to suggest that we move our start time to later in the day so that she could sleep. But, right at 10 a.m., per the original plan, a beautiful, melodic voice sang out, "I'm here!" With a huge smile on her face, Meryl hugged me, then did an amazing job with the narration, bringing the Arctic story of motherhood to life. We walked out of our building and down the stairs, holding hands until we got to her car. And off she went to meet her son for lunch. In my mind, Meryl Streep is the definition of a wonderful human—and the perfect, caring mother of four to tell our unique story of motherhood. [26]

Over the next eight months we completed our film and, following our new model, engaged a host of partners who would benefit from its release. With Shaun's sales acumen, we, along with Warner Bros. and IMAX Corporation, released **To The Arctic** using a robust worldwide campaign of cross-collateralized advertising and promotion that allowed the subject of the effects of climate change on polar bears, caribou, and walruses to be shared and appreciated by millions of viewers in over 75 countries.

As part of this massive crusade, we partnered with The Coca-Cola Company and the World Wildlife Fund to create a multi-year education and fundraising campaign that would support efforts to create an MPA in northern Greenland twice the size of Texas. In their ad campaign, called Arctic Home, Coca-Cola used our spectacular footage of MB on special Coca-Cola cans. "Little did MB know that she'd become the poster child for her species," joked Shaun.

Coca-Cola's award-winning TV and print ads promoted the film, as did the Arctic Home PR campaign, website, special events, social media, and digital ads. With all the partners singing the same tune for six months, the campaign really moved the needle. Millions of people were moved to act. "Let's save the polar bear," they agreed. They cared! Because of this revolution-

26 Meryl Streep is the most highly honored actor of all time, with 21 Academy Award nominations and 3 wins.

> **"I have so much admiration for [Greg MacGillivray], and his team, and how they have captured sort of impossible subjects and made them available to us in the most vivid ways. It's unimaginable that they can capture this stuff. I'm so glad to be part of it."**
>
> —MERYL STREEP ON *TO THE ARCTIC*

ary campaign and the film's outstanding qualities, **To The Arctic** received the Best Film of the Year award from the Giant Screen Cinema Association.

A Mission-Based Campaign

Then, in parallel with the release of **To The Arctic**, Barbara and I announced the establishment of the One World One Ocean campaign, with its mission of fostering awareness and mobilizing support for the restoration and protection of the world's oceans. We began by donating $5 million to fund a 30-year ocean media campaign. **To The Arctic** was the campaign's first release. Our concept was simple. Just as Jacques Cousteau opened people's eyes to the beauty of the ocean through the medium of TV, we want to open hearts and minds using IMAX films, feature presentations, television specials, and new media programming.

In **To The Arctic**, we found a simple message to take home with us. A mother polar bear will do anything to protect her cubs, including taking the offensive against a predatory male twice her size; but she is powerless against the threat of a changing natural environment that risks turning their way of life on its head. The Arctic Ocean serves as the thermometer of our world. With its cold-water runoff supercharging the currents of the great ocean conveyor belt that moderates weather everywhere, and with the polar ice cap acting as a climate-balancing shield that reflects 80 percent of the sun's energy back into space, it's easy to see how regional climate changes can end up impacting the entire Earth, and all of us who live on it.

Even during our lifetime, the polar bears that use this ice to survive may need to look for another place to live—but with films like **To The Arctic**, produced in a new partnership with IMAX and Warner Bros., we were doing what we could to raise awareness and inspire change.

(FACING PAGE) Our boat captain, who had tracked polar bears for 40 years, said, "this mother is the smartest bear I've ever followed. She conserves energy, hunts skillfully, and continually protects her cubs from predators." The mother and her cubs stayed with us for five days.

New Guinea and the Biggest Fish

SURF

HOLLYWOOD

IMAX ENTERTAINMENT

MISSION

> "The Jawi we would bring back to Sawinggrai was a more mature boy, a braver boy. At only 13, he was now a boy who could put into perspective how his village's reef impacts, and is impacted by, the larger world."

For our next conservation film, I wanted to connect with kids everywhere by featuring a young island boy of color named Jawi. What I didn't anticipate was how tough it would be for the 13-year-old to leave home, even for a month. Hugging his uncle, Yesaya, and his buddies Gibson and Jacob, Jawi felt like he was saying farewell forever. They all cried. The boy went inside the cabin of our departing boat and cowered in a corner for 30 minutes.

Jawi would come to realize that the whole purpose of IMAX is to go big or go home. To do it—to push past your limits, to get to the top, to see the other side of the world—requires creativity, bravery, and a sense of adventure. Jawi had all of that in spades; he just needed a moment. He was about to go big.

The IMAX format allows us to really see vast, breathtaking places. These are the places that we often find ourselves describing with superlatives: the highest, the most remote, the hottest, coldest, largest. These are places audiences wish they could visit, but might never get to.

In an idyllic wonderland, **Journey to the South Pacific** tells the story of a unique floating classroom—a boat—that teaches islanders about the importance of their ocean's health. Jawi and our team would board the 100-foot MV *Kalabia* (originally funded by Conservation International) to educate the children of West Papua. (The project is now underwritten by an independent Indonesian foundation.) In its

first life, the trawler was used for illegal tuna fishing and confiscated by authorities. It was given a new life after being completely refurbished and outfitted with classrooms, libraries, and a paint job that echoed both the local arts and the wonders of the sea. Literally and figuratively, Papuan educators got on board, and soon the *Kalabia* was island-hopping through the region, providing a precious opportunity for kids in 132 island villages to experience hands-on education of the unusually fun kind.

Remarkably, though children in West Papua grow up in the water, many hadn't had the chance to see the reefs with the aid of a mask and snorkel.

"It opened up their world to reefs in a whole new way," noted my son and the film's producer, Shaun. "You see these kids come alive out there." This palpable exhilaration over education became a linchpin of the production.

I fell in love with Indonesia in an emotional, beyond-words way in the 1980s, when I spent more than a year there, diving and making a series of four IMAX films. On my first visit to West Papua, I'd lived in a thatched hut in a Dani village; but now I found myself in Jawi's village of Sawinggrai, population approximately 150, one of the last truly isolated places on our increasingly interconnected Earth.

When I returned years later, I was more enchanted than ever. I loved the warm, caring people and I remained fascinated by the cultures that govern by consensus and community decision-making. I was blown away by how the elders actively taught the young people both their traditions and the responsibility for taking care of the oceans. "Sasi" they call it. Even here, locals already have embraced change, including halting dynamite fishing and establishing marine protected areas (MPA), where damaged reefs and fish populations have made a thrilling comeback.

(FACING PAGE) Thirteen-year-old Jawi was afraid of sharks, but once we showed him how docile the whale sharks were, he had to resist hugging them.

Journey to the South Pacific

FILMED IN: 15 PERFORATION/70MM
RELEASE DATE: November 27, 2012
NARRATED BY: Cate Blanchett
SCORE BY: Steve Wood
100% on Rotten Tomatoes

"Spectacular documentary footage . . . It's amazing the water doesn't spill into the auditorium."
—THE WALL STREET JOURNAL

"We've played this film for the past seven years, anytime we need a huge attendance!"
—OMNIVERSUM THEATRE, HOLLAND

Life Aboard the Kalabia

Our boat's first stop was the Misool Eco Resort in the MPA. In this protected environment, Jawi saw his first seahorse and orangutan crab, along with hawksbill sea turtles; stonefish; a school of gregarious fish called lined sweetlips; a pregnant, docile wobbegong shark; and giant, graceful manta rays feeding on "plankton soup" and endless schools of anchovies. In the past, Misool suffered from overfishing but, amazingly, has rebounded thanks to proactive management. In fact, this entire region has just been established as Indonesia's first "conservation province," with the hope that more of the 34 provinces of Indonesia will follow. After filming this MPA success story at Misool, Jawi and our team set sail for Cenderawasih Bay, two days away, a place where Jawi would have two of the best experiences of his life.

The Leatherback's Last Stand

"Leatherbacks love high-energy, big-wave beaches!" These words from the science advisors rang in our ears as we approached Wermon Beach, one of the most remote beach spots I've ever seen. From the safety of the boat about 200 yards offshore, we were able to appreciate the primordial nature of the rugged coastline. I reassured the crew: "The open-water swells have gone down to three or four feet now, so the shore break should only be six to seven feet."

But my seasoned surfer assessment did little for their confidence. We needed to transport our team of eight people, including Jawi, plus 23 pieces of heavy, expensive IMAX camera equipment onto the beach in one inflatable dinghy. We could all see the mist at the shore from the breaking waves. Though we knew there were four local villagers waiting onshore to help us, it was a slim consolation. This could get dicey.

It took our valiant red Zodiac six rather harrowing trips to shore, timing the waves, to get the cameras, lights, generators, and ten rolls of 65mm film through the surf, onto the beach, and into the outstretched arms of the waiting villagers.

And this was no ordinary beach. A nearly four-mile stretch right out of *Jurassic Park*, the raw jungle abutting it reminded me of Conrad's *Heart of Darkness*. Hundred-foot-tall trees were rooted in the narrow beach that is the age-old habitat of the critically endangered Pacific leatherback, the largest of the seven species of sea turtles: leatherback, olive ridley, Kemp's ridley, green turtle, loggerhead, flatback, and hawksbill. Citing a 6 percent decline in population every year, most scientists call this beach "The Last Stand of the Pacific Leatherback." Here, they are protected from egg poachers, dogs and other predators.

These huge, prehistoric turtles return to this beach every two years to lay their eggs, 100 per clutch, four or five clutches per trip. Their ability to navigate 12,000 miles, slowly swimming halfway around the world, has long confounded even the most experienced scientists. After the fist-sized hatchlings are born on this lost-in-time beach, the tiny newborns spend less than an hour awkwardly flippering their way down the sand to their new ocean home before swimming all the way to California and Oregon. A full 15 years later, the females somehow make their way back to the exact beach where they were born to give life to their own offspring. This fact was incomprehensible to Jawi, and we figured that he wouldn't be the only one in awe. The story of the leatherback is one of the most awe-inspiring events in all of nature. We wanted to tell that story, hoping to help save the species.

Once we reached shore, we heard a humming emanating from the forest—a shrill, unearthly whine that grew in amplitude as we approached the impenetrable edge of green. We were being welcomed by millions of insects, chanting, "We're glad you're here so we can nibble you to death!" As if the warnings about crocodiles in the river weren't enough, we were face to face with insects that were even fiercer than the no-see-ums in Mexico!

There appeared to be no easy way in: no road and no trail. We lugged our cases of IMAX equipment for a mile to get to the one-room hut that we would call home for the next three days. We had the impression that no outsider had ever been here before. And why would they, with 90-degree heat and an equal dose of humidity? This was not Club Med! As we walked along the beach, every footstep was a plunge into thick, dark sand. For the next five hours, we labored. Faces became zombielike and I could practically read the crew's minds: "I chose this career over a law degree? What a romantic, idiotic notion!"

We finally reached our hut, which was in a clearing cut from the jungle. Dusk had fallen and rangers began their night patrol to find and protect the birthing, nesting turtles. We lay down on the floor of the ranger station, eight of us "sleeping" in a 12' x 12' space on a blue tarp stretched over wooden planks. One of our crew labeled it "a mattress turned to 100% firm." Those humming insects did their best to destroy us, crawling over our bodies all night. One the size of a golf ball navigated my chest until I grabbed it and threw it against the wall with a satisfying *splat*! I don't think any of us slept for more than 10 minutes at a time.

A little after midnight we got a call on our radio receiver: "A leatherback is nesting 350 meters east and getting ready to lay her clutch." We roused ourselves for the 20-minute hike to the turtle, careful to keep our headlamps set on red so the turtle would not get distracted and stop her egg laying. We had been briefed by our University of Papua turtle conservationists, so we knew that the turtles would stay away from white lights, but they couldn't see red. When we reached the female, she was already well into her egg laying. What a sight; it was breathtaking. Almost the size of Cindy's Volkswagen Bug back in Laguna, she sat atop a mound she'd built after digging a nearly five-foot-deep hole into which she dropped one egg after another. The huge globs of mucus hanging from her deep black eyes looked like tears but had nothing to do with distress; they actually protected her eyes from the sand flying off her flippers. University scientists Willy and Betuel guided us as we worked under the eerie red glow to capture this miraculous event in IMAX film and digital formats.

The science team carefully hoisted the turtle high enough to record her weight at 600 pounds—well below the species' 1,200-pound record but impressive enough for us! Her length and width were measured and her PIT tag (an ID chip installed on an earlier trip) scanned. After coming all this way and overcoming so many obstacles, we made our way back to our ranger rest station, our work complete. This magnificent event moved us all.

Morning came quickly. Since we'd gotten all our shots on our first of three nights, we began the long trek back down the beach, cautiously anticipating millions of sand flies. Tiny as they are—you can't even see them—they inflict the nastiest of bites that produce unforgettable itchiness. But our end goal propelled us; on the waiting boat were showers and food. Getting out to the *Kalabia* proved no less difficult than any other part of this shoot. The six-foot-high waves were rolling in like clockwork and there was only one spot, at the end of the beach, where we could get our Zodiac in and out safely. Between one set of waves, our boat turned sideways and almost capsized. It again took six trips back and forth. I am not sure how we managed to hold onto everything in that crazy struggle, but I can say with certainty that we refused to spend one extra minute on that

(RIGHT) A baby leatherback turtle, beginning its first trip across the Pacific.

(ABOVE) A difficult location. (BELOW) The largest of turtles, the leatherback, giving birth to its young. (BOTTOM) Jami admires the newborn leatherback turtles, hatched after an incubation period of 60 days, buried in their soft egg sacks beneath the sand.

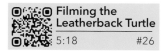

Filming the Leatherback Turtle
5:18   #26

bug-infested beach. Happily, we left with much more than sand-fly itches to remember. We will always have memories and film footage of one of our greatest ocean ambassadors. We steamed off in the *Kalabia*, headed for Jawi's second monster.

Swimming with Sharks

"He's scared!" our Papuan translator said. Jawi was scared of all sharks because his grandfather had nearly lost an arm to one. Jawi also knew that these were not just any sharks. That night, illuminated by our spotlights, swam whale sharks, the largest of them all.

They came to the bagans of Cenderawasih Bay, fishing platforms hovering like UFOs at the ocean's surface. The fishermen scrambled in a delicate balancing act around the deck, raising and lowering the nets. Strong lights around the edges of the bagan shone down into the dark waters and attracted large schools of small anchovies, at which point the nets were raised, usually overflowing with little fish. Although sharks are considered to be only moderately intelligent, the whale sharks of Cenderawasih have figured out that the bagans can provide something close to a free late-night supper.

After the sun came up, Dr. Mark Erdmann, the senior marine advisor for Conservation International in Indonesia, told us about the whale shark. He said it was the largest fish in the sea, that it stayed in the bay year-round, and that it had no interest in eating people. Jawi didn't buy it. For our first hour of filming, he watched silently, studying carefully. I quickly appreciated why Jawi was afraid. First, there was their size; after whales, they are the largest animals on earth. Accurate measurements are sparse, but records show average lengths of 30 to 40 feet, with satellite tracking and other scientific reports recording whale sharks at more than 60 feet long. The largest are estimated to weigh 66,000 pounds, rivaling the dinosaurs. Second, you had to consider their style of filter feeding. Like baleen whales, megamouth sharks, and basking sharks, whale sharks capture tiny plants and animals in filtering pads at the back of their throats. A whale shark's 3,000 tiny, vestigial teeth can't bite anything; but the suctioning force of the water pulls everything in front of them right into their wide-open, mammoth maws that can reach up to five feet in width.

Mark told me that whale sharks can't accidentally swallow a person. Even if you got past the filtering pads, their throats are too narrow. But that was easy to forget when three of them came straight for me out of the dark blue. They were headed toward something behind me—a net filled with squirming, delicious anchovies. I had a large RED EPIC camera in a black fish-eye case, which I knew would protect me a little like a gladiator's shield, but still I was as nervous as Jawi. Three of the ocean's largest fish, like a fleet of Porsche 911s

(ABOVE) Islands in Waigeo are mushroom-shaped limestone surrounded by healthy coral reefs. (BELOW, CLOCKWISE FROM UPPER LEFT) Shaun shows kids a photo of the boat, *Kalabia*; the *Kalabia* became a floating classroom to educate the children of West Papua about ways to improve the ocean's health; the teachers engage through games and are spreading practices that will lead to a sustainable use of the island's aquatic resources; Jawi, at left, with his best friends; the *Kalabia* is playfully painted to attract even the youngest of students. The teachers make learning fun.

with their hoods up, moved steadily toward me. They passed me by, brushing against my knee, while retracting their tiny eyes a full one and a half inches to avoid damaging their lenses.[27]

Minutes later, another two swam directly toward me, acting like enormous wood chippers as they expelled leftover morsels from huge slatted gills on either side of their bodies. They were vacuum cleaners on steroids, and they kept coming, sucking, not turning away. I was trapped. The camera lens was almost touching one shark's lips, capturing a birds-eye view of its gaping mouth.

I felt like helpless biblical Jonah right before he was swallowed by the whale. My swim fins were working double time but they were not enough to counteract the sucking force of the whale shark. I finally had to reach out and push away from the shark's jaw, hoping not to piss it off. Its hide was sandpapery in one direction, seal-soft in the other. I shoved myself backward, away from the constant sucking. By then, I was out of air and had to get to the surface. I watched as a second one, a 25-foot monster, gently wound its body around me as he made his way toward the nets. I started laughing, underwater, and couldn't stop. By all rights, being in such close proximity to a shark the size of a whale should put fear and trepidation into the stoutest of hearts. But my heart was filled with joy. What a gift I was being given. It was bizarre, it was incongruous, and it was one of the sweetest moments I have experienced in the ocean.

Maybe Jawi heard me laughing through my snorkel, or maybe he had simply seen how much fun Barbara, Brad, Mark, and I were having, but eventually, he relaxed. Like a true water warrior, he slid into the water, but when he came nose-to-mouth with his first whale shark, he made a beeline for Mark's protective back. Soon, though, he was having the time of his life, diving next to those creatures and doing all he could not to full-on hug them. You could see his reflex to instinctively reach out, or even to hop aboard for a spin. This was particularly funny because, when we had earlier warned him about not touching or riding the whale sharks, Jawi had looked at us like we were crazy. But there was no denying it: The smile on his face lit up the water around him, and clearly told the story of his new favorite underwater friends. Pretty soon, we could hear him too, giggling through his snorkel.

The entire day was like that. I stayed in the water with my team and characters, shooting the gentle (I now know) whale sharks, sometimes nine at once, who made a daily habit of visiting the fishing platforms. There, the thankful fishermen believed that the whale

(ABOVE) The whale shark sucks in its prey. (RIGHT) The children of West Papua joyously live as one with their seas.

shark brought them good luck. Tourists also have discovered the ritual and now pay the fishermen for the opportunity to witness this

South Pacific Montage
3:19   #27

amazing animal. Even the scientists agree that this interaction is a win-win-win: The whale shark is protected and fed (and not killed for its fins, to serve in the popular Chinese shark fin soup); the villagers are able to earn money for high school scholarships for their children; and, the fishermen have a new source of revenue.

We spent two days in the water with the whale sharks, a treasured experience that we all—but perhaps Jawi more than anyone else—will remember forever. It was the icing on the cake of a voyage where Jawi had learned that every reef system is a model for how humans can make sustainable, ecological, life-saving, planetwide choices, no matter where they live. By the end of our journey, Jawi had become an inhabitant of the planet.

During the making of this film, we were able to act as Jawi's extended family. We watched as this kid went from a homesick child who contracted malaria and recovered to a boy who now stood taller as his coming-of-age story unfolded, and he learned about how he could take ownership of his home ecosystem. For Jawi and us, this journey was a once-in-a-lifetime experience, a phrase we use often to describe our filmmaking adventures. The other one is this: I have the best job in the world.

When we released the film in partnership with IMAX Corporation, it ignited a worldwide concern for the health of the reefs and the importance of educating those who live near them. We are told that the film helped push the Indonesian government toward naming West Papua their first "conservation province" and promoting the development of sustainable jobs and a more long-term fisheries management plan.

---

27 When we were out of the water, Mark told me how the whale shark can navigate so well when its eyes are so far apart. The fine-tuned spatial swimming skills are accomplished through a band of electronic sensors on the chin. Plus, their high-tech eyes are probably good for close-up vision, since they can switch from stereoscopic—for three-dimensional sight, like ours—to monocular. That means they can use just one eye to see very clearly, but with reduced depth perception. They also can rotate their eyes, which, combined with the lateral placement, means they can get nearly a 360-degree field of view.

THE PURPOSE-DRIVEN FILM

Humpbacks: A Rare Positive Conservation Story

"It's hard to convey what it's like when a whale sings. The sound goes directly to your middle ear and pulses through your tissues. The reverberations are so strong that you can actually feel the air vibrating in your lungs."

—HOWARD HALL, DIRECTOR OF UNDERWATER PHOTOGRAPHY

In 2014, we traveled to Tonga, a South Pacific nation of 170 islands with a strange secret: Tongans rarely swim because they believe that evil lurks under the water in the dark unknown. That's what makes Ali Takau so interesting. When he was just four, his father threw him into the water so that he'd learn to swim. As a result, Ali loves the water and its creatures and, as soon as he was able, became a licensed dive master and whale boat guide. His Polynesian island monarchy was one of the locations we'd chosen to feature, along with Alaska and Hawaii, in our documentary, **Humpback Whales**.

Ali's hometown was once a whaling village. As recently as 60 years ago, his great-grandfather would harpoon humpbacks to provide oil for lamps and to feed his family of 20. Today, thanks to an international whaling ban in 1966, the humpback population has swelled from near extinction—somewhere between 5,000 and 20,000—to an estimated 100,000 worldwide. Now, Ali shudders at the very thought of killing humpbacks, making this one of the few happy conservation stories in the world.

Our purpose at MacGillivray Freeman Films is to help people to appreciate nature through science, through learning. In one moment, one image, one sound, one "something," another kid, even another adult,

can see science and conservation in a new light. With this film, that "something" was that IMAX cameras were made to shoot whales. These gargantuan creatures, some of the earth's largest mammals, would be shown, life-sized, on giant screens, inviting school kids to fall in love.

Of the 90 species of whales, it's my opinion that humpbacks are the coolest because they breach with exuberance, playfully launching out of the water and slamming back down, and to top it off, they sing! Unfortunately, they don't do those beguiling things at the same time.

Humpback Planet

There are about fifteen regional populations of humpbacks, and they inhabit all of our oceans. From June to November each year, the beautiful, sheltered bays of Tonga become a honeymoon paradise for the mating and calving humpbacks, and every morning, Ali says goodbye to his mom, his wife, and his young son and walks a mile down to the dock. From there, at 7:30 a.m., five Dolphin Pacific Diving Company tourist boats depart to track the humpbacks. Ali loves these giants of the sea and he loves to bring people out to meet and photograph them. He loves to see visitors overcome with joy after their first experience near these magnificent animals. Tears come to his own eyes at the thought of killing a female humpback or her calf for any reason.

(FACING PAGE) The Tongan humpback stars. (ABOVE RIGHT) Ali Takau and son. (PRECEDING SPREAD) Over the years, as a tip-of-the-hat thank you to our dedication to surfing, I've tried to include this beautiful, natural sport in each of our films. Alana Blanchard, Ehukai Beach Park, Oahu, Hawaii.

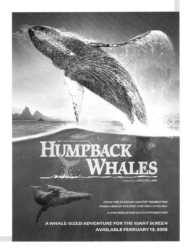

Humpback Whales

FILMED IN: 15 PERFORATION/70MM

RELEASE DATE: February 13, 2015

NARRATED BY: Ewan McGregor

SCORE BY: Steve Wood

100% on Rotten Tomatoes

Jackson Hole Wildlife Film Festival–Global Embassy Showcase in 20+ countries

Giant Screen Cinema Association Award: Best Film of the Year

Humpback Whales offers stunning shots that are both intimate and immense . . . It offers the kind of awe-inspiring sequences that CGI can only dream of." *—BOSTON GLOBE*

Humpbacks have come to Tonga's shallow waters for centuries to mate, give birth, nurse, and train their young for the rigors of the long migrations ahead. Maternal humpbacks give more than 100 gallons of fat-rich milk a day to their calves who in turn gain as much as 100 pounds per day.

Then, as the ocean warms in summer, these humpbacks begin their southerly migration along the Tonga Trench, the second deepest on earth, heading for the krill- and plankton-rich Antarctic where they replenish their energy by eating all day. At this southern restaurant, humpbacks sift through the cold waters, their brush-like baleens straining out the tiny phytoplankton, consuming tons each day. They again move north as winter approaches, returning in June to the protected waters of Tonga, far from the orcas, or killer whales, that would otherwise prey on their calves. Ali and his team wait to greet them, looking forward to sharing their magnificence with Tongan schoolchildren and tourists, who are sure to fall in love with these graceful giants.

Nursery School

Every day, we headed out with Ali on the boats and stayed there from before dawn until dark, hour after hour at the ready, rocking and rolling and watching and waiting.

Finally, after motoring around for more than a week, a mom and calf were sighted breaching. We loved the breaching, but were touched by how palpable the bond was between mother and calf. We could feel the female's instinct for motherhood and the calf's deep connection to her mother. This bond has to be ironclad because a humpback mother is a calf's only constant. What made us laugh most, though, was nursery school! We watched Mom teaching baby how to breach. Mom would pop up, and a few seconds later, baby would pop up. Mom slapped her

fluke onto the water's surface, and *thwack*, baby slapped the surface. Mom: *Thwack*. Baby: *Thwack*. Once baby got the hang of it, just like any baby learning anything, it thwacked and thwacked and thwacked. It just couldn't get enough.

We spent about four and a half hours with this pair, both topside and underwater. The experience was fun, sweet, and endearing, and it somehow provided more of a personal glimpse into humpback lives than anything we'd seen so far. I couldn't imagine what it would be like for either one of them, after a year together, on the day that baby took off to be on its own, to start its own adventure.

Forging a New World Order

Tonga is a deeply religious country. The tiny town of Matamaka, population 72, has five separate churches. The color of school children's uniforms tells you which religious school they attend. Everywhere, Sunday's focus is on family and church, and by constitutional law, no one can work except taxi drivers, who ferry people to church. These customs account for strong friendships among neighbors and contribute to national unity. They also explain the ability of the entire country to change direction instantly, to abandon, for example, a strong cultural tenet like whaling in favor of a more enlightened, sustainable effort. The unity of Tonga's people allowed them to redefine their heritage and cement a new legacy.

I loved seeing how families spend time together in Tonga. They talk, play games, and enjoy their beautiful, peaceful islands. Tongans appreciate their country, its intimacy, its welcoming nature. For the visiting humpbacks, Tonga is a sanctuary with a human culture that has embraced them. There are humpbacks carved in wood in homes, marketplaces, restaurants, and airports. The humpback is Tonga's unofficial national symbol.

Tonga, one of the sanctuaries of the humpback whale, where they can mate, give birth, and nurse their young.

MICHELE HALL

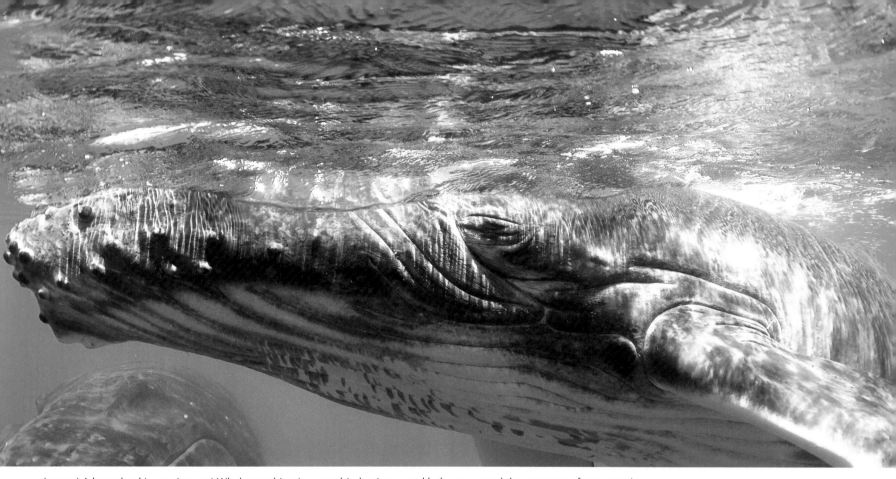

(ABOVE) A humpback's eye. (BELOW) Whale watching is now a big business, and helps to spread the message of conservation.

Although other whaling nations, particularly Japan, Norway, and Iceland, continue to pressure the Tongan government to lift its ban on whaling and begin the killing again, Tonga's king has stood firm and the country has successfully shifted its paradigm from a whaling nation to a whale-watching nation. A study by the International Fund for Animal Welfare (IFAW) found that each humpback whale in Tongan waters was worth $20,300 a year, or $1 million in tourism dollars during its lifetime, to the Tongan economy. Regardless of the statistics, the country is a shining example of how change can bring humans into alignment with their environment, and this story brought me great joy.

Making *Humpback Whales*
4:10   #28

Hawaiian Humpbacks Go A-Courting

For humpbacks in the Northern Hemisphere, travel schedules are reversed. In winter, humpbacks return to the Hawaiian Islands to do as their cousins do in Tonga: mate, give birth, and raise their young. Especially popular are the calm, shallow waters near Lahaina, on the island of Maui. So, we followed them. During this leg of our adventure, my daughter, Meghan, spent three weeks with us training to be a production manager, which I think is the hardest job on the crew. Her magical, velvet-touch participation, along with MacGilli-luck, made this one of our best shoots ever.

On our first predawn outing, things looked bad. The wind whipped through the channel between Molokai and Maui and we wondered when (and if) to leave the harbor. I asked Tad Luckey, the owner and captain of our boat, whether he thought we'd be able to find the humpbacks with all the wind and whitecaps. I loved his reply: "You're sure to find a lot more out there than you will here in the harbor!" Tad also thought it might be calm on the north side of Lanai, so we set off. After a rough crossing, we arrived to find the water perfectly glassy, with 100-foot underwater visibility. We watched and waited for about four hours, and then, suddenly, two humpbacks, a male and a female, appeared right next to the boat, circling each other. At first we thought that the female was using the boat as a protective shield to evade the advancing male, but then we noticed that she was circling him at times as well. Dr. Jim Darling, a leading whale researcher, told us that this was actually a courtship ritual, and that they were getting to know each other. I asked whether this was something he saw all the time, and Jim answered with a wink, "Oh, yes; about once every 10 years I might get this opportunity."

The whales stayed with us for 90 minutes, as cameraman Jason Sturgis photographed underwater and our helicopter cameraman,

(LEFT) Howard Hall gets close to the tail.

265

(ABOVE) On that calm day near Lanai, the humpbacks seemed to enjoy entertaining us with their many skills, including breaching (RIGHT).

Ron Goodman, who'd flown out to meet us within 20 minutes of our call, shot a whole roll of IMAX film from the air.

It was an exhilarating dance to behold, but it wouldn't be the most intense one in the courtship department. We would also get to photograph a surface active group, better known as a heat run. Our team was alerted to the action by Rob Walker, aka Eagle Eye, who spotted about 200 seabirds and an agitated surface two miles away. As we sped toward the frothing water and what we thought were eight spouting whales, the usually laconic, even-tempered Tad and his wife, Cindy, practically hopped in excitement. Our crew had no idea what to expect, but Tad and Cindy told us that what was unfolding was going to be extraordinary. By the time we arrived, the number of males had grown to about 15. We had front-row seats.

During a thrilling, high-speed chase, multiple males chase one female, hoping to gain her attention and affection. As they jockey for position next to the female, they lunge at each other, ram their bodies in terrific bloody collisions, pound their tail flukes, and snort like crazy. Thankfully, our gear was able to deal with the level of intensity. To keep the camera steady on the bow of Tad's boat, we had rented two stabilization rigs. They could move in three directions, and housed a gyro, a computer, and motors to keep the camera level. This device would allow us to get steady shots most of the time and keep our IMAX theater audience from getting seasick.

After three intense hours across about 10 miles of ocean, the chase came to an end. All in all, between 20 and 30 males had participated. Tad and Cindy said this was the biggest heat run they'd seen in 25 years. We hoped that the male who remained in the lead had won the contest and, presumably, the right to breed. But as is the case with all humpbacks, their intimate moments remained private. What plays in Maui stays in Maui. Scientists, like Jim and his associate Dr. Meagan Jones, are still studying, every day during the season, these hidden activities.

Whale Song

Few stories from the animal kingdom have stirred our hearts and minds like the discovery of whale songs. The sounds were first picked up in the early 1950s by a US naval operation that was listening for Soviet submarines. Mysterious, haunting "voices" were coming from the depths of the ocean, and no one could explain what they were.

Eventually, biologists recorded these melodic and strange songs, and linguists became mesmerized by them. They wondered how and why whales would produce such eccentric musical interludes. Some of the most complex vocalizations known in the animal kingdom, these songs are composed of a series of unique sounds repeated in distinctive patterns. Years later, scientists would discover that only the male humpback sings, and from a specific position. He begins a slow, arching dive—the origin of the name "humpback"—and then falls still. With his head down, he points his tail, or fluke, at an upward angle of about 45 degrees, and can remain there, "singing," for 20 minutes or more, until he needs to surface for air. He might repeat the same song for hours.

Dr. Fred Sharpe told us that sound travels five times faster underwater than it does in the air. "Humpbacks can project their sounds over hundreds or even thousands of miles," he said. "They have incredible hearing, so they can probably listen to lots of individuals at once." The idea that animals thousands of miles away match their songs to one another must have significance; and it will be glorious when we understand it more fully. But in the meantime, we have to be mindful of filling our oceans with mechanical sounds from boats or sonic blasts that can mask this crucial communication network.

Saving Whales
3:46   #29

Saving the Humpbacks

In our film, some of our most heart-pounding footage was shot during a disentanglement effort for a whale from Alaska that arrived in Hawaii with fishing gear and rope slicing through the blubber around its tail. We were able to send our helicopter to locate the whale and witness the teamwork that in all likelihood saved its life. Remembering Kubrick's advice to never walk away from a sequence until it's perfect, we returned to Maui a year later and filmed re-creations of the rescue boat and disentanglement process. This allowed us to edit and perfect the final, heroic humans-save-the-animals ending to our film. The rescue team was elated: "We feel lucky that we saved that whale."

We felt lucky, too. When **Humpback Whales** premiered in 2015, everything we had gone through proved to be worth the effort. We had celebrated the beginnings of the humpback whale's recovery from near extinction, proving once again that good science works! We also raised awareness about today's continued threats to these magnificent creatures. The film became the highest-grossing IMAX film of the year and won the GSCA Best Film of the Year award. Our sponsor and business partner on the film, Pacific Life, led by Jim Morris, Bob Haskell, and Tennyson Oyler, received positive reactions from this investment and connection to their brand. It was a win for everyone, especially the whales.

Dreaming Big:
A Mission of Education

"We were hired to solve a problem: not enough kids think about engineering as a career. If young people are to connect with engineering, our film has to be an emotional people story about using engineering in creative, adventurous ways."

By 2015, our work had become synonymous with preservation, conservation and nature. We'd taken our cameras through tight spots in nearly inaccessible and sometimes dangerous locations. We'd shown what was happening in pristine, fragile ecosystems across the world. But my kids, Shaun and Meghan, thought we could go further.

It was true that the power of the IMAX screen, teamed with important societal needs and movements, could result in gains for the world. So, logically, we opened ourselves to campaigns that companies, governments, and individuals were already engaged in, worthwhile causes with interesting, exhilarating visual possibilities, hoping to lend our IMAX muscle in 250 world markets to educate and inspire audiences.

Dream Big was the first project we did in this category. Ironically, it would require shooting in more outdoor locations than any film we had ever done. The film's initial concept came from the American Society of Civil Engineers (ASCE), a group of 150,000 civil engineers who have been trying to solve a major societal problem: It's a fact that engineering is not attracting enough of the most innovative, creative, and diverse students. Various engineering societies have tried repeatedly over the past two decades to rectify the situation, creating advertising and educational campaigns of their own—but nothing had moved the needle. So, with the guidance of ASCE's Jane Howell Lombardi, we

started with the root of the problem: American kids don't think engineering is cool, fun, or, frankly, interesting.

Shaun assigned our side of this challenge to Mary Jane Dodge, a MacGillivray Freeman senior project director who has worked with us for the past four decades. She knows her way around science museums, having spent 20 years working in several across the country, especially the Museum of Science in Boston. She and Jane developed an ambitious, long-range, multitiered plan. It started with engaging many specialized engineering groups and societies, members of which would later volunteer at local science centers to support the film when it was released. It included educational curricula, volunteer coordination, and layers of ancillary planning so that the film could dovetail with annual engineering events and continue to unfold for years after the film was completed. The plan, featured on the DiscoverE.org website, allowed us to reach kids and their parents all over the world with the click of a button. It was peer-reviewed by a group of engineering experts—and then, the hard work truly began. Mary Jane and Jane took this plan on the road to find promotional and financial partners to share in its mission.

Bechtel Corporation was acutely aware of the need to attract more diverse students to engineering and had a vested interest in our plan. They joined us on this journey.

For me, the challenge was to design and write a film that would inspire middle and high school students. During a research phase that was perhaps the lengthiest of any we'd embarked on, we scoured ten years' worth of ASCE civil engineering journals for profiles of engineers. We interviewed more than 40 engineers, convened a 14-person advisory board, defined a set of major goals and, from those goals, developed concepts for the film. When we tested those concepts on twelve- to

(FACING PAGE) Engineers designed the Golden Gate Bridge in San Francisco to be inspected, maintained and painted every day.

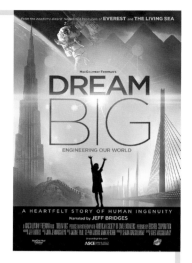

an underwater robot. They were up against the finest and best-funded university programs in the country, including the presumptive champion, MIT. After encountering serious technical malfunctions that they overcame using unforgettably creative solutions, the ragtag team, against all odds, prevailed against and dethroned MIT.

Steve continues: "At a meeting with our clients, I proposed reenacting this story for **Dream Big**. Because it has such close parallels to the most important person in my own life, I couldn't tell the story without choking back tears. Although the clients were lukewarm about the idea, Greg believed in its strength and persisted for two years, never losing faith in the power of this inspiring story. When the stakeholders saw the completed movie, they finally got it. And loved it. The movie has succeeded beyond everyone's expectations, and has motivated thousands of young people to choose engineering as their career."

How Engineering Stole Our Hearts

The story began in Phoenix, Arizona, when high school teacher Fredi Lajvardi dreamed up a program to get kids interested in engineering. He began to "play" with engineering by starting an after-school robotics program at Carl Hayden High School, where as many as 80 percent of the students lived below the poverty line.

Every day this class met, kids got to build robots from scratch. They funded their projects through book drives and bake sales and kept their expenses to a minimum. The program became more and more popular. After a few years, Fredi told his team about a national Remote Operated Vehicle (ROV) competition that would take place at the University of California, Santa Barbara (UCSB, my campus!). The format required robots to complete ten tasks on an underwater course. The team voted enthusiastically to enter and to build a brand-new underwater robot.

One leader of the team was a straight-A student named Angelica Hernandez, whose parents had come from Mexico when she was six. She had learned English and was one of the high school's best students. She studied endlessly, worked at part-time jobs to help her family, and was one of Fredi's favorite people. Angelica's enthusiasm helped push the team to successfully complete the difficult task of building "Stinky," named for its strong smell of plastic glue. Stinky had cost all of $800 in parts. It wasn't pretty or elegant, but it worked and it was ready. They drove the finished robot to UCSB. The students didn't take their chances very seriously since they were competing against teams from much more affluent high schools and universities. There, Stinky became the great underdog—and it all started with a leak. Stinky stopped cold during the test run the day before the competition. The students stayed up all night and jiggered an ingenious last-minute fix, using tampons to soak up the water and keep moisture from reaching

seventeen-year-olds, what came to the fore was fascinating. We learned that none of them wanted a desk job. The boys tended to envision a career of adventure and challenge, often overseas. Girls, with few role models in engineering, weren't sure how they'd fit in; but most wanted a job that was "helpful to other people" and that included adventurous challenges. (One young girl, admittedly an outlier, hoped that her career would allow her to dress up, wear high heels, and bring her dog to work.) Because the ratio of American engineering graduates is weighted by a factor of 4:1 toward males, one of our goals for the film was to pique the interest of young women. Even more stark were statistics showing that so few African American and Hispanic women had been exposed to engineering as a career that hardly any were pursuing this option. Our expert advisors encouraged us to seize this opportunity. But how?

Protect the Dream

Looking back, our editor-writer Stephen Judson thinks that the answer was in the mantra that I adopted: "We typically start each film with a simple idea that needs to be defined and fleshed out," he said. "In the case of **Dream Big**, we began with only a title and a goal. Throughout the development process, Greg repeated that the film would be about creativity. Engineers are creative problem solvers. Engineering is a great chance to use your imagination. To become a good engineer, you don't need to be a walking slide rule—a math nerd. If young people are to connect with it, the film cannot be the celebration of magnificent engineering marvels. It has to be an emotional story about young people using engineering in creative ways."

In our research, Steve came across an extraordinary documentary called **Underwater Dreams**, about a group of underserved high school students who entered a national competition to design and build

the electronics. It was a Hail Mary pass. But the next day Stinky completed nine of the ten required underwater tasks—more than any other robot—before shorting and dying. The team still didn't realize they'd won until the evening banquet.

When the team returned home, they became Phoenix's new hometown heroes. They, along with Angelica, appeared on David Letterman's national talk show and were interviewed in the newspaper. Their story became the year's David versus Goliath inspiration. To make the story even better, the whole process kicked off Angelica's engineering career. She was chosen to be her graduating class's valedictorian, went on to study mechanical engineering at Arizona State, was granted a DACA deferment, then graduated from one of our best schools, Stanford, where she earned a master of science degree, and now works in clean energy. "The thing I take away the most from Fredi," she says now, "is the belief that you can do anything."

Emotional, personal, and unexpected—this was the perfect dramatic finish to our film, the kind of surprise that every film needs. And at its core was an amazing young Hispanic woman. But it surprised me that a few of our advisors thought differently. They raised several objections. First, they questioned the optics of the fact that several of the students were illegal immigrants. Second, they questioned the validity of the area of focus, noting that robotics is not a traditional area of civil engineering. Finally, while we viewed the techniques that the underfunded team used as inventive and an example of engineering in action, a few advisors questioned whether they were appropriate for a film aimed at families and young children. This pushback generated long, heartfelt discussions about whether we should include this inspirational story in the movie, but I refused to give up. Perhaps channeling Jim Freeman's gift of persuasion, I kept pushing and finally won over our advisors.

When we shot the re-created competition sequence (since the event had already passed), we used many of the real players, including Fredi and Angelica. Once edited, the sequence, which appeared at the end of the film, became the hit segment. People like David Keighley from IMAX called it "one of the best sequences ever done in an IMAX movie" and the most emotional one he'd ever seen.

How Teachers Can Inspire
3:42　　#30

Women in Engineering

ASCE had no problem introducing us to other incredible, intelligent female engineers. We hoped that by including them in the film as role models, more girls and young women would be inspired to discover their "inner engineer." According to the kids in the audience, it did the trick. One little girl said simply, "If you watch this, you'll turn into an engineer."

(ABOVE) Filming in San Francisco. (BELOW) Our team and new cameraperson, two-year-old Kellan, in Scotland. (BOTTOM) Inspirational teacher Fredi Lajvardi (far right) and the team.

Our opening story featured Menzer Pehlivan, a Turkish woman who at age 13 had experienced a 7.4-magnitude earthquake centered about 62 miles (100 kilometers) from Istanbul. Menzer's family was forced to evacuate its Ankara apartment building, and although they escaped unharmed, the girl was moved by the devastation the earthquake caused. More than 30,000 people lost their lives that day and hundreds of thousands were left homeless. "That was the seed," she said, "that planted in my head early on that I would become a civil engineer focusing on seismic safety." Easier said than done; in Turkey, as in so many countries, engineering was a male-dominated pursuit. Menzer's teachers told her that it simply wasn't possible, but her grandfather told her otherwise, and encouraged her to do anything she set her mind to.

Today, Menzer works in Seattle as an earthquake engineer, testing and building earthquake-resistant structures. Menzer also is living proof that an engineer can love fashion and style. Her mother is a dress designer, and Menzer loves dressing up. She said that a young student in a **Dream Big** audience took one look at her "feminine" outfit and assumed she was an actor. Menzer was quick to set the record straight. "You can be an engineer and wear heels and dresses and be a 'girly girl,'" she said, "or you can be the opposite. It doesn't matter." We watched as she and the other women in **Dream Big** defined, and redefined, engineering in the minds of today's students. Menzer had created the role of a female engineer in Turkey—and then stepped into it. Now she was able to pay it forward.

Another remarkable engineer who upended the stereotype was Avery Bang, then the thirty-something CEO of Bridges to Prosperity. Our crew fell in love with Avery from the moment we met her. This intelligent, well-intentioned young woman believes that "no one in the world should suffer poverty because of isolation." We joined her on the stunning island of Haiti, in a remote area where people were cut off from services by the treacherous Grand Anse River. Residents drowned every year just trying to get to school, work, or the doctor. When Avery's team completed construction of a footbridge over the river, we were able to witness the joy on the faces of the residents as they ran across that bridge for the first time. We understood in that moment how Avery must feel on every project.

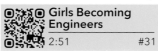

Girls Becoming Engineers
2:51   #31

Monuments to Innovation

In addition to telling stories of personal achievement, we knew that a giant-screen film about engineering had to showcase giant examples of jaw-dropping or mind-bending engineering concepts. We traveled the globe to find them.

In central Scotland, we captured footage of the Falkirk Wheel, an ingenious rotating boatlift that replaced nine of eleven water locks and that now connects the Forth and Clyde Canal with the Union Canal.

We followed a Mississippi high school team to Australia as they competed in the World Solar Challenge Race, a 1,900-mile trek from Darwin to Adelaide. This contest is a research project in motion, showcasing the world's most efficient vehicles powered by the sun.

And, of course, you can't shoot an engineering film without a nod to humanity's most astonishing engineering feat: the Great Wall of China, the largest structure ever built. Our tour guide at this location was Steve Burrows, an engineering visionary from England. During our time together, Steve addressed the social and cultural preconceptions about the field, saying, "The engineers I've known are some of the weirdest, wackiest, most interesting people I've met, and they come from all walks of life. The one thing we share is this inner desire to shape the world. If you become an engineer, you can put your stamp on history." The Great Wall stands as a testament to that legacy.

Making a Difference

When **Dream Big** premiered at the national meeting of ASCE in Portland, the 900 engineers in attendance were moved and thrilled by the experience. Several came up to thank Barbara and me for the film. One said, "You've achieved a miracle—you've made us look human!" It is true that engineers are thought to be nerdy, sedate, and not much fun to be around; but that couldn't be farther from the truth, and I think our film proved that.

The "engineered" three-year rollout began with several initiatives launched during the first year of the film's release. These included: 1) getting the movie into IMAX theaters around the world; 2) booking television and radio interviews for our four main characters; and 3) pitching and placing printed news articles to share our engineering stories with the broader public. Then, in the second year, more than 250,000 people attended private screenings organized by engineering organizations in locations where there was no IMAX theater. In year three, to accompany the continued IMAX release, the team focused on getting video versions of the film out to every school in America, grades 6 to 12—some 110,000 in all. At most screenings, a volunteer ASCE engineer attended, answering questions and engaging students with hands-on activities. This push continues today; plans include a follow-up effort featuring a suite of educational outreach activities and screenings, lectures, videos, and social media components.

As we go to press with this book, we are busily conducting research for a second IMAX film about engineering. As ASCE says, we've finally found a way to move the needle—and, as Shaun and Meghan brilliantly convinced me, that the power of IMAX storytelling was the key!

(ABOVE) Every construction needs an engineer, especially a roller coaster. Here, engineer Menzer Pehlivan shows her class how engineering can be fun.
(BELOW) Angelica Hernandez helps glue together parts of the soon-to-be-champion robot Stinky, named for its distinctive smell.

CHAPTER 24

Brand USA:
A Mission of Exploration

"Our Sistine Chapel is Yosemite. Our Big Ben is Wyoming's Devils Tower. The halls of our Louvre are at the base of waterfalls, in caves hung with stalagmites and stalactites, and in Yellowstone's hot springs. America's national parks are our national treasures; they are our pride and joy."

In 2007–2008, the US economy experienced one of its downturns, and Americans had to grapple with what came to be known as the Great Recession. Unemployment, bank failures, and a plummeting stock market affected everyone; but, ironically, it led MacGillivray Freeman Films to one of the best opportunities in decades in the form of a series of three films that helped the world.

Preparing for the downturn, the incoming Obama administration invited business leaders to a brainstorming session in Washington to find ways to get Americans back to work. One solution arose from the tourism industry leaders who observed that, for decades, other countries had advertised themselves as tourism destinations, but not the United States. Would a tourism-promoting "destination package" create more jobs at restaurants, hotels, airlines and car rental facilities? The group agreed to give it a try. An unprecedented public-private partnership, now called Brand USA, would be the test vehicle.

Approved by Congress and funded by a slight increase in the price of tourist visas added to donations from the travel industry (with no tax dollars!), Brand USA developed ad campaigns in conjunction with agencies in 25 countries. After a few years, tourism numbers rose significantly, creating thousands of new American jobs and helping in

a small way to get us out of the recession. In 2014, as a next step, Brand USA hired our team to create an IMAX film promoting America. We didn't have a moment to lose, since the perfect subject, our National Park Service, was approaching its 100th birthday.

I've always believed that in the United States, our most precious treasures reside in the great outdoors. Our mission for **National Parks Adventure** was to produce an IMAX film and accompanying educational campaign that would both promote the National Park Service and increase park attendance during the anniversary years of 2016–2017. As we developed our concept, we pinpointed places and stories that would surprise and thrill audiences. We narrowed our list down to the parks that would be the most photogenic on IMAX screens and searched for unusual stories about lesser-known parks. After settling on about 30 of them, I realized that we had a chance to invite audiences to actually engage with the parks, capturing the fun and immersive ways that the parks speak to adventurers, artists, athletes, and others looking for a physical, aesthetic, or spiritual challenge. And this goal led me to Conrad Anker.

Conrad is not only one of the world's most talented rock, ice, and alpine climbers, he is also a wonderful role model and father. Conrad was the perfect ambassador to host a tourism trip through a series of natural wonders, because he is an expert in how to play in our parks. He has also been an inspiration, to me, for years for one reason.

In September 1999, Conrad and his climbing partner, Alex Lowe, were in the Himalaya to climb Tibet's 26,000-foot peak, Shishapangma. As they began ascending the mountain, they were struck and consumed by a massive avalanche that injured Conrad and, tragically, killed Alex. Alex and his wife, Jennifer, had three wonderful boys. Over the next two

---

(FACING PAGE) National Park Service Ambassador Conrad Anker climbing at Michigan's Pictured Rocks National Lakeshore.

(ABOVE) I'd seen an aerial still photo of the Prismatic Pond at Yellowstone, but when we requested permission to shoot with a helicopter there, the NPS contact said no, we could only shoot with the crane there—no drone or helicopter shots, due to the noise and enjoyment disruption the motorized equipment would cause for visitors. I could sympathize and crossed that location off my flight shot list. Then, when the helicopter team finished, on my review video was a brief shot of the pond. I asked the pilot, Cliff Fleming, "How'd you get this?" He said that his permitted flight path took him over the pond, and on one pass at dawn, no one was around to be disturbed so they turned on the camera. "Don't walk away until it's perfect" was Cliff's mantra as well. (FACING PAGE) Rachel Pohl flexes.

years, Conrad assumed some of his best friend's fatherhood responsibilities. Unexpectedly and over time, Jennifer and Conrad fell in love and married, and Conrad adopted the boys. As the family began this new chapter, they were bolstered by wilderness areas near their Montana home and across the country. I loved this story of fatherhood, of acceptance of responsibility, of a manning up kind of courage, and thought it would work well in our inspirational film.

Conrad was thrilled to get my call, and later commented that "much of the best climbing in the United States is in national park sites, so as climbers we feel an obligation to be stewards. It's been said that the parks are America's best idea, and I'm confident in saying we have the best parks in the world. The wonderful message of this film is that our beautiful parks are approachable by everyone."

I had to agree. In many countries, the aristocracy and royalty own and sequester the most beautiful places. But in America, our national parks belong to all of us, including (and perhaps especially) the generations to come. That's why we rounded out the adventure team with Conrad's stepson, Max Lowe, and their family friend, Rachel Pohl.

Artist Rachel Pohl grew up in Montana, going to Yellowstone for "as long as I can remember, and climbing boulders when my mom wasn't looking for just as long!" The utterly alien landscape of red rock at Utah's Canyonlands was burned into her memory at age five and shaped who she would become. Then she met Max. Having grown up with two celebrated climbers as fathers, Max was exploring the high and the wild before he could even walk. As an adult, he has taken off in a distinctively personal direction, becoming an accomplished outdoor photographer, writer, and filmmaker.

National Parks Adventure

FILMED IN: 15 PERFORATION/ 70MM AND DIGITAL

RELEASE DATE: February 12, 2016

NARRATED BY: Robert Redford

FEATURING: Conrad Anker, Rachel Pohl, Max Lowe

SCORE BY: Steve Wood

100% on Rotten Tomatoes

Highest Grossing Documentary, 2016

Giant Screen Cinema Association Award: Best Film of the Year

"[MacGillivray's] latest documentary is a testament to dauntlessness and vision.... Exhilarating.... The film is sure to delight anyone who appreciates top-flight nature documentaries."

–THE HOLLYWOOD REPORTER

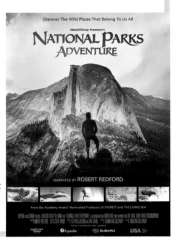

During the production, Conrad stepped back a bit, allowing the kids to take center stage. He still acted as our guide and role model, but he let Max and Rachel helm the adventure.

They definitely turned up the heat by paying tribute to edgy challenges. At Devils Tower, Rachel, Max, and Conrad faced compromises. To get permission to film, with our giant cameras, the first involved the team's meeting with National Park Service staff along with more than 20 tribal elders and leaders, because Devils Tower, also called Bear Lodge, is sacred to the Lakota Nation and other northern Plains Indians. Conrad is calm, contemplative, and compassionate. At this meeting, he gained their respect and agreed not to shoot aerials near the mountain and never to climb all the way to the top. While we didn't mind those constraints, we still had to get our heavy equipment up the rock. I had chosen a 5.10d classic crack climb called El Matador because the edges were so well defined in the afternoon light. In order to capture bird's-eye views of the three climbers using their body parts as levers and jamming hands and feet at jigsaw tilts into the fissures, we hired Michael Brown.

A climber and a cinematographer, Michael had worked with us on **The Alps** and a film in production, **Return to Everest**. He knew how to manage complex rigging: he'd clip it to his harness and attach our innovative tripod variation, nicknamed the wall-pod, in order to provide the overhead perspective. Brad Ohlund, our director of photography, later joked that "it was far from the easiest way to get the camera up on the cliff, but in this case, it was the best way." Without a helicopter, it was actually the only way.

Our American Treasures

2:28 #32

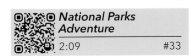

National Parks Adventure

2:09 #33

It was also super cold. "The clouds would roll in, and we'd sit on a ledge waiting and waiting for the right light," Max recalled. Or they'd wait for lightning to pass. Or for snow to quit. Above all else, the climb was challenging, requiring every crack-climbing technique in the book. It tapped all of Rachel's skills, but she powered through. "That climb would have been hard if I could have felt my hands; but not only were my legs maxed out, my fingers were completely numb! It really spoke to the theme of endurance." Which was exactly the kind of adventure we were looking for.

America's Best Idea Ever
1:00   #34

Ice Climbing

One of the most exceptional locations we found was discovered by a twist of fate. For our winter sequence, we had scheduled a three-week shoot in Yellowstone, and through the National Park Service, had reserved snow coaches, hotel rooms, and support staff. The shoot was all set up and looking perfect; except that, a month before our trip, Yellowstone still didn't have enough snow. Every day, I would check the web-cam mounted on the lodge's roof, hoping for a snowfall. No snow! Two weeks before the shoot, I panicked. After an emergency meeting, our 20-person production team began scouring the country for backup options. Niagara Falls, frozen over and stunning, was one possibility. Places in Colorado, like Ouray, were tempting because of their sheer beauty. Then, one day, production assistant Becky Jameson brought in photos of icefalls at Pictured Rocks National Lakeshore, along Lake Michigan. No one on our team had seen or heard of these sculpturesque icefalls. We hired a Michigan-based photographer to go out the next day, photograph these mysterious falls, and digitally transfer the photos to us so we could make a value judgment. Turned out, it was the real deal!

Shaun called the place a fantasyland; and, since Yellowstone was still snowless and, yes, ugly, we booked the trip. Designated a national lakeshore in 1966, Pictured Rocks is the very definition of a hidden gem. Three seasons a year, it boasts sandstone cliffs, caves, natural archways, and dunes that draw local visitors. But not many people see the place coated in ice during the winter.

When we arrived, it was 20° below zero, which, for you nonmeteorologists, is 52° colder than freezing. Let me mention again that

The Trials of Filmmaking
4:00   #35

I hate the cold! Every morning at 6 a.m., in the frigid darkness, we would hook sleds laden with equipment to the 20 snowmobiles we'd hired to get us onto the frozen lake. We hauled lights, generators, and the IMAX 3D Solido and 2D cameras. By 8 a.m., everything was in place,

(LEFT) In all of our films, I try to give the audience moments of WOW that will make them drop their popcorn.

279

and we began filming. Or trying to. One camera literally froze up; film snapped; lenses crystallized. Much of the equipment just said "no."

Of course, the people were cold, too; but their focus was on getting the shots. They threw up a tent and snuggled the cameras under electric blankets. When that wasn't enough, they added a propane heater at full-blast, which brought the tent up to about 50°. Still, the people stayed outside. As I watched the climbers ascend the icy waterfalls, I knew how miserable they must be. But just look at them, I thought to myself. Here, in the harshest of places, they're climbing something exquisitely beautiful, just to show it to the world. This is adventure!

It was one of the most difficult filming locations we'd chosen in a long time, and yet it was magical. And it only got more so. On our final day of filming—a beautiful, sunny, windless day—our guide mentioned a secret cave nearby. It was about noon, and I was only halfway through my slate of climbing shots, so I asked Barbara to go with him to take a look. When I saw the images they'd captured, I actually yelled. Barbara's photos were stunning, and I hollered for the most beautiful cave I'd ever seen. We'd made an entire movie about caves years before, and I hadn't known about this amazing place. The cave was pristine. Adorned with icicles hanging from the ceiling and frosty crystals all over the icicles, it reminded me of a Tiffany glass house. I gathered everyone together at our original location on the lake and announced a change in plans. "Let's wrap here immediately, take what we need—lights, generators, dollies, 3D camera—and get up to the cave as fast as we can, because who knows how long these crystals will last? They may be gone in hours!"

Within minutes, we were at this new location and filming one of the most beautiful places I'd visited in my years of photography. The only footsteps were ours, so we were careful not to disturb anything, including the icicles. We tried to leave the cave as pristine as we'd found it. It remains one of the best 3D locations I've ever encountered. Later, in the editing bay, editor Mark Fletcher and I knew we had to set that scene to Jeff Buckley's beautiful, haunting rendition of "Hallelujah."

I will remember that shoot for my entire life for two reasons. First, of course, it was a once-in-a-lifetime experience. Second, though: I actually got frostbite on the bottoms of my feet. For the next three months, I had no feeling in the skin of my feet and toes. For an avid surfer, this was bad news, as I couldn't feel my surfboard as I rode a wave. But, considering the adventuring images we captured, it was totally worth it.

The Camping Trip That Changed a Nation

A high-octane experience like this is only possible because of naturalist John Muir, who in 1903 went camping in Yosemite Valley with President Teddy Roosevelt. It was this visit that inspired the foundational mechanism that would protect and manage our country's natural wonders. Muir argued that it would be an incalculable loss if these "temples of nature" were to be hunted, logged and mined into oblivion. Roosevelt agreed and returned to Washington, D.C., fired up to argue for the protection of our American wilderness.

To commemorate this pivotal meeting of two visionaries, we went to Yosemite's Mariposa Grove, the very spot where the two men first camped. Using seasoned actors who play these characters in historical re-creations, we shot a sequence that placed them in the middle of devastating beauty. We shot wide so as not to distract viewers with mustaches or costumes. We wanted to place the audience in the majestic setting that inspired the real-life event that ultimately allowed our country to protect these lands forever, creating the first National Park system in the world.

But Roosevelt already knew the unlimited value of nature, because of a personal tragedy. In 1884, his wife and mother died on the same day! Deeply distraught, he moved into the wildlands of the Dakotas, and there, for two years, surrounded by the beauty of the landscape, found solace and redemption. After meeting with Muir, not only did Roosevelt resolve to protect Yosemite, he also would sign orders to create five more national parks, 18 national monuments, 55 national bird sanctuaries and wildlife refuges, and 150 national forests. This president also enacted The Antiquities Act, a precursor to the park service that obligated federal agencies to preserve "scientifically, culturally, and historically valuable sites," and authorized the president to designate national monuments. Roosevelt told the people, "We are not building this country for a day. It is to last through the ages."

In 1916, President Woodrow Wilson would sign The Organic Act, which established the National Park Service. Today, there are 423 national park sites totaling a whopping 84 million acres. Hundreds of millions of people visit them annually. Most hike or picnic, activities that Rachel finds perfectly appropriate. "You don't have to do anything quite so bold as we do to find joy in the parks," she says. "There are so many ways to have fun."

That's a Wrap

Going into this project, we knew that it would be one of the last giant-screen documentary films made on film. We were on the cusp of a full conversion to digital, but I view this indelible, transitional moment as a precious time capsule that celebrates this moment in the parks' history in an everlasting way. Centuries from now, on the 200th or 300th birthday of these parks, our images will still be around, preserved on

(FACING PAGE) Rachel in the most astonishing cave I've ever seen.

15/70 film (or 24K digital resolution!). I found it fitting to make a film about preservation using celluloid film, the longest-lasting recording medium humans have ever invented. There was only one person I wanted to narrate this story: Robert Redford. An actor renowned for his connection to America's wilderness, he told us about the drive up the valley on his first trip to Yosemite. He was eleven years old and had just recovered from months of bed rest following a mild case of polio.

"We went through that tunnel and came out at Inspiration Point and I said, 'Wait, wait, wait a minute. I don't want to look at it; I want to be in it.' I think that's when my passion for nature and the environment began. There's something about solace in those places," he concluded, "something almost spiritual in the power of our parks." It seemed like millions of people agreed, because the film became that year's best-attended documentary worldwide.

To further broaden the reach of our campaign, Shaun made a deal with the Travel Channel to fund and release, with several screenings, eight MFF-produced half-hour TV shows called "America: The Beautiful." The many releases proved to be force multipliers, weaving our messaging into a single-timed wave of awareness. Tourism increased at the national parks and, as those tourism business leaders had predicted, elsewhere.[28]

The Music Man

Once **National Parks Adventure** proved that a beautiful, you-are-there IMAX film was capable of encouraging millions of people to visit America, Brand USA wanted us to create a second and a third film. The team suggested a film focusing on the history of American music. While pairing music with poetic visuals can move viewers on the purest emotional level, with Brand USA's idea, we faced a new kind of challenge: How could we possibly introduce people to America's vast musical landscape in a 40-minute film? Ken Burns has told the stories of jazz and country music brilliantly, but he had about 10 TV hours to do it!

My solution was to follow two musical characters who were separated by 100 years: Louis Armstrong and Aloe Blacc. Armstrong's path from New Orleans to Chicago to New York City provided a way to personalize our story. Aloe Blacc would follow in Armstrong's steps, visiting places and people who shaped America's musical history.

Aloe earned a bachelor's degree from USC and got a great job, but was later laid off. Years later, during the Great Recession, while

---

28 From 2013 to 2016, Brand USA created jobs in the US tourism business by successfully utilizing TV and print ads. But Oxford Economic's independent (third-party) analysis of the success with our IMAX campaign was an eye-opener. The return on investment was calculated at a 32 to 1 ratio, adding 52,000 incremental jobs with almost $9 billion in economic impact. Stunning!

(FACING PAGE) Rachel Pohl inches up Devils Tower, Wyoming.

America's Musical Journey

FILMED IN: 15 PERFORATION/ 70MM AND DIGITAL

RELEASE DATE: February 16, 2018

NARRATED BY: Morgan Freeman

FEATURING: Aloe Blacc, Jon Batiste, Gloria & Emilio Estefan, Dr. John, Ramsey Lewis, Willow Osborne, the Flying Elvi, the Fisk Jubilee Singers

Giant Screen Cinema Association Awards: Best Musical Score and Best Sound Overall

sleeping on the sofa at his sister's house, he wrote the song "I Need a Dollar"—because he really did! The song took off and made him a star. While touring the world, he met rapper Maya Jupiter in Australia, and after a telephone romance, they fell in love, married, and now have two children. Aloe's next songs, "Hello World" and "Wake Me Up," made him an international celebrity.

The heart of our film became the intertwining of these two stories, separated by 100 years but connected by America's powerful musical heritage. In the 1920s, as Louis Armstrong and 6 million other African Americans sought work outside the Jim Crow south, they traveled north and west, bringing their accents, their cuisine, and their music with them. The moral of the story was that music expresses what it means to be American.

Venturing Into America's Wild

With the first two Brand USA films having captivated audiences in over 300 theaters, we went full steam ahead with

Why New Orleans is Cool
2:52   #37

plans for the third, which would shine a light on the American wilderness, its hidden national treasures, and the role of Native Americans in creating, understanding and preserving those special places. Fortunately, we found two wonderful characters: John Herrington, the first Native American astronaut to orbit the planet and Ariel Tweto, an Alaskan Inuit and the popular star and coproducer of the Discovery Channel series *Flying Wild Alaska*. Because indigenous peoples had always lived close to the land and depended on it for everything from food to shelter to medicines, Ariel and John fully appreciated the connections between all living things. This native wisdom is now called TEK, or Traditional Environmental Knowledge. **Into America's Wild** celebrates the indestructible bond between humanity and nature.

(LEFT) The new sport of flyboarding in Miami. (FACING PAGE) Utah's natural treasures.

Nature Deficit Disorder

Richard Louv, the author of the bestseller *Last Child in the Woods*, has devoted years to exploring the larger questions of why nature is so important to us. In his book, he coined the term "Nature Deficit Disorder" to describe what he saw as an emerging disconnect with nature. Today, most of us live in cities, so we've become walled-off from the natural world. He theorized that, when we spend too much time indoors with our omnipresent screens, we start to think of nature as something foreign and separate from our own lives, and that this has real consequences for our health and well-being. Indeed, a number of recent scientific studies have demonstrated that one of the best ways to lessen stress, boost cognition, and lift one's spirits is to get outdoors. A 2015 study published by the National Academy of Sciences found that a simple 90-minute walk in the wild actually altered brain activity and calmed the prefrontal cortex, where whirling thoughts often churn. Maybe that's why, as author Walter Isaacson reported, when he wanted a boost of creativity, Apple creator Steve Jobs took a walk in nature!

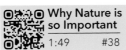
Why Nature is so Important
1:49   #38

(FACING PAGE) Ariel Tweto takes children into the Alaskan wilderness, to experience nature first hand, in **Into America's Wild**. (ABOVE RIGHT) Sports are a great way to engage with nature. (PRECEDING SPREAD) Ariel in wonder, Antelope Canyon.

Into America's Wild

FILMED IN: 15 PERFORATION/70MM AND DIGITAL

RELEASE DATE: FEBRUARY 12, 2020

NARRATED BY: MORGAN FREEMAN

"There's no need to wait for your next trip to get an outdoor-adventure fix. **Into America's Wild** takes viewers to untamed landscapes in seven states."

—WESTWAYS MAGAZINE

Over the years, these films about America, helped by concentrated multimedia campaigns, increased tourism dramatically. Says Brand USA's Chris Thompson, "The films bring the USA to life, allowing viewers to truly immerse in our culture through destination experiences. They have helped to increase travel dreaming and positive perceptions of the United States around the world far beyond our wildest expectations."

My Purpose-Driven Life

> "Humans don't mind hardship, in fact, they thrive on it; what they mind is not feeling necessary."
>
> —SEBASTIAN JUNGER, *TRIBE*

There are times when I think back to the first movie dates Barbara and I enjoyed together. In the dark, when we'd sit down close to each other and hold hands, my chest—my heart—would grow warmer. I didn't know why, but the feeling was miraculous. I'd cherish that warmth and then, further along in the film, I'd gain confidence and take a chance. Since I had such a difficult time expressing my feelings verbally, I'd write the word "love" in her palm, spelling it out with my finger, then she'd copy me on my palm. Neither of us had experienced these feelings before so it was a bit terrifying, like we were edging into an unknown, mysterious place. Did others have these magical sensations? Or were these feelings uniquely ours alone? One thing we did know was that we enjoyed the sensation.

Since that lovely time decades ago, I've learned that time goes quickly, which explains why my study of Stanley Kubrick taught me never to waste it. Like he showed to me, I try to use every minute. As you jam your days with goals, striving to bring lasting purpose to your time on Earth, defending what you love, working to perfect your craft a bit more, you'll "feel necessary"—something celebrated author Sebastian Junger (*The Perfect Storm*) has concluded that our tribe needs. It's then that you also find the confidence to finally kick back, relax, and enjoy the beauty of life that's all around you every day.

Now, many days in Laguna end with that soothing, relaxing evening glass-off, a dying of the wind, settling of the waves, and an enveloping stillness. To take advantage of one such entrancing evening, Barbara and I paddled our lightweight stand-up paddleboards (SUPs) out through the kelp beds to beyond the surf line and sat quietly holding hands, enjoying the serenity of the ocean's rise and fall. We laid back on our boards, our feet dangling, and soaked in the last of the warm California sun, sharing stories of Shaun, Meghan, and our five grandchildren.

Suddenly the calm was interrupted by the hissing of a fin gliding by, followed by another, and finally by a leaping dolphin trailed by her calf. We were surrounded by almost two dozen bottlenose dolphins who were in a playful mood and very curious about us! We stood up and paddled alongside them. They seemed to like being with us. After five minutes of this miraculous joy, I told Barbara, "I'm paddling to shore and I'll get video of this. Stay with them!" The lovely encounter continued for 20 minutes, just 200 yards from our house, where I videotaped their leaps near Barbara's board. Then, thankfully, after I'd gotten a couple great shots, just like that, they moved on, another reminder of how amazing (and fleeting) life can be, especially if you only let it come to you.

Our Nature, Even as Kids

Years ago, during one amazingly transformative summer, when I was about seven, my parents drove us to Yosemite National Park to enjoy the beauty of that protected place. After an impressive week among the towering sequoias, Dad had to get back, so we took the coastal route home. By then, most beaches in California had been developed and were open to the public. They seemed protected, just like our new favorite place, Yosemite. But I came to learn that conservation means more than simple access. As we drove by Bolsa Chica Beach near

(FACING PAGE) Capturing images such as this in IMAX 70mm film has been an honor over the past 47 years. Kodak claims we've used 7½ million feet of their camera film and more than 40 million feet of their printing stock, the most of any company. They say I've personally shot more 70mm film than anyone, even David Lean, estimated at about 5 million feet of film!

Huntington, we were shocked to see that it had become a dumping spot for beer bottles and cans. It didn't take long for it to be nicknamed "Tin Can Beach." I found it heartbreaking to see the piles of trash accumulating. It depressed us so much that day, that my sister and I started to cry. Could our cherished Little Corona Beach near our home end up like this?

Soon, this otherwise beautiful, quarter-mile-long beach was little more than a garbage dump, and locals recognized the potential for a more widespread problem. The community began to discuss putting rules in place to protect these special natural environments.

At the same time, surfing beaches, many of which I loved, were being closed off to us. Stanley's Diner, a beautiful reef break I'd enjoyed many times in the Santa Barbara area, was destroyed by the expansion of Highway 101. Killer Dana, a big wave spot at Dana Point that my sister and I surfed often with Dad, was replaced with a harbor. Salt Creek Beach and Trestles were closed, and hundreds of other spots came under threat from development by entrepreneurs and investors eager to profit from Southern California's growing popularity.

But then, a paradigm shift began. The public increasingly viewed all untamed, underdeveloped land as treasures much like Yosemite and our other national parks. People accepted the idea that it was our job to watch over these places, to ensure that they were not overused and abused. All of us had to be stewards of the land and beaches.

In the 1970s, as Jim, Bud, and I were starting work on **Five Summer Stories**, we included strong themes of environmental protection. Soon thereafter, inspired by the first Earth Day, the first *Whole Earth Catalog,* and the pressure brought to bear on Congress by conservation groups, our representatives passed 24 environmental protection laws. President Nixon signed those bills into law, thus jump-starting my passionate career in protecting the environment and conserving nature through films which remind us of our public ownership rights to these treasures of nature.

When we finished **Five Summer Stories**, in 1972, our forceful environmental message included one story, called "Closed Out," which took to task developers, exploiters of the ocean and all those who would change the coastal environment for the worse. We used that film to raise money in support of Proposition 20, the California Coastal Act, which was passed soon thereafter and ensured access to California's beaches.

It was at this point that Jim and I decided that at least half of our movies should be about conserving nature. We committed ourselves to educating the public at large about what could go wrong—and how far-reaching the toll would be—if we were to lose the health of our oceans. Thus began our unending quest to finance, produce, market,

(FACING PAGE) President Teddy Roosevelt and environmentalist John Muir in our recreation of their pivotal 1903 campout in Yosemite's sequoias.

and distribute around the world—including in about 200 IMAX museum theaters—this message of concern and caretaking of the environment. How selfish would it be for our generation to horde the benefits of nature and leave our descendants empty-handed? If I get to surf pristine waves, if I get to paddle next to frolicking dolphins, why shouldn't my great-grandchildren?

Also during this time, our little village of Laguna Beach began to push to save our immediate environment from the developmental boom that would engulf all of Orange County. Bookstore owner, James Dilley, created the Laguna Greenbelt, to save the rolling hills and animal habitats surrounding our town, and the Marisla Foundation and other groups began inventing ways to save our ocean and sea life. Today, Laguna Beach boasts a Greenbelt and a Bluebelt, with protected areas that have beautified and safeguarded our surroundings.

Our company was an active participant in establishing these sanctuaries and, more than 30 years after Jim's death, we decided to extend our mission by creating an ocean media campaign called One World One Ocean. This campaign would work in tandem with the nonprofit MacGillivray Freeman Films Educational Foundation to step even more proactively into the ring. With renowned environmental filmmaker Chris Palmer now at the helm as president of both, it's really working. When we team with like-minded companies of international scale, as we do on every IMAX film, we multiply our impact and educational reach. Our successful campaigns include social media and IMAX films, targeting kids and adults. We're happy to report that we have driven attention, love, and enlightenment toward the endangered wild places in the ocean and on land. We generate more than 14 billion media impressions per year and are thrilled to have the support of more than 1 million social media followers.

In one example, the king of Ghana attended our IMAX film **Coral Reef Adventure** and saw vividly on the giant screen how some coral reefs in Fiji were struggling and dying due to soil runoff from shore. One of Fiji's forests had been clear cut, allowing the soil, no longer held by tree roots, to wash down the river and blanket the reef with silt, smothering its view of sunlight and killing the animals that lived inside the coral. When the king clearly observed the silt in the river in our helicopter photography, he vowed to change Ghana's forestation policies.

Why Save the Ocean? 1:38 #39

Teddy Roosevelt discovered, and modern-day scientists, including Dr. Sylvia Earle (one of our key board members), have proven that the battle for nature's protection never ends. The allure of financial profit to real estate developers or politicians gains the upper hand over common sense far too often. That's why our company will do its best to produce an ocean or land conservation film at least once every two to three years for the next 30 years. I think that we all understand intuitively that the overriding goals of humanity are to honor beauty, strive for serenity, and appreciate that which is bigger and more divine than our individual selves. As John Muir said, "In every walk with nature one receives far more than he seeks."

The Importance of Family

Over the years, Barbara and I vowed to always do things together, especially in our free time. And it has worked! Our love is deep and the respect that we have for each other is stronger now than ever before. We love sports, and when we have free time with our kids we ski, surf, swim, play volleyball, or mountain bike.

After my mom died, my dad stayed in their house in South Laguna and I would have a weekly breakfast with him. One day he said, "I think I need to find a smaller place. The house feels way too big." When I asked him where he'd want to live, he answered, "Somewhere in downtown Laguna, near you guys. I'd like to be able to walk to the market, the restaurants, the movies."

When we got together the following week, he told me that a search for a downtown apartment hadn't gone well. The places he'd seen were in poor condition. Basically, they'd be no fun to live in, which was an important consideration for my dad.

"You know, we've got two apartments above our house," I said. "Would you ever consider moving . . . " Before I could finish asking the question, a huge grin spread across his tanned face. "Geez, Greg, I thought you'd never ask!"

I had to laugh; and then I doubled down on my offer of an apartment. "I lived rent-free with you and Mom for 26 years," I said. "Seems to me it's only fair that you get the same deal. Barbara and I won't charge you rent for the first 26 years!"

Every morning, for the next three years, my dad, our dog, Paige, and I walked the half-block from our house to the Orange Inn to have breakfast and shoot the breeze. These were some of the best times I had with my father. Growing up with him was fun and informative, but these moments near the end of his life were richer and filled with more astute observations than ever. In his last years on the planet, I learned more from my father than in all the years we'd lived under the same roof. He was an unusual, well-educated and completely positive person. He shaped my life more than anyone else.

Three years later, when we learned of my dad's brain tumor, our priority was to make his final months really fun. We took a luxury cruise in Tahiti, with 19 family members visiting the beautiful Society Islands. When we got back from Bora Bora, we threw a party for 300 at Laguna's Surf & Sand Hotel. Some of Dad's best friends put on skits, did impersonations, sang, and danced. I know my dad loved those tributes; every day, I still see the smile on his face as he enjoyed their humor.

Optimism: A Self-Fulfilling Prophecy
by Stephen Judson

"Meeting Greg, people get right way that he's a friendly people-person, perennially cheerful and optimistic. But how did Greg become Greg? For starters, his dad was a great guy and a bit of a raconteur. He could graciously make each person feel valued. He used to drop by our office unannounced with several buddies in tow and take them on a tour, stopping at every office to explain with gusto why Matthew Muller (or whoever) was a wonderful person and an indispensable genius.

"Greg always stressed that the foundation of every business is relationships—something he absorbed from his dad. After teaching school, Greg's dad became a developer, building houses on spec. He knew about rolling the dice. He had an unmistakably sunny can-do take on life that was echoed by Greg's optimistic approach to running his own company. Time and again, when a case could be made for caution, Greg went the opposite direction, taking risks and forging ahead. He approaches life as if it's a grand adventure.

"At the memorial service for Greg's dad, the church was packed. Greg acted as host, welcoming each speaker with poise and calmly sharing his own reflections. It was a remarkable feat of grace under pressure to honor the man whose cheerful optimism first sparked Greg's career. As for sustaining that career, his dad had nothing to do with it. Nothing and everything."

For the Love of Filmmaking
3:10   #40

Learning From the Best

When I took the risk to shoot movies, because I had no way to learn, I decided that the best avenue was to emulate filmmakers I admired. Starting when I was 13, I watched a number of people producing surfing and skiing films; but three filmmakers stood out: John Severson, Bud Browne, and Bruce Brown. John's films were the most artful, Bud's were the most action-packed, and Bruce's had the best and most comical stories. I respected the way they developed sequences, edited and used music, and told stories. I studied their movies inside and out, taking notes as I watched the films, even dissecting every scene in standout films like **The Endless Summer**.

All three of my mentors are gone now. Bud Browne had been like a father figure to me during his last thirty years, and our strong friendship endured until his final days at age 96. I paid tribute to Bruce Brown when I delivered an address of appreciation at the 50th anniversary of **The Endless Summer** in 2014 at a spectacular event in Huntington Beach.

And when we were filming **Humpback Whales**, Barbara and I were able to take John and Louise Severson out for dinner in Lahaina, Maui, where they lived, about a year before John died. That evening, I tried to express to John what an inspiration he had been to me and

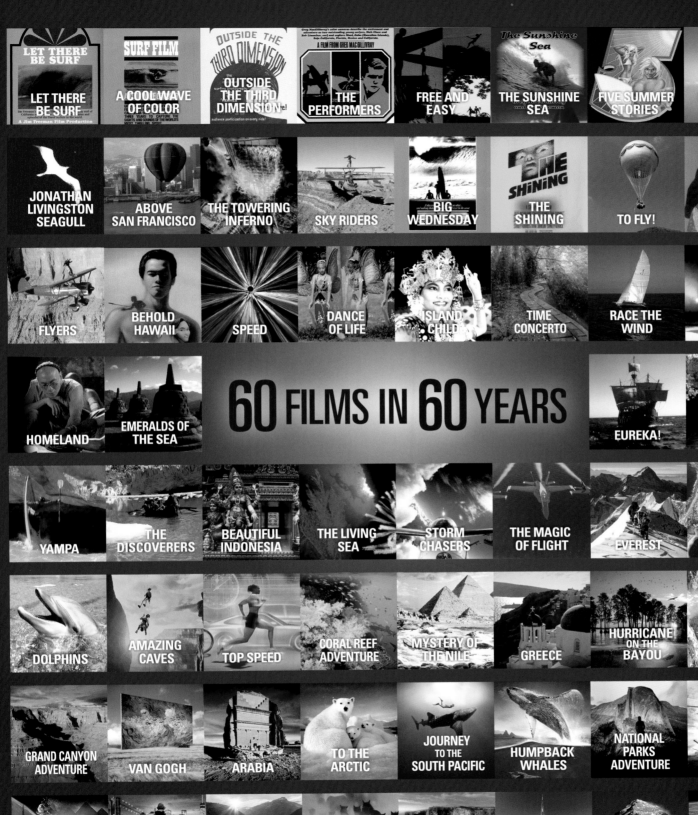

60 FILMS IN 60 YEARS

LET THERE BE SURF
A COOL WAVE OF COLOR
OUTSIDE THE THIRD DIMENSION
THE PERFORMERS
FREE AND EASY
THE SUNSHINE SEA
FIVE SUMMER STORIES
CLEARED FOR TAKEOFF

JONATHAN LIVINGSTON SEAGULL
ABOVE SAN FRANCISCO
THE TOWERING INFERNO
SKY RIDERS
BIG WEDNESDAY
THE SHINING
TO FLY!
WONDERS OF CHINA

FLYERS
BEHOLD HAWAII
SPEED
DANCE OF LIFE
ISLAND CHILD
TIME CONCERTO
RACE THE WIND
TO THE LIMIT

HOMELAND
EMERALDS OF THE SEA
EUREKA!
NEIGHBORS

YAMPA
THE DISCOVERERS
BEAUTIFUL INDONESIA
THE LIVING SEA
STORM CHASERS
THE MAGIC OF FLIGHT
EVEREST
ADVENTURES IN WILD CALIFORNIA

DOLPHINS
AMAZING CAVES
TOP SPEED
CORAL REEF ADVENTURE
MYSTERY OF THE NILE
GREECE
HURRICANE ON THE BAYOU
THE ALPS

GRAND CANYON ADVENTURE
VAN GOGH
ARABIA
TO THE ARCTIC
JOURNEY TO THE SOUTH PACIFIC
HUMPBACK WHALES
NATIONAL PARKS ADVENTURE
WE, THE MARINES

DREAM BIG
AMERICA'S MUSICAL JOURNEY
INTO AMERICA'S WILD
OUT WHERE THE WEST BEGINS
IRELAND
DREAM BIGGER
RETURN TO EVEREST
OCEAN PLANET

(CLOCKWISE, FROM THE TOP LEFT): The Hanalei Pier, our second love; Barbara shows our first grandchild, Charlie, how to ride waves; Jim & I always loved the Kauai rainbows; shooting the 30-foot tides in Nova Scotia, 1994; Charlie, Greta, and Rosie; our view to joyous surf; Bora Bora; Bud Browne, me, Bruce and Pat Brown; Hawkeye Patterson's art; our Laguna home.

so many others, between his beautiful films, his graphic and artistic style, and his founding of *Surfer Magazine*, the first surfing periodical.

"When I was a teenager, I loved and voraciously studied all your films," I told him proudly over cocktails, listing them aloud. "**Surf**, **Surf Safari**, **Surf Fever**, **Big Wednesday**, **The Angry Sea**, and **Pacific Vibrations**!" John was impressed, but then, with that playful lift of an eyebrow, he smiled. "You forgot one." I was embarrassed and couldn't believe it. He grinned, knowing he had me, and completed the list with **Going My Wave**. What a playful wit.

John's artistry really did shape the way that I make movies. His graphic design skills, his wonderful photographic eye and his artful use of music were ahead of their time in the overall world of filmmaking. At dinner that night, I was able to thank him for what he'd taught me and I think he felt the love. In historical newsreel films I've seen, Franklin Roosevelt often tilted his head back and lifted his eyebrows in a smile that seemed to let you into his thinking. John did the same, especially later in life. He was in a happier place than the John I knew back in the late sixties. He seemed relaxed, content with his life, and truly happy. It was a joy up until the end to see the gleam in his eyes when he expressed a devious thought or joke. Even today, I miss these wonderful mentors.

"Why Not?"

Back in 1963 when Barbara and I were seniors, our annual senior class play, a big event for our high school, was written as a compilation of eight comedic dramas from all areas of entertainment. My contribution was a seven-minute film comedy—a black-and-white slapstick homage to silent-era melodramas. The evening was titled "Why Not?"

Following that eventful Greek summer of 1975 when Cindy left Jim, I was editing **To Fly!** and Jim was searching for himself. For months he seemed lost, unable to get his bearing, find his true north. I told him, take time, don't come to the office, escape your daily routine and find a new Jim. At the same time we were planning the largest encore screening schedule for **Five Summer Stories**—beginning in April 1976, and we needed a new highlight sequence to entice repeat customers. Jim said, "What if I make a short film about the new skateboarding craze?" I said "Why not?" hoping that he'd find his north in this challenging and newly focused goal. And it worked. Jim changed, became happier, even more creative, and really turned on to life. Taking that chance was transforming. This new Jim, more fun than I'd even experienced in 12 years of friendship, would only have a few more months to soar. But he died as a completely reborn human, changed for the better.

Just as Jim had, I have always believed that hard work has its own rewards. Do your good work now; don't leave it for tomorrow. Fill yourself up with challenges and projects today and you'll be happy until your last day on this beautiful Earth, just as Jim was.

About Once a Decade, I Write to Jim to Take Stock

Dear Jim,

I hope you don't mind but I'm writing a book about all our fun adventures we had in those early years when we were both discovering the possibilities of life. Remember when we traveled to Hanalei Bay that first time and you were struck by the dramatic clouds, the myriad rainbows, and the cascading waterfalls? Today, it's much the same, where you can feel the "ohana" and "aloha" of the old Hawaiian culture. You'd love it. It would make you happy to know that Billy and JoAnn Hamilton raised Laird—and then Lyon—there in the beautiful Kauai surf.

And, back in Laguna, Cindy and Barbara are both happy and fulfilled, even though they still cry often thinking of the fun times missed, the adventures with you not taken. And for myself, I've tried to make you proud with each of our films, always searching for a more original or imaginative way to tell a positive story. Your idea of always reaching for perfection—that elusive A+—is still the hallmark of our MF films. Filmmaking was indeed harder without you, but we as a team made it work.

You'd be delighted to know that the IMAX format prospered, in spite of the hundreds who predicted that it would die like Cinerama did. It's grown to be the most significant theater format in the world!

One big disappointment over the years is that Kodak retired our favorite film stock, the adored Kodachrome. You loved those rich blues, deep solid reds and that jump-off-the-screen contrast. Cindy even named her cat Kodachrome and Paul Simon wrote a catchy song about the film, pleading to all that would listen, "Mama, don't take my Kodachrome away." Unfortunately, they did just that! I became one of the last photographers to use it before its final film lab closed in 2010.

And though your sister, Barbie and mom Velma, are now gone, I was able to take them to Huntington Beach in 2000 when we were jointly honored by the surfing industry with its highest honor—a star on the sidewalk at surfing's Walk of Fame. Your mom and sister were so proud of you. Our friends—and collaborators—Bud, Drew, Gerry, David, and Jericho were there too, and each gave your mom a big hug.

Because our belief in IMAX was validated by millions of happy customers, several big name companies tried to buy our small company. I was tempted to sell, but I remembered our adage of "passion over profit." So, I've stayed independent and in little Laguna for the past 25 years since those generous offers came in. And, none of us regret it. Our films continue, even after so many decades, to be our strongest love and our most satisfying passion.

And now our kids, my family is running the business as you would have recommended. In fact, Shaun and Meghan possess many of your verbal skills. They love to engage people, as you did, in "dream adventures"—films which will inspire and let our audience appreciate more fully the unmistakable beauty of the world.

*Jim, thank you for all you gave to me. This year we are celebrating the 50th anniversary of **Five Summer Stories**. Remember that wild, electrically charged premiere in Santa Monica? People still revere this film, its honesty, its humor and its unflinching portrayal of the elegance and sheer poetry of surfing.*

Jim, there have been so many adventures, wonderful people, and heart-moving stories—perhaps five hundred over the years—and I feel that you've been there for each one. Hopefully, there will be five hundred more over the next years. Thanks for being our guiding light. We all love you. —Greg

(CLOCKWISE FROM TOP) At San Blas, Mexico, Rich Chew, Bob Limacher, and I learned new ways to get my van stuck; Shaun and I enjoyed Fiji soft-coral diving; Barbara and Cindy in the Sea of Cortez; **Everest** billboard at Times Square, 1998; Blane Kia, the star of **Behold Hawaii**.

(CLOCKWISE FROM RIGHT) After Jim's accident, David Nuuhiwa and his girlfriend, Heather, thoughtfully visited me at the office; this was my lightweight hand-held camera on **The Sweet Ride**; favorite friend Bobbie Poledouris joined us in Hawaii as we filmed **Big Wednesday**; Herbie Fletcher in the green-blue water at Maile, Hawaii; Meghan learns early.

DAVID & HEATHER SEPT 1976

Acknowledgments

I've found a joy in working in the weirdest art form ever conceived. Perhaps because you never end up with what you set out to find, the filmmaking process is more similar to a demolition derby than a meticulously planned assembly line. Even so, when Jim and I took on **Jonathan Livingston Seagull** we were confident. But as work proceeded, we learned far more about filmmaking and dealing with others fairly in business than we had ever expected. As we learned different truths on each project, Jim and I had realized that it's the striving for perfection that is so captivating, so enjoyable. From the time I couldn't wait to re-edit sequences after several screenings of my first commercial film in 1964 to the continual pursuit of a slightly better way to tell an emotional story of Ireland in 2021, the fun of creation can also be contagious. Just as Jonathan strived for perfection in flight, becoming the Horatio Alger with wings, all our collaborators, year after year, find themselves reaching toward higher stars. They've learned to share in those joys I have grown to adore. With all our films, we tried to reach higher, go further, dive deeper. We never knew whether we'd succeed, but as Jim Freeman always said, it's that "uncertainty factor" that makes trying so much darn fun. And because hundreds of talented craftspeople contribute, the final result can never be claimed by one person. The celebrated auteur theory of one central author never really made much sense, but you do need one person to say, "Hey, it's really good. Let's stop here!" Over the following pages are listed those collaborators who have shared in my joy of filmmaking and it is for them that I devote this book of stories.

Cherished Members of the MFF Family

Getting together in Kauai with lifelong friends, Billy, Pierre, Jenny, Laird, Lyon, Mark, Phil, Jeff, and Anne always feels like a joyous reunion where the stories get better, the waves bigger, and the parties more outrageous. It was at this group's insistence that I started this book. It's always a struggle to leave. Thank you to them.

Many friends helped me with this book. First, Natalie Redwitz utilized her UCLA English degree, Jeff Blyth his deep understanding of storytelling, and Nadine Hoffman her sense of organizing a story arc to help edit the lengthy text that I had dictated as I walked the beautiful beaches of Laguna. Then, Howard Hall, Stephen Judson, Graeme Ferguson, Brad Ohlund, Billy Hamilton, Gerry Lopez, Corky Carroll, Paul Holmes, Nelson Tyler, Richard Bach, Sam George, Matt Warshaw, John Milius, Taylor Cole White, Elise Title, Cindy Hartman, Ana Hurley, Shaun MacGillivray, Meghan MacGillivray, and Barbara MacGillivray all added expertise in their areas of understanding. Jeff Girard, the brilliant art director of The Surfer's Journal, who has guided our company's ads and outreach for 30 years, made it look beautiful and fun to read.

And finally, I thank our insightful editor, Karyn Gerhard at Earth Aware, for her skillful help wrangling this project into its final shape, and to our esteemed publishers, Raoul Goff and Roger Shaw.

I'd also like to thank the many team members who for decades have guided our productions and ensured the quality of our films. These people have promoted them, sold them, and produced educational add-ons at such an intensity and with so much care that they have become our next-generation industry leaders. Special thanks to: My first "hired-hand" Miss Tracey, and then Bill Bennett, Harrison Smith, Pat Gilluly, Rae Troutman, Kristi Anderson, Elizabeth Williams, Cheryl Real, Terresa Ferreira, Linda Halopoff, Jeff Blyth, Alec Lorimore, Rob Walker, Matthew Muller, Susan Wilson, Nancy Finley, Kathy Almon, Tori Stokes, Debbie Bergin, Janna Emmel, Bob Harman, Mike Lutz, Patty Collins, Lori Rick, Doña Harman, Mary Jane Dodge, Jack Tankard, and many more who can be found in the following list.

The Early Years

MacGillivray Family: Alex, Betty Gaye, Gaye, Lisa, Grammy Wood • Bob Moore • Bob Limacher • Rich Chew • Richard Harbour • Mark Martinson • Jim Freeman • Richard Hovey • Dell Haughey • Bill Bennett

1976

Francis Thompson • Robert Young • Arthus Zegart • Jeff Blyth • Bernardo Segall • Tom McGrath • Alexander Hammi d • Richard R. McCurdy • Sam Shaw • Philip D. Schwartz • Art Scholl • Frank Tallman • Peter Walker • Kurt Stehling • Bob Wills • George Nolan

1983

Blaine Kia • Kanani Velasco • Peter Kalua • Kimo Kahoano • Henry Kapono Ka'aihue • Nona Beamer • Al Harrington • Rick Whiting • Deborah Roberson • Kristi Anderson • Lorelei Hammond • Cay Cannon • Liz Perry • Maile Semitekol • Chris Upham • Melissa Kim • Grace Niska • Basil Paledouris • Alec Lorimore • Matthew Muller • Stan Lazan • Brad Ohlund • Bruce McGregor • Mark Dawson • Ted White • Marvin Foster • Brian Keaulana • Michael Tongg • Chuck Everts • Mark Mangini • Mike Minkler • John Kruse • William Pine • John Wash • David Keighley

1984

Steven Henschel • James Foster • David Lester • Jody Rosenthal • Stephen Judson • Martina G. Young • Wylie Stateman • Evans Wetmore • Thomas Walsh • Merrily Murray-Walsh • Frank Cotinola • Craig Newman • Shaun MacGillivray • Meghan MacGillivray • Doug Williams

1989

Jon Boorstin • Paula S. Apsell • Jeffrey W. Kirsch • Susanne B. Simpson • Christopher Reyna • Richard Kiley • Carmen Flores de Tanis • Scott Price • Steve Koflanovich • Nina Ananiashvili • Irek Mukhamedov • Derek Hart • Matvey Shatz • Ludmilla Lopukhova • Mike Hoover • Randy Rossi • Ray Baum John Parsons •

• David Barlow, Ph.D. • Karl Sabbagh • Deane Rink • Tony Yaniro • Werner Braun • Randy Grandstaff • Walt Shipley • Beverly Johnson • Maria Walliser • Roger Brown • David Douglas • Scott Hering • Carl Lewis • Cheryl Real • Virginia Murray • Liz Ervin • Liz Mercado • Dan Butts • Bob Beattie • William Grant • Queene Coyne • Brigid Sullivan • Sue Kantrowitz • Terry Landau • Roger L. Nichols, M.D. • Richard Michalak • Libby Woolems • Tracy McCandless • Angela Margolis • Kathy Almon • Anne Marie Casavant • Janna Emmel • Alison Logan • Jayne Hall • Debbie Fogel • Ken Teaney • Jo Ann Carlson • Dwayne McClintock • Geoff Williamson • Jeff Girard • Bob Auguste • Jacquie Tankard • Jeff Mart • Myles Connolly • Scott Ganary • Marco Markovich • Alice Casbara • Dan Muscarella • Dr. Robert Eather • Dr. Louis Herman • Dr. Ellen R. Stofan • Dr. R. Stephen Saunders • Eric De Jong • Adam Pack

1995

Hal Holbrook • Curt Schulkey • Taj Teffaha • Jeffrey Sudzin • Dick Wilkinson • Manny Hernandez • Jerome Olsen • Paul Taylor • Jeanette Connolly • Bill McLeod • Dr. Robert C. Sheets • Dr. Naomi Surgi • Dr. Frank Marks • James McFadden • Greg A. Bast • Dr. Howard Bluestein • Dr. Margaret A. LeMone • Dr. Daniel W. Breed • Bruce Miller • Roger Holzberg • Tim Cahill • Meryl Streep • Sting • Ron Bartlett • David Fanning • Chuck Davis • Bob Cranston • Mark Thurlow • Steve Ford • Gay Browning • Tim Drnec • Harry Hauss • Lee Parker • Chuck Nicklin • Dr. Robert Ballard • Dr. Milton Love • Jennifer Saitz • Dr. Bruce H. Robison • Dr. Judith Connor • James A. R. McFarlane • Dr. Steven K. Katona • Jennifer Rock • Stephanie K. Martin • Francis Toribiong • Dr. William Hamner • Laura Martin • Julie Packard • Mimi Drummond

1998

David Breashears • Mike Lutz • George Harrison • Robert Schauer • Teresa Ferriera • Paula Viesturs •

Linda Marcopulos • Dr. Cynthia Beall • Dr. Roger Bilham • Dr. Kip Hodges • Lori Rick • Dr. Charles Houston • Dr. Christopher Scotese • Dr. Bradford Washburn • Bob Harman • Elizabeth Cohen • Beck Weathers • Broughton Coburn • Audrey Salkeld • Dr. James Fisher • Lhakpa Norbu Sherpa • Sumiyo Tsuzuki • Robert Mehnert • Araceli Segarra • Ed Viesturs

2000

Christopher N. Palmer • Chat Reynders • Lowell, Blake and Associates, Inc. • Pierce Brosnan • Patty Collins • Grace Atkins • Doug Merrifield • Anne Marie Hammers • John Anderson • Pete Zuccarini • Eric Anderson • Bernd Würsig, Ph.D. • Kathleen Dudzinski, Ph.D. • Alejandro Acevedo-Gutiérrez, Ph.D. • Randall Wells, Ph.D. • Peter Tyack, Ph.D. • Whitlow Au, Ph.D. • Dean Bernal • JoJo the Dolphin • Sam LaBudde • Dale Beldin • Mike Kirsch • Paul Curtis • Bob Stewart • Mark Krenzien • Jimmy Smits • Andrew DeCristofaro • Dana Prieto • Peter Sharpe • Roy Disney • Bill Owens • Joe Van Bonn • Jeff Clark • Grant Washburn • Jay Moriarty • Sue Campbell • Steve Sillett • Jim Spickler • Joe Jennings • Troy Hartman • Bryan Iguchi • Steve Wood • Lindsey Buckingham • Cris Andrei • Thomas Conroy • Scotty Guinn • Dan Dickman • Durinda Wood • Nancy Finley • Chris Blum • Morgan Ohlund • Rick Tiedeman • Jim Surette • Ron Goodman • Andy Sych • Cliff Fleming • Jim Gavin • Harry O'Connor • Jake Brake • Mike Kitahara • Jeff Jamison • Chris Baird • Andrew Loschin • Marshall Garlington • Ann Scibelli • Mel Bucholz • Ralph Milliken • Jim Garber

2001

Liam Neeson • Jack Stephens • Justin Hayward • John Lodge • Nancy Holler Aulenbach • Hazel Barton • Mael Lamberton • Gordon Brown • Luc Moreau • Scott Davis • Douglass McDonald • DeVere Burt • Dave Duszynski • Kit Anderson • Mary Kaye Kennedy • Dr. Jacqueline Belwood • Dr. Barbara

Flagg • Lance Milbrand • Earl Wiggins • Allison Chase • David Schultz • Mark Chapman • Rick Bridges • Courteney Hall • Scott Janush • Alan Markowitz • Harrison Smith • Mike Clark • Ken Richards • Tim Allen • Lucas Luhr • Marla Streb • Stephen Murkett • Glen Pitre • Peter Coleman • Carl Beyer • Ann Putney • Kaeran Sudmalis • Cornelia von Bühler • Michael Payne • Kana Goto

2003

David Crosby • Stephen Stills • Graham Nash • Michele Hall • Mark Conlin • John Heiney • John Dunham • Jean-Michel Cousteau • Rusi Vulakoro • Richard Pyle • Tracey Medway • Maria João Rodriguez • Rob Barrel • Cat Holloway

2005

Jordi Llompart • Reed Smoot • Laura Vidiella • Scott Hoffman • Michael O'Donnell • Mike Speaks • Pasquale Scaturro • Saskia Lange • Mohamed Megahed • Myriam Seco • Michel L'Huillier • Dennis Delestrac • Martin Schloemer • Almuth Itzen

2006

Nia Vardalos • Georgette Alithinos • Maria Alithinos • Sandra Stokes • Phil Clarke • Susan Wilson • Niki Martin • Jeff Horst • Jennifer Leininger • Pat McBurney • Victoria Stokes • Nadine Ferdousi • Brooke Nance • Dr. George Vougioukalakis • Dr. Irene Nikolakopoulou • Pagona Kolomvotsou • Fragoula Georma • Frank Corcoran • Craig Barron • Krystyna Demkowicz • Tim Sassoon • Chris "C. B." Brown • Johnathan Banta • Jeremy Nicolaides • Jenn Bastian • Scott Boyett • Amanda Shaw • Jim Fields • Tab Benoit • Allen Toussaint • Marva Wright • Joseph "Chubby" Carrier, Jr.

2007

Bettina Wild • Roger Taylor • Brian May • John Harlin III • Daniela Jasper • Adele Hammond • Dr. Bruno Messerli • Siena Harlin • Beatrice Messerli • Robert Jasper • Dr. Christine Pielmeier • Roland Baumgartner • Samantha Spaeth • Cindy

Olson • Phil Glutz • George Buhlhann • Heinz Muller • Gerold Biner • Robbie Andenmatten

2008

Stefan Lessard • Robert Redford • Peter Gleick, Ph.D. • Wade Davis, Ph.D. • Tara Davis • Robert F. Kennedy Jr. • Kathleen "Kick" Kennedy • Shana Watahomigie • Cree Watahomigie • Regan Dale • Dr. Kristin Kuckelman • Anthony Yap • Tanya Shuman • Nikki Kelly • Steve Fisher • Doug Lavender • Justin Bergler • Joshua Kjorven • Leonard Reynolds • Jack Cruikshank • P. J. Connelly • Orville Sisco • Liz Ferrin • Chris Rainier • Katie MacGillivray • Anne Tassinello • Patricia Keighley • Jason Stearns • Paul Fraser • George Wendt • Carter Beauford • Dave Matthews • LeRoi Moore • Boyd Tinsley • Tim Reynolds • Greg Leisz • Richard Hardy • Mike Hamilton • Bruce Flohr

2010

Helen Mirren • Robert Lacey • Neal Allen • Marwan A. Alireza • Fouad Al Humoud • Hala Al Houti • Russel Bowie • Mark Hunstable • Hamzah Jamjoom • Robert Adams • Housam Al Mahde • Kieran Humphries • Tarek Taher • Phil Rothwell • Jim Thomas • HRH Prince Turki Al Faisal • HE Abdullah Nassif • Dr. Abdullah H. Masry • HE Faisal Al Muaammar • Khalid Al Maeena • Dr. Farhan Mizami, OBE • Jim Benedict • Terry Liskevych • Dale Kriebel

2012

Paul McCartney • Tom Campion • Greg Foster • Daniel White • Adam Ravetch • Sarah Robertson • Karsten Heuer • Leanne Allison • Simon Qamanirq • Bjorne Kvernmo • Zach Grant • Jason Roberts • Florian Schulz • Ragnheiður Gröndal • Beth Fitchet Wood • Annie Toth • Mark Humphrey • Irving Barrios • Kurt Schaefer • Gerald Mantonya • Tim Amick • Erin Hill • Amrit Khalsa • Toby Wallwork • Jason E. Paul • Steven C. Amstrup, Ph.D. • Dafna Tobi • Andrew E. Derocher, Ph.D. • Christopher Krenz, Ph.D. • Kenneth R. Whitten •

Geoffrey York • Mose Richards • John Downer

2013

Cate Blanchett • D. J. Roller • Jawi Mayor • Menas Mambasar • Jacob Sauyai • Yesaya Mayor • Gibson Sauyai • Ferdiel Ballamu • David Stuart • Stuart MacFarlane • Nydia Ponsen • Samuel de Castro-Abeger • Vance Wiese • Dale Stokes, Ph.D. • Marc Ostrick • Jonathan Shaw • Matt Amick • Vincent Waythomas • J. R. Racine • Michael Roderick • Rick Gordon • Brenda Carlson • John Daro Karen Nichols • Daniel Rapo • Alex Rapaport • Jamie Hinrichs • Molly Malloy • Kimberly Helling • Kristina Gonzales • Debbie Bergin

2015

Ewan McGregor • Calum Graham • Kevin McCarey • Steven Burnette • Josh Dono • Amanda Fisher • Fred Sharpe • Jim Darling • Roger Payne • Jan Straley • Bob Haskell • Tennyson Oyler • Ali Takau • Meagan Jones • Ed Lyman • Tad Luckey • Aaron Pelman • Sarah Wilson • C. Scott Baker • Phil Clapham • Michael Donoghue • Pieter Folkens • David Mattila • Susan Nash • Michael Gil • Sarah Bedolfe • Shauna Badheka • Anne Marie Block • Justin Veizbicke • Joe Carrier

2016

Mark Fletcher • Tom Garzilli • Mike Day • John Barrett • David Zucker • David Stanke • Chris Thompson • Anne Madison • Don Richardson • David Whitaker • Karyn Gruenberg • Jake Conte • Renee Mason • Aaron Wodin-Schwartz • Sarah Kay • Becky Jameson • Conrad Anker • Max Lowe • Rachel Pohl • Joseph Wiegand • Lee Stetson • Marie Antoine • Jim Camp-bell-Spickler • Ryan Hudson • Eric Porter • Kristan Culbert • Cooper Dendel • Michael Brown • Nick Savander • Adriene Wyse • Keith Bronsdon • West Chambless • David Fortney • Dustin Farrell • Peter Chang • Violet Angell • Josh Helling • Matt Irving • Kyle Rott • Andy Shillabeer • Marty Reed • Chris Bolfing • Christian Straub • Joe Alaniz • Wendy Smith •

(ABOVE) Our growing family. (FOLLOWING SPREAD) Bixby Ranch, a saved treasure.

Edwin Escalante • Steve Denicola • Christine Van Ness • Tom Murphy • Michael Olmert • Mark O'Malley • Merle Dickinson • Donald Leadbetter • Alexa Viets • Brian Holst • Doña Harman • Mike Meeker • Caroline Beteta

2017

Jane Howell Lombardi • Christine A. Williams • John Jennings Boyd • Grady Candler • Wayne LaBar • Melissa Mason • Hector Gika • Sharelle Walker • Felipe Mendoza • Alex Falk • Keith Melton • Nick Lantz • Jamey Warner • Erin Douglas • Andrew Gough • Sam Gutierrez • Tami Hinson • Brandon M. K. Lane • Jonathan Wallace • Tim Mendez • Justin Ostensen • Chris Newman • Menzer Pehlivan • Angelica Hernandez • Avery Bang • Steve Burrows • Fredi Lajvardi • Stephen D. Bechtel Jr. • Patrick J. Natale • Thomas W. Smith, III • Charlene Wheeless • LeeAnne Lang • Amy Ochs • Cassandra Watson • Gene Hackman • Frank C. Kostenko • Tom Campbell • Terry Brown • Kristin Donan

2018

Aloe Blacc • Victoria McGinnis • Gavin Massey • Marty Rhett • Nick Bianchi • Natalie Redwitz • Talbot Solenberger • Bill MacLeod • George Green • Aaron Harper • Charles Wiggins • Charles Steve Rhea • John Witherspoon • Maya Jupiter • Jon Batiste • Dr. John • Irma Thomas • Willow Osborne • Gloria

Estefan • Emilio Estefan • Susi Mai • Brandon Niederauer • Ramsey Lewis • Keb' Mo' • Lil Buck • Donnetta "Lil Bit" Jackson • Pause Eddie • Lani Richmond • Alexandra Farah • Jefferson Wooley

2020 to 2022

H. Scott Salinas • Mike Brown • Nick Peterson • Jason Sturgis • Deshan Evans • Ana Hurley • Harisa Lalić • Joshua Martinez • Fernando Lara • Gabe Montgomery • Nick Walker • Bryce Reif • Karsu Nalbantoglu • Jonthan Bird • Leena Gundapaneni • Jeff Heacock • John Herrington • Ariel Tweto • Jennifer Pharr Davis • Shaun Martin • Paul Rogers, Ph.D. • Emma Faye Rudkin • Richard Louv • Melissa Nelson, Ph.D. • Rosalyn LaPier, Ph.D. • Jenny Roe, Ph.D. • Christopher Neale, Ph.D. • Laura Barnes, Ph.D. • Stephen Aron, Ph.D. • Tom Osborne, Ph.D. • Mehdi Boukhechba, Ph.D.

Endless Thanks

Don King • Roger Holzberg • Miguel Angel Trujillo • Peter Kragh • Tim Housel • Neguine Sanani • Richard Bangs • Mike Peralta • Daniel May • Jan Baird • Paul Atkins • Ralph Mendoza • Stephen Venables • Jason Rosenfield • Kelly Tyler • Craig Naylor • Bob Kresser • Bob Talbot • Peter Parks • Ron Fricke • James Neihouse • Osha Gray Davidson • Sean Phillips • Jill Osmon • Robbie Huntoon • White Oak Associates •

K2 Communications • B. J. Worth • Michael J. Cudahy • Audubon Nature Institute • Rodney Taylor • Mark Olshaker • David Giró • Adam Moos • Michael Graber • Bernat Aragonés • Byron McKinney • Bill Reeve • Patrick Williams • Ryan Kresser • Paul Mockler • National Science Foundation • Alex G. Spanos • Karyn Noles Bewley • Wes Skiles • Dea Berberian • Tom Cowan • Alexander Biner • Khalid Zainal Alireza • Steve Dorand • Hugh Renfro • Michael Stearns • Peter Metzdorf • Rich Gelfond • Dennis Earl Moore

MacGillivray Freeman Films
PO Box 205
Laguna Beach, CA 92652
www.MacGillivrayFreeman.com

Follow us on Instagram: @MacFreeFilms
Follow us on Facebook: @MacGillivray Freeman
Follow us on Twitter: @MacFreeFilms

CHAIRMAN **Greg MacGillivray**
PRESIDENT **Shaun MacGillivray**

One World One Ocean is an ocean media campaign
presented by MacGillivray Freeman Films and
MacGillivray Freeman Films Educational Foundation

www.OneWorldOneOcean.com

Follow us on Facebook: @OneWorldOneOcean
Follow us on Instagram: @1World1Ocean
Follow us on Twitter: @1World1Ocean

MacGillivray Freeman Films is donating all proceeds from the sale
of this book to marine conservation: Oceana, Surfrider Foundation,
and One World One Ocean.

All photos courtesy MacGillivray Freeman Films, except where noted.

Page 12 film frames from *Big Wednesday* © 1978 Warner Bros.
All Rights Reserved.

Page 82 excerpt courtesy of William Finnegan, *Barbarian Days*,
Penguin Random House

Page 188 "Love Is The Seventh Wave" lyrics © Sony/ATV Music Publishing
LLC. Written by Gordon Sumner.

Page 204 excerpt courtesy of Beck Weathers, *Left for Dead*,
Penguin Random House

Page 204 excerpt courtesy of Jon Krakauer, *Into Thin Air*,
Penguin Random House

Page 249 photo of Coca-Cola can © 2011 The Coca-Cola Company.
All Rights Reserved.

IMAX® is a registered trademark of Imax Corporation.

Oscar® and Academy Award® are registered trademarks of the
Academy of Motion Picture Arts and Sciences.

All best efforts have been made to secure permissions for photos and
text; any omission is unintended.

EARTH AWARE

An Imprint of **MandalaEarth**
PO Box 3088
San Rafael, CA 94912
www.MandalaEarth.com

Find us on Facebook: www.facebook.com/MandalaEarth

Follow us on Twitter: @MandalaEarth

Library of Congress Cataloging-in-Publication Data available.

ISBN: 978-1-64722-736-4

CEO **Raoul Goff**
PUBLISHER **Roger Shaw**
VP OF MANUFACTURING **Alix Nicholaeff**
SENIOR PRODUCTION MANAGER **Greg Steffen**
SENIOR PRODUCTION MANAGER, SUBSIDIARY RIGHTS **Lina s Palma-Temena**

Mandala Publishing/Earth Aware Editions, in association with Roots of Peace, will plant
two trees for each tree used in the manufacturing of this book. Roots of Peace is an
internationally renowned humanitarian organization dedicated to eradicating land
mines worldwide and converting war-torn lands into productive farms and wildlife
habitats. Roots of Peace will plant two million fruit and nut trees in Afghanistan and
provide farmers there with the skills and support necessary for sustainable land use.

Manufactured in China by Insight Editions

10 9 8 7 6 5 4 3 2 1